"LET US VOTE!"

"Let Us Vote!"

Youth Voting Rights and the 26th Amendment

Jennifer Frost

NEW YORK UNIVERSITY PRESS
New York

NEW YORK UNIVERSITY PRESS
New York
www.nyupress.org

© 2021 by New York University
Paperback edition published 2023
All rights reserved

References to Internet websites (URLs) were accurate at the time of writing. Neither the author nor New York University Press is responsible for URLs that may have expired or changed since the manuscript was prepared.

Library of Congress Cataloging-in-Publication Data
Names: Frost, Jennifer, 1961- author.
Title: "Let us vote!" : youth voting rights and the 26th amendment / Jennifer Frost.
Description: New York, N.Y. : NYU Press, 2021. | Includes bibliographical references and index.
Identifiers: LCCN 2021011856 | ISBN 9781479811328 (hardback) | ISBN 9781479827244 (paperback) | ISBN 9781479811342 (ebook) | ISBN 9781479811335 (ebook other)
Subjects: LCSH: Voting—United States. | Youth—Political activity—United States. | Voting age—United States. | Political culture—United States. | United States—Politics and government.
Classification: LCC JF831 .F76 2021 | DDC 324.6/208350973—dc23
LC record available at https://lccn.loc.gov/2021011856

This book is printed on acid-free paper, and its binding materials are chosen for strength and durability. We strive to use environmentally responsible suppliers and materials to the greatest extent possible in publishing our books.

Manufactured in the United States of America

10 9 8 7 6 5 4 3 2

Also available as an ebook

For my students,

past, present, and future

CONTENTS

ABBREVIATIONS

AFL-CIO American Federation of Labor–Congress of Industrial Organizations

AYD American Youth for Democracy

CIO Congress of Industrial Organizations

CORE Congress of Racial Equality

CTA California Teachers Association

CUE New Jersey Student Committee for Undergraduate Education

ER Eleanor Roosevelt

ERA Equal Rights Amendment

FDR Franklin Delano Roosevelt

JFK John F. Kennedy

LBJ Lyndon Baines Johnson

LUV Let Us Vote

MCLVA Minnesota Coalition to Lower the Voting Age

MFDP Mississippi Freedom Democratic Party

NAACP National Association for the Advancement of Colored People

NEA National Education Association

NSA US National Student Association

RFK Robert F. Kennedy

ROTC Reserve Officers' Training Corps

SCLC Southern Christian Leadership Conference

SDS Students for a Democratic Society

SNCC Student Nonviolent Coordinating Committee

UAW United Auto Workers

VAC Voting Age Coalition of New Jersey
VISTA Volunteers in Service to America
VOTES Vindication of Twenty-Eighteen Suffrage
YAF Young Americans for Freedom
YFC Youth Franchise Coalition

Introduction

"We're old enough so let us vote"

In 1969, pop musicians Tommy Boyce and Bobby Hart released "L.U.V. (Let Us Vote)." "It's been a long time getting' here; A change is comin' and it's very near." Their first claim to fame was writing songs for a popular television show about an imaginary, Beatles-esque band, The Monkees, yet this song was far from just fun and frivolous. It was the campaign theme song for a grassroots student organization, Let Us Vote, founded that year in California.

The song had a focused aim—winning voting rights for young people—and it made an argument in support of that aim emphasizing young people's education and maturity.

> L.U.V., I'm talking 'bout you and me
> And changin' things peacefully
> We're old enough so L.U.V.

It offered an optimistic message about the possibilities for social and political change at the end of the 1960s.

> Let us vote!
> It's time that we all made a contribution
> Come on and let us vote
> It's a solution

Boyce and Hart's song never achieved great popularity at the time (although it did make the *Billboard* chart), and few remember it today. But the story behind this song and how it was used to mobilize and organize is evidence of the 30-year struggle for youth voting rights in the United States.

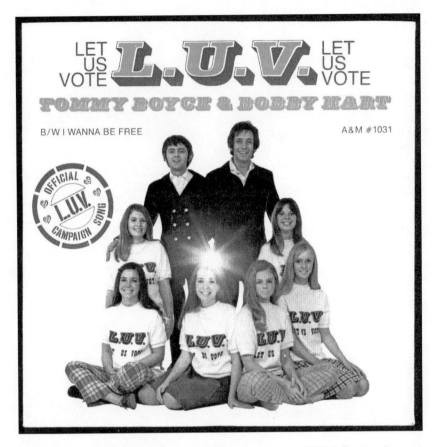

Tommy Boyce and Bobby Hart, "Let Us Vote," single cover, 1969. LUV Collection. Courtesy of Holt-Atherton Special Collections Department, University of the Pacific Library.

Paying attention to Boyce and Hart's "Let Us Vote" illustrates how Americans, old and young, Democrat and Republican, in politics and culture, built a movement and momentum for the 26th Amendment to the US Constitution. This amendment, ratified in 1971, gave the right to vote to 18-, 19-, and 20-year-olds, and it marked the last time that the United States significantly expanded and protected voting rights. Although historians, legal scholars, and political scientists have written persuasively about various aspects of this topic, there is only one book-length historical overview.[1]

Historical neglect of this important topic has given rise to a misinterpretation about how the 26th Amendment came about. Most scholars attribute its achievement to "top-down" efforts by politicians rather than "bottom-up" campaigns or a movement by young people themselves. This interpretation certainly has a basis in fact. Jennings Randolph, Democrat from West Virginia, has rightly earned the title "Father of the 26th Amendment." Starting in 1942 as a member of the House of Representatives and then continuing in the Senate, Randolph made it his goal to achieve voting rights for 18-, 19-, and 20-year-olds. In 1971 he fulfilled that goal, when his proposed constitutional amendment became the law of the land. "I'm the one who lowered the voting age, you know," he said in a later interview. "I gave 18-year-olds the vote," he added, reinforcing the top-down interpretation. "I'm proud of that."[2]

Correctly crediting proponents in Congress for their contributions, however, has led to a lack of recognition of or respect for the role of young Americans as well as their many other older allies. "The Twenty-sixth Amendment was not sought by and was of no interest whatever to the eighteen-year-olds to whom it granted the vote," dismissed one scholar.[3] This claim that young people had little interest or involvement in winning the right to vote does not stack up against the historical evidence or the memories of participants. With the 50th anniversary of the penultimate amendment to the US Constitution upon us, I hope this historical study can begin to do justice to a major advance toward democracy and equality in the United States.

How and why calls and claims for youth suffrage emerged, proceeded, and succeeded over a 30-year period are the overarching questions for this book. Understanding who participated, their arguments and strategies, their conflicts and coalitions, and developments on the local, state, and national levels helps to explain the success of youth voting rights specifically. These answers also can illuminate the process of political change more generally.

The 26th Amendment was the result of a sustained struggle for youth suffrage, beginning in the early 1940s and lasting to the early 1970s. Although calls for lowering the voting age well predate the mid-twentieth century, these 30 years mark a period of consistent advocacy and action. Only in the crucial last phase of 1969 to 1971 did a national movement emerge. Putting those years within a longer time frame allows us to see how individual efforts and organized campaigns built the movement over three decades. During the 1940s and 1950s a few prominent figures and organizations pushed for youth voting rights nationally and locally. In the second phase of the 1960s the numbers and locations of proponents expanded exponentially and energized the existing efforts. These developments culminated in the youth franchise movement.

This longer, more expansive story makes it clear that youth voting rights were achieved not only through the actions of politicians but through the interrelationship of top-down and bottom-up forces. Proponents with political power—US leaders (including presidents, both Democratic and Republican), state officials, and members of prominent national organizations—interacted with Americans involved in campus and community organizing. They communicated and cooperated in myriad ways, directly and indirectly, across three decades. Participation from proponents in government, within organizations, and at the grassroots contributed to the political mobilization that led to this historic change.

A broad and bipartisan coalition characterized this mobilization. In the making from the start, this coalition came together formally in late 1968 and early 1969 as the Youth Franchise Coalition. This coalition included well-known, older, multi-issue organizations and groups such as the National Association for the Advancement of Colored People (NAACP) and National Education Association (NEA) and new ones dedicated solely to the issue of youth voting rights, like Citizens for Vote 18 and Let's Vote 18. Together they worked to lower the voting age to 18, shaping and sustaining the successful movement.

Over time these proponents advanced numerous arguments for youth voting rights. Young Americans fulfilled citizenship responsibilities and so deserved the rights of citizenship. They had the maturity and education to vote. Their participation would strengthen democracy and government in the United States, and many more. Revealed and reflected in the chronology of the youth suffrage struggle—from World War II to the Vietnam War—was the most influential argument: "Old enough to fight, old enough to vote." In 1942 the draft age for military service reduced to 18, yet voting remained a right gained only at 21. This profound unfairness and injustice propelled early proponents. The poignant rallying cry grew louder with the Korean War and louder still with the American war in Vietnam.

These efforts and campaigns and the eventual movement also involved a range of strategies on the local, state, and national levels. Supporters initially pursued legislation, specifically constitutional amendments at both the state and federal levels. But later they engaged in education, organizing, lobbying, litigation, and cultural politics. The complicated structure of the US government—with a separation of powers between the states and the federal government and among the three branches of the federal government—plus the need to build grassroots support necessitated this range of strategies.

This multiplicity—of participants, organizations, arguments, and strategies—could have fragmented the youth franchise movement and undermined its effectiveness. The opposite happened. This multiplicity made the movement. It meant people had many points of entry and helped to transform isolated efforts and state campaigns into a national movement by 1969. And multiplicity gave the movement flexibility and energy in the final phase leading up to victory with the 26th Amendment in 1971.

By charting this 30-year history of how and why the United States has a voting age of 18, one conclusion is obvious: the 1960s were pivotal. Progress toward achieving youth suffrage built on the decade's many social movements, political achievements, legal developments, and three additional constitutional amendments. Success came within the context of the 1960s, not at any earlier point in the 30-year effort.

This success owed much to the African American struggle for civil and voting rights. "The Civil Rights Movement was a borning struggle," activist, singer, and scholar Bernice Johnson Reagon has argued.[4] It is well known that the freedom movement offered inspiration and impetus for all the activism that followed, including the student, antiwar, feminist, and other movements. Taken together these movements created the circumstances and context during "the sixties" that made youth voting rights seem and in fact be possible. As proponent and Youth Franchise Coalition founder Paul J. Myer notes, "I think the confluence of civil rights and other issues began to form a cauldron of passion and activity that made it very hard for politicians to simply treat the vote as a nice thing to give. It forced politicians to not just put out statements but to actually act. That's where we were coming from."[5]

This familiar story about the profound influence of the freedom movement on the sixties takes a pragmatic twist with regard to youth suffrage. Civil rights organizations, leadership, and lobbyists were central to forming and furthering the youth franchise movement. Even more, civil rights legislation, legal arguments, and court decisions in the 1960s provided the legislative and legal path for the 18-year-old vote. Youth vote advocates and activists certainly drew inspiration from the freedom movement. They also got lessons in politics and policymaking and a concrete, practical way to achieve their goal.

The decade of the 1960s was pivotal to the achievement of youth voting rights in another way. It was during the sixties that young people committed to their own and others' enfranchisement came to the fore. Student and youth groups started to organize campaigns on campuses and at the state and local levels. Single-issue youth suffrage organizations spread. Given that youth activism is one of the defining characteristics of the sixties, it makes sense that this was the decade when young Americans built a movement to lower the voting age. Individual and collective efforts among youth can be found in earlier decades. But just as the sixties generation contributed to changes in so many aspects of American life, they took the struggle for youth suffrage in new, politically advantageous directions.

In turn the youth franchise movement needs to be understood as a "sixties movement." That it hasn't been can be explained partly by the larger scholarly neglect of this topic. Another reason is that the standard narrative of the sixties simplifies, truncates, or mischaracterizes the decade's events and developments. As a result few historical surveys of the 1960s include the 26th Amendment, much less the movement that achieved it. A sign of this inattention is that early editions of one important history misnamed it (since corrected!) the "Thirty-sixth Amendment to the Constitution."[6] British historian of the global 1960s Arthur Marwick observed fifteen years ago that "too little attention is still given to the way in which young people, at the age of eighteen, were given the vote."[7] His observation still holds true, even if "given" doesn't quite capture how the 26th Amendment came about.

The absence of that story, the proponents, and their movement from our histories of the 1960s means we miss one of the most consequential changes of that transformative decade. I did so myself, until recently. Twenty years ago I published a book on the 1960s and started teaching a course titled "Making Sense of the Sixties" (a title borrowed from a 1991 PBS documentary series). Only in 2014, after offering that course many times, did I teach about the 26th Amendment. I remember preparing my last lecture on the legacies of the sixties, when I realized, "Wait, didn't young people get the right to vote?" Fortunately we assign as a required reading a brief chronology of the decade courtesy of David Farber and Beth Bailey, which includes the amendment.[8] From that moment I knew I wanted to research and write this history.

As it turns out this history offers a different perspective on the 1960s. Placing the movement for youth voting rights alongside other sixties movements and in its proper context challenges the standard narrative and reinforces revisionist interpretations of the decade in several ways.

The standard narrative presents the chronology of the 1960s as a discrete decade from 1960 to 1970. In fact some early histories end even earlier, in 1968 or 1969, at just the time the struggle for youth suffrage became a movement. Similarly, activism among high school students "peaked between 1968 and 1973," Gael Graham found.[9] Describing this period as "the sixties" rather than "the 1960s" already indicates a broader timeframe and defines, as John D'Emilio does, "an era organically bound together by events, outlook, and mood." Adopting the revisionist concept of the "long sixties" further brings into view the youth franchise movement and the 26th Amendment. D'Emilio, Wini Breines, and Andrew Hunt have argued for expanding our chronology. These historians have made the case that movements emerging in the later 1960s and into the 1970s, like women's liberation, gay liberation, and Vietnam Veterans Against the War, were sixties movements. They, like youth suffrage, need to be included in our histories of the era.[10]

Importantly, including these movements and their social and political impact changes the standard narrative, the story we tell of the era. According to this initial version of events the early "good" sixties of the civil rights movement and a young President John F. Kennedy devolved into the late "bad" sixties of defeat in Vietnam and riots in the streets. This so-called declension interpretation of the 1960s, as identified by Breines, can be seen in book titles. *Coming Apart*, *The Unraveling of America*, and *Years of Hope, Days of Rage* are just a few.[11] But when these later movements and their accomplishments are understood as a product of the 1960s, the last years of the decade and the next look much, much brighter. The success of the youth suffrage movement and achievement of the 26th Amendment in 1971 mean a major expansion of American democracy came right at the end of the "long sixties." The declension interpretation fits only some developments during the decade and misses many others. So why then does this interpretation have such power?

The origins of the standard narrative's story of decline can be located in the politics of the sixties. The era has long been understood as an important period for liberalism, the dominant political philosophy of the time, and radicalism, with a "new left" coming onto the scene. Liberals in the Democratic Party started the decade with political power and plans for reform, while young radicals in the Students for a Democratic Society (SDS) sought to realize a more democratic and equal America. But in 1968 Democrats lost the presidency, and SDS began to fracture. Early histories focused on politics—whether center or left—featured this defeat and downfall. More recently, conservatism has come to be recognized as a significant political force during the decade. Those political histories trace a contrasting story arc, of a rising right wing in the Republican Party.[12]

Even so, because of its political dominance, "liberalism's rise and fall" remains the standard narrative of the 1960s. There are good reasons for viewing liberal politics in this way. The early high hopes—even hubris—of liberals to achieve reform raised expectations and then failed to deliver, in large part due to the decision of a liberal president, Lyndon B. Johnson, to escalate the American war in Vietnam. Both conservatives and radicals during the decade defined themselves against liberals and fiercely criticized their failures. As Allen J. Matusow summarizes, "In a few short years, optimism vanished, fundamental values emerged to divide the country, social cohesion rapidly declined, and the unraveling of America began."[13]

By focusing on youth voting rights and the 26th Amendment, however, this book tells a different story about liberalism over the "long sixties." It was mostly liberals who led the efforts, supported the campaigns, and joined the movement to establish the right of Americans aged 18 and up to vote. They were young and old, from both major political parties, and in all sorts of organizations and groups. Those of the sixties generation who participated in the youth franchise movement expressed a new kind of liberal politics. Coming of age alongside civil rights and new left activists, they shared many of the same commitments. To young Americans as political actors. To an inclusive democracy. To achieving civil rights and racial justice. To ending poverty and the war in Vietnam. To creating change through grassroots organizing and electoral politics. Contrary to Matusow's summary of liberalism at the end of the sixties, these liberals stayed hopeful, forged a coalition, and attained a constitutional amendment that advanced first-class citizenship for young Americans and benefited every constituency in the nation.

The 26th Amendment was a consummate liberal achievement. The right to vote has both intrinsic and instrumental value. It represents our inclusion in the democratic polity and provides the means to be heard and achieve our aims within it. While the pillars of liberalism—a capitalist economy, welfare state, democratic institutions, and civil liberties—lead to a certain set of policy preferences—economic regulation, social programs, and electoral reform—liberalism is more than policymaking. Kevin Mattson puts it well. It is "a humanist project committed to pushing people to think beyond the interests of the self" and to "the core values of pragmatism and pluralism."[14] In their struggle for youth suffrage, proponents carried this project forward. "In the final analysis," said Edward J. Forand in 1969, "we want to push the idea of negotiation, compromise, and, over all, a sense of human compassion to bring everyone together."[15] Forand and his peers show the persistence and success of liberal reform, despite significant failures and criticism on all sides, into the 1970s.

Still it cannot be denied that the politics and policies of the 1960s put all liberals on the defensive for decades to come. They did because when liberals were in power, as Terry H. Anderson reminded us, all the key conflicts in American history reemerged. Democratic inclusion versus exclusion, states' rights versus federal power, peace seeking versus war mongering, ideals of equality versus the reality of inequality, and individualism versus community. Youth voting rights intersected with all of these conflicts. During these years Americans questioned and contested "the very nature and meaning" of their nation, Anderson concluded in his textbook on the sixties.[16] A more inclusive American democracy through expanded voting rights, including for youth, was one answer. Such answers made this era one of the most transformative in US history. It is a legacy still being fought over.

In the 50 years since, the 26th Amendment has often been seen as an easy, even unremarkable achievement. True, extending the right to vote to a new group of Americans was not a radical change to "politics as usual." And three decades is half of the 72 years women fought for equal suffrage in the United States. Even a proponent like Dennis Warren, who helped to create Let Us Vote in 1969 and collaborated on its theme song, emphasized the relative ease and speed. "Being a student of history, I thought that we would be the catalyst and that it would take years and years." But that wasn't the case. "Things started falling together in a way you could never imagine. It really was serendipity in many respects."[17]

"Serendipity" is one way to see the achievement of the 26th Amendment. It's true that proponents, like Randolph Jennings, Paul Myer, Edward Forand, and Dennis Warren, and their cause found and fit the historical moment. But as the saying goes, "Chance favors those who prepare." And proponents of youth voting rights had been preparing for decades.

PART I

"It's been a long time gettin' here"

1942–1962

1

Franchise of Freedom

It was during the darkest days of World War II that Congressman Jennings Randolph first proposed a constitutional amendment to lower the voting age to 18. It was October 1942, nearly a year after Imperial Japan attacked the US naval base at Pearl Harbor and the United States entered the war. In the months after December 7, 1941—"a date which will live in infamy," as President Franklin D. Roosevelt famously declared—the United States experienced a relentless series of military losses in the Pacific. The US territories of Guam, Wake Island, and the Philippines fell to the advancing Japanese forces, as did the British colonies of Hong Kong, Malaya, Singapore, and Burma. Meanwhile, in Europe, Nazi Germany and Fascist Italy controlled most of the continent as well as North Africa. The German assault on the Soviet Union also pressed forward. By September 1942 the Axis Powers had conquered the most territory they would hold during the war.

At this crucial time President Roosevelt addressed the nation and the need for more troops in a radio fireside chat. "With every passing week the war increases in scope and intensity. That is true in Europe, in Africa, in Asia, and on all the seas." "All of our combat units that go overseas must consist of young, strong men who have had thorough training," argued the president. "The more of such troops we have in the field, the sooner the war will be won, and the smaller will be the cost in casualties." Laying out his case, Roosevelt considered lowering the military draft age from 20 to 18 an absolute necessity. "We have learned how inevitable that is—and how important to the speeding up of victory."[1] He called upon Congress to make this change.

Jennings Randolph, a Democrat from West Virginia serving in the House of Representatives, responded to Roosevelt's request with his support and a stipulation. For a committed New Deal Democrat, Randolph's support for FDR was unsurprising. Swept into the House of Representatives in 1932 along with FDR's presidential victory, he signed his letters,

Representative Jennings Randolph with First Lady Eleanor Roosevelt, 1930s. Jennings Randolph Collection. Courtesy of the West Virginia State Archives.

"Your 'New Dealer' for all the years!" He forged close bonds with both the President and First Lady Eleanor Roosevelt. Still, if the draft age must drop to 18, he felt it should be matched by a lowered voting age. "Who will say," he asked about young Americans, "they are old enough to use bullets, but too young to use ballots?"[2]

A political idealist, Randolph believed in the power of government to promote the common good, and he was strongly committed to the democratic process. "If America speaks and if the spirit of the country says action must come," he pledged in early 1942, "you'll find a hearty and hasty response in Congress."[3] He was a powerful orator, and he loved to tell stories. The son and grandson of Democratic politicians, he was named after Populist firebrand and three-time Democratic presidential nominee William Jennings Bryan, a family friend.

Throughout his life Jennings Randolph never wavered in his loyalty to the Democratic Party or his commitment to small "d" democracy. As Jane Eisner writes, he used to carry in his pocket a list of important political decisions throughout history that came down to just one vote. If a listener expressed doubt about why anyone should vote, when one vote hardly mattered, he would pull out his list and start reading.[4] In 1942, feeling keenly responsible for helping to pass the amended draft bill, Randolph made it his lifelong goal to extend what he called the "franchise of freedom" to youth in return.

On October 21, four days after the House voted to make 18- and 19-year-olds eligible for the draft, Randolph proposed his first constitutional amendment to lower the voting age. He was to repeat this action ten more times over his long career in Congress. He was not the first to do so, and he was not alone. Many members of the House and the Senate joined Randolph along the way. In 1942 and 1943 proposals came from Democratic representative Victor Wickersham of Oklahoma, Republican senator Arthur Vandenberg of Michigan, and Randolph's Democratic Senate colleague from West Virginia, Harley Kilgore, among others. Support for youth voting rights was bipartisan and bicameral from the very start.

During World War II proponents—with Randolph at the forefront—laid the foundation for the next 30 years of advocacy and activism around youth voting rights. They advanced arguments and strategies. They allied across political and partisan differences. These activities did not just occur at the national level. Events on the home front indicated the importance of state and local action for the 18-year-old vote. It became clear that both top-down and bottom-up forces were necessary. The interactions of proponents with political power and at the grassroots shaped this first phase of efforts to lower the voting age nationally and locally. And together they achieved the first success in 1943.

Advancing Arguments

In advancing their arguments for enfranchising young Americans, proponents focused first on the fairness of matching the ages for voting and for the draft. Michigan senator Vandenberg purposely introduced his proposal for a constitutional amendment at exactly the same time the amended draft bill came up for debate in October 1942. He aimed to extend the "privilege of the ballot" to the very same men "who would be inducted into the fighting forces under the pending bill." "If young men of 18 are to be drafted to fight for their country, they should be able to vote for the kind of government the country is to have."[5]

Jennings Randolph expanded on this argument at a House subcommittee hearing in October 1943, the very first on the 18-year-old vote to be held in Congress. Like Vandenberg, Randolph "strongly" felt the draft was "one of the very cogent reasons" for lowering the voting age. The "impact of war has lifted, through the process of the draft, from our home front millions of young men and women in the age bracket of 18 to 20," he testified. He offered statistics on the number of American men fighting overseas who could not vote: 25 percent of the Army, 37 percent of the Navy, 50 percent of the Marine Corps were aged 18 to 20. And each had a story.

> Private John McEachern, of Roxbury Crossing, Massachusetts, went into the Army at 18. As a paratrooper at 19 years of age, he lost his life in North Africa fighting. Private Everett Sparks, of Marietta, Ohio, left his home and parents at 20, and today lies buried somewhere amidst the cruel and drifting mists of Kiska, or on the agonizing fogbound island of Attu.

"Who shall say," Randolph asked passionately "they were not old enough to have been voting citizens of the America for which they gave their lives?"[6]

Several days after Randolph introduced his resolution in the House, Harley Kilgore entered his own joint resolution in the Senate. In justifying his stance, he endorsed Vandenberg's position and echoed Randolph's passion. "While our young soldiers are preserving and restoring democracy on the battlefronts of the globe, how can we fail to give them at home the same right for which they are fighting so valiantly abroad?" Elected in 1940, Kilgore was in his first term as senator from West Virginia. A liberal supported by organized labor, Kilgore posed "the proposition 'if he's old enough to fight, he's old enough to vote,'" a rallying cry that would resonate far and wide.[7]

"Old enough to fight, old enough to vote" became the foundational argument for the campaign to lower the voting age to 18. That the responsibility of military service and bearing arms for one's country earned the right to vote had been heard before in US history. The Civil War crucially advanced the link between soldiering and voting, with 19 northern states enfranchising soldiers in the field in time for the election of 1864. The first instance of "absentee" voting, this development secured the right to vote away from home and set a precedent for the soldier vote during World Wars I and II. Voting soldiers still needed to have attained the age of 21. But following the Civil War, Marcus Bickford argued for the 18-year-old vote for "native-born white citizens" at the New York State constitutional convention of 1867. "We hold men at 18 liable to the Draft and require them to peril their lives in the battlefield."[8] In return, they deserved the right to vote.

Departing from their historical predecessors, Kilgore, Vandenberg, and Randolph recognized women, noncombatant men, and citizens of all races as entitled to the vote equally with military men. Vandenberg carefully worded his amendment. It would allow all "citizens" aged 18 and up to vote, "thereby making it applicable to girls as well as youths."[9] Kilgore's amendment would enfranchise seven million young Americans aged 18 to 20. He commented on those serving in the military and working in war and farm production, and he included women in both categories. He complimented them for their vital contributions to the war effort. "In a word, 90 per cent of these 7,000,000 young citizens are devoting their full time energies to the defense of the nation." The vote rightfully belonged to "our youthful defenders in foxhole, factory, and farm," Senator Kilgore finished with a flourish.[10]

The foundational argument was not the only argument proponents advanced.[11] Kilgore and Randolph further argued that young Americans had the maturity to vote. "If they are mature enough to fight for their country, they are mature enough to vote for the preservation of its institutions," contended Kilgore. "Youth, old enough to fight and die for their countries, are, assuredly, mature enough to participate in the processes of government," reinforced Randolph.[12] Randolph had a good basis for his judgment, as he had taught journalism and public speaking and coached sports at Davis and Elkins College in West Virginia before launching his political career. "When I was teaching I found that the group from 18 to 21 in the classes over which I presided had well-ordered minds."[13]

For the two congressmen from West Virginia, the expansion of public education crucially contributed to young people's readiness for voting. They believed American public education, just as originally intended, laid the foundation for good citizenship. "Advances in education in the past thirty years and the deepening understanding of national affairs among young people of today are matters of general knowledge," asserted Kilgore. To Randolph youth were "in most instances as intelligent and as well informed as men and women many years their senior."[14]

Randolph also pointed out that by the mid-twentieth century what it meant to be 18, what the accrual of those years signified, had changed. In modern America, events and developments moved faster. "Stepped-up methods of communication," "the increased tempo of transportation," the very "processes of civilization" sped up the maturation process for young people. In the 1940s 18-year-olds had the attributes and awareness of "the youth of the country, shall we say, 25, 50, or 100 years ago at the age of 21." "I don't believe we should be tied down to any tradition, which in this instance I believe to be meritless, which would continue the voting age at 21 rather than 18," Randolph asserted.[15]

Implicit in Randolph's discussion was the understanding that the fixing of age markers and the construction of their meanings evolved over time and place. The voting age, like all age categories, was determined not by biology or chronology but by social processes.[16] In 1867 New Yorker Marcus Bickford conveyed this same understanding at his state's constitutional convention, commencing with biblical references. "Under the Jewish economy, the age of majority was fixed at twenty-five. Now, sir, the age in which we live, in this fast age, men arrive to maturity both in body and mind at a great deal earlier period than formerly."[17]

Bickford's "fast age" of the nineteenth century accelerated age consciousness and distinctions in American society. More ways to know and prove age, such as birth certificates, were required over time.[18] Never in doubt, however, was the political meaning and significance of age 21, at least for white men. For Bickford and his peers, reaching the age of enfranchisement earned a political right and exercising that right became a rite of passage.[19] Depending on one's gender, race, location, and historical moment—on whether one was included or excluded from the franchise—being 21 years old or of "voting age" came to signify adulthood, maturity, and full American citizenship. Proponents of youth voting rights during World War II sought to make age 18 signify the same.

In making their arguments these early proponents referenced not only present-day conditions but also the past and the future. They considered youth suffrage to be part of a larger national story: the progress of American democracy. They harkened back to the founding of the republic. "The right to vote is more precious than diamonds," Senator Kilgore exclaimed in 1943. "It is the hard, unshatterable, granite core upon which the greatness of America is founded." For Kilgore, the recognition that "We the People," popular sovereignty, formed the basis for the government of the United States went together with great respect for citizen participation in politics. The "extension of the vote to our 18-year-olds is a real test of our devotion to the democracy we profess. It will be proof positive that we Americans can practice what we preach."[20]

These World War II proponents also connected youth voting rights to other suffrage reforms in US history. Randolph called attention to the most recent reform: the enfranchisement of women with the 19th Amendment in 1920. "I can remember, as a young man, listening to heated debate in my State on the subject of woman suffrage."[21] The battle over women's suffrage in West Virginia was controversial and close, with ratification approved by only one vote in the State Senate. With that victory, West Virginia became the 34th of 36 states needed to ratify the 19th Amendment. Randolph had turned 18 just days before his state's suffrage battle was won, a date well within his and others' living memories. "Naturally, I recall the arguments against woman suffrage which were hurled at me when I called the legislature in special session in 1920 to ratify the amendment," John J. Cornwell, former governor of West Virginia, wrote Randolph. Overcoming those objections, West Virginian women "have been most active in politics since they obtained the privilege of voting." Of youth, Cornwell suspected "the same will be true."[22]

Proponents of youth voting rights during World War II were counting on this. They strongly believed that the political participation of 18-, 19-, and 20-year-olds was needed to strengthen US democracy and government and ensure the future of the nation. "Youth's point of view should be made a part of today's vast undertakings and important discussions of the future," Randolph proclaimed in 1943. Lowering the voting age to 18 would lead to "an infusion of new thoughts and plans" into the nation. Kilgore could not resist an effusive extension of the metaphor. "The infusion of 7,000,000 young voters into the body politic will be a blood donation that as a nation we owe to our Uncle Sam."[23] Yet both men knew that multiple arguments and memorable metaphors would not get their amendments passed. They needed a constitutional strategy.

The Law of the Land

These World War II–era proponents of the 18-year-old vote were comfortable with amending the US Constitution. Carrying on a tradition in American constitutional thought, they considered the federal constitution to be a living document, amenable to change as conditions warranted. They understood the amendment process laid out in the Constitution, which required a joint resolution passed by two-thirds of both houses of Congress and then ratification by three-quarters of the states.

They also knew how earlier suffrage reforms had been achieved. As Randolph indicated the achievement of women's suffrage through the 19th Amendment remained their first point of reference. It was the most recent expansion of voting rights, and they modeled their resolutions on it. They worded their proposed amendments for youth suffrage nearly identically. The 19th Amendment states, "The right of citizens of the United States to vote shall not be denied or abridged by the United States or by any State on account of sex." They substituted "age" for "sex" and qualified the age of citizens to be 18 and older.

Seldom heard in these early congressional debates and discussions was that this wording also followed that of the 15th Amendment, the very first voting rights amendment in the US Constitution. Ratified in 1870, the 15th Amendment introduced a national conception of a right to vote and extended the franchise to African American men following the Civil War. It was the third of three Reconstruction Amendments. Passed as part of reconstructing the country on a new, interracial basis, these amendments abolished slavery (the 13th Amendment) and established national citizenship (the 14th Amendment). The 15th Amendment states that the rights of US citizens to vote cannot be "denied or abridged . . . on account of race, color, or previous condition of servitude."

The phrasing of all three suffrage amendments is similar and similarly stated in the negative. During the 1943 House hearing on Randolph's voting age amendment this question came up. "I was wondering," asked one congressman, "why it is in the negative form." He read the resolution aloud. "It is really in the negative form, isn't it?" Representative Emanuel Celler, Democrat from New York, responded. "I think the amendments to the Constitution relating to suffrage are couched in the negative."[24] Celler was right. Rather than affirmatively guaranteeing voting rights, the 15th, 19th, and later 26th Amendments prohibited their denial or abridgement, and that difference matters. The negative wording limited the scope of congressional action to ensure enfranchisement and opened up other bases for disenfranchisement, such as literacy tests and poll taxes.

The 14th Amendment also had implications for suffrage. Section 1 related to "the privileges or immunities of citizens of the United States," specifying rights to "due process" and "equal protection of the laws." Section 2 addressed the apportionment of representation in the House with attention to voting rights. It provided a punishment for states that practiced disenfranchisement, for it would reduce a state's representation in Congress in proportion to the number of disfranchised citizens. If enforced this clause may have helped to protect Black voting rights, but it never was. Section 2 also inserted for the first time "male" and "twenty-one years of age" to modify "citizen." Sex and age qualifications related to voting rights now were in the US Constitution. The introduction of the word "male" struck a blow to early women's suffrage advocates. They then tried unsuccessfully to include "sex" in the 15th Amendment.

In the early 1940s, apart from Black civil rights activists and their allies, the 15th Amendment was largely ignored and certainly not enforced to protect Black voting rights. Given his membership in the Republican Party—the "party of Lincoln"—Senator Vandenberg believed the 14th and 15th Amendments to be "the heart of the Constitution so far as the colored citizen is concerned." He admitted, however, that for "seventy years there has been a large measure of evasion in their acknowledgment."[25]

Randolph also recognized this evasion and lack of enforcement around the 15th Amendment. In the early 1940s, in his position as chair of the House Committee on the District of Columbia, he was working on another constitutional amendment: to provide representation in Congress and in the Electoral College to the "voteless" citizens of Washington, DC. This effort raised the issue of racial disenfranchisement because nearly a third of DC's citizenry were African American. Randolph's position put him at the intersection of three twentieth-century suffrage struggles: for African Americans, Washington, DC, and youth.

What was needed was action on the part of Congress, as the civil rights movement and advocates of other political reforms had long argued. But setting aside the politics of race and of party, the US Constitution made such action contentious.[26] As is true for American government as a whole, the Constitution divides power between the federal and state governments with regard to determining election regulations and voting qualifications. Fierce debates occurred during the original drafting and ratification of the Constitution and with the 14th, 15th, and 19th Amendments, with most of the ferocity coming from the champions of states' rights. They adamantly opposed what they saw as a federal incursion on the power of the states to set suffrage qualifications and regulate elections.

Two constitutional provisions were at the center of these debates. Those championing state sovereignty over voter qualifications cited Article 1, Section 2: "The House of Representatives shall be composed of Members chosen every second year by the people of the several states, and the electors in each State shall have the qualifications requisite for electors of the most numerous branch of the State legislature." For proponents of federal power Article 1, Section 4 was most pertinent: "The Times, Places and Manner of holding Elections for Senators and Representatives, shall be prescribed in each State by the Legislature thereof; but the Congress may at any time by Law make or alter such Regulations. . . ." So the power to regulate elections belongs to the states in the first instance, but the Congress "may" step in.

Yet qualifications for voters and regulations for elections are not necessarily the same thing. At the Constitutional Convention the Founding Fathers affirmed suffrage qualifications as the basis of republican government, and as such they "ought not to be left to be regulated" by Congress.[27] In *Minor v. Happersett* (1875), the Supreme Court confirmed that the "power of the State in this particular is certainly supreme until

Congress acts." Historically, Congress did act with the 15th and 19th Amendments. It also enacted the 17th Amendment, ratified in 1913, which provided for the direct election of senators.

The conflict between states' rights versus federal power would continue throughout the 30-year campaign for youth voting rights, but proponents could quote Article 1, Section 4 and the precedent set by earlier suffrage amendments. On this basis Randolph and his colleagues contended that Congress had the power to lower the voting age. There were some differences among these first resolutions. Representative Wickersham's proposed amendment held for youth voting only in federal elections, while the others covered elections at all levels of government. But they all agreed that a US constitutional amendment was the way to go. Now they just needed to convince their congressional colleagues, as well as their fellow citizens, to make youth voting rights the law of the land.

Voters of the Country

A remarkable shift in public opinion over 1943 aided this prospect. "Sentiment for Lowering Voting Age Gaining," headlined George Gallup's article in the *Washington Post* in September 1943. Gallup reported on the results of three surveys conducted in January, April, and September, during which support for the 18-year-old vote grew from 39 percent to 42 percent, then to a clear majority of 52 percent in just nine months. The director of the American Institute of Public Opinion attributed this rise to "the wartime drafting of young men, and the cry that if a man is old enough to fight at 18, he is old enough to vote."[28] The rise also showed how the advocacy of political elites could have an impact on public opinion. Among "the voters of the country," Randolph happily reported, "there has been an increased sentiment for this type of resolution."[29]

Polling also showed bipartisan and broad geographical backing. Gallup called attention to the latter, as the latest survey "indicates no great difference by areas." Support ranged from 53 percent on the East and West Coasts to 50 percent in the central states, with 52 percent in the South. That region, the pollster noted, "appears no more strongly in favor of the change than the average for the country."[30] For George Gallup in 1943, if not for us today, this finding was very much unexpected. He had assumed the southern states would be more favorable toward youth voting rights than other regions of the country. And he made this assumption because the first state in the nation to enfranchise 18-year-olds had already done so the previous month, August 1943. That state was Georgia.

At the center of this turn of events was the newly elected governor Ellis G. Arnall. Emerging victorious in 1942 out of a bitterly fought campaign against the demagogic and anti–New Deal incumbent governor Eugene Talmadge, Arnall was a southern liberal. Only 35 years old when he took office, Arnall became the youngest governor in the United States. He ran on a reform platform to rout out corruption in state government as well as strong support for the New Deal. Yet Arnall was a segregationist. Even so, during his tenure in office, Arnall softened the "orthodox" southern stance on Black voting rights and successfully abolished the poll tax, alongside his support for youth voting rights. Backing from an array of state organizations and grassroots groups made these moves toward greater democracy in Georgia possible.

When Governor Arnall joined Representative Randolph as a witness at the October 1943 hearing in the House of Representatives on lowering the voting age, he told the subcommittee "we had an interesting experience in Georgia last August." He went on to explain how the state had enfranchised 18-, 19-, and 20-year-olds. At his prompting the General Assembly passed an amendment to the state constitution earlier that year. When the amendment was put to the voters on August 3, 1943, they ratified it by a margin of more than two to one.[31] This success repaid and rewarded the many students who contributed to the groundswell of grassroots support for Arnall's gubernatorial race the previous year.

"Probably the most zealous workers in the campaign to elect Ellis Arnall Governor of Georgia are students of the state," editorialized the *Augusta Chronicle*. College newspapers endorsed, and campus clubs electioneered. "Georgia Students Want Arnall." "Vote for Arnall and Save Our Schools."[32] Such prominent student political involvement raised awareness about the lack of youth voting rights in Georgia. "It is true that the majority of them cannot vote because they have not reached voting age," one journalist observed. "But the folks back home . . . make no bones about respecting their opinions." With the backing of their family members, students were "making the political powers stand up and take notice."[33]

University of Georgia students welcome Governor Ellis Arnall in his hometown of Newnan, Georgia [1944]. AP photo. Atlanta-Journal Photographs Collection. Courtesy of Special Collections & Archives, Georgia State University Library.

Georgians in newspaper editorials, opinion columns, and letters to the editor also took notice and overwhelmingly endorsed youth voting rights. Endorsements using the "old enough to fight, old enough to vote" argument came from the Veterans of Foreign Wars and the American Legion in Georgia. A second argument emphasized the "greater honesty and purer idealism" of youth.[34] Both arguments appealed to the labor liberals in the Congress of Industrial Organizations (CIO) in Georgia, and the state CIO Council endorsed youth suffrage. The right to vote belonged to "young people who are old enough to fight and die for their country." Moreover, "the enthusiasm and ideals of young men and women of this age group will bring new energy to democracy in Georgia." The CIO regional director promised Arnall that his union colleagues would come out to the polls and vote for ratification.[35]

Referendum voters fulfilled the CIO's promise. "Especially am I delighted that Georgia leads the nation in lowering the voting age to 18," Arnall declared. "We have let the world know that we have faith in our young people."[36] Although he didn't specify white young people, others did. According to one student newspaper youth suffrage made "approximately 160,000 white boys and girls eligible to vote." After all, reported the *Atlanta Constitution*, "Negro youths could not vote in white primaries."[37] Less than direct on the racial implications of the 18-year-old vote, Arnall immediately announced his intention to carry this campaign to the rest of the country.

Seeds of a National Coalition

"Georgia last week became the first state to adopt the doctrine of 'fight at 18, vote at 18,'" noted *Newsweek*, and it happened under "the leadership of the youthful Gov. Ellis G. Arnall, who is only twice 18 himself."[38] Within two weeks of the August referendum two members of the Senate Judiciary Committee weighed in: "Georgia's Action Brings Federal Amendment to Fore." Work finally would begin on the joint resolution sponsored by Senator Vandenberg earlier that year. "Georgia Started Something," the *Atlanta Constitution* crowed.[39]

Public awareness and political action for lowering the voting age grew markedly over 1943. Twenty-nine states, in addition to Georgia, introduced constitutional amendments that year. Also important was the role of American veterans, the League of Women Voters, and labor unions. Evident in Georgia's ratification campaign, they were essential to any future successes. The voting age "should be adjusted now, while we are at war," contended the president of the United Auto Workers (UAW). All states should "follow the example of Georgia."[40] State and local CIO councils in Michigan and Ohio passed resolutions and started petition drives. Such crucial organizational backing needed to be built from the bottom up. Together with events in Georgia, developments across the country revealed the seeds of a national coalition for youth voting rights.

Support definitely existed on the left of the American political spectrum. Norman Thomas of the Socialist Party indicated his approval for lowering the voting age to match the draft age and to balance the increasing proportion "of old folks and tired folks."[41] When Senator

Harley Kilgore explained his proposal for a constitutional amendment in 1943, he did so in *Spotlight*, the official magazine of American Youth for Democracy (AYD). The AYD's progressive program included "champions the right to vote at 18."[42] This commitment had a history. The AYD, newly formed in 1943, grew out of the Young Communist League, the youth wing of the Communist Party USA, and as early as 1934 the league considered youth enfranchisement a priority. Kilgore urged "all believers in youth and democracy" like AYD "to give their active support" to his proposal in Congress and encouraged state-level initiatives. "Let the other states promptly follow Georgia's courageous lead!"[43]

Organizations definitely were. The most important and influential was the National Education Association (NEA). Founded nearly 100 years earlier, NEA provided an organized voice for public school educators across the country. As such, it had been part of early debates and reforms to reorganize schooling according to age-related grades, adding to the social awareness and impact of age categories in the United States.[44] NEA leaders emerged as strong advocates for lowering the voting age during World War II.

In making their case they advanced multiple arguments. Military service, war work, equal justice, and fairness all earned youth voting rights. But—hardly surprisingly—they emphasized educational attainment most of all. "The 18-year-olds of 1943 are much better equipped to assume the responsibility of voting than the 21-year-olds who were vested with suffrage at the beginning of our Republic," argued NEA president Edith B. Joynes. Contemporary youth were better educated and informed, while "a goodly percentage" of their predecessors "signed their names with a mark."[45] NEA *Journal* editor Joy Elmer Morgan contended that young Americans were well prepared for voting due to "the effectiveness of education for citizenship" and "the emphasis on the study of current affairs" in American public schools. After all, US public schools were established in the first place to educate and train citizens for democracy.[46]

One procedure often promoted in civic education was student discussion and debate, and what better way to enlighten students, parents, and communities about youth suffrage? During World War II and after, local schools sponsored debates. The winners, losers, and their arguments received respectful attention in local newspapers.

"Debaters Want Voting Age Lowered; Advance Good Reasons" head-lined an article on a 1943 Connecticut debate.[47] American university and high school students engaged with the issue during the 1944–1945 school year, when the national debate topic was "that the Voting Age be reduced to 18 years." Given that education for democracy entailed both theory and practice, debating the 18-year-old vote was a perfect, if para-doxical, exercise. Students were engaging in democratic practice over whether or not democratic theory should extend to themselves.

Answering yes was First Lady Eleanor Roosevelt, who came out in favor in her popular daily newspaper column, "My Day" in early 1943.

> If young men of eighteen and nineteen are old enough to be trained to fight their country's battles and to proceed from training to the battle-fields, I think we must accept the fact that they are also old enough to know why we fight this war. If that is so, then they are old enough to take part in the political life of their country and to be full citizens with voting powers.[48]

She expanded the foundational argument of "old enough to fight, old enough to vote" to include not just training but also knowledge and understanding, two vital attributes for American voters.

Eleanor Roosevelt's statement of support for the 18-year-old vote not only appeared in her widely syndicated column, which she signed "E.R.," but also received attention from the Associated Press and other news outlets. "Mrs. Franklin D. Roosevelt, whose daily newspaper column often gives hints of policies under discussion in Administration circles, declared today that the voting age should be lowered to 18."[49] Although her husband may in fact have been a supporter, FDR never said so. ER expressed her support from 1943 on.

Committed to social justice and a consummate coalition builder, ER participated in a wide array of activities and organizations and inter-acted with others who shared her views. She had a long-standing interest in young people and worked closely with the youth movement in the 1930s and 1940s, including the Young Democratic Clubs. She followed the progress of New Deal projects in the state of West Virginia and fre-quently visited with Representative Randolph. A member of the League of Women Voters since its founding, ER wholeheartedly agreed with the league's commitment to voter education and participation. She also supported the American Civil Liberties Union, cofounded by her good friend Roger Baldwin, who joined her in 1943 in endorsing "Old Enough to Fight, Why Not to Vote?"[50] Over the next three decades, all of these parties would help to progress youth suffrage.

Eleanor Roosevelt belonged to another future coalition member: the NAACP. Since its founding in 1909 the NAACP has been a long-standing force for the expansion of voting rights for all American citizens. At the time, under the leadership of executive secretary Walter F. White and with committed youth organizer Ella Baker as the director of branches, the association's agenda necessarily prioritized ending the disfranchisement of African Americans in the South rather than enfranchising youth. Yet together with the rest of the civil rights movement, the NAACP's voting rights activism in communities, through the courts, and in Congress prepared the ground for the 18-year-old vote.

During the Second World War civil rights activists and organizations—not just the NAACP—challenged discrimination and disfranchisement on many fronts. They won a ban on employment discrimination in the war industries and a Fair Employment Practices Committee to investigate violations. They sought to remove voting rights restrictions like the poll tax. Understood as a restriction of voting rights based as much on class as race, the poll tax was criticized by President Roosevelt and advocacy groups and was repealed in a few states. But anti–poll tax advocates ran into opposition in the Senate and at the Supreme Court. In 1944 a major success for voting rights did occur with *Smith v. Allwright*, which FDR's first appointment to the Supreme Court, Justice Hugo Black, decided with the majority. This case culminated the NAACP's legal challenges to the Democratic Party's "white-only" primary elections as violating the 14th and 15th Amendments.

Proceedings around the poll tax and white-only primaries played out in Georgia. Under the leadership of Ellis Arnall, anti–poll tax victories stacked up. The 1943 youth suffrage amendment suspended the poll tax for voters 18 to 20 years of age. The state waived the poll tax for members of the armed forces in the election of 1944. Then the next year Arnall achieved the abolition of the poll tax. In response the *New Republic* hailed him as an exemplar of "bold progressivism."[51] Moderating such acclaim for Arnall, these changes were not expected to increase the Black vote in Georgia, but the end of the white-only primary might make a difference. In 1944 Reverend Primus E. King of Columbus, Georgia, sought to implement *Smith v. Allwright* by participating in his state's Democratic Party primary. He was prevented from doing so. With the support of the cofounder of the local NAACP, King went to federal court and won at every level.

The number of registered African American voters in Georgia subsequently rose tenfold, but they confronted a campaign of white violence and intimidation, including a terrible mass lynching in July 1946. Afterward a young Martin Luther King, a student at Morehouse College, wrote a letter to the editor of the *Atlanta Constitution*. "We want and are entitled to the basic rights and opportunities of American citizens," he argued, including "the right to vote; equality before the law; some of the same courtesy and good manners that we ourselves bring to all human relations."[52] Adding his voice to the rest of the civil rights movement, the 17-year-old King sought racial justice for and from his fellow citizens. Much was at stake, the *New Republic* concluded. "What happens in Georgia in the next two years will have a profound effect on the kind of peace we are able to make, as well as the kind of postwar world."[53]

2

Youth's Own Future

With World War II's end in sight delegates to the 1944 Democratic National Convention met in Chicago to nominate President Roosevelt for an unprecedented fourth term. Youth suffrage was on the agenda. Governor Arnall proposed, "as one of the planks of the platform, that we believe in extending to these young people the right to participate in elections."[1] American Youth for Democracy sent the convention an impassioned statement of support. Young women and men were "now fighting for democracy." The nation, in return, owed them "a fuller measure of that democracy." "Young people," argued AYD, "have an unprecedented interest in all public affairs. This interest grows from knowledge of the fact that youth's own future is being shaped by this war and by our ability to establish a secure postwar world."[2] Yet Arnall and AYD's aim to affect the Democratic Party platform in 1944 did not come to be.

The postwar future envisioned by AYD also did not come to be. Instead, during the second half of the 1940s, the United States ended a world war and entered a cold war. Although World War II spurred support for youth voting rights, the Cold War cut both ways. Proponents considered youth voting rights consistent with the United States as the world's bastion of freedom and democracy against the totalitarianism of the Soviet Union. They extended the foundational argument of "old enough to fight, old enough to vote" when the Cold War necessitated continuing the military draft. But opponents of lowering the voting age justified their stance within the context of the Cold War as well, and growing anticommunism at home and abroad undermined liberal and leftist advocates of voting rights.

Opponents had already succeeded in slowing the momentum for the 18-year-old vote that emerged during World War II. The groundbreaking 1943 congressional hearing, featuring Governor Arnall and Representative Randolph, adjourned after just these two speakers. Randolph and Arnall's approach and arguments proved unpersuasive to members of the subcommittee, particularly the chairman, Emanuel Celler.

A New Yorker, liberal Democrat, and supporter of Black civil rights, Celler became Randolph's fiercest foe on this issue in the House of Representatives. He objected most to lowering the voting age with a federal constitutional amendment rather than on a state-by-state basis. Of Congress, he said, "we are not a mere funnel through which could be poured an amendment to the Constitution of the United States."[3] Over the next decade Celler moved from chairing a subcommittee to heading up the full House Judiciary Committee. He held this powerful position from 1949 to 1952 and then again after 1955, during years when Democrats held a majority in the House of Representatives. From this position Celler blocked efforts to lower the voting age until 1970.

The actions and arguments of opponents, like Celler, help to explain why achieving youth voting rights took three decades. Just as support was bipartisan, so too was the opposition. It also spanned the same demographic and geographic spectrum. Opponents could be found across the country, among young Americans, educators, women, journalists, and public figures. They opposed campaigns at both the state and national levels during the 1940s and 1950s. As a result, proponents could claim few victories in these years. But they did not give up, and they achieved some important firsts at the national level.

The Opposition in Congress

The October 1943 hearing on Jennings Randolph's proposed constitutional amendment provided opponents in Congress with their first opportunity to make their case. When he had the floor Representative Celler focused on countering the foundational argument. Military service and voting, he later observed, "are as different as chalk is from cheese."[4] At the hearing he challenged Randolph's contention that the voting age should match the draft age. "Let us suppose—and God forbid—that the exigencies of war would turn against us . . . and we would have to reduce the draft age to 16, as is the case in Germany today. Would you say the voting age should likewise be reduced to 16?"[5] Randolph rejected this idea and restated his reasons for the 18-year-old vote. But Celler did not back down. For him, revisions to the fixity and meaning of any age marker called into question all age distinctions.

He was joined in this line of reasoning by another member of the subcommittee, Representative Sam M. Russell, a Texas Democrat. When questioning Arnall, Representative Russell pushed this line to the point of preposterousness.

> You speak of the age of 18, and you say that a boy of 18 is doing his bit and rendering service as a soldier. Why don't you make the voting age 17? Aren't you discriminating against the 17-year-old boys? There are thousands of boys of 17 in the service, and some of 16, and some of 15, and I saw in the paper there was one of 12, I think.

Arnall answered by admitting that the age of citizenship was "arbitrary," but that one needed to be set, and, as Randolph stated, 18 was fair and right.[6]

Celler and Russell both went on to reinforce why 21 should remain the age qualification for voting. Russell argued that as young people mature from age 18 to 21, they are "in better condition, mentally, judicially, and otherwise, to pass on what are the best interests of the country!" Arnall could not resist pointing out that "by the same reasoning we could say that a man from 21 to 25 will grow more mature and be better qualified to vote." For Arnall, 21 was just as arbitrary an age as 18 or any other, so additional factors, like military service and high school graduation, should be considered in justifying 18 as the voting age.[7]

Celler took a different tack in the hearing and looked back to the past. He cited the fact that "our constitutional fathers recognized that the common law handed down over the centuries set the age of majority at 21." He made the historically correct point that the original US Constitution did not set any age qualifications for voting—those were left to the states alongside other suffrage qualifications—but did for federal office holding. Only with the 14th Amendment, ratified in 1868, did the age of 21 appear in the Constitution, as did the word "male." Celler told his colleagues that the Constitution affirmed "in the fourteenth amendment, the age of 21 as the age of majority."[8]

In pushing back against Arnall and Randolph's arguments, Celler and Russell made clear what they saw as the most important issue at stake:

states' rights versus federal power. In pursuing a federal amendment to enfranchise 18-, 19-, and 20-year-olds, proponents were proposing "an abridgement of the powers of the States." Russell confronted Randolph directly. By adopting such an amendment, "then you have killed any constitutional action on the part of the individual States relating to the matter."[9] Randolph parried, pointing out that the amendment process requires ratification by three-quarters of the states. This requirement meant "the final decision does rest with the States." With this requirement, Arnall added, there "were adequate safeguards" to ensure "democratic processes."[10]

Some congressmen at the subcommittee hearing considered the governor's stance contradictory. After all, Arnall advocated a federal action that would deny to the rest of the states the power to determine age qualifications for suffrage, a power his own state of Georgia had just used. Celler later reminded his colleagues that "the States can act first, if they will."[11] The opposition's insistence on individual state action to achieve youth voting rights turned out to be an effective way to block youth suffrage in Congress for decades to come.

Beyond the Capitol

Opponents outside of Congress joined these representatives in criticizing the value of lowering the voting age. Those at the state level assumed, like Celler, the states would act first. Yet of the 29 states that like Georgia introduced constitutional amendments in 1943, none succeeded. Most of these amendments died in committee, although a few lived longer. In New York, for example, the Assembly passed the measure but the State Senate failed to take action. The Maine Senate vigorously debated the issue, but the voices of the opposition dominated. One state senator pointed out that there were only two supporters at the committee level and one was "a member of the Communist Party." If the voting age was going to change, another believed it should be raised and not lowered![12]

Whether politicians, public figures, or parents, opponents did not think military service warranted the franchise. Several offered a variation on Celler's chalk-and-cheese argument. "The very qualities which makes them good in battle—their daring and lack of caution—would be against them in voting," expressed one.[13] Missed in these criticisms was that proponents' foundational argument focused on balancing the rights and responsibilities of citizenship. It was not aimed at equating the qualifications and qualities of soldiers and voters.

Americans against the 18-year-old vote also agreed with congressional opponents that 21 remained the appropriate minimum age for voting. Twenty-one, the New York City Bar Association reminded, "is the traditional age at which a person attains majority and the additional three years add that much more to the knowledge and experience of the voter."[14] Conservative economist Alfred P. Haake presented this argument on the libertarian radio program, *Wake Up, America!* "The law says any person under 21 is a 'legal infant,' not responsible for all his acts. . . . Wisdom and sound judgment come only after living with the realities of adult life." As "evidenced by the phenomenal political success of Hitler, Mussolini and Franco," Haake warned ominously, young voters would be "fertile soil for demagogues."[15]

More measured opponents found fault with the maturity and capabilities of teenagers as well. In a 1943 readers' poll conducted by the *Woman's Home Companion*, 61 percent opposed lowering the voting age. "Youths of eighteen are much too immature to vote intelligently."[16] This viewpoint could be found among young people themselves. Sidney Silvian, a high school senior from Cincinnati, Ohio, noted that "at what age a person is politically developed" was open to question. But he was certain that older Americans had joined the workforce at a younger age than was currently the case, given expanded opportunities for high school education. Unlike 21-year-olds in the past, an "18-year-old of today does not have the social experience of a wage earner to enable him to vote wisely." Silvian introduced another counterargument. Age—unlike race and sex—never constituted a permanent barrier to enfranchisement: "to assert that the 18-year-olds represent some special group . . . is a false illusion."[17] In three short years, they would be able to vote.

George Gallup's analysis of his September 1943 poll showing majority support for youth suffrage suggested another reason for opposition: partisanship. Party politics had figured in the expansion of suffrage in the past. After the Civil War the Republican Party pushed the 15th Amendment out of a principled commitment to full citizenship for African Americans. At the same time Black enfranchisement would help to build the Republican Party in the South. A similar partisan calculation was assumed to be at work with youth suffrage. Given that political support for the Democratic Party was higher among younger voters than older ones, Gallup hypothesized that a new constituency of teenage voters would "lean strongly toward the Democratic side and swell the ranks of that party much more than of the GOP." Thus, backing from Republicans for youth suffrage was "unlikely."[18]

Gallup was wrong on both counts. The youth vote could and would swing to the Republican Party as well as to Democrats. And several very important members of the Republican Party continued or committed their support after World War II. Some 14 proposals for lowering the voting age came to Congress, and nearly 100 to the various states through 1952.[19] Republicans as well as Democrats brought these forth, including the first Republican president in two decades. But another president announced his support even earlier, becoming the first US president to do so.

A Presidential First

On a chilly, windy April 6, 1946, in Chicago, President Harry S. Truman participated in a commemoration and celebration of Army Day. The day's events included a parade and speeches before a crowd at—appropriately enough—Soldier Field. During a brief press conference, the president said "he favored giving 18 year olds the right to vote, if they prepare themselves, because they had proved in time of war that they are entitled to the rights of citizenship."[20] With Cold War threatening, the timing of Truman's statement was telling. The president set off a "political flurry over the wisdom" of youth suffrage. The Democratic National Committee followed up with a survey of opinions within the party. Respondents favored lowering the voting age by four to one.[21] Young Democrats advocated for the issue at both the state and national levels.

Although he followed in FDR's footsteps, Harry Truman took a stance on the 18-year-old vote that his predecessor never did. When President Roosevelt died on April 12, 1945, Vice President Truman inherited overseeing the end of a global war and an uneasy transition to a postwar world. Truman had joined the Democratic presidential ticket only in 1944 and served just a few months before Roosevelt's death. As the new president struggled to find his footing in a turbulent geopolitical environment, he also found himself on shaky ground domestically. Both developments influenced the path and progress of youth voting rights in postwar America.

At home, the political dominance of the Democratic Party, which had held the White House and Congress since 1933, faced serious challenge. War weariness, economic instability, and a labor strike wave characterized the immediate postwar period. The party that had delivered the New Deal and directed American participation in World War II became a target. The intensifying Cold War abroad increased the political backlash. Conservative candidates in both parties used a combination of anti–New Deal, anti–civil rights, and anticommunist rhetoric very effectively. The midterm election of 1946 racked up historic losses for Democrats, especially liberals and progressives, and turned both houses of Congress over to the Republicans. One winner was Richard M. Nixon, who deployed accusations of communist connections, or "red-baiting," to defeat his Democratic opponent. One loser was the consummate New Dealer Jennings Randolph. Youth suffrage had lost its foremost champion in the House of Representatives, although a future champion, Montana Democrat Mike Mansfield, won reelection.

The Senate still held supporters of youth voting rights. Randolph's fellow West Virginian, Senator Harley Kilgore, won reelection in 1946, and he would again in 1952. Kilgore remained committed to many of his liberal, prolabor ideals, and he was red-baited in his last Senate campaign. His connections during the war years opened him up to such accusations. One was his 1943 article on lowering the voting age for AYD's *Spotlight*. Later named a communist organization, AYD disbanded in 1949. Kilgore successfully countered these charges, but only by taking a strong stance against the Soviet Union and the civil liberties of American communists.[22] He continued to support youth voting rights, however. And he introduced his constitutional amendment once again with the new Congress in January 1947. Senator Arthur Vandenberg did the same, after securing his fourth term in the Senate. As during World War II, the question of the draft age shaped their stances.

US draft policy was in a state of flux during the transition from world war to postwar and then to cold war. Was the nation at war or at peace? What needs did the nation have for military personnel, particularly in the era of nuclear weapons, and how to fulfill them? Ideas were floated for an all-volunteer military and universal military training. Key constituencies for the Democratic Party conveyed their criticisms. Labor unions opposed a draft in what was ostensibly peacetime. Civil rights organizations objected to continuing "the Jim Crow draft" for a segregated military. At one point, in 1947, President Truman let the draft expire, but that did not last long. It was reinstated in June 1948 with a draft age of 19.

The next month Truman abolished racial discrimination and paved the way for ending segregation in the armed forces, one of the many landmark and long-awaited recommendations of his President's Committee on Civil Rights. Its 1947 report "To Secure These Rights" was forthright on this principle. "The injustice of calling men to fight for freedom while subjecting them to humiliating discrimination within the fighting forces is at once apparent."[23] Truman's draft and civil rights moves lent unpredictability to the close presidential election of 1948. But in a dramatic comeback, and despite the defection of southern segregationists, or "Dixiecrats," voters returned Truman to the White House and a Democratic majority to Congress.

With the outbreak of the Korean War in 1950 the Cold War got hot, fueling debate again about appropriate ages for the draft and for voting. The Truman administration sought to lower the draft age back down to 18, as in World War II. The "nation's mothers" took action, according to Newsweek. They "bombarded" Congress "with letters and telegrams, all sounding the same call to arms: Don't take my boy away until he's older."[24] For Carroll D. Kearns, a Republican congressman from Pennsylvania, if the draft age changed back to 18, it should be accompanied with the 18-year-old vote, enacted either by the states or by federal amendment. A former educator, Kearns credited the "study of current affairs" and "classes in problems of democracy" in the nation's schools for "have properly enlightened the youth of our country." "Give Youth the Right to Vote!" editorialized the women's magazine, Redbook.[25]

Appeals for youth voting rights continued after the establishment of universal military service in 1951, with a draft age of 18 1/2 years. The first one came from Eleanor Roosevelt. Since her husband's death ER had maintained her commitments to public affairs and to youth. Just as President Truman signed the universal military service bill into law in June 1951, she offered her support in her "My Day" column. The new law "has sharpened up the question of a change in the voting age" and the unfairness of youth not having "a voice in the government." ER once again urged "granting to young men and young women this right of participation in their government."[26]

A Congressional First

The combination of the Cold War with the Soviet Union, war in Korea, and a new military draft kept youth suffrage a topic of news and politics heading into the 1952 presidential election. That year, Senator Blair Moody, Democrat from Michigan, offered a joint resolution. He was fulfilling an obligation of the office he now held: the Senate seat of Senator Vandenberg, who had died the year before. A former journalist and war correspondent with the *Detroit News*, Senator Moody made multiple arguments for the 18-year-old vote before a subcommittee of the Senate Judiciary Committee in June 1952. Youth's military service, education, knowledge of government, politics, and current affairs, critical thinking, and contributions toward "a better tomorrow" all merited the franchise. "A young person can learn the ways of democracy best by taking part in the decisions which shape its future," Moody maintained.[27]

Participating alongside the Michigan senator at this hearing were early proponents, Ellis Arnall and Harley Kilgore, the subcommittee chair. Both men added new arguments to their old ones. Arnall spelled out the success of Georgia's experience with voters 18 to 20 years of age. "They exercise a very informed opinion," he asserted. But when Moody asked if he "could interject civil rights" into the discussion—connecting Black and youth suffrage—Arnall shut him down. Harley Kilgore, facing reelection and soon red-baiting, advanced an anticommunist argument totally absent from his earlier advocacy. Young people would not go "astray after false gods such as communism," he believed, if "they have a voice in our political life."[28] In a report issued by Kilgore, the Judiciary Committee recommended the resolution to the Senate. Although nothing resulted, the report included a recent statement from the Republican frontrunner for president, Dwight D. Eisenhower.

President Eisenhower became the decade's most prominent proponent of youth voting rights. As a candidate in 1952 he offered his endorsement just 12 days before the June subcommittee hearing. "I believe if a man is old enough to fight he is old enough to vote."[29] As party leader in 1953 he supported a Republican National Committee initiative to lower the voting age. The GOP saw an electoral opportunity. Ike had won a larger proportion of the youth vote than had any Republican presidential candidate since 1936 and was very popular among 18- to 21-year-olds.[30]

Ike's first year in office, 1953, brought more proposals before the now Republican-dominated Congress and subcommittee hearings in the Senate. A proponent on the other side of the aisle, Senator Hubert H. Humphrey, Democrat from Minnesota, offered a statement in favor of his own joint resolution, later reprinted in *Redbook*. "There are many good reasons for the passage of this amendment, and I have seen no opposing arguments which meet the test of logic and civic concern." He stated the key arguments and summed up in stirring fashion. "Youth ought to have a voice in determining its own future. What is more, youth has a definite contribution to make to the future of our whole country." Senator Humphrey also shared his strong agreement with the president.[31]

In 1954 President Eisenhower went even further, using his second State of the Union Address to call for congressional action.

> For years our citizens between the ages of eighteen and twenty-one have, in times of peril, been summoned to fight for America. They should participate in the political process that produces this fateful summons. I urge Congress to propose to the States a constitutional amendment permitting citizens to vote when they reach the age of 18.[32]

This presidential call for an amendment was a historic first and signaled a commitment far firmer than Truman's favorable statement eight years earlier.

President Eisenhower's actions and arguments undoubtedly advanced youth voting rights during the 1950s. His status as Allied Commander during World War II, achievement of an armistice in the Korean War in July 1953, and ongoing Cold War leadership lent legitimacy to his use of the foundational argument. Republican National Chairman Leonard W. Hall affirmed this fact. "I am further convinced of it by the views of the President, who after all, led the greatest army of youth ever assembled during World War II."[33] From Eisenhower's experience as president of

Dwight D. Eisenhower, president of Columbia University, with students, Low
Memorial Library, ca. 1948. Manny Warman, photographer. Courtesy of University
Archives, Rare Book & Manuscript Library, Columbia University Libraries.

Columbia University, just prior to running for the Oval Office, he knew
young people well and believed their maturity and education had much
to offer. His cabinet, including Vice President Richard Nixon, gave their
support.

With the president's backing, the 18-year-old vote became a priority
in Congress in 1954. Proponents geared up for debating and decision
making. The 18-year-old vote had been approved by a plurality of the
nation's secretaries of state at their convention the year before. NEA officially endorsed it, as did many state CIO councils, and public attention
gravitated to the issue. Opinion polling found 58 percent of adults, 64
percent of 18-, 19-, and 20-year-olds, and 90 percent of military servicemen under 21 favoring youth enfranchisement. College students in
favor encouraged peers and parents to write Congress.[34] *Parents' Magazine* ran a forum that featured support from Georgia's current governor,

the Democratic Party's national leadership, and the NAACP's Walter White. Due to the Cold War, White argued, "an imperiled world has made American youth more mature and more concerned about political issues."[35]

Newspaper editors took stands. The "children of the atomic age live in the shadow of terrible responsibilities and burdens," editorialized the *New York Post*. "It seems reasonable to give them a larger voice in shaping policies that may quite literally mean life or death for them." The *Post*'s rival *New York Times* opposed. "Eighteen Is Too Young," headlined its editorial, which echoed Sidney Silvian's counterargument that age is a fluid category and a characteristic shared by all. "Eighteen is not a hopeless age or condition. If we live, as most of us do, we get over it all too soon."[36]

The opposition held firm and even got a new recruit. Harry Truman had changed his mind. "The more a man knows, the more intelligently he can vote," Truman said, the day after Eisenhower's State of the Union Address. "I do not think he has that knowledge at 18; 21 is a better age; 24 would be still better."[37] In the House of Representatives, Celler attempted to hijack the agenda by introducing his own constitutional amendment prohibiting 18- to 20-year-olds from voting. So that "no one who has not reached the age of 21—that is the age of maturity—can be given the right to vote." In the midst of the Cold War and in memory of world war, Celler offered what would become his oft-repeated, ominous warning. "The teen-ager is likely to take the extreme point of view," and thus posed a danger, a counterargument also advanced by Alfred P. Haake. "Hitler, Mussolini, Stalin all gave the teen-agers the right to vote and herded them into line."[38]

Over in the Senate proponents brought the proposed amendment to the floor for a debate and vote on May 21, 1954. It was the first debate and full vote on lowering the voting age to be held in Congress. Proponents had advanced their constitutional strategy further than they had on any previous attempt. Senator William Langer, a North Dakota Republican and chairman of the Judiciary Committee, opened debate on his joint resolution. He made the case for the 18-year-old vote, emphasizing the foundational argument within the context of the Cold War. Young men and women deserved the franchise, because "whenever and wherever future wars are fought by the United States, those 18, 19, and 20 years of age will be pressed into service." Langer also summarized proponents' progress over the past decade, admitting these efforts "have had a somewhat rocky road thus far."[39]

The road got rockier when Senator Richard B. Russell, Democrat from Georgia, began to speak. He first interrupted Langer with a comment about "the largest country which allows 18-year-olds to vote—the Soviet Union." Russell tried to discredit Langer's proposed amendment with this comparison. "I do not think Russia affords a very good illustration of democratic elections." With this red-baiting interruption, the senator from Georgia linked youth voting rights—and proponents—to communism, a tactic also deployed against civil rights and organized labor. Russell then led off the opposition with his own speech and a states' rights argument. He noted his state's adoption of the 18-year-old vote as the correct process for setting suffrage qualifications. "I do not propose to vote to coerce any other state of the Union to follow the example of my state." In loaded language he alleged that Langer's resolution would "have the Federal power invade the several States." He warned of "centralized control of Federal elections" and feared "for the future of government by the people."[40]

Buttressed by similar opinions from his southern Dixiecrat colleagues, Russell also received support in the debate from a northern member of his party: Senator John F. Kennedy. In the second year of his first Senate term, Kennedy personally approved of youth voting rights. He believed "the maturity and wisdom of those in this age group is not to be deprecated." But the Massachusetts Democrat advocated for political action only "if it were supported by the experience and demand of many States."[41] Kennedy's future vice president, Senator Lyndon B. Johnson of Texas, also voted "nay" on the proposed amendment to lower the voting age.

Russell's heightened states' rights rhetoric came at a significant historical moment. "We have gone a long way in diminishing the power of the States," Russell opined. "States are fast losing their identity as units of government."[42] The date mattered. It was only four days since the US Supreme Court had issued its decision in *Brown v. Board of Education*, declaring segregation in America's public schools unconstitutional. "All riled up over the court's decision, the Southern Democrats had to let off steam in some way," reported *Newsweek*. "So they blocked the amendment in the Senate."[43] Those southern senators who, like Russell, spoke and voted against lowering the voting age became authors of the so-called Southern Manifesto to defy the Supreme Court's decision in *Brown*. Along with other political figures, they were architects of "massive resistance" to school integration in the South.

In the end more senators sided with Langer than Russell, but not enough to reach the two-thirds necessary for a constitutional amendment. Defending segregation, the southern senators voted "to penalize American youth for an act of justice done to another segment of the population," observed the *New York Herald Tribune*.[44] The vote would have been enough to pass a regular bill, and Russell believed "the present Supreme Court would have seen fit to try to enforce this as a simple statute." He expressed relief that the 18-year-old vote had come as a constitutional amendment and not a legislative statute.[45]

The Senate debate and vote in May 1954 revealed the intertwined fates of civil and voting rights for African and young Americans. Opponents of youth suffrage explicitly entwined them early, while proponents would do so in the future. A mass movement for civil rights and voting rights needed to come first.

3

Make Democracy Live

Less than six months after the first congressional vote on youth voting rights failed to win a two-thirds majority, the 1954 midterm elections illustrated the importance and impact of Black voting rights. That election brought a victory for the first African American to represent the state of Michigan in Congress. Charles C. Diggs Jr., a Democrat from Detroit, beat his Republican opponent nearly two to one. With his slogan "Make Democracy Live," Diggs received strong support from the Black community. "If this victory is to be viewed in the full perspective of our progressing times," he announced, "I say to you that our election as Michigan's first Negro congressman was democracy in its finest hour—a victory for the Constitution and the Bill of Rights."[1] When Diggs entered the House of Representatives in January 1955, he became one of only three Black members of Congress. But, with his optimism and energy, he hoped to make a difference.

Thirty-one years old and a veteran of World War II, Diggs embodied the spirit of the growing civil rights movement. He identified himself with "those of us who are dedicated to the fight for the liberal cause and those peoples throughout the world who battle for freedom and equality among men."[2] As a Michigan state senator he had supported and sponsored legislation against racial discrimination. He worked on a bill to establish a state-level Fair Employment Practices Commission, which passed after he had left for Congress in 1955. Diggs strongly believed that "the right of Negroes to vote is key to the racial problem." He fought for the franchise where African Americans were denied it, and he urged those who had it "to get out and vote more."[3]

For Diggs, the power to shape American politics and policy through the vote belonged to all American citizens, including youth. "Throughout my 16 years of service both in the Michigan legislature and in the United States Congress," he recalled in 1966, "I have been a strong advocate of voting rights for 18-year-old citizens." "America's youth," he

believed, had "the right to help determine the Government whose actions and decisions it is morally and legally obligated to support."[4] While
he was in the Michigan State Senate in the early 1950s, youth suffrage
was on the legislative agenda. These experiences meant Diggs entered
Congress committed to civil and voting rights for African and young
Americans and ready to act.

Diggs symbolized the vital connection between youth and Black voting rights, as did other proponents. For the NAACP's Walter White,
"common justice" entailed for all Americans the right to "fight for
preservation of freedom through the ballot." Of young people, White
observed, "we need their idealism."[5] Over the 1950s the civil rights
movement grew in strength and size and achieved the first civil and voting rights legislation of the twentieth century. In the process the freedom
movement paved the way for youth voting rights. Smoothing the path
were significant developments at the state and local levels and among a
new generation of young Americans.

The Freedom Movement

Representative Diggs's congressional career began in 1955 with "civil
rights the major issue in our national and international life," as he put
it.[6] Civil rights leaders and activists continued to focus attention on
the injustices and inequities of the second-class citizenship endured by
African Americans. Using legal arguments based on the 14th and 15th
Amendments in court and direct action and demonstrations in the
streets, they challenged racial inequality in its many forms—segregation,
disfranchisement, discrimination—and in many ways. Despite unrelenting white racism and resistance, with setbacks accompanying every civil
rights success, they persisted.

Diggs involved himself immediately. He introduced bills and forged
alliances in Congress. Halfway through his first year in office, he joined
with eight colleagues to press for immediate action on 44 pending civil
rights measures. These measures addressed segregation, employment discrimination, and the "protection of human rights."[7] Diggs helped with
fundraising for civil rights organizations, including the NAACP. In one
of his first speeches in Congress he paid tribute to Walter White, who
died in March 1955. He then worked with incoming NAACP executive

Representative Charles Cole Diggs Jr., 1958. Harris & Ewing
Photographic Studio. Courtesy of the Collection of the US House
of Representatives.

secretary Roy Wilkins. Diggs regretted that White would not see "the
100th anniversary, in 1963, of the Emancipation Proclamation, when it is
hoped that the more dramatic struggles of his people will be resolved."[8]

The young representative soon garnered national attention. He got
requests to appear at public events and political rallies all over the country. He made an estimated 200 such appearances in his first term in

office. "He used to get . . . mail from all over the country from Negroes who believed he was the Congressman for all the Negroes in the United States," recalled one of his office staffers.[9] He still hosted his family's "House of Diggs" radio show—current events interspersed with gospel music—which had helped him to build a public profile and get elected in Detroit. He spoke frequently to the Black and mainstream press, and the *Chicago Defender* dubbed him "Dynamic Charles Diggs."[10]

Coming of age in the northern civil rights movement, but with family connections in the South, Diggs participated in challenges to racial inequality in both regions. One demanded his immediate attention. "It was on May 17, 1954 that the United States Supreme Court held that segregated education was inherently unequal," Diggs reminded. "There are many dates to be remembered. Of the more recent ones especially memorable to the oppressed, May 17, 1954, will take its place beside January 1, 1863, the date of President Lincoln's Emancipation Proclamation."

The timing of *Brown v. Board of Education*, with the initial decision in 1954 and implementation order in 1955, coincided exactly with the start of Diggs's congressional career. "In the field of race relations, this constituted a break-through fully as significant as the explosion of the first atom bomb," he argued.[11] He joined with colleagues in the House of Representatives to condemn the Dixiecrats' Southern Manifesto defying *Brown*. He defended the Court's decision as constitutional and consistent with the 14th Amendment's guarantee of "equal protection of the laws" to all citizens.[12] Diggs kept apprised of the slow progress of school desegregation due to the massive resistance of white southerners. He also sought to aid desegregation struggles like the Montgomery, Alabama, bus boycott over 1955 and 1956, where Rosa Parks and Dr. Martin Luther King Jr. rose to national prominence.

Diggs remained active on the voting rights front as well. Within a decade after *Smith v. Allwright* over one million African Americans, about four times the number in 1944, had qualified to vote in the South.[13] Achieved through voter registration drives, citizenship education programs, and "get out the vote" campaigns, these gains were real. They were not great, however, given that a majority of southern Blacks were still disfranchised. To counter disenfranchisement Diggs advocated using Section 2 of the 14th Amendment. Although never enforced, Section 2 would reduce a state's representation in Congress in proportion to the number of disenfranchised voters. He pledged to challenge the seating of representatives "whose elections were obtained by unconstitutional and illegal denial of the right to vote."[14]

Because of *Brown v. Board of Education*, desegregation became the freedom movement's most visible goal in the 1950s, but voting rights remained fundamental. Diggs agreed. He sought to end the poll tax and "assure the right to vote to all citizens." When an intensifying campaign of white intimidation and violence in the South led to the 1955 murders of civil rights leader Reverend George W. Lee and 14-year-old Emmett Till in Mississippi, Diggs got involved. In both cases the killers got away with murder, and Diggs attributed the blatant injustice of the justice system to Black disfranchisement. "I have some legislation in already to give the Justice Department the right to intervene in Civil Rights Cases."[15] Federal intervention and the right to vote were needed to correct the frequent, flagrant miscarriage of justice in the United States.

The Torch of Freedom

When Representative Diggs honored the life of the NAACP's Walter White early in his first year in Congress, he had faith that White's legacy would inspire "succeeding generations to brighten the torch of freedom, for the sake of all men, and to keep it fired always to its full flame."[16] With those succeeding generations in mind, Diggs proposed his very first bill. It was for the 18-year-old vote. On January 5, 1955, just two days into the first session of the 84th US Congress, Diggs proposed House Joint Resolution 12. It called for a constitutional amendment to lower the voting age to 18 and was immediately referred to the House Judiciary Committee. He received praise from *Ebony* magazine. "He let it be known that he would be active on his first day in office when he introduced a bill to extend voting rights to 18-year-olds." The magazine profiled his political rise in Michigan and his promise as a national leader on civil rights and other issues. "How he will measure up . . . only time will tell." But Diggs already showed he "had not been too young to make history."[17]

The state of Kentucky also made history in 1955 when it became the second state in the nation to lower its voting age to 18. The General Assembly of Kentucky met every two years. It approved a constitutional amendment for the 18-year-old vote in both 1952 and 1954. In between, the Kentucky CIO Council among other organizations signaled support. Governor Lawrence W. Wetherby opposed the amendment. He felt "teenagers are likely to have their minds busy with problems other than those of government and good politics." Young Kentuckians respectfully disagreed and went on the record as proponents. In editorials and letters to the editor, they advanced all the usual arguments. One letter ended with a plea. "Make us proud of our state. Trust us. We won't let you down." Voters appeared to have heard. On November 8, 1955, they approved the amendment by over 85,000 votes, which Governor Wetherby had to admit was "substantial." Although he disagreed with the measure, "our people have spoken, and I shall willingly abide by their mandate."[18]

In other states, including Kentucky's neighboring state of Illinois, proposals to lower the voting age met with uniform failure. With futile fanfare, governors in Massachusetts, New Jersey, New York, and South Carolina announced their support in 1954 and 1955. The Illinois House of Representatives refused to progress a referendum to lower the voting age in 1955. "It is nonsense to believe that the 'course of a nation or a family should be set by its 18 year olds,'" argued one state representative.[19] In Oklahoma voters overwhelmingly defeated a 1952 referendum, and South Dakota citizens rejected two referenda, just barely in 1952 but decisively in 1958.

The Hoosier State held out the possibility for success. Like that in Kentucky, the Indiana General Assembly met biennially. Bills were introduced in 1943 and passed in 1945. But the state constitution required a second vote in the subsequent session before the referendum could go before the voters. The question arose again in 1951. "Why not let them vote?" asked an Indiana woman. "I belong to the League of Women Voters and when the time comes to register our grassroots convictions I'll be ready."[20] In 1953 the General Assembly did approve the 19-year-old vote, but it needed to do so again in 1955. A veteran and farmer, 27-year-old Birch Bayh brought his best energies to bear. Newly elected to the state assembly in 1954, he could not win a second sessional vote from his colleagues unconvinced of the political maturity of 19-year-olds. This experience did not shake Bayh's own conviction. "Even as we disagreed, I think one learned," he recalled. Learning how to bring into coalition "a legislative body from the ages of twenty-four to seventy-one" would contribute to his future career in Congress.[21]

Despite these defeats in the mid-1950s and opposition from groups like the General Federation of Women's Clubs, proponents persisted, and they kept youth suffrage before politicians, the press, and the public. President Eisenhower is a good example. After the failure of Senator Langer's May 1954 resolution, Eisenhower expressed his disagreement with the Dixiecrats' debating points. "To my mind the issue of States rights there was mistakenly brought up."[22] Yet their argument affected him. When he called for a constitutional amendment to lower the voting age in his 1955 State of the Union Address, he specified for federal elections. Running for reelection the next year, he reiterated his support and his reasoning. "I really believe that we tried to delay too long their taking a very serious and vital part in the running of our country. As I tried to explain it to them—I used to at Columbia—if I am 60 and they are 20, they certainly own 40 years more of the future than I do."[23]

On the issue of youth voting rights—although not limited to federal elections—Charles Diggs was on the same side as the president; the same could not be said for civil rights. Eisenhower refused to endorse the *Brown* decision in 1954 and remained silent on the Montgomery Bus Boycott over 1955 and 1956. Diggs also held Ike's administration responsible for failing to advance its own civil rights bill in 1956. Civil rights leaders felt similarly about Eisenhower. As the NAACP's Roy Wilkins summed up, "President Eisenhower was a fine general and a good, decent man, but if he had fought World War II the way he fought for civil rights, we would all be speaking German today."[24]

President Eisenhower was finally forced to take a stand when Arkansas governor Orville Faubus refused to allow nine Black students to integrate Central High School in Little Rock in 1957 and precipitated a major racial crisis. The president dispatched federal troops to the city, the first such federal military intervention in southern race relations since the Civil War and Reconstruction nearly a century before. But it did not solve the problem. Efforts to integrate continued to be met with "daily acts of violence" for years afterward. Diggs followed up on this racial flashpoint in 1959. Students were still "being beaten, kicked, spat upon, cursed and otherwise mistreated," and Diggs asked the president to deploy his "personal diplomacy" at home as well as abroad. "There is no place," he argued, "where the need is greater than here in America."[25]

If Eisenhower's stance on desegregation was weak, he stood strongly for voting rights, as shown in 1957. "With his right to vote assured," Ike said, "the Negro could use it to help secure his other rights."[26] After his reelection in 1956, the administration's civil rights bill was reintroduced in Congress. The legislation would establish a Commission on Civil Rights, a Civil Rights Division in the Department of Justice, and the authority of the Justice Department to intervene in violations of both civil and voting rights. In hearings, civil rights activists testified to race terror in the South. Escaping punishment for the Lee and Till murders had emboldened white supremacists, and federal intervention was desperately needed.

In June the House passed the civil rights bill intact. Over in the Senate, however, majority leader Lyndon B. Johnson brokered a compromised bill. Gone was federal intervention in civil rights violations, such as white resistance to school integration, while violations of voting rights guaranteed a jury trial for the white offender. Since white juries were not going to punish one of their own, the jury trial amendment made the voting rights measure mostly meaningless. Civil rights advocates, northern liberals, and the Republican Eisenhower administration, including Vice President Richard Nixon, objected. Still the jury trial amendment passed with support from northern Democrats like Senator John F. Kennedy.

Civil rights advocates inside and outside Congress felt they had no choice but to support the compromised bill. Martin Luther King's new organization, the Southern Christian Leadership Conference (SCLC), did. Even the NAACP did. Driven by Wilkins and Clarence Mitchell, head of the NAACP's Washington Bureau and legislative director of the Leadership Conference on Civil Rights, the decision was controversial. But it was the first national legislation to protect Black civil and voting rights since Reconstruction. As Wilkins said, "a start is better than standing still."[27] Eleanor Roosevelt agreed. "This is never very satisfactory," she wrote in her "My Day" column, "but I think the civil rights bill with the amendment would be a small step forward and I hope it will become law."[28] The revised bill passed Congress in August, and President Eisenhower signed it into law in September.

In addition to casting a vote for the Civil Rights Act of 1957, Diggs became the first African American appointed to the House Committee on Foreign Affairs, and he served on the House Committee on Interior and Insular Affairs. At the time, this often overlooked committee oversaw policy on American Indians and multiple territories, including Alaska, American Samoa, Guam, Hawaiʻi, Puerto Rico, and the US Virgin Islands. His presence on that committee allowed him to take part in another victory for youth voting rights. Diggs would have been aware that the Territory of Guam passed the 18-year-old vote in 1954, and the Territory of Alaska did the same for the 19-year-old vote in 1956. In 1958 the House committee approved the Territory of Hawaiʻi's lowering the voting age to 20. The popularity of the measure in Hawaiʻi and President Eisenhower's endorsement contributed. When Alaska and Hawaiʻi became states in 1959 they brought voting ages of 19 and 20 into the nation. These developments, together with Kentucky, meant four states and one territory had a voting age below 21 by the turn of the decade of the 1960s.

For proponents like Diggs youth voting rights were part of a larger freedom struggle. To make democracy live for young Americans, they needed a dedicated movement. The civil rights movement had set the example. Youth involvement in culture and politics in the 1950s prepared them to follow.

The Voice of Youth

The cultural impact of young Americans was already being felt due to those born just before as well as during the "baby boom." Beginning with the end of World War II and lasting into the 1960s, a dramatic rise in the birth rate added 76 million young people to the US population. Born and raised at a time of economic growth and prosperity for many Americans, they and their older siblings benefited from greater opportunities for high school and higher education. They also participated eagerly in the era's growing consumer and popular culture. With 90 percent of families owning a television set and 80 percent having an automobile by 1960, many enjoyed watching their favorite television shows and even driving cars. Young people developed their own tastes in fashion and music, creating distinctive youth lifestyles.

In turn their sheer numbers, consumer dollars, and myriad actions profoundly influenced American culture in the 1950s and 1960s.

Adults—from their parents to politicians—were paying attention. Discussions and debates about the meaning and significance of the new youth culture occurred in politics, the media, and academic scholarship. Young Americans responded with their own views, stated in mainstream and college newspapers and through their activities, clubs, and organizations. They expressed a clear age and generational consciousness. Although in the 1950s few linked cultural and political change or called for lowering the voting age, many lauded civic and political involvement of all sorts. At the very least, they and their adult advocates saw such involvement as training for adult citizenship. In the process, they helped to make the case for their generation—broadly defined—having the right to vote at 18.

One place they did this was in "The Voice of Youth" column launched by the *Chicago Tribune* in 1957. It would be a place "where young writers may display their skills, express beliefs, or develop ideas."[29] With this column's launch, *Tribune* editors continued the twentieth-century media's role of popularizing age consciousness and peer group identity in the United States.[30] The column reflected the importance given to the American teenager even before the first of the baby boom generation reached that chronological marker.

Advertisers, marketers, and the media popularized "the teenager" in the 1940s, rebranding the term "adolescent" that originated in the nineteenth century.[31] These terms defined a period of time between childhood and adulthood as a distinct stage of development. During this stage, young people were understood to be forging their own identities apart from parents and families. Popular experts, like anthropologist Margaret Mead as well as psychologists and other social scientists, contributed to this understanding through their academic work and public outreach. "The Voice of Youth" allowed Chicago-area students to present their own perspectives on what it meant to be a "teen-ager."

"Where do we draw the line between adolescence and adulthood?" asked one student. "It is a spiritual and mental development as well as physical. The road to maturity is rocky." Titling her column "Help, I'm Growing Up," this young woman revealed the profound influence of turn-of-the-century psychologist G. Stanley Hall's idea of adolescence as stormy and stressful.[32] Another Chicago student expressed the emotional upheaval she felt at this new stage of development, but she also acknowledged the positive aspects. "I began to experience a keen sense of independence and a realization of my inner self."[33] That mix of uncertainty and excitement appeared often. "In this time a teen finds himself in a world full of problems, realizes his responsibilities, and discovers his potentialities."[34]

In offering their own definitions of teenagers, the *Chicago Tribune's* "Voice of Youth" columnists pushed back against what they saw as derogatory definitions offered by adults. "Many a time I have heard the question, 'What is the younger generation coming to?'"[35]

> Is a teen a person who is interested in rock 'n' roll, the opposite sex, and drag racing? . . . Are teen-agers identified by their too tight skirts, too much makeup or leather jackets? All of these things seem to be synonymous with the name "teen." Many adults bemoan this is the generation that will rule America in a few years.[36]

The "adult world," wrote one student, assumes "their children are money mad, distrusting and mad for Elvis Presley," the celebrated and controversial rock and roll singer.[37]

In voicing their views, these contributors took on two very different stereotypes of contemporary youth: the juvenile delinquent and the Beat. "Hello. My name is Teen-ager. I live everywhere from Manhattan to San Francisco. People look at me and call me clown, hoodlum, delinquent," began one young man.[38] "We teen-agers are members of the so-called beat generation," noted another.[39] "The 'beat generation'—that's what they call us. We are a generation of war babies who grew into a defiant, anti-intellectual, energetic generation," argued a female student, the year after Jack Kerouac's *On the Road* (1957) was heralded as the novel of the Beat generation. "And how do we come to be called the 'beat generation'?" She blamed the mass media.[40] As it turned out, inaccurate, adverse media framing of young Americans wouldn't end with the 1950s.

Due to these negative associations, some of the columnists resented and rejected the teenager label. "Many young people do not like being called teen-agers, and I am one of those persons. Too many adults have come to look upon teen-agers as bad," while "the good ones are often overlooked."[41] "The majority of teens who enjoy rock 'n' roll are clean living, civic minded young men and women," argued one young man.[42]

"The Voice of Youth" columnists demonstrated their civic-mindedness when they wrote about social and political concerns. "We are tomorrow's leaders, and as such we will be faced with the tremendous task of bringing peace to a strife torn world whose problems we didn't create."[43] "Our beat generation, the future leaders of the world, must unite and procure an everlasting peace," wrote another Chicago student.[44] These sentiments were shared with other student writers for the *Chicago Tribune* and showed up in college newspapers across the country. Young Americans revealed their informed opinions about a range of issues as they readied for political leadership and full citizenship.

Student writers addressed a wide range of current events and issues over the 1950s and early 1960s. Juvenile delinquency, poverty, free speech, and other civil liberties were just a few. Cold War concerns received great attention. College newspapers covered international developments and national debates and decisions. Often these were reprints of articles from mainstream newspapers or syndicated columns, but student journalists also wrote their own pieces. Closely followed were changes in military draft and training policy, given how highly relevant it was for their generation. Nuclear weapon policy and strategy loomed large as well. After antinuclear activists and pacifists founded the National Committee for a Sane Nuclear Policy (SANE) in 1957, campus chapters sprang up. Their activities received coverage.

Dominating student columns and campus headlines alongside the Cold War was civil rights. College newspapers around the country dedicated stories, editorials, and opinion pieces to the struggle for African American civil and voting rights. And they balanced national civil rights stories with local ones. They covered racist incidents on campus. Reports were published on the problem of racial discrimination in housing both on and off campus in the North and the progress of racial integration in southern colleges and universities. To inform and educate their peers about the issues, student journalists announced and analyzed campus lectures about civil rights law, policy, and politics from their own professors as well as visiting scholars and public figures.

Column inches were dedicated to student action around civil and voting rights in both the North and the South. For decades college chapters of the NAACP had been active on historically Black and predominantly white college and university campuses and in surrounding communities. Their support of legal cases to integrate higher education and campaigns to increase the number of Black faculty members received press attention. The Columbia University chapter of Students for Democratic Action appeared on the front page when it sought to use the injustice of the Emmett Till murder and trial to "fight discrimination against Negroes in the South." Instead, one member urged "cleaning up our own back yard." "There's enough work to be done in the North," reported the campus paper, "right in our own community."[45]

Voters of Tomorrow

In commenting on crucial current political events and issues, student writers conveyed the wide range of campus and civic political activities available to young people. Civil rights lectures, for example, were sponsored by campus organizations ranging from student governments and law school forums to chapters of the NAACP, the Young Democrats, and the YMCA. Youth engagement with campus and civic organizations was certainly not new in the 1950s. But the Cold War expanded opportunities in schools and communities for young Americans to learn and practice democratic citizenship. At the forefront of these initiatives was NEA. "More time is being given to citizenship units" in the school curriculum, reported a superintendent of schools in Kansas, Evan E. Evans, in the *NEA Journal* in 1950.[46] If the United States stood for freedom and democracy in the world, it needed to ensure its citizens did too.

Youth themselves made the case. "Our generation, upon coming of age, will be faced with many problems," stated a columnist for "The Voice of Youth." "The young people of today must learn to understand and practice the principles established by the Constitution; they must assume responsibilities and become faithful citizens of a democratic society."[47] This Chicago student, who wanted to become a high school teacher, regarded knowledge of US history to be a must for every citizen. She also recognized that both theory and practice needed to be part of any citizenship curriculum. Another student, who hoped for a career in politics, agreed. He pointed out how "experience in leadership" at school allowed students to gain "practical knowledge which could be used when they were turned out into the world."[48] A Columbia University student put it succinctly: "Education + Experience = 1 Citizen."[49]

Discussion, debate, and decision making in the classroom and in competitions still proved a useful way to integrate citizenship theory and practice. National debate topics, as with the 18-year-old vote in 1943, focused on politics and governance and required debaters to express their opinions in the form of well-reasoned arguments.

Student elections gave them an opportunity to act on their opinions. "There is no better civic training than the exercise of the vote," contended Senator Hubert Humphrey in 1953.[50] Young people could tell him they were already in training. "The teenagers of today are the voters of tomorrow," reported a North Carolina high school newspaper, and "they get a 'kick' out of carrying on a campaign and voting." When they reach "civic voting age," they will know how "to pick candidates of their choice as leaders of their country."[51] College newspapers similarly promoted elections for student government. They provided a platform for candidates and published returns, including voter turnout. High turnout was hailed, and low turnout was lamented, as when only one-third of students voted in Seattle University's 1955 elections. Despite being "begged and exhorted," they did not bother to "vote to get their voice heard," complained a fellow student.[52]

US local, state, and national elections were followed on campuses as well, and students engaged in various ways. At some colleges and universities students of voting age could register and even cast their ballots on campus. Straw polls were conducted to allow all students—with or without the franchise—to convey their choices. "Get-out-the-vote" campaigns involved students, with youth affiliates of the political parties, the League of Women Voters, and the NAACP participating. They registered voters, canvassed neighborhoods, launched letter-writing campaigns, and offered to babysit or help with transport on Election Day. In 1956 students at a Maryland high school took part by ticketing cars with "ARRESTED—Are you guilty of Failing to Register? Do it today! Vote November 6."[53] Eleanor Roosevelt that year paid "tribute to all the teenagers who enlisted in the campaign for getting out the vote" in her column, an estimated one million "Teenage Election Volunteers."[54]

Young Americans also volunteered for community-based civic activities and programs. One of the most prominent was the YMCA's Youth and Government program. Founded in New York in 1936, the program sponsored student legislatures modeled on those of their states. They met once a year and discussed, debated, and decided on bills. "Teen-agers in the model legislatures of a dozen states are instigating useful legislation—and learning how democracy works in the process," noted *Reader's Digest* in 1948. Thomas C. Desmond, a New York state senator, described the YMCA program as a "Seedbed for Leadership."[55] And an issue regularly taken up by these budding leaders was youth suffrage.

Should the Voting Age Be 18?

In 1954, following President Eisenhower's "bombshell" endorsement, the popular teenage magazine *Seventeen* ran its first story on lowering the voting age. The author, Natalie Gittelson, asked her readers "how, *you*, the young people yourselves, feel about this grave, exciting possibility of being catapulted into political adulthood at this early teen age." Despite her off-base definition of 18 as "early" in the span of teenage years, Git-telson respected her readers' opinions. She presented all of the major arguments for and against lowering the voting age through the voices of young people themselves. At the end of the piece she included a survey to gauge support for and opposition to the 18-year-old vote.[56]

Although *Seventeen's* initial article on the issue, it was not the last, and the magazine often covered and cheered youth involvement in politics. "You don't have to be twenty-one" to learn about a candidate or volunteer for a campaign. "You don't need to wait for that birthday." Other articles presented ideas on how to "pep up politics" and get "hep on Democracy."[57] *Seventeen's* use of such teenage slang reflected an ef-fort to establish a positive connection between contemporary youth cul-ture and politics.

Young Americans in favor of the 18-year-old vote advocated for their generation. They repeated the reasons for youth enfranchisement heard before, including their military service, education, and knowledge of government, politics, and current affairs. In 1953, when the Junior States-men of America organized a petition to amend California's constitu-tion lowering the voting age, high school students sounded off. "If we are going to be drafted we should be given a voice in the action." "My brother went into the Navy at 18; he had to wait to vote but not to fight. We want to vote now." "We study government in class and conduct our own elections, and I'm more interested in politics now than I'd be after a three-year recess." "Today's youth is getting a good education and I think they know more about national and world affairs than a lot of adults."[58]

For youthful proponents, the foundational argument continued to be central, but its masculinist focus could cause confusion. Although older advocates, like President Eisenhower and Representative Diggs, always included women in their vision of youth voting rights, some young people were less certain. "I'm not sure about girls, but if boys at 18 are old enough to fight they are old enough to vote," stated one of the California high school students.[59] At Whitworth College in Spokane, Washington, several female students were confused by the slogan. When discussing whether 18-year-olds should be allowed to vote, they asked, "You mean girls, too?" "This might after all be the solution," quipped a campus newspaper reporter: "let the male gender do the actual voting when 18 and the fairer sex can tell them who to vote for."[60] But most youth understood the foundational argument as gender inclusive, balancing citizenship rights and responsibilities.

Building on this understanding, teenagers pointed out the responsibilities their age group fulfilled beyond that of military service. Like earlier advocates, they believed employment, marriage, raising families, and paying taxes should be balanced with voting rights. "Half of [high school] graduates go to work and three years is too long for them to wait to vote on things that affect their lives." "Many young people are marrying at 18 and if they are old enough to have families they should have the privilege of voting."[61] They were right. The average age of marriage declined during the 1950s to 22 for men and 20 for women, and these young families, in turn, contributed to the baby boom.[62] "Eighteen-year-olds are considered old enough for other responsibilities equally as great—government jobs, work in the armed services—so why shouldn't they vote?" asked a North Carolina college student.[63]

These updated versions of the usual arguments appeared in student newspapers across the United States, as did discussions of the meanings attached to the ages of 18 versus 21. What age determined adulthood was debated, and the ages entitling other citizenship rights were in flux. "21 is purely arbitrary; nothing makes a man more mature by the simple fact of the celebration of his twenty-first birthday," observed Cornell University student and future journalist Andrew D. Kopkind.[64] "There has been much controversy recently concerning the proper age at which one should be allowed to vote, drive, and serve his country," wrote a Chicago student in "The Voice of Youth." "The problem facing today's youth," she asked, "is what is an adult and how can I become one?" Her answer: "Becoming an adult does not require a prescribed length of time."[65]

These young Americans called attention to the variations in rights granted to different ages of different sexes in different states, highlighting the arbitrariness and constructedness of age markers and meanings. Through these discussions they demonstrated an awareness of what they shared in common as an age cohort, from a culture of their own to the lack of full citizenship. Increasingly, they explicitly, if self-consciously, identified as a generation. Proponents of youth voting rights contributed to and benefited from this growing generational consciousness. So, too, did the new president in the new decade of the 1960s.

4

Change Is in the Air

The new decade and the new president, John F. Kennedy, held out great hope for "action and progress" on many fronts.[1] This hope was conveyed in the Democratic administration's political agenda, called the New Frontier. The three years of Kennedy's presidency, from 1961 to 1963, definitely demonstrated action and progress. Many, including African Americans in the freedom movement, young people, and liberals, sought even greater action and swifter progress. JFK's reputation as a liberal icon initially soared and then later suffered as aspects of his politics and governance gained greater scrutiny. Yet the Kennedy administration operated within a Cold War context and with a Democratic Party still filled with conservative southern Dixiecrats. Given these continuities, the change initiated in the early 1960s was not insignificant.

It helped that civil rights activists kept their eyes on the prize, as a civil rights song goes, and stayed steadfast in their goal of achieving racial equality in politics, society, and the economy. They still sought to eradicate segregation and expand employment opportunities across the country. On the voting rights front, they pushed to end disfranchisement in the South and further Black registration and voting in every region. In 1960, new student-led organizing campaigns seized the moment and sped up momentum. As students, youth, and their older allies worked to secure Black civil rights and voting rights, they prompted discussions at the local, state, national, and even international levels about who is an American citizen, citizenship rights and responsibilities, the importance of the vote, and voter qualifications.

This work and these discussions progressed the intertwined fates of voting rights and full citizenship for African and young Americans. Signs of change were everywhere, with some real successes along the way. Youth of all races—born just preceding and as part of the baby boom—were an important part of these developments as the sixties got started.

John F. Kennedy 1960 presidential campaign pamphlet.
Courtesy of the John F. Kennedy Presidential Library and
Museum, Boston.

Leadership for the Sixties

Just two days into the new decade, John F. Kennedy launched his campaign for president. From then on JFK's campaign connected his candidacy to the 1960s. Campaign slogans such as "A Time for Greatness 1960," "Leadership for the '60s," and "A New Leader for the '60s" captured that connection. JFK's speech accepting the Democratic nomination and introducing the idea of a New Frontier did the same. "We stand today on the edge of a New Frontier—the frontier of the 1960s."[2]

Cementing this connection was his performance at the first presidential debate and the first ever to be televised. His Republican opponent, Vice President Richard Nixon, based his case for the presidency on his experience in Congress and in the White House. Only four years younger, Kennedy pointed out that both he and Nixon won their first elections to the House of Representatives in 1946 and then to the Senate in 1952. "The question is of experience. The question also is what our judgment is of the future," JFK contended. He went on to catalogue the Democratic Party's record of reform, particularly in social policy. "The question really is which candidate and which party can meet the problems the United States is going to face in the 1960s."[3]

Kennedy placed himself in the tradition of the Democratic Party, President Roosevelt, and President Truman, but he also pressed forward to the future. In the process, he secured the support of Eleanor Roosevelt. ER had maintained her role in the Democratic Party in the postwar period. She shaped the party's commitments and candidates, platforms and policies. Initially she did not support Kennedy. At the party's convention in 1960 she seconded the nomination of Adlai Stevenson, although three of her sons were in Kennedy's camp. Yet as a loyal party member, she endorsed JFK once he secured the nomination. After watching the first debate—"a milestone in TV history"—she "felt honesty in Mr. Kennedy." "If Mr. Kennedy can project himself thusly often enough he will persuade a large part of what has been called the independent vote," she wrote in her newspaper column, "and that would be a great accomplishment on his part."[4]

During the campaign Kennedy courted key constituencies of the Democratic Party. He reached out to organized labor and secured the endorsement of the merged American Federation of Labor–Congress of Industrial Organizations (AFL-CIO). His Catholicism drew voters who shared his faith, and the party's platform pledging a higher minimum wage, federal aid to education, and equal pay attracted teachers and wage-earning women. Kennedy's running mate for vice president, Lyndon Johnson, shored up southern support. They also needed the votes of African Americans. The campaign engaged in direct outreach and publicity to Black newspapers, churches, and communities. But a delicate balancing act was required to bring in both Black voters and southern white voters.

Kennedy also appealed directly to young Americans, as seen in a January 1960 profile in *Seventeen* magazine. "Youth has its own advantages," he told his interviewer, an 18-year-old from California, "vitality and adaptability and freshness. Youth doesn't mean folly, age doesn't mean wisdom" were his proverbial words.[5] His campaign held dedicated youth rallies. To his audience, he asserted "this is your election" and "change is in the air." He identified the nuclear fears created by coming of age in the context of the Cold War. "I do not want to be President of a destroyed world perishing under the mushroom clouds of nuclear holocaust," he told an Oregon audience, and the Democratic Party platform promised nuclear arms control.[6]

Projecting youth and vigor—despite suffering from chronic illness— JFK campaigned energetically. When he won the election by less than one percent of the popular vote, it was evident that every vote for the Democratic ticket had counted. At age 43, Kennedy became the youngest candidate to win the White House.

Delivering his inaugural address on January 20, 1961, hatless and coatless in the cold, the new president emphasized the future, generational change, and renewal. "Let us begin anew. Let the word go forth from this time and place, to friend and foe alike, that the torch has been passed to a new generation of Americans." The speech focused on US leadership and the Cold War, so his famous call summoned all to struggle against communism. "And so, my fellow Americans: ask not what your country can do for you—ask what you can do for your country." But this call to service inspired Americans, especially youth, beyond the Cold War. They would come to work for many causes, volunteering locally as well as globally. Through his words and image, Kennedy expressed a mood of hope and idealism that came to define a decade and a generation.

JFK's actions told a different story. As a member of Congress he had been in the conservative wing of the Democratic Party. He had voted for legislation to undermine civil liberties spurred by domestic anticommunism and for the jury trial amendment designed to undercut the Civil Rights Act of 1957. These stances were among the reasons why ER initially opposed his bid for the White House.[7]

Kennedy also had not supported and in fact spoke out against the constitutional amendment lowering the voting age when Senator Langer's resolution came up for a vote in 1954. JFK's nay vote jettisoned the opinion he had expressed to the *Harvard Crimson* just a month before. He told a journalist from his alma mater that the states should act before Congress did, but he added an assurance. "When the amendment is presented for vote on the floor of the Senate, I will vote for it."[8]

Both before and after his vote against the resolution, the senator from Massachusetts received letters from curious and concerned young constituents. In an exchange of letters in early 1954 with a female student from Ayer asking his view on youth voting rights for "the members of my class and myself," Kennedy responded.

> In my opinion, this is a decision which should continue to be within the jurisdiction of the individual states, inasmuch as each state is better able to judge the qualifications of its voters. Of course, I have personally come in contact with many young people below the age of twenty-one who are as well qualified to consider the merits of the various candidates for public office at that time as they would be three years later.[9]

Other letter writers were much more critical. "I was surprised that you joined southern Senators to defeat President Eisenhower's proposal to reduce the minimum voting age to 18," wrote a young man in 1955. Especially given a recent opinion poll of Massachusetts voters showing 76 percent in support, "I am unable to understand the basis of your negative vote." A response came not from Kennedy but from Theodore "Ted" Sorensen, then in his 20s and JFK's chief legislative aid and speechwriter. Sorensen sent Kennedy's remarks on the Senate floor during the 1954 debate over the resolution. He also pointed out constitutional amendments should not be "engaged in so lightly and so frequently." And factors like polling data would not determine the position of "a conscientious Senator, particularly when it comes to amending the Constitution."[10]

So John F. Kennedy won the White House without the record on Black and youth voting rights that proponents would have wanted, but 1960 still held clear signs of change. JFK's words and actions during the campaign, developments in Congress, and the Democratic Party platform held potential for progress. Election wins for Democrats meant the party now controlled both the executive and legislative branches of the federal government. Charles C. Diggs was reelected for the third time to his Michigan seat in the House of Representatives. And after a 12-year absence from Congress, Jennings Randolph of West Virginia returned, this time to the Senate. Following up on his 1958 special election victory, he won a full Senate term in 1960. To his new position he brought his old priorities, including youth voting rights. This priority got a push in 1960 when American Samoa lowered its voting age to 20. Change could happen.

Steps toward Change

One change that year, even before the November election, was further civil rights legislation. Over 1959 and 1960 the 86th Congress worked on what would become the Civil Rights Act of 1960. In a repeat of what happened with the Civil Rights Act of 1957, opponents spent months engaged in "southern hacking," as the *Washington Post* called it. Envisioned to fill the gaps in the 1957 act, the original bill had seven provisions. These provisions included affirmation of the Supreme Court decision in *Brown v. Board of Education* as "the law of the land"—which of course it was—and federal enforcement of school desegregation orders to avoid another Little Rock crisis. Another provision aimed to prevent and prosecute bombings against homes, churches, and schools associated with the freedom movement. All were eviscerated over time. Even the heart of the bill, which focused on voting rights and registration, was enfeebled.[11]

Yet the Civil Rights Act of 1960 had some positives. It provided for the appointment of voting referees, although how that would work in practice was open to question, and for the preservation of voter registration records. Evidence from these records would enable civil rights advocates to demonstrate systematic racial inequalities with voter registration in the South. The Democratic ticket—both Senator Kennedy and Senator Johnson—voted "yea" on the bill, as they had for the 1957 act. As weak as the eventual act was, Kennedy and Johnson also ran on a Democratic Party platform that pledged considerable progress on civil and voting rights.

The platform's civil rights plank did not call for the full-scale removal of segregation in public accommodations, as civil rights activists would have wanted, but it did in education. Southern school districts would be required to submit a plan of compliance with the *Brown* decision, with a first step taken by 1963, the 100th anniversary of the Emancipation Proclamation. With Democratic control of the executive branch, the federal courts would be used "to prevent the denial of any civil right on grounds of race, creed, or color" and the Commission on Civil Rights strengthened. A Fair Employment Practices Commission also would be forthcoming, modeled on the FDR-era committee and state-level commissions like the one in Diggs's Michigan. Finally, Democrats would "use the full powers provided in the Civil Rights Acts of 1957 and 1960 to secure for all Americans the right to vote" and take "whatever action is necessary to eliminate literacy tests and the payment of poll taxes as requirements for voting."[12]

"Hail Demo Plank as Step Forward," announced the *Chicago Defender* after the Democratic National Convention. The civil rights plank "went far beyond the expectation of Negro leaders." It was "bold," "magnificent," and "a ringing triumph for the cause of human rights." Not every delegate felt the same when asked. "Go to hell," responded an Alabama Dixiecrat delegate. "No comment." "This is the most tremendously far-reaching and far-sighted document ever adopted in the history of the party," Representative Diggs remarked.[13] Diggs at first supported Missouri senator Stuart Symington's candidacy, as did fellow Missourian president Truman. But by the time of the convention Diggs was in Kennedy's camp, along with a majority of the Michigan delegation. Diggs notably accompanied Kennedy to an NAACP-sponsored event just as the convention opened. In the general election Michigan ended up in the Democratic column.

As did Jennings Randolph's state. West Virginia played a pivotal role in the Democratic nomination process. JFK's primary win in the Moun-

President John F. Kennedy designating Frederick Douglass's home as a part of the National Park System. Senator Philip A. Hart on left and Representative Charles C. Diggs Jr. on right. Oval Office, White House, Washington, DC, September 5, 1962. Abbie Rowe, photographer. Courtesy of the John F. Kennedy Presidential Library and Museum, Boston.

tain State gave his campaign a boost at the right time, in May 1960. West Virginia, predominantly Protestant and with a prominent union presence, revealed that JFK's religion and wealth did not prevent wider appeal. In a state suffering economic distress and high unemployment due to the mechanization of coal mining, he promised voters "a program to assist West Virginia to move forward." Kentucky and Pennsylvania too were "states that desperately needed the attention and assistance of the Federal Government," Kennedy argued. But there was no state "harder hit by technological change and subsequent chronic unemployment than West Virginia."[14] The Democratic Party platform included a plank on "Aid to Depressed Areas." It assured "action to create new industry in America's depressed areas of chronic unemployment." "Stricken communities deserve the help of the whole nation."[15]

The New Frontier encompassed all these proposals the Democrats sought to enact and helped the party win some 70 percent of the Black vote. In such a close race, the significance of this supermajority was not lost on African Americans. Two months after the election, on December 30, 1960, Martin Luther King addressed an audience in Tennessee. "It is pretty conclusive now that the Negro played a decisive role in electing the president of the United States, and maybe for the first time we can see the power of the ballot and what the ballot can do." This reminder of the importance of Black voting rights did not end there. "Now we must remind Mr. Kennedy that we helped him to get in the White House. We must remind Mr. Kennedy that we are expecting to use the whole weight of his office to remove the ugly weight of segregation from the shoulders of our nation."[16]

Signs of Change

Just two months into President Kennedy's term in office, the Republican opposition assailed the administration for "being the greatest 'do-nothing' administration in the history of our Republic." In his response, Senator Randolph took the opportunity to do some assailing himself. "Whatever criticisms may fairly be leveled against President Kennedy and his administration, and there are precious few to date, that of being a 'do nothing' administration is not one of them." He explained that JFK had sent 29 messages to Congress on legislative matters already.[17]

The New Frontier indeed entailed significant reform. Hundreds of measures were enacted, including new employment, education, and environmental laws. In 1961 the Peace Corps was founded, with Charles Diggs a committed advocate of this "exciting program."[18] Later that year brought the establishment of the President's Commission on the Status of Women, with Eleanor Roosevelt as chair until she passed away in 1962. The commission issued its report on what would have been her 79th birthday. Its investigations helped to achieve greater gender equity and ignite the modern feminist movement.

These achievements of the early years of the 1960s and Kennedy's time in office overlapped with two historic amendments to the US Constitution: the 23rd and 24th. The 23rd Amendment gave the disfranchised citizens of Washington, DC, the right to participate in presidential elections. Congress passed the amendment in June 1960, and the Democratic Party platform urged ratification by the states. "The capital city of our nation should be a symbol of democracy to people throughout the world."[19] It was ratified in 1961. At one point in the legislative process the joint resolution that became the 23rd Amendment contained an anti–poll tax provision. Five states still had this egregious economic restriction on the franchise: Alabama, Arkansas, Mississippi, Texas, and Virginia. It would take the 24th Amendment to prohibit the poll tax as a qualification for voting in federal elections.

President Kennedy appealed for the abolition of both poll taxes and literacy tests in his State of the Union Address in January 1962. He affirmed that "a strong America requires the assurance of full and equal rights to all its citizens, of any race or of any color."[20] To accomplish this aim, he believed constitutional amendments were necessary. He recognized that the process of amending the Constitution was a slower process than legislating by statute. But an amendment avoided the accusations of unconstitutionality that could be directed at laws, which also took time to resolve. It took three years and a unanimous Supreme Court decision, *United States v. Raines* (1960), to validate key provisions in the Civil Rights Act of 1957, for example. The civil rights arguments that the 14th and 15th Amendments gave power to Congress to abolish poll taxes and literacy tests—even if Congress was convinced—would certainly have been challenged in court. That amendment passed in 1962 and was ratified in 1964.

The 23rd and 24th Amendments were ratified by three-quarters of the states, although without the support of certain southern states. These changes to the US Constitution had taken over two decades to achieve, but they benefited all Americans by expanding and protecting voting rights. They demonstrated the commitment of the president, Congress, and a supermajority of the states to enable, if not ensure, citizens to exercise their right to vote. As Senator Estes Kefauver, Democrat from Tennessee, stated, the aim was "to remove some obstacle which prevents or endangers full expression of the popular will through the ballot box."[21] The combination of the civil rights movement and the close 1960 election had prompted political leaders to consider constitutional reform to achieve this aim. Rethinking and remaking the Constitution in even more significant ways was on the new decade's reform agenda.

During Kennedy's first year in office, Kefauver chaired Senate subcommittee hearings on proposed constitutional amendments related to elections and voting. Held less than two months after the ratification of the 23rd Amendment, the hearings investigated three reforms in addition to abolishing the poll tax: eliminating the Electoral College, changing presidential and vice presidential nomination procedures, and establishing the 18-year-old vote. Of these, only poll tax abolition had JFK's full support and so moved forward as an amendment to the US Constitution. Presidential leadership mattered.

And in the early 1960s it was too often lacking in confrontations between civil rights activists and defenders of white supremacy, when nonviolence came up against violence. The Freedom Rides exposed this lack of leadership in Kennedy's first year in office. Initiated by the Congress of Racial Equality (CORE) in May 1961, the Freedom Rides brought attention to the South's lack of compliance with Supreme Court rulings dating from 1946 and 1960 outlawing segregation on interstate buses and stations. Interracial groups of activists rode the buses and met with virulent white racism and mob violence en route. It took two weeks for the administration, led by the president's brother, Attorney General Robert F. Kennedy, to overcome their own opposition to the Freedom Riders and begin to take action to protect them physically. RFK also hesitated to protect them legally and uphold their constitutional rights. Activists from other civil rights organizations soon joined the protest. The rides and the retaliations, including imprisonment, continued for months until finally in September the executive branch issued an order enforcing the court decisions and thus the law.

The Freedom Rides were the most dramatic demonstration of the administration's hesitant response to events in the freedom movement. In siding with activists they risked alienating southern white supremacists in Congress and the country and jeopardizing the New Frontier. The situation truly changed, however, on June 11, 1963, when Kennedy addressed the American people on civil rights. White resistance to integration of the University of Alabama and to civil rights protests in Birmingham and elsewhere pushed the president to take a forceful stand. "One hundred years of delay have passed since President Lincoln freed the slaves, yet their heirs, their grandsons, are not fully free." In eloquent terms, he laid out long-standing racial inequalities and what was needed to rectify them, including the right to vote. "Next week I shall ask the Congress of the United States to act, to make a commitment it has not fully made in this century to the proposition that race has no place in American life or law."[22]

Just hours later a white supremacist shot and killed Medgar Evers, Mississippi's first NAACP field secretary, outside his home in Jackson. For some, especially young civil rights activists, JFK's commitment came too little and too late. Others expressed appreciation that it came and came convincingly.

Blueprint for Action

For a constitutional amendment lowering the voting age, JFK's commitment never came. He signaled support when the issue was raised for the District of Columbia, but DC is not a state. At the Senate hearings on electoral reform in 1961, Assistant Attorney General Nicholas Katzenbach repeated the president's position. "The administration, while thoroughly believing in the competence of 18-year-olds to discharge their civic responsibilities as voters, is of the view that this judgment should continue to be left to the States."[23] Members of Congress had different views. Four Senate and three House joint resolutions were proposed in the months preceding the hearings. They again represented bicameral, bipartisan, and broad geographical support for lowering the voting age. In the Senate two proposals came from Democrats and two from Republicans, representing the states of Illinois, New York, Tennessee, and of course West Virginia.

The senator from West Virginia led off the discussion of his Joint Resolution 71. "I have for many years been an active proponent of a constitutional amendment granting the right to vote to 18-year-olds." Jennings Randolph recounted his history of proposing amendments as a member of the House of Representatives and participating in House hearings in October 1943. He asked that Georgia governor Ellis Arnall's statement from that hearing be inserted into the current record. Senator Randolph then presented his arguments. He pulled back from his first and foremost argument. "Old enough to fight, old enough to vote" he no longer believed was "the strongest or most relevant position that can be advanced."[24]

He focused instead on another of his favorite arguments: how youth suffrage would fully realize democracy for both individual citizens and the nation as a whole.

> With the 15th amendment, we abolished the restrictions of race, color, and previous condition of servitude, as with the 19th amendment we abolished the restriction of sex. There remains but one medieval vestige, Mr. Chairman, that which defines the estate of manhood as the age of 21. This criterion, originally predicated upon the age of attainment of the requisite skills of strength for personal combat, is an anomaly in the 20th century.[25]

Whether historically accurate or not, Randolph's explanation for the traditional age qualification of 21 resonated.

In reformulating his arguments Randolph recognized the contemporary context of the early 1960s. As civil rights activists and advocates made clear, voting was the most vital democratic right. It certified full citizenship status, conferred the power to change society, and constituted the consummate democratic act. Randolph had long felt this way about the "franchise of freedom." In his home state his reputation as "a liberal" and his "consistent position on civil rights" gained him respect among "all West Virginians who believe in democracy as traditionally defined, but not always practiced, in America."[26] The close election of 1960 made even more credible his contention that every vote counted. They did in the new states of Alaska and especially Hawai'i, which required a recount. Randolph heralded "our two newest States" for their lower voting ages of 19 and 20. "These younger States are more vibrant." As was contended with the western states and women's suffrage in the late nineteenth century and early twentieth, Randolph commented, "I think they are pioneering in this field of thought."[27]

Additional witnesses testified over the seven days of hearings, including the respective chairmen of the Democratic and Republican National Committees. Youth members of the two parties had called for lowering the voting age. "The 18-year-old vote was always an issue for Young Democrats," recalls Spencer Oliver, active in the Young Democratic Clubs starting during his undergraduate years at Texas Christian University. "It was one of our main issues, one of our main objectives."[28]

At the hearings the two party chairmen concurred on making the 18-year-old vote the law of the land. But echoing the long-standing conflict between states' rights and federal power over suffrage qualifications, they contrasted on how to do so. "I think it should remain for the State to decide," contended Democrat John M. Bailey. "I would rather prefer it to be done as a constitutional amendment at the national level," confirmed Republican William E. Miller.[29]

A student from Findlay College in Ohio also appeared. He reported that the 1960 White House Conference on Children and Youth, which he had attended, had endorsed youth enfranchisement because "the 18-year-old citizen was mature enough to assume the duties of full citizenship." Aware of the concerns over juvenile delinquency, he contended that it "should not be considered as an argument against the 18-year-old's right to vote." "We should not charge the many with the failures of the few." He also deemed it "unfair" that high school students' interest and preparation for politics "must wait until the age of 21 to be applied."[30]

The high point of his testimony, however, referenced the president. "This generation of Americans has a burning fire of interest in the affairs of state."

> Let me urge you, Senators, to take the means of keeping it lighted. In his momentous inaugural address, President Kennedy said: "Ask not what your country can do for you, but what you can do for your country." By providing the youth of this Nation with the right to vote, you will have answered the President's call to action.[31]

This strategy of passionate persuasion found a receptive audience among the senators, although they knew very well where Kennedy, like Democratic Party chairman John Bailey, stood on the issue. Lowering the voting age was a state not a federal government matter.

JFK did contribute to youth voting rights in one key way: his President's Commission on Registration and Voting Participation, established in March 1963. Concerns about lower voter turnout and "apathy" in the 1960 presidential election—less than 65 percent of the electorate cast ballots—stood alongside long-standing voting restrictions, such as the poll tax and literacy tests. "In a country with our educational system and our great tradition, we have to do much better," Kennedy contended.[32]

The commission was to investigate the reasons why citizens did not vote and issue "recommendations for increasing citizen participation in Government through the exercise of the right to vote."[33] It had representatives from the two major political parties, the League of Women Voters, the United Auto Workers, and academic scholars, such as pioneering political scientist Victoria Schuck. The UAW and affiliated unions, represented by Roy L. Reuther, had favored lowering the voting age since World War II, and Professor Schuck inspired her students "to become immersed in politics, to run for electoral office, to have a strong civic sense, and to take political activity very seriously."[34]

When the commissioners presented their "blueprint for action" on November 26, 1963, the 18-year-old vote was one of the recommendations. They pinpointed the three-year gap between high school graduation and gaining the franchise as the problem. By the time they turned 21, "many young people are so far removed from the stimulation of the educational process that their interest in public affairs has waned. Some may be lost as voters for the rest of their lives." They also called for greater civic education in the schools to cover registration, voting, and "the importance of a single vote to the American way of life." Randolph could not have agreed more, except with the process the commissioners recommended for lowering the voting age: "Voting by Persons 18 Years of Age Should Be Considered by the States."[35]

This recommendation did fit with the president's position, but shockingly and sadly he was not there to receive it. John F. Kennedy was assassinated only four days before the commission submitted its report. His remarks upon acceptance of the report had already been drafted, and he had decided to continue the commission for another few months to initiate the implementation of its recommendations. JFK never heard the answer to the question he posed. "What accounts for the widespread failure to exercise democracy's most fundamental and precious freedom?" The reasons were both psychological and legal, the commissioners concluded.[36] Nor did he hear the new president, Lyndon B. Johnson, pay tribute to "his deep commitment to the principles of democracy."[37] The president's brothers could, however. Robert Kennedy stayed on as Johnson's attorney general until he successfully ran for the Senate from New York in 1964. Edward Kennedy had been elected to the Senate from Massachusetts in 1962, as had Birch Bayh from Indiana. As the decade continued, all three would become important advocates for lowering the voting age.

Another, less well-known advocate connected and contributed to the work of the President's Commission on Registration and Voting Participation. Joseph S. Dolan, a student at the University of Connecticut, sent a term paper on lowering the voting age to the commission chair. He then submitted a full report on January 1, 1964. Dolan explained that he became interested in the issue as a high school student and built on that interest over the next few years. "When I first heard about this idea, I thought it was absurd," he admitted. "But after two years of research . . . I realized what an excellent cause it was."[38] He also realized that research and writing were not enough to win youth voting rights. So in 1962 he cofounded the first student organization dedicated solely to the excellent cause of youth suffrage.

PART II

"A change is comin' and it's very near"

1963–1967

5

Agenda for a Generation

Joseph Dolan had big plans for VOTES. The organization he cofounded with Joline Breton in the summer of 1962 would work for youth enfranchisement in the state of Connecticut. The name—Vindication of Twenty-Eighteen Suffrage—may have been convoluted, but the acronym was catchy. VOTES could have begun just on Dolan's campus of the University of Connecticut at Hartford and the main campus at Storrs, where Breton was a student. Instead VOTES started as a statewide organization "to demonstrate that college and high school-age youths have a responsible interest in government and should be allowed to vote," as she put it.[1] They sought support from youth as well as adults.

With a 25-page constitution drafted by Breton, officers from four different colleges, and three categories of membership, the new organization was ambitious. The officers all had participated in student government, clubs, or civic organizations and brought that knowledge and experience with them. They divided the state into ten districts, with district headquarters to "handle communications and publicity for their districts." Since Dolan served as the president of VOTES, his campus at Hartford would house the central headquarters and be the "spotlight of attention and publicity."[2] VOTES was the first single-issue, student-led organization dedicated to the 18-year-old vote.

In a decade known for student activism, VOTES received little notice. Overshadowed by the Student Nonviolent Coordinating Committee, Students for a Democratic Society, and Young Americans for Freedom, to name just a few organizations, VOTES does not have a place in popular memory of the sixties or in the history books. But its founding in 1962 marked a significant moment, when the efforts of a few prominent figures and organizations for youth voting rights in the 1940s and 1950s moved into a new phase. VOTES was more than an effort. It was an organized, planned campaign, with a political strategy and a goal. During this second phase of the 1960s, support for youth suffrage grew within a context of increasing student activism around a range of issues, on high school and college campuses, and in local communities across the nation.

VOTES, or Vindication of Twenty-Eighteen Suffrage

VOTES signaled a shift among students from support for youth voting rights to organized campaigning. Since World War II student activists in the youth wings of the political parties and multi-issue organizations, like American Youth for Democracy, had expressed their support in print and in person. Although these efforts were important and helped to demonstrate youth interest in their own enfranchisement, they did not lead to a focused, formal organization until VOTES in 1962. That this development occurred in the new decade of the 1960s mattered. Joe Dolan, Joline Breton, and VOTES members understood they were starting something new.

They also knew that lowering the voting age in Connecticut would be a challenging task. It had been considered and quashed in each state legislative session of the 1950s. In 1954 concern over juvenile delinquency contributed to opposition. At a set of subcommittee hearings, testimony on the problem of "teenage hoodlumism" preceded discussion of lowering the voting age. The results were predictable. "Delinquency Hurts Plan to Lower Voting Age to 18," headlined the *Hartford Courant*.[3] Moreover, like other states, Connecticut's process for amending its constitution was complex and would "take considerable time." "In Connecticut, this would require action by the State House of Representatives in 1955, action by the Senate and the House in 1957 and then approval by a majority of the voters in either a special or regular election held after that."[4] Four to five years would pass before 18-, 19-, and 20-year-old citizens of the state could cast their first ballot.

Still the early 1960s held out hope. In 1961 John M. Bailey, the longtime Democratic powerbroker in Connecticut, had been rewarded with the position of Democratic National Committee chair for his early support of President Kennedy. Lauded for his "great experience with young people in Connecticut" and being "well qualified to give your impression of their capacity for voting," Bailey endorsed youth voting rights at the 1961 Senate hearings. Between public education and the mass media, "the young people of 17 and 18 are more cognizant of the issues," he argued. They also gained practical experience with student government and mock presidential elections. "In Connecticut the schools have done quite a good job," Bailey asserted, "in having high school polls."[5]

VOTES proved Bailey's point as they prepared their campaign in Connecticut. In August 1962 they held their first formal assembly. They sent out invitations. They delivered the VOTES constitution to Connecticut's attorney general and the secretary of state, Ella T. Grasso. They received well wishes for their convocation from the governor, two city mayors, and members of the state's congressional delegation. "I support your objective wholeheartedly," wrote one congressman, while Secretary Grasso requested a report on the proceedings. The Connecticut League of Women Voters planned to send a representative, as did the Young Republican Clubs of Connecticut.[6]

Speakers at the convocation included VOTES officers and members as well as a local attorney, John A. Berman, who provided "a history of Teenage Suffrage." For context, he cited citizens voting at 18 in Georgia, Kentucky, and Guam, at 19 in Alaska, and at 20 in Hawai'i, although he missed out on American Samoa's recent 20-year-old vote. He called for popular support to make this change in Connecticut possible. Concluding on an optimistic note, he posited that "it looks as through this period of apathy is over."[7]

Each of the student speakers articulated one of the arguments for lowering the voting age. Treasurer Arthur Fournier asserted that students' political knowledge and awareness meant that "in many instances 18-year-olds are more capable of exercising the vote than their parents." Member Jack Kerlin addressed the time gap between high school graduation and voting. "When one's interest is highest, he must delay his rights of citizenship for three long years." This delay was an injustice, according to VOTES vice president Lou DiFazio. Youth were already assuming the responsibilities of adults; in fairness, they should have the same rights. He then pushed this point further than had earlier proponents.

Failing to act on youth voting rights, DiFazio argued, was "as contrary to our Constitution as denying Negroes the right to vote in the South."[8] This point of comparison was a new and powerful one for advocates of youth suffrage. Earlier proponents, such as Charles Diggs, Jennings Randolph, and Eleanor Roosevelt, were committed to voting rights for both

African and young Americans. They connected these two twentieth-century suffrage struggles as part of realizing the promise of American democracy. Yet when making their arguments, they could not assume their audience accepted the righteousness of Black re-enfranchisement and thus advance claims for youth on the same basis. In 1962 the VOTES vice president could, at least in Hartford, Connecticut. The civil rights movement of the 1940s and 1950s had prepared the ground for youth voting rights activists in the 1960s.

The VOTES arguments were astute and ardent, but the audience at the VOTES assembly did not bear out attorney Berman's optimism about the end of apathy. Only half of the expected 100 supporters showed up. Cofounder and secretary Joline Breton did not deny her disappointment at the poor attendance, and she "criticized the apathetic and indifferent attitude of the movement's opponents."[9] The *Hartford Courant*, for one, could be counted among the opponents. The newspaper's negative coverage of the effort in the 1950s continued into the new decade. "18-Year Vote Rally Draws Small Audience," headlined the *Courant*'s article. "Students Address 'Throng'" was the sneering subtitle.[10]

Even if the "campaign to win the 18-year-old vote got off to a less than stellar start," Joe Dolan stayed positive. Two months later he characterized the convocation as a "success," and compliments later came their way as a group "spouting with intelligent, alert, go-getting youth."[11] VOTES set its sights on 1963, when the Connecticut General Assembly would be back in session.

The year 1963 also would bring Dolan's commitment to contribute to the work of JFK's Presidential Commission. He expanded on his earlier research, so that his final 1964 report encompassed "The Results of a 3-year Study on 18-Year-Old Suffrage."[12] He acknowledged his sources of information, including the United Nations, the Governor's Office in Guam, and Alaskan and Hawai'ian state officials, and admitted he had learned a lot. "If a vein of optimism is detected in this report it is because this writer at the age of seventeen possessed a negative attitude towards lowering the voting age to 18. This is no longer true." Even so, Dolan admitted, "there is a great deal unknown about 18 year old voting."[13]

Recapping his findings in 34 pages plus seven appendices, he repeated the commission's recommendation for lowering the voting age. He also reinforced its rationale. "The three years of stagnation between the time one graduates and the time one enters the electorate has caused incalculable harm to participation and interest in our political affairs."[14]

In his conclusion Dolan put his political research, writing, and action into the larger context of his generation and the president who had inspired him. "This report has its origins at the time of the ascendency of the late John F. Kennedy to the White House; it is in his spirit that it is written; and coincidentally enough, its ending came at about the time of his tragic and sudden death." Like the Findlay College student from Ohio who testified at the 1961 Senate hearings, Dolan referenced Kennedy's inaugural address. He was certain that when JFK "asked us to do something for our country, when he said there were so many, so willing, and so able to seize the 'burden and glory of freedom,' he was thinking of young people in particular." Exactly those "aged 18, 19, and 20" who would be enfranchised if the VOTES campaign succeeded.[15]

Student Movements

Joseph Dolan and his fellow VOTES members were not the only American students inspired to participate in political activism in the early 1960s. Right at the start of the decade, in February 1960, African American college students started a dramatic sit-in movement in Greensboro, North Carolina. Their protest against segregation in public accommodations and facilities swept the South. Sit-ins in some 78 southern communities involved an estimated 70,000 students. Out of this movement came a new civil rights organization founded in April 1960. The Student Nonviolent Coordinating Committee (SNCC) used direct action—"putting your body on the line"—to challenge racial inequality.

SNCC inspired students across the country, including members of the Students for a Democratic Society (SDS). Emerging from its forerunner, the Student League for Industrial Democracy, SDS adopted this new name in 1960 and aimed to rejuvenate the US left after recent anticommunist attacks. The year 1960 also brought a student movement on the right wing of the political spectrum: Young Americans for Freedom (YAF). SDS on the left and YAF on the right expressed great concern about political apathy and disengagement among their peers, which VOTES also encountered.

Despite these concerns the three student organizations and their founding statements captured the attention of their peers. In keeping with its name, SNCC's statement—as prepared by Reverend James M. Lawson—focused on nonviolence. "We affirm the philosophical or religious ideal of nonviolence as the foundation of our purpose, the presupposition of our belief, and the manner of our action. Nonviolence, as it grows from the Judeo-Christian tradition, seeks a social order of justice permeated by love." For SNCC, nonviolence was the basis, means, and end of their movement. YAF's Sharon Statement was similarly short and sweet but emphasized personal and economic freedom under capitalism. SDS issued its much longer, multipart Port Huron Statement two years later. Considered a political manifesto for a "new left," it was initially drafted by University of Michigan graduate Tom Hayden and then collaboratively revised by SDS members. "We are people of this generation, bred in at least modest comfort, housed now in universities, looking uncomfortably to the world we inherit."

After the introduction—boldly titled "Agenda for a Generation"— SDS members placed a section on values, which SNCC and YAF also foregrounded. YAF considered "foremost among the transcendent values is the individual's use of his God-given free will," while SNCC connected the value of nonviolence to many other meaningful values. "Through nonviolence, courage displaces fear. Love transcends hate. Acceptance dissipates prejudice; hope ends despair. Faith reconciles doubt. Peace dominates war. Mutual regards cancel enmity. Justice for all overthrows injustice." SDS saw the process of "making values explicit" to be the "initial task in establishing alternatives." They proposed as an alternative to the present US political and economic system "participatory democracy." SNCC activists also pursued a true democracy in which people share in the decisions shaping their lives, a long-held political purpose of their mentor, Ella Baker. In the meantime these young people—many, like Hayden, had already reached voting age—urged and assisted participation in representative democracy through voting and electoral politics. SDS called for a new Democratic coalition, shorn of the Dixiecrats, to end "the perverse unity of liberalism and racism."[16]

Democracy, nonviolence, freedom—activists in SDS, SNCC, and YAF expressed and explored these values through the student organizations they named for them. They were joined by other young Americans engaged in questioning their society and their place in it. They were all "someone-in-search of himself," suggested a columnist in the *Chicago Tribune*'s "The Voice of Youth."[17] "When we are thrown to our own resources, we are forced to become acquainted with ourselves," asserted a young man, and "we begin asking: 'Who am I? What is my purpose in life?' It is when we are alone that our natural impulses help us go into the world and accomplish something."[18] Some looked to folk music and musical artists like Bob Dylan and Joan Baez to find themselves and define their values and social standards. Others looked to social and political reform. "We must stand up and be counted for what we believe! We must dare to be different," contended another columnist. "It does take courage to move against the stream, but why not try?"[19]

Personal reflections and social reform occupied students on college campuses. Encompassing the baby boom generation and those born a few years before, about 45 million Americans turned 18 between 1960 and 1972. The number of college students escalated. From three million students enrolled in 1960, colleges and universities had 10 million enrolled in 1973. Expanded opportunities for higher education allowed more young people to further their academic learning and thinking. For many this experience meant a prolonged period of time apart from their parents and with their peers. Campus life fostered a flourishing exchange of ideas and values and a shared youth culture. One of these young Americans was Paul Minarchenko (now Myer).

Campus Life

Paul Minarchenko did not take for granted his opportunity to go to college. "I was a first-generation college student. No other Minarchenko or Rusciano family member had gone beyond high school." Of Ukrainian and Italian heritage, Paul grew up in Linden, New Jersey. His father, a World War II veteran and machinist, ran the municipal garage there. "The decision to go to college was not something that received a great deal of thought," he recalls. "I was a typical 'C' student" and hoped to have a career in music. When he confessed his conflict between college and music, his high school guidance counselor laughed at him. "You've got to be joking; you will be lucky to get a job pumping gas!" For Paul, "that was the tipping point. Afterward, I was determined and announced my intention to go to college." In 1962 he ended up at nearby Newark State College, a teachers college located in Union, New Jersey. "It was a short commute, very affordable," and, most importantly, "they accepted me."[20]

At first commuting from home in his Volkswagen bug, Paul started spending more and more time on campus. Breaking the rules, he started staying overnight with friends in the men's dormitory. In his second year he could afford to legitimately live in the dorms, aided, yes, by a part-time job pumping gas. By his third year, like many college students across the country, he chafed against the rules and restrictions imposed by on-campus housing.

At this time universities and colleges had a policy of *in loco parentis*, which meant administrators were considered parents away from home and students were subsequently treated like children. Undergraduates, women especially, were closely monitored, and any rule violations risked expulsion. Students, individually and through their student governments, started to call for greater freedom and responsibility and to challenge such rules as curfews and dress codes. Indirect challenges to *in loco parentis* also began to occur, as overcrowding on campus sent more students, like Paul, into housing off campus. "Feeling that dorm life was too restrictive, I joined with three very close friends and fraternity brothers to rent a two bedroom apartment very near the campus."[21]

He thrived in the college environment. He enjoyed his history major and hanging out at the student union, drinking coffee and playing bridge. He pledged a fraternity and played both soccer and golf. He participated in student government right from the start. In the fall of 1962 he represented his freshman class. In the spring of 1963 he ran for vice president. "I believe that the Student Organization is one of the most important groups in this institution," he said in his official candidate statement. "I feel that I am capable of fulfilling the responsibilities and duties which accompany the office of vice-president."[22] A ringing endorsement came Paul's way. "During my four years at this college, I have yet to meet a freshman with more promise or drive," maintained the president of the Men's Athletic Association. "His maturity and sense of values are a tribute to himself and the entire student body."[23] Paul won the election, but barely—by 59 votes. Every vote had counted.

He put his time in student government to good use. He became involved in the National Student Association and attended regional and national conferences. Despite its covert funding and use by the CIA—revealed in 1967—the US National Student Association (NSA) backed liberal public policies and adopted progressive positions on issues like civil rights. "Higher Education in a Democracy" was the theme of the 1963 eastern regional conference, where student leaders called for greater federal government support for colleges and universities. "Going to my first national NSA conference, I was at first worried that a guy with a name like Minarchenko from a small state school in New Jersey might not fit in." But he needn't have worried. "In the end, there was a passionate sense of shared commitment to achieve common goals. I left that first conference energized and believing that students could make a difference."

With his political awareness and involvement growing, Paul gravitated to causes and organizations beyond student government, including SDS. He fully agreed with the ideals and values expressed in the Port Huron Statement. "Young people speaking out on matters of public policy and international relations and what a civilized world should be: peace, justice, liberty for all." He decided that one way he could speak out was through his campus newspaper, the *Independent*, which he considered to be "a largely ineffective campus voice." Paul started as a reporter. Then in his third year, in October 1964, he was elected managing editor. Along with the staff, he sought "a major change in philosophy and leadership" for the newspaper. By December he was editor-in-chief. "It was the beginning of a new day," he felt. His efforts focused on the *Independent* "becoming an influential and respected pro-active student voice."[24]

Under his leadership one of the first issues the *Independent* championed was funding for higher education in New Jersey. Among the wealthiest states in the country, New Jersey ranked 6th in per capita income but 48th in per capita spending on higher education. And it showed. Overcrowding, lack of facilities, and too few faculty members plagued Newark State College as well as other institutions. Paul and his fellow students set out to change that. They formed the New Jersey Student Committee for Undergraduate Education (CUE). "A College must grow to meet the needs of a student body," Paul editorialized. "Facilities and faculty do not just appear. Money must be made available." "Unless citizens of this State desire a change," he warned, "an injustice will be done to the youth of New Jersey."[25] Over the next year CUE held rallies and a 22-hour vigil at the state capitol in Trenton. As CUE coleader, Paul addressed the state legislature. They won early support from the governor and eventually further funding.[26]

CUE's activism mirrored what was happening with the student movement nationally. Students at more American colleges and universities were protesting the conditions of campus life as well as the quality of classroom teaching. Like CUE, organized students also sought to shape politics and policy beyond campus. A major win for student rights on campus in fact came from student civil rights activism off campus. During the sit-in movement, students at Alabama State College took part. Because of their participation, six students, including St. John Dixon, were expelled without a hearing. They challenged their expulsion through protest action, including a mass rally addressed by Martin Luther King and in the courts. With the help of the NAACP and other lawyers and arguing that the 14th Amendment guaranteed students due process, they won a consequential victory. In *Dixon v. Alabama State Board of Education* (1961), the federal appeals court decided that public colleges and universities could not use *in loco parentis* to deny students their constitutional rights as citizens.[27]

The simultaneity and significance of the movements for civil rights and student rights meant Paul's years as editor of the *Independent* "were exciting times." Bob Dylan's 1964 song "The Times They Are a-Changin'" reflected this sentiment. "It was the turbulent sixties and I was in the middle of it," Paul recalls. The apartment he shared with friends provided a base for their activities and activism. "Although the apartment did serve as an occasional party venue, with our growing maturity and student leadership roles, the place became a frequent gathering place for serious deliberations and planning of activities and events."[28] They also invited and hosted student leaders and activists from around the country, including SDS's Tom Hayden. Paul's political knowledge and network grew.

The *Independent*'s articles covered the major political issues of the day and the campus and community activism around them. Paul's editorials contained a clear, politically progressive perspective. His staff believed

Paul J. Minarchenko, of Newark State College and the New Jersey Student Committee for Undergraduate Education (CUE), calling for increased higher education funding at the New Jersey State House, 1965–1966. Governor Richard J. Hughes on left, and Barry Metzger, of Princeton University and CUE, on right. Courtesy of Paul J. Myer.

the newspaper "received a gift of strength through the personal integrity of its editor-in-chief."

> Paul has courage. He has the fortitude to speak when others would remain silent, to act when others would hesitate, because he has attained that level of personal knowledge which allows a man to believe in himself and makes it necessary for him to uphold his convictions.[29]

Paul's convictions were shared by his friends and compatriots at Newark State College and beyond. "I am young and inexperienced," exclaimed a Chicago high school student, "but does this excuse me from doing something, no matter how small for my country? Of course not!"[30] To uphold their convictions, students around the country participated in political organizing and direct action on campuses and in communities.

Campus and Community Activism

Student activism on civil rights bridged college and high school campuses and local communities. After all, SNCC began with four students from North Carolina Agricultural and Technical College challenging segregation at a Woolworth's store lunch counter in Greensboro. In Savannah, Georgia, after the arrest of high school senior Carolyn Quilloin (now Coleman) and two other students during a March 1960 sit-in, the local NAACP launched a boycott of downtown stores. The following year the city repealed segregation at lunch counters. "Savannah was one of the first cities in the South to desegregate," Coleman later said. "We felt that this was the beginning of the modern day civil rights movement. We laid our bodies down as bridges that others might walk over into freedom, and the struggle continues."[31] The lunch counter sit-ins expanded into "play-ins" at city parks, "read-ins" at public libraries, and "watch-ins" at movie theaters, demonstrating how racial segregation permeated every possible public space in the South.

Direct action against segregation in southern communities sparked the consciousness and commitment of student activists everywhere, as did challenges to disfranchisement. When SNCC called for protests on Election Day 1960, students in the NAACP, CORE, SDS, NSA, and other organizations joined in answering the call. To demand action on Black voting rights, they marched to local voting polls and campaign headquarters. "March in '60 so that all may vote in '64!" "Free Elections in America—in the South, North, and Washington, DC."[32] "College students throughout the United States paraded in many cities, including San Francisco," reported the *Stanford Daily*.[33] In Washington, DC, SNCC affiliates at five nearby colleges held an election vigil outside the White House until Kennedy was announced the winner. "After picketing, we went to the Democratic Headquarters to congratulate on their victory . . . we made it known that we remember the platform planks."[34]

These Election Day protests connecting campus and community were just one instance of collaboration among students on civil rights. They conducted fundraising drives and invited civil rights organizers to speak on campus. During civil rights crises, like the 1961 Freedom Rides, students "activated our phone trees, called the Justice Department, implored friendly members of Congress to intervene, sent telegrams of protest."[35] With civil rights an early focus, SDS opened a southern office in Atlanta with Tom Hayden to report directly on activity across the region. Hayden reported on the murderous violence that met SNCC's organizing in McComb, Mississippi, in the fall of 1961. Staying dedicated to nonviolence in spite of physical attacks, SNCC activists and local people were "digging in, and in more danger than nearly any student in this American generation has faced." "When do we begin to see it all not as remote," Hayden asked, "but as breathing urgency into our beings and meaning into our ideals?"[36]

As the decade continued, more young Americans across the nation began to see and to take action on civil rights in myriad ways. While growing up in San Jose, California, in the 1950s, Les Francis knew about the civil rights movement, especially developments around school integration in the South. "I was aware," he recalled, "but uninvolved." It was an experience during his freshman year at San Jose State College that truly raised his consciousness about race. He decided to pledge a fraternity in the fall of 1961, seeing it as a path into student government. When it came to signing the pledge form, however, he noticed it incorporated a statement of the fraternity's racial exclusion policy. He signed the form but quickly regretted it. Les felt deeply that "those types of restrictions should not exist" and quit the fraternity a day after pledging. "That was a defining moment for me."[37]

Also important to his growing knowledge and understanding of race in America was a sociology course Les took in his sophomore year with Dr. James E. Blackwell, a talented and transformative teacher. Dr. Blackwell's research focused on racial inequalities in social institutions, including education. It was the young professor's first academic job and "a critical time" for him. Bridging campus and community, Blackwell became president of the San Jose chapter of the NAACP, boosted its membership, and battled against racial discrimination in local housing, employment, and recreation. Racists retaliated against his activism by burning a cross in his yard. "We were outspoken about the goals we had articulated to change the pattern of race relations in San Jose," Blackwell remembered.[38]

One significant change in California's pattern of race relations, the Rumford Fair Housing Act of 1963, which prohibited discrimination against homebuyers and tenants, was targeted for toppling by Proposition 14 in November 1964. Sponsored by the real estate industry, Prop 14 would repeal the Rumford Act, allowing realtors and landlords to once again discriminate. It was opposed by the civil rights movement and liberal Democratic leaders, such as Governor Edmund G. "Pat" Brown. Martin Luther King spoke out against it on visits to California, and college students like Les mobilized against it.

"We walked precincts and knocked on hundreds of doors in neighborhoods around downtown San Jose; but, it was to no avail. Our fellow Californians, including many Democrats and independents, sanctioned racial discrimination when they approved Proposition 14."[39] One of these Californians was Republican Ronald Reagan, then readying himself to run for governor in 1966. Of voting age at 21, Les cast his first ballot in the 1964 election. Within three years Prop 14 would be declared unconstitutional. But its passage served as reminder of white resistance to civil rights in the North as well as the South. By the mid-1960s it was clear that white supremacy was a national problem that needed national solutions.

Participants in Mississippi Freedom Summer understood this well. In 1964, under the leadership of Robert Moses, SNCC as part of the Council of Federated Organizations, a coalition of civil rights groups, recruited nearly 1,000 northern, mostly white student volunteers to come to Mississippi. "Mississippi, the snake-pit of America," characterized Charles Diggs.[40] The volunteers would contribute to voter registration campaigns and citizenship education through Freedom Schools. Along with the student volunteers, the project ideally would bring the attention of their northern peers, parents, press, and politicians—including the new president Lyndon Johnson—to protect civil rights activists and punish their murderers and assailants. Even before the project officially began, three organizers, James Chaney, Michael Schwerner, and Andrew Goodman, were kidnapped and later confirmed killed. The stakes could not have been higher.

Student volunteers for the Mississippi summer project testified to the profound impact of their experience. Witnessing the conditions of oppression and violence in the South and the commitment of organizers and residents changed their lives. Mario Savio, a student at the University of California, Berkeley, felt this way. At Berkeley he had allied with the University Friends of SNCC. He participated first in their inner-city tutoring program and then in a mass sit-in and arrest in San Francisco to demand fair, nondiscriminatory hiring. Even so Freedom Summer was "the trigger for very deep change," he recalled. "SNCC and the other black workers in the South liberated themselves. In the process they helped liberate us."[41] When he and other volunteers came back to Berkeley in the fall of 1964, they dedicated themselves to spreading the word about the dangerous and dire situation in the South and supporting local organizing.

"It was a really active summer," Berkeley CORE member Jack Weinberg noted, "and everybody was saying 'In the fall when the students return, things are really going to happen.'"[42] The flashpoint became the issue of free speech on campus. The free speech movement arose to protest a long-standing campus ban on nonstudent-government political activity, including civil rights organizing. In a series of confrontations with the university administration and campus and local police, student activists demanded their rights of citizenship. Over the fall semester they held rallies, sang civil rights songs and folk songs—aided by folksinger Joan Baez—and heard speeches from the likes of Weinberg and Savio. After the administration revoked an agreement, Weinberg articulated his famous adage "you can't trust anyone over 30." Savio's speech before the occupation of the administration building also gained fame. "There is a time when the operation of the machine becomes so odious, makes you so sick at heart, that you can't take part."[43]

Less famous but very relevant to youth voting rights was an exchange between the student protestors and Seymour Martin Lipset, a well-known and supportive faculty member. Lipset's research drew on political science and sociology to examine the conditions that made democracy possible. When he spoke at one of the free speech rallies he explained his opposition to the movement's protest tactics with reference to his theory of pluralism. A pluralist democracy allows diverse interest groups to compete within the political system, so he believed that "civil disobedience is only justified in the absence of democratic rights." Of course, as student participant Ellen Sewell later put it, "the system can't work if people can't actually vote." As Lipset urged the crowd to express their concerns by taking part in democratic pluralism, they yelled back, "But we can't vote!" "And he looked, and he looked out at the whole crowd," Sewell recollected. "You know, he took that seriously. So then, he started a different tact because he realized he couldn't get very far with that argument."[44]

Although aware of youth disfranchisement, Berkeley students did not take up the issue of the 18-year-old vote at the time. They focused on achieving democratic rights on campus and succeeded. Across the country, apart from members of VOTES, few college and youth activists were focused yet on youth voting rights off campus. Many more prioritized the civil and voting rights of African Americans, citizenship rights with life and death consequences. Of necessity, the restoration of these rights demanded the attention of the nation and dominated the middle years of the 1960s.

6

Consent of the Governed

It took more than a year after President Kennedy sent his civil rights bill to Congress to achieve the Civil Rights Act of 1964. And then more than another year to achieve the Voting Rights Act of 1965. This relatively slow pace of legislative change on civil and voting rights occurred in the context of a series of swift-moving events and developments. JFK's assassination and Lyndon Baines Johnson's ascendency to the presidency in November 1963 altered political dynamics in the nation's capital. In and beyond Washington, DC, civil rights activists mobilized a mass movement and multiplied their campaigns for racial equality. The interaction of bottom-up grassroots activists and top-down government actors achieved the Civil Rights and Voting Rights Acts. These two pillars of "America's Second Reconstruction" reinforced the 14th and 15th Amendments of the first Reconstruction. They prohibited segregation in public accommodations and discrimination in employment and voting, including literacy tests.

Neither quickly nor easily achieved, these two pieces of legislation were not inevitable. Over 1963, 1964, and into 1965, opponents in Congress deluged the bills with amendments. "Our enemies tried to hamstring it with no less than 140 separate amendments," the NAACP's Roy Wilkins noted about the 1964 Act.[1] Southern senators also dragged out debate with record-breaking speeches. Organized by Georgia senator Richard B. Russell, the filibuster lasted for 75 days, the longest on record and replete with states' rights rhetoric. Civil rights advocates negotiated and lobbied on Capitol Hill, while civil rights activists organized and protested across the country. They were met with white violence and hostility at every turn.

Even the well-recognized peak moment of the modern civil rights movement revealed the perils of this period. To spur action on Kennedy's original civil rights bill, the interracial March on Washington for Jobs and Freedom took place on August 28, 1963. Before some quarter million marchers, Martin Luther King gave his stirring "I Have a Dream" speech. "I have a dream that one day this nation will rise up and live out the true meaning of its creed: 'We hold these truths to be self-evident, that all men are created equal.'"[2] Two weeks later white racists shattered that dream by bombing the 16th Street Baptist Church in Birmingham, killing four young women. Civil rights campaigns continued to confront such murderous violence in Alabama, in Mississippi, as during Freedom Summer, and in other states over 1963, 1964, and 1965.

King captured this intensifying conflict between the forces of racial progress and reaction in his March on Washington speech when he reminded Americans of "the fierce urgency of now." "Now is the time to make real the promises of democracy," he insisted. "Now is the time to rise from the dark and desolate valley of segregation to the sunlit path of racial justice."[3] As Kennedy, Johnson, and civil rights supporters in Congress realized, the Civil Rights Acts of 1957 and 1960 had failed to do this. The task before them was to craft and pass new federal legislation to end segregation and disenfranchisement and establish democracy and justice for all—or at least more—Americans.

With this political process unfolding, the first of the baby boom generation turned 18 in 1964 and the matter of youth voting rights arose again. A few young and adult Americans raised this question in tandem with the discussions, debates, and demonstrations over the reenfranchisement of African Americans. President Johnson was one of them. He reminded his fellow citizens of "one of the basic principles upon which this nation was founded, the principle of government by the consent of the governed."[4] To achieve the consent of the governed, voting laws needed to change.

The president disclosed his support for lowering the voting age when he delivered his proposal for voting rights legislation to Congress in 1965. "Frankly, I would like to have included in the message a provision that would permit all people over 18 years of age to vote." Johnson was well aware of the issue and the debates surrounding it. He had recently received the President's Commission on Registration and Voting Participation 1963 report, which recommended that states adopt the 18-year-old vote. A decade earlier he had rejected a resolution to lower the voting age through a constitutional amendment when it came up for a Senate vote. The arguments for, against, and over the appropriate strategy to achieve youth voting rights were well known to LBJ. "I should have liked to go further if I thought I could have without a constitutional amendment," he added.[5]

But the president and members of Congress understood an amendment necessary to enfranchise young Americans. Although several voting age proposals were introduced in the 89th Congress, they did not progress. The focus in 1964 and 1965 needed to be on restoring through legislative statute the full citizenship rights of African Americans already recognized by the 14th and 15th Amendments.

Civil Rights Act of 1964

A week after President Kennedy addressed the American people on the civil rights crisis in June 1963, he sent his bill to Congress, where it stalled for months. Civil rights leaders kept pressing forward. "The hundreds of thousands who marched in Washington marched to level barriers," King emphasized in an essay in the *New York Times Magazine* in September. "They summed up everything in a word—NOW." He underscored the urgency of the historical moment. "The long-deferred issue of second-class citizenship has become our nation's first-class crisis." New legislation was needed to curb the crisis. "Everything, not some of the things, in the President's civil-rights bill is part of NOW."[6] Diggs anticipated King's argument earlier that summer. "The Negro is no longer content with moderate progress toward first-class citizenship and demands complete freedom now."[7]

On November 27, 1963, the new president echoed Diggs and King's exhortations. Just five days after the terrible tragedy of Kennedy's assassination, President Johnson addressed Congress and the nation. He sought to assure grieving Americans that the government was in steady hands. The country would "continue on our course," particularly on civil rights. "No memorial oration or eulogy could more eloquently honor President Kennedy's memory than the earliest possible passage of the civil rights bill for which he fought so long," he announced. "We have talked long enough in this country about equal rights. We have talked for 100 years or more. It is time now to write the next chapter, and to write it in the books of law." He left no room for doubt about where he stood. Like civil rights advocates and activists across the country, he wanted action. When advised privately that civil rights was a "worthy" but "lost" cause, LBJ characteristically responded, "Well, what the hell's the presidency for?"[8]

Over the next seven months he used the powers of the presidency to push for what became the Civil Rights Act of 1964. Credit belongs to LBJ and Nicholas Katzenbach, his deputy attorney general, but also to Emanuel Celler in the House and Everett Dirksen, Republican from Illinois, in the Senate. Proudly hailing from the party and state of President Lincoln, Dirksen swung enough Republican votes to close debate in the Senate, ending the filibuster. His speech paraphrasing Victor Hugo helped to win the day. "Stronger than all the armies is an idea whose time has come."[9] The NAACP's Clarence Mitchell and his ally in the Leadership Conference on Civil Rights, Joseph Rauh, also played prominent roles. They developed legislative strategies with civil rights advocates, the White House, and congressional leaders, especially Senators Hubert Humphrey of Minnesota and Mike Mansfield of Montana. And they effectively deployed them, earning Mitchell the nickname of "the 101st Senator."

Through all these efforts, the civil rights bill was far more comprehensive than those that came before. Diggs attributed this "comparatively strong administration package of civil rights legislation" to organizing and protest. He believed that "prior to the Birmingham demonstrations, they were going to be satisfied [with] tightening up voting machinery and to extend the life of the civil rights commission."[10] Instead, the Civil Rights Act as eventually passed had eleven titles, "the most expansive civil rights measure in modern times," recalled Wilkins.[11] Celler had used his position to broaden JFK's original bill, with provisions promoted by civil rights advocates. Politicians enacted the Civil Rights Act, but the mobilized forces of the freedom movement had envisioned every element.

The heart of the omnibus bill was desegregation. "Either integration and peace or status quo and violence," Diggs had warned the year before. "Take a choice," and Congress did.[12] Title II outlawed discrimination on the basis of race, color, religion, or national origin in public accommodations, and Title III prohibited state and local governments from denying access to public facilities on the same basis. Segregated parks and pools, lunch counters and libraries—accepted as part of southern life—

now violated the law of the land. Title IV enforced the desegregation of public schools and empowered the Justice Department to act. Ten years after *Brown v. Board of Education*, with still only 10 percent of southern African Americans students attending desegregated schools, the federal government finally recognized its responsibility to fulfill their rights.[13]

Title VII set into motion equally significant changes by prohibiting discrimination in employment on the basis of race, color, religion, sex, or national origin. Leaders and members of civil rights organizations and labor unions had worked against discrimination and for equal opportunity in employment through many means over many years. Fair Employment Practices Commissions at the national and state levels, as in Diggs's Michigan, were just one. Boycotts against businesses and demonstrations against governments that refused to hire African Americans were another. Civil rights campaigns in Birmingham and elsewhere targeted the racist hiring practices of downtown stores and city government. The March on Washington for Jobs and Freedom put jobs first. As Diggs cautioned, "If the gap of income median between Negroes and whites is not closed, the interest of our total society will be in danger."[14] Title VII undoubtedly opened up the American workplace, and for a brief period of time that gap began to diminish.

Titles V, VI, IX, and X provided additional mechanisms to support and strengthen the civil rights of African Americans. Title V focused on expanding and extending to 1968 the Commission on Civil Rights, established with the 1957 act. It added a "clearinghouse function" to the commission's investigation and reporting duties, allowing for greater communication of its findings. Title VI forbade discrimination by entities receiving federal funds, and Title IX facilitated moving civil rights cases from segregationist state courts and all-white juries to the federal court and, ideally, fairer trials. Title X established the Community Relations Service to provide federal assistance in resolving discrimination cases at the state and local levels.

The Civil Rights Act of 1964 did not prioritize voting rights. As Wilkins put it, "If we gave the South such an opening it would do what it had done in 1957: agree to support voting provisions, then wreck everything else."[15] But the ratification in January of the 24th Amendment prohibiting poll taxes for federal elections signaled progress, as did several significant victories in court around legislative apportionment.

Starting with *Baker v. Carr* (1962), the Supreme Court decided in favor of plaintiffs seeking equal protection under the 14th Amendment for equal political representation. Through *Gray v. Sanders* (1963) and *Reynolds v. Sims* (1964), the Court developed the "one person, one vote" doctrine, with Justice Hugo Black at the forefront. In this way the Supreme Court expanded federal intervention in state voting practices.

Titles I and VIII of the Civil Rights Act smoothed the path for more. Title I barred the unequal application of voter registration requirements. More a statement of principle, this provision did not provide pragmatic solutions. For example, Title I did not eliminate literacy tests, which in the hands of white supremacists prevented Black voters from registering. It also did nothing about economic or physical reprisals against African Americans for registering—or attempting to register—to vote. Title VIII required the collection of statistics on registration and voting. Building on the 1960 act, these statistics would allow the Commission on Civil Rights to demonstrate systematic racial inequalities with voter registration in the South.

These provisions mattered, however they did not measure up to what was needed to realize the promise of political equality. "To walk unafraid to the ballot box and cast a free vote remains still a myth in most of the South," affirmed King.[16] Much was at stake. "Something must be done now," argued Diggs, "or the Negro people will lose faith in whites and alienate themselves from the cause of democracy."[17] These leaders' statements were being proven daily on the ground by civil rights activists in the South, revealing the necessity of further legislation on voting rights and, equally importantly, its enforcement. After all, as Wilkins reminded, the "act would not implement itself."[18]

Freedom Votes

Mississippi Freedom Summer was under way when LBJ signed the Civil Rights Act into law in July 1964. This historic signing took place just eleven days after Mississippi summer project organizers James Chaney, Michael Schwerner, and Andrew Goodman went missing. "The kids are dead," Robert Moses told stunned project volunteers finishing their training in Oxford, Ohio, before heading to Mississippi. "When we heard the news at the beginning, I knew they were dead." "There may be more deaths," Moses warned, releasing the volunteers from their commitment to continue given the critical situation in Mississippi.[19] The vast majority did continue. "We are more determined than ever to go," University of Iowa student Mike Kenney told his campus newspaper. "If we are able to stay the summer without getting killed, it will be a big step."[20] Together with Council of Federated Organizations staff and visiting clergy, lawyers, and medical personnel, student volunteers like Kenney engaged in community organizing with tens of thousands of local residents across the state. The priority was voting rights.

During Freedom Summer the project worked on voter registration, citizenship education, and the formation of a new political party, the Mississippi Freedom Democratic Party (MFDP). "It was clear that the Freedom Movement would make no positive headway in Mississippi until the racial composition of the electorate was radically changed," argued a founding document of the MFDP. Less than 7 percent of eligible African American Mississippians were registered to vote. Those who tried to register were time and again turned away or turned down. Even if they succeeded in registering they were subjected to "mob violence," "vigilante action," and "organized economic freeze-outs." "The long history of systemic and studied exclusion of Negro citizens from equal participation in the political processes of the state grows more flagrant daily."[21]

The Mississippi summer project exposed to the nation that exclusion and the white violence directed at enforcing it. Although the Civil Rights Acts of 1957, 1960, and now 1964 provided some protection for Black voting rights, the legislation assigned the task of enforcement largely to the Department of Justice and the federal courts. Limited personnel to prosecute and the delaying tactics of the defense plagued these cases. "This judicial approach is strictly a long-range proposition," argued Leslie W. Dunbar, a leader of the biracial Southern Regional Council's Voter Education Project, based in Atlanta. "It's a matter of years and years." White supremacists in Mississippi acknowledged as much. Politics was "white folk's business" and ending racial discrimination in voting would not happen until the Attorney General "Bobby Kennedy comes down here with some Federal marshals," one white resident told the *New York Times*.[22]

As a consequence, official Black voter registration numbers hardly budged over the months of Freedom Summer. But the Mississippi summer project pursued additional activities and a bold strategy. After all, 1964 was a presidential election year. LBJ was running in his own right to win the Democratic nomination and the White House. Building on a 1963 Freedom Vote, project activists sponsored interracial MFDP meetings and conventions in parallel to the all-white Mississippi Democratic Party's primary election. They registered freedom voters, nominated freedom candidates, and decided on a freedom platform. The Mississippi Freedom Democrats also sent delegates to the Democratic National Convention in August to challenge the unjust selection and seating of the state party's official delegation. With this strategy the MFDP demonstrated both the demand for Black voting rights and the denial of those rights by the state's white Democrats.

At the Democratic National Convention in Atlantic City, New Jersey, the MFDP contested the right of the all-white delegation to represent Mississippi. Ella Baker, now director of the MFDP's Washington office, contended that "all Democrats who can register and vote with freedom are now challenged as never before."[23] They made their case before the Democratic Party's Credentials Committee, later broadcast across the nation. The delegation's vice chair, Fannie Lou Hamer, had endured economic and physical reprisals for her voting rights organizing. She testified to a brutal beating she received in county jail in 1963, which left her with lasting injuries. "All of this is on account of we want to register, to become first-class citizens. And if the Freedom Democratic Party is not seated now, I question America." The gripping testimony of Hamer and others gained little ground. Johnson and national Democratic Party leaders chose to seat the entire all-white Mississippi delegation, offering only two seats to the Freedom Democrats. As Hamer put it, "We didn't come all this way for no two seats."[24]

What party leaders saw as a compromise, the Freedom Democrats and supporters considered to be a betrayal of the MFDP's just fight against racially based political exclusion. It also betrayed "the one party" in Mississippi that has "pledged its loyalty, unconditionally, to President Johnson and the principles for which our national party stands," telegrammed Representative Diggs and 23 Democratic congressmen to the president.[25] Although King, Wilkins, and Joe Rauh suggested accepting the compromise as a practical solution, Freedom Summer volunteers and other student activists saw it very differently. Moral principles and party politics appeared to be wholly incompatible. They were "heart-broken and bitter" after Atlantic City, one member of SDS recalled.[26] This experience undermined enthusiasm for the election of President Johnson among some student activists, reflected in their slogan "Part of the Way with LBJ."

But in November 1964 many, many more Americans were "All the Way with LBJ," and he defeated his Republican challenger Barry Gold-water in a landslide. Johnson and his running mate, Minnesota senator Hubert Humphrey, won over 60 percent of the popular vote, with an even higher margin of victory in the Electoral College. They secured the support of the citizens of Washington, DC, newly enfranchised by the 23rd Amendment. Their push for the Civil Rights Act of 1964, which Goldwater voted against, won 94 percent of the Black vote for the Democrats. They also received the youth vote, with 72 percent of voters aged 18 to 29 casting their ballots for the Democratic ticket.[27] Goldwa-ter's reputation as a conservative reactionary and extremist, particularly on the military use of nuclear weapons, did not help him with young Americans.

As chair of Young Citizens for Johnson-Humphrey, Senator Birch Bayh of Indiana helped his party win this voting bloc. Still youthful at age 36, Bayh energetically campaigned on college campuses and at loca-tions across the country during the 1964 election season. He appeared at events for young voters with the popular folk singers Peter, Paul, and Mary. In his speeches Bayh reassured his audience that they need not fear nuclear war or a retreat on civil rights. "Young America is destined to live tomorrow. We're not going to turn back the clock of history."[28]

White voters in the South vehemently disagreed, and only in John-son's own state of Texas did the Democratic ticket get a majority of the white vote. Goldwater swept South Carolina, Georgia, Alabama, Missis-sippi, and Louisiana as well as Arizona, his home state. What LBJ had predicted after signing the Civil Rights Act had come true. "We just delivered the South to the Republican Party for a long time to come," he told an aide.[29] Ensuring and expanding the African American vote for the Democratic Party became a political necessity. Voting rights leg-islation needed to become the political priority.

Voting Rights Act of 1965

President Johnson and his fellow Democrats knew further legislation and its enforcement were needed to re-enfranchise African Americans in the South. The ongoing voting rights activism of all the civil rights organizations—NAACP, SCLC, SNCC, CORE—had made that clear. The MFDP made it undeniable. But LBJ and his administration were not in a rush, given the very recent achievement on civil rights. "It's just not the wise and politically expedient thing to do," Johnson told a frustrated King after the 1964 election. At the same time the president earlier had told his acting attorney general Nicholas Katzenbach to start preparing. "I want you to write me the goddamndest, toughest voting rights act that you can devise."[30]

In the new year of 1965 Martin Luther King made his move by joining SCLC to an ongoing voting rights struggle with SNCC and local citizens in Selma, Alabama. He arrived in the city on January 2, 1965, and addressed members of the movement at a local church that same evening. "Today marks the beginning of a determined, organized, mobilized campaign to get the right to vote everywhere in Alabama," Reverend King preached from the pulpit. "Give us the ballot!" As he concluded, the audience cheered and started singing "We Shall Overcome."[31] The popular anthem of the modern mass freedom movement, the song symbolized solidarity, religious faith, and hope. "Oh, deep in my heart, I do believe—we shall overcome some day."

The next few difficult months demonstrated that "some day" was still a long way away. While activists tried to register in groups or peacefully protest, white supremacists fought back with all the weapons they had. Mass arrests and mass assaults using electric cattle prods, billy clubs, and baseball bats took place over many weeks. King himself was punched in the face, arrested, and jailed. "THIS IS SELMA, ALABAMA," he wrote in a public appeal. "THERE ARE MORE NEGROES IN JAIL WITH ME THAN THERE ARE ON THE VOTING ROLLS."[32] This unrelenting white resistance and violence led up to the fatal shooting of young Jimmie Lee Jackson in late February. To honor his memory and take their voting rights message to the Alabama state capital, activists promised to march the 54 miles from Selma to Montgomery.

On Sunday, March 7, 1965, the marchers set off from Selma. They soon encountered a wall of sheriff's deputies and state troopers at the Edmund Pettus Bridge. Within minutes of an order to turn around, the marchers were viciously attacked. Media reports and broadcasts of "Bloody Sunday" catalyzed the consciences of Americans. Numbering in the thousands, volunteers came to contribute to the voting rights movement in Selma. Another march to Montgomery was planned to finish what had been started. Demonstrations in solidarity and sympathy were held on countless college campuses and in over 80 cities. "The mournful, determined tones of 'We Shall Overcome' rang out from Miami to Seattle," reported the *New York Times*.[33]

Protestors also picketed the White House, singing "We Shall Overcome" and carrying signs urging the president to "Go All the Way LBJ." Finally, he did. He announced he would soon be sending voting rights legislation to Congress. On the evening of March 15 he explained and justified this step in the most moving and meaningful speech of his presidency. "At times, history and fate meet at a single time in a single place to shape a turning point," he reflected. "So it was last week in Selma, Alabama." Before Congress and the country, President Johnson reasserted the "right of every American to vote in every election" and related how this bill would protect that fundamental right. "This bill will strike down restrictions to voting in all elections—federal, state, and local—which have been used to deny Negroes the right to vote."

The climax of speech came midway through. "What happened in Selma is part of a far larger movement which reaches into every section and State of America. It is the effort of American Negroes to secure for themselves the full blessings of American life." Johnson recognized African Americans in their communities and organizations as the drivers of political change. He also realized the crucial role of their fellow citizens. "Their cause must be our cause too," he vowed. "Because it is not just Negroes, but really it is all of us, who must overcome the crippling legacy of bigotry and injustice." Then he repeated the refrain so often sang by members of the freedom movement in moments of hope and hardship. "And—we—shall—overcome."[34] Those in attendance burst into applause over 30 times during the speech, and this refrain brought them to their feet.

Beyond the Capitol Building, responses ranged from equally enthusiastic through more restrained to openly hostile. More than a few
southern congressmen boycotted the speech. At the University of Colorado, students believed LBJ had waited too long. "It is a sad commentary on American politics that Congressmen and presidents . . . must be
confronted with blood to awaken their senses."[35] Watching the televised
speech in Selma, Martin Luther King and leaders of the movement were
stunned to hear that evocative refrain from a president, especially one
from the South.[36]

Now with the full support of the federal government and federal
troops, they prepared to finish the march to Montgomery. The interracial and interfaith Alabama Freedom March proceeded over five
days, with 25,000 participants and representatives from all of the civil
rights organizations. The march culminated in a rally at the Alabama
state capitol building on March 25. "We are on the move now. Yes,
we are on the move and no wave of racism can stop us," proclaimed
King. Of the voting rights bill, he pronounced, "We want immediate
passage."[37]

Although Congress did not pass the Voting Rights Act of 1965 immediately, the legislation moved through much more quickly than the
Civil Rights Act and was even more of an omnibus bill. In its final
form the Voting Rights Act had 19 sections. Section 1 introduced the
purpose of the act: to enforce the 15th Amendment. "No voting qualification or prerequisite to voting, or standard, practice, or procedure
shall be imposed," specified Section 2, "to deny or abridge the right of
any citizens of the United States to vote on account of race or color."
Literacy tests were understood to be a disenfranchising device and
prohibited.

Because the 24th Amendment barred poll taxes for federal elections,
many wanted the Voting Rights Act to do the same for state and local
elections. As with the 18-year-old vote, LBJ would have liked to have
added that provision but feared both "would bog the bill down."[38] In the
end, the act empowered the attorney general to challenge the constitutionality of state and local poll taxes and abolished the accumulation of
any back poll taxes.

Federal remedies to racial discrimination in voting were substantially strengthened across a number of sections. Sections 3, 6, and 13

buttressed federal litigation efforts, and Sections 6, 7, 9, and 13 provided for federal examiners to determine voter eligibility and qualifications. Section 8 allowed for the appointment of federal poll watchers to support the work of examiners.

Most controversially, the act targeted those states, localities, and officials where racial disenfranchisement was most rife. Section 4 laid out a formula for determining which political units would be in "coverage," and Section 5 required that any changes to their voting rules needed "preclearance" from federal authorities. But both sections expired after only five years, under the optimistic assumption they would no longer be needed in 1970. Sections 11 and 12 outlined civil and criminal sanctions against individuals who prevented eligible voters from casting their ballots, including through intimidation and threats.

Over five months, members of Congress—liberal and conservative, Democrat and Republican—amended, debated, filibustered, and compromised. Opponents objected to what they saw as federal encroachment on states' rights to determine voter qualifications. The bill "would make constitutional angels weep," observed Senator Samuel J. Ervin Jr., Democrat from North Carolina. Citing Article 1, Section 2 of the US Constitution, he asserted the power of the states to set suffrage qualifications and regulate elections, regardless of the 15th Amendment.[39] (Or, he could have added, the 19th Amendment.) Even some supporters, like Attorney General Katzenbach, considered the best option to be a constitutional amendment, given that the bill would empower the federal government to suspend and supervise state suffrage practices.

But not LBJ or the key players who also had helped to pass the Civil Rights Act. Emanuel Celler, Everett Dirksen, Vice President Hubert Humphrey, Roy Wilkins, Clarence Mitchell, Joe Rauh, and the Leadership Conference on Civil Rights believed the 15th Amendment provided the needed authority. After all, they could cite Section 2 of the amendment. "The Congress shall have power to enforce this article by appropriate legislation." In their view and that of the vast majority of Congress, the Voting Rights Act of 1965 was just such "appropriate legislation." The Supreme Court agreed and upheld the act's constitutionality the following year.

The Fight Goes On

President Johnson's signing ceremony on August 6, 1965, symbolized the alliance of bottom-up activism and top-down action that achieved the Voting Rights Act. Nearly all the key players in passing the act witnessed the signing, as did Thurgood Marshall, lead lawyer for the NAACP's lawsuit in *Smith v. Allwright* (1944). SNCC chairman John Lewis also attended. A veteran of the student sit-in movement, the Freedom Rides, and the long voting rights struggle in Selma, Lewis had spoken at the March on Washington and suffered a skull fracture on Bloody Sunday. He was all too aware of the high price paid by activists, past and present, for basic voting rights protections. So too was another attendee, Rosa Parks. Forced out of Montgomery and now a resident of Detroit, Parks worked in the congressional office of Charles Diggs's colleague, John Conyers. Back in February Diggs had led a delegation to Selma that included Conyers. Their demand to remove "once and for all any racial restrictions on exercising the franchise" had now been met.[40]

"Today the picture has improved," wrote an 18-year-old activist from Mississippi, summarizing the impact of the Voting Rights Act six months on. Earnestyne Evans felt she'd been in the freedom movement all her life. "I became active just after my junior year in high school. That was in the summer of 1964 when college students and other volunteers from around the country came down south to help with local voter registration campaigns." She knew how few African Americans were registered to vote. "My father was one of the few, I'm proud to say." She participated in the Freedom Summer campaigns. Now there was a federal registrar in her county and the literacy test had been stopped. By the end of 1966 more than half of all African Americans in the South had registered to vote. "But an act of Congress doesn't change everything," Evans cautioned. More progress was needed. And "with the help of SNCC and other organizations, the fight goes on."[41]

The fight also continued for youth voting rights, which would have fully enfranchised Earnestyne Evans. Teenagers were paying attention, as evidenced in "The Voice of Youth" column in the *Chicago Tribune*. "The question of who is eligible to vote is much publicized and discussed by young Americans today," wrote a young woman. In "A Plea for the Polls," she presented her case for youth suffrage and promised "change if we teens were allowed to light a little of our own election fire."[42] "It is about time that 18 year olds have a voice in their government," declared a male high school student.[43] In 1965 alone some 50 proposals to lower the voting age were introduced in about half of the state legislatures.[44] All failed to progress. At Connecticut's constitutional convention that year, delegates considered and overwhelmingly rejected proposals for voting at 18, 19, and 20. This rejection indicated that members of VOTES had made little headway in their home state.[45] Despite these defeats, in 1965 American Samoa lowered its voting age further, from 20 to 18, and Micronesia instituted the 18-year-old vote.

Proponents of youth enfranchisement raised the question in Congress several times that year. After the passage of the Voting Rights Act, Representative Lester Wolff, Democrat from New York, prized this "major step toward extending the franchise to those who have previously been unable to participate in the basic act of free government—the right to vote." In the first year of his national political career, he was "proud to have been in Congress when this milestone legislation was added to the fabric of our democracy. There remains, however, a group of American citizens—8 million strong—who are flatly denied the right to vote in all but four States of the union."[46] As had others before him, Wolff connected youth and Black voting rights. In fact, the Voting Rights Act, specifically its renewal in 1970, would directly pave the way for the 26th Amendment, which he would strongly support. Wolff, alongside other congressional proponents, connected youth voting rights to two other developments in 1965: the war on poverty and the war in Vietnam.

7

Challenge of Citizenship

In 1965, as a new congressman from New York, Lester Wolff introduced his first bill to lower the voting age. A volunteer for the Civil Air Patrol during World War II, a successful journalist and businessman, and a liberal, Wolff had been a Republican until the party nominated Barry Goldwater for president in 1964. The nomination of the conservative Goldwater sent Wolff to the Democratic Party, and he made his first bid for the House of Representatives that year. In an upset victory he defeated his opponent, who "was to the right of Genghis Khan," Wolff joked.[1] His shifting party allegiance indicated the partisan political sorting then under way. Republicans increasingly identified as ideologically conservative, while liberals were more at home in the Democratic Party. Wolff came to Washington, DC, after LBJ's landslide election, with Democrats in control of both houses of Congress and an era of liberal reform under way.

Over the middle years of the decade, 1964 to 1966, President Johnson sent to Congress a raft of reforms to realize what he called "the Great Society." He announced this aspiration before an audience of college students in Ohio. "And with your courage and with your compassion and your desire, we will build a Great Society. It is a society where no child will go unfed, and no youngster will go unschooled. Where no man who wants work will fail to find it."[2] The president elaborated on his agenda in another speech before students, this time at the University of Michigan. The most transformative civil and voting rights legislation since Reconstruction in the nineteenth century was just the start. The Johnson administration also oversaw the largest expansion in the welfare state since the New Deal of the 1930s. With the ambitious aim of eliminating poverty in America, LBJ launched a "war on poverty." As a result Wolff cast his first votes in Congress for the Voting Rights Act and the creation of Medicare and Medicaid, national health care programs for elderly and poor Americans.

In this political context the 18-year-old vote seemed possible. "I firmly believe our young people between the ages of 18 and 21 deserve the right to vote," the new congressman stated in October 1965. "In these times, we cannot afford to be without the voice at the polls of a segment of our society that has served us honorably and well." Wolff complimented young Americans for contributing to initiatives like the Peace Corps and the war on poverty. "As Peace Corps volunteers they are bringing a new image of America—the image of a compassionate and friendly people—to other nations of the world," he observed. "As volunteers in the war on poverty, they are helping to eradicate the evils of poverty and want where they exist in this country."

Wolff recognized another service young people were providing the country. "Perhaps most significant of all, they represent our national security in the rice paddies and jungles of Vietnam. Some have given the ultimate sacrifice." Wolff entered Congress in the same year that President Johnson decided to escalate the American war in Vietnam. Like his predecessors in the White House, Johnson saw the war through a Cold War lens and justified his decision as necessary to contain global communism. In doing so Johnson broke promises made during the 1964 presidential campaign. "We are not about to send American boys nine or ten thousand miles away from home to do what Asian boys ought to be doing for themselves." But he did, ordering the first American ground troops—age 18 and up—to Vietnam in March 1965.

Young men and women "are being asked to do more for our Nation than ever before in our history," Wolff contended, "and they are meeting the challenge of citizenship with maturity."[3] Wolff was right. Young Americans were inspired to contribute to as well as criticize and counter these developments at home and abroad. In the process of practicing and demonstrating citizenship, they came to feel the effects of disfranchisement until age 21 more deeply, as Newark State College student Paul Minarchenko experienced.

In 1965 Paul sought to meet the challenge of citizenship through his campus newspaper and his political activism. Under his editorship the *Independent* ran stories on academic freedom, the civil rights movement, the war on poverty, and the Vietnam War. "We cannot help but be impressed with our college's role in the shaping of President Johnson's 'Great Society,'" Paul editorialized in 1965. "Let us hope (and work) that we are capable of meeting the challenge which our society presents."[4] During his senior year, with graduation coming up in the spring of 1966, Paul began to think about his next step. He knew he didn't want to become a teacher, but he was still committed to making a difference. "In my fourth year, when we were sort of getting ready to leave the cocoon of the university and had to go out into the real world, many of us had lots of debates as to what we should do."[5] Those debates would take him to Washington, DC, and his next challenge.

To Eradicate the Evils of Poverty and Want

President Johnson's Great Society encompassed many new policies and programs designed to improve the quality and standard of living for all Americans. At the center was the war on poverty. Johnson declared an "unconditional war on poverty in America" in his first State of the Union Address in January 1964. As with civil rights, he presented this priority as carrying on the legacy of his predecessor, JFK. At the time studies showed that poor Americans constituted one-fifth of the national population, about 36 million people. The civil rights movement and two publications—Michael Harrington's *The Other America* in 1962 and Dwight Macdonald's review in the *New Yorker* in 1963—put the problem of persistent, hard-core poverty on the national political agenda.

For solutions, the Johnson administration could have looked to civil rights leaders. They had proposals to address poverty and economic inequality for all Americans. Four of the ten demands of the 1963 March on Washington for Jobs and Freedom focused on economic issues. Barring employment discrimination was one, which Title VII of the Civil Rights Act helped to achieve. Another demand sought a minimum wage higher than that enacted during the Kennedy administration as well as a New Deal–style jobs program. "A massive federal program to train and place all unemployed workers—Negro and white—on meaningful and dignified jobs at decent wages."[6] But the Johnson administration considered full-scale public job creation too costly and requiring too much government planning and direction.

Instead, believing "blocked opportunities" were the predominant cause of poverty, policymakers and lawmakers prioritized education, job training, and job "readiness," especially for youth. Programs such as the Jobs Corps and the Neighborhood Youth Corps would allow poor Americans to see and take advantage of "economic opportunity." As a result, the 1964 legislation that enacted the war on poverty was the Economic Opportunity Act, which established the Office of Economic Opportunity to oversee it. Early childhood education, through Head Start, and adult education and literacy programs were fundamental to the war on poverty and generally well received nationally and locally.

They were definitely well received at Newark State College. Given the college's teacher-training mission, faculty and students, including Paul Minarchenko, paid attention to these new federal initiatives. They also participated in them. "War on Poverty Is Aided by Newark State Students," trumpeted a 1965 headline in the *Independent*. "The student army, now well over 200 strong, fights poverty of educational opportunities in the front lines, as tutors of disadvantaged children in surrounding school systems."[7] Educational initiatives like this fit the understanding of Great Society legislation as social investment, as did the Elementary and Secondary Education Act and the Higher Education Act. Passed in 1965, these acts provided federal funding, greater student access, and new programs to enhance American education at all levels. A former teacher himself, LBJ saw them as the "roots of change and reform."[8]

To highlight the historical significance of this new federal education legislation, the president traveled to his alma mater, Southwest Texas State College, to sign the Higher Education Act into law. Sharing a mission of teacher training with Newark State, Southwest Texas State provided a welcome audience for the president and the First Lady on November 8, 1965. Reminiscing about his college years from 1927 to 1930, Johnson remembered how "the seeds were planted from which grew my firm conviction that for the individual, education is the path to achievement and fulfillment; for the nation, it is a path to a society that is not only free but civilized; and for the world, it is the path to peace—for it is education that places reason over force."[9]

Rosalyn Hester (now Baker) was in the audience. In her sophomore year, majoring in political science and speech and pursuing her teaching credential, Roz remembers the signing. "LBJ was a good-sized man, somewhat larger than life, and he brought a lot of prestige to the college. He was very interested in education. We felt very honored to have

President Lyndon B. Johnson returns to his alma mater, Southwest Texas State
(Teachers) College, to sign the Higher Education Act, November 8, 1965. Frank Wolfe,
photographer. Lyndon B. Johnson Collection. Courtesy of the University Archives,
Texas State University.

a president from our school." She "grew up in a family of teachers" and
enjoyed debate and public speaking. "I was a very opinionated child
when I was growing up." At Southwest Texas State, she got incredibly
involved in campus activities. Over the years, Roz took part in band,
debate, sorority life, and student government. As a liberal critic of the
Dixiecrats—her college racially integrated only in 1963—she joined the
Young Republicans. "I didn't last though," she recalled.[10]

Most prominently, she participated in the Texas Student Education
Association. A student affiliate of NEA, "its purpose is to provide members with experience and education about the work of local, state and
national teachers' professional organizations."[11] Roz served in her local
college chapter and as an officer at the state level. Her involvement contributed to her recognition in *Who's Who among Students in American
Universities and Colleges* in her junior and senior years. In this way Roz
aligned herself with NEA, the principal organization supporting the
educational initiatives of the war on poverty and the Great Society.

NEA and Student NEA joined with the NAACP, NSA, UAW, and other organizations in endorsing and assisting another federal program, Volunteers in Service to America (VISTA). Often called the "domestic Peace Corps," VISTA involved Americans aged 18 and up in myriad service activities and community projects in rural and urban areas all over the country. VISTA recruited vigorously on college campuses. As editor of his college newspaper, Paul Minarchenko proposed inviting a VISTA speaker to campus for the recruitment drive in 1965. "This government-sponsored group is seeking five thousand volunteer workers to live in poverty stricken areas and assist people for one year," he explained. Articles in the *Independent* supported those students "willing to give a year of their talents and energies to help the poor help themselves."[12] In the process, volunteers on the local level found that participation in the war on poverty and the civil rights movement often overlapped.

Challenging Racial and Economic Inequality

College students involved in a new SCLC project intended as much. Launched in 1965, the Summer Community Organization and Political Education Project extended the organizing model used during Freedom Summer in 1964. The project targeted political disfranchisement, educational inequality, and poverty in selected counties throughout the South. Students at a particular college formed and fundraised for their own group. Then they "adopted" a county for summer organizing and future support. "You are here because history is being made here and this generation of students is found where history is being made," Martin Luther King told the summer volunteers. In addition to voter registration and education, student organizers were to initiate community projects by working with the war on poverty. Although federally funded, war on poverty programs were implemented locally. SCLC believed these programs would never reach African Americans in the South without "outside assistance . . . due to the recalcitrance of the local white power structure."[13]

College students and graduates who sought social change around class and race inequalities also joined SDS's community organizing. In late 1963, inspired by the civil rights movement, SDS members decided to take their campus activism in a new direction—into communities.

Through their Economic Research and Action Project and with initial funding from the UAW, they set out to build "an interracial movement of the poor" to end poverty and extend democracy in America.[14] Over the next few years, new left organizers established thirteen community projects in predominantly Black, white, and racially diverse neighborhoods. The largest, most successful, and longest-lasting projects were located in Chicago, Newark, Boston, and Cleveland. In each of these cities organizers and community members worked with—and against—the local war on poverty. They believed that "the official effort would be a token in comparison with the real needs" and that they could be "frontline soldiers in a *real* war on poverty."[15]

Their starting point was to ensure the participation of poor Americans. They could cite a provision for the federal Community Action Program mandating that local poverty agencies and programs be "developed, conducted, and administered with the maximum feasible participation of residents of the areas and members of the groups served."[16] Yet the exact meaning of "maximum feasible participation" was open to interpretation. Cities like Newark and San Francisco proved more amenable to participation. But cities such as Chicago and Cleveland excluded poor residents from planning and decision-making structures. Joining in grassroots protests with civil rights and other community activists, SDS's projects demanded that officials fulfill the rhetorical promise of participation by increasing low-income resident representation on local governing boards.

Although their demands were never fully met, these campaigns mattered for youth voting rights. Elections ended up being one way of selecting representatives for the local war on poverty boards. Held in designated "poverty spots," these elections had some similarity to regular elections but differed in how they defined eligibility. Voters had to meet an income requirement and identify themselves as poor. These voter qualifications constituted "a pauper's oath" and unsurprisingly contributed to very poor turnout, with the average participation rate far less than 10 percent.[17] A number of cities, however, included a new, noteworthy qualification. For poverty board elections in Boston, Cleveland, Chester, Pennsylvania, Huntsville, and other cities, the voting age was 18. In Kansas City it was 17.[18] Lowering the voting age for these elections made sense, given the war on poverty's youth focus. By taking an opening for participation in the war on poverty and seeking to make it real, SDS's projects, together with local activists and Office of Economic Opportunity officials, advanced the idea that young Americans deserved to have a voice and a vote.

Coming to the same conclusion and aware of the SDS's Newark project, Paul Minarchenko spent the spring 1966 semester immersed in the community. Instead of completing the required practicum for student teachers, he convinced the college administration to let him work in a war on poverty program. A forerunner of Upward Bound, the program prepared and assisted low-income high school students for college. "I had a very different education being in an urban slum, the Ironbound section of Newark, where I was one of the few white people there." The work and witnessing such stark poverty and prejudice had an impact. "We didn't have a political agenda. We were there to help people. But it became very obvious that there were barriers to helping them at the local level and those barriers were essentially political. That was part of my education about the importance of the 18-year-old vote."[19]

After this experience and about to graduate, Paul asked "what could I do to change or make things better?" Meeting and impressing an official from the US Department of Labor got Paul a job with the US Employment Service, a division of the Manpower Administration. "The Labor Department was a major player in implementing President Johnson's domestic policy initiatives and I was excited to have the opportunity," Paul remembers. "I hoped I would have more power to help people."[20]

Now knowing he was off to Washington, DC, he took some time to reflect on his life's meaning and purpose. Putting pen to paper, he wrote down where he stood at age 22 on June 21, 1966.

> This date marks the date of my dedication to live the remaining years of my life in service to my country. The inspiration which has led to my commitment is the words of the late John F. Kennedy, president of the United States of America. Although at this time of my development I lack the formal and informal knowledge and experience to achieve my goal, I vow to actively pursue a path which will allow me to acquire the necessary attributes which will aid me, and those I serve, to become an effective and honorable leader.[21]

But he faced a significant hurdle before he could begin his service in national politics and government. With his college deferment at an end, Paul was drafted to fight in the Vietnam War.

In the Rice Paddies and Jungles of Vietnam

Facing the reality of the draft and the very real possibility of fighting in Vietnam was an experience shared by all the men of Paul's generation. Yet due to deferments only a small proportion served. Of the 27 million men who came of draft age during the American war in Vietnam, less than 10 percent, 2.5 million, served in the military. Since class and race shape education and employment opportunities—which in the 1960s provided deferments—up to 80 percent of the US military came from working-class and poor backgrounds. A significant proportion were racial minorities.[22] Paul's experience matched that. "I was drafted and ordered to report for an induction physical. I still recall the fear I felt as I joined mostly young black men for the bus ride to Fort Holabird in Maryland. I was certain that I would soon be off to Vietnam." In the end he failed the physical and, unlike his less fortunate fellow draftees, took "a lonely surreal bus ride home."[23]

While a student and editor at Newark State College, Paul had followed and published news of the war. Within two months of LBJ's decision to escalate with expanded bombing and ground troops, the war in Vietnam appeared in the pages of the *Independent*. "Do we belong in Viet Nam," asked a student in April 1965, "or should we leave?" His age cohort urgently needed to engage with this question. "This is no debate over the dress code, over whether or not there should be more freedom given to students," he emphasized. "This is a pressing question of the future of mankind for generations to come!"[24]

The next month, Paul helped to organize, moderate, and present at an open forum cosponsored by the campus newspaper and the Committee of Concern for Peaceful Solutions in Vietnam. Again he used his editorial to spur his peers to attend and learn more about this "issue of vital concern to each and every American." "Across the nation the Vietnam issue has been debated," he wrote, "the political and military wisdom questioned." As it was by him. "Is the policy presently being carried out in Vietnam necessary or wise?"[25] At the forum he participated in a panel of history majors. Scheduled for nine o'clock in the evening, the very well-attended forum lasted until three in the morning.

Already by then new left activists in and around SDS had gained prominence in the antiwar movement. Students made up the largest group among the diverse coalition of Americans opposed to the war, and SDS thinking and strategies about the war and how to stop it were influential. An early strategy involved education, specifically "teach-ins," inspired by the civil rights sit-ins. The first teach-in took place at the University of Michigan in March 1965, with students, including SDS members, and professors meeting to discuss the history of Vietnam and US intervention. Although not called a teach-in, Newark State's open forum in May was structured similarly and occurred just after a National Teach-In held on over 100 campuses across the country.

The teach-ins politicized students to take further action against the war. Many did on April 17, 1965, when SDS sponsored the first anti–Vietnam War demonstration in Washington, DC, and drew more than 25,000 protesters. Old and young, traditional pacifists and progressive citizens took part. Activists from the Berkeley free speech movement attended. Robert Moses drew on his experiences in SNCC and Freedom Summer to connect the struggles for civil rights and against the war. Community participants in SDS's projects connected the war on poverty, advocating "Welfare Not Warfare." SDS president Paul Potter's speech indicted the immorality of US foreign policy. Joan Baez and Phil Ochs sang. These events were just the start of what would become the largest and longest-lasting antiwar movement in US history.

Soon the foundational argument of the youth voting rights effort—"old enough to fight, old enough to vote"—was voiced again. In Congress a few of Lester Wolff's colleagues joined him in advancing this argument. "We are asking our young soldiers to die for our democracy; yet we deny them an electoral vote in the operation of that democracy," asserted Representative Benjamin Rosenthal of New York in 1965.[26] This argument came from both supporters and opponents of the war. Representative Richard Fulton from Tennessee demonstrated this fact. In advocating for the 18-year-old vote, Fulton repeated the Johnson administration's Cold War rationale for sending American troops to Vietnam. As he declared in 1965, "We are calling on them to give their lives in a remote but important region of the world where Godless communism threatens world peace and security and they are prepared to offer the ultimate sacrifice to protect the freedoms which we hold so sacred."[27]

In 1966, when Representative William D. Ford, Democrat from Michigan, introduced his resolution to lower the voting age, he reminded his House colleagues "that 21 is not the cutoff age used when we sent soldiers to fight and die in Vietnam." He recalled proponents among Michigan's congressional delegation, citing Senator Vandenberg and quoting Senator Moody.[28] And he could have mentioned Representative Charles Diggs, who reiterated his support that year. "The average age of our nation's citizens is growing younger every year, while the average of the electorate is rising," he reminded. Democracy demanded the inclusion, not exclusion, of young Americans in the electorate.[29]

Later that year voters in the Great Lakes State had the opportunity to decide what they thought of the 18-year-old vote. Proposed first in 1943, frequently over the 1950s, and again with the state constitutional convention in 1961–1962, youth suffrage had been on the political agenda in Michigan for over two decades. By June 1966 the state legislature approved with the necessary two-thirds majority a referendum for the November elections. Both political parties endorsed the referendum, including Republican governor George Romney. The leading union in the state, the UAW, continued its long-standing support. But the most active and vocal constituency in the campaign for Proposal No. 1 were Michigan youth.

The Michigan Campaign

Young citizens, most prominently college students, participated in all aspects of the 1966 campaign to lower the voting age to 18. They lobbied and testified at hearings to win the two-thirds majority in the legislature in the first place. They recruited allies for the referendum on high school, college, and university campuses. College students also founded organizations to fight for the referendum, like Youth Equal Suffrage, which had the winning acronym of YES and was chaired by Andrew Marks, a student at Central Michigan University.

The campaign's chief organization, Michigan Citizens' Committee for the Vote at 18, was student led and affiliated with the NSA. "This is basically an issue of and for youth," argued James Graham, the committee chair. "So that leaves the real campaign up to us."[30] The Michigan Citizens' Committee represented student governments from 20 campuses across the state, plus the Michigan Federation of College Republicans and the Young Democratic Clubs of Michigan. "We hope to raise the necessary funds and manpower," a member of the coordinating committee stated, for "collective action on the 18-year-old-vote referendum."[31] "The student governments at all these universities have made campaign contributions," noted Michael P. Wood, the state coordinator, "an unprecedented move in student government history."[32]

As Election Day drew closer, Michigan students ramped up their campaign. They circulated leaflets and bumper stickers. They hosted lectures. They pressed for favorable newspaper articles and claimed editorials were running three to one in their favor. Again and again the foundational argument was foremost in these articles and editorials as well as letters to the editor. One reporter for the *Michigan Daily* considered "the familiar 'old enough to fight, old enough to vote' argument" to be a convincing one in 1966. What he called "the 'fight-vote' causists" would "attract far greater attention this year, due primarily to the Viet Nam war. At no time in recent history have the moral and social implications of the draft been more acutely felt."[33] This article came with a *Chicago Sun-Times* Bill Mauldin cartoon illustrating this very point. A US Army sergeant in Vietnam crawls through the jungle to consult with his commanding officer, only to be turned back. "I'm sorry, Sergeant, but the law says you're too young to vote. Now get back to your men."[34]

Despite its prominence, proponents did not emphasize the foundational argument in a full-page newspaper advertisement published just two days before the election. Instead, their primary argument addressed the social and historical construction of age categories and meanings. "21 IS AN ARBITRARY AGE . . . in the 18th century we adopted 21 because of tradition. That tradition was partly based on the fact that a man couldn't become a knight until he was 21." Recognizing that a chronological marker for voting needed to be fixed somewhere, they asked, who bears the responsibilities of citizenship? "The arbitrary line should be drawn to include citizens who do share in the government's burdens."[35] The ad then enumerated all of the responsibilities young Americans already fulfilled, including being subject to the draft and to paying taxes.

Bill Mauldin cartoon published in the *Chicago Sun-Times*, 1966. Chicago Sun-Times Special Collections. Copyrights held by and courtesy of the Pritzker Military Museum & Library (PMML), Chicago.

Further familiar arguments appeared from proponents and in the "Vote YES on Proposal No. 1" advertisement. The ad included the usual argument about young people's educational attainment, awareness of political issues, and preparation for political participation. "They have a real stake in government today," stated a spokesman for the Michigan Citizens' Committee. "They have always been intensely interested in the issues of education, poverty and civil rights."[36] The ad also connected youth voting rights to the progress of democracy. "IT IS NOT A RADICAL CHANGE . . . the trend toward extending suffrage is in the American tradition." The ad listed earlier expansions of the electorate. "Today Negroes, women and non-property owners have won their right to vote. Four states already have a voting age under 21."[37] The time had come for young citizens to participate in political decision making.

Michigan proponents offered an additional, novel argument for the 18-year-old vote. "THE GAP BETWEEN 18 and 21 LEADS TO FRUSTRATION AND APATHY . . . it is to the benefit of both the democratic and educational processes to lower the voting age to 18."[38] This contention combined two earlier viewpoints. The first came from Joseph Dolan and JFK's Commission on Registration and Voting Participation: the three-year gap delayed and discouraged later voting by youth. The second came from activists in SDS and YAF: political apathy plagued their generation. But the Michigan referendum campaign broadened these views. By connecting youth disfranchisement to frustration, this argument revealed the impact of recent youth activism in the antiwar, civil rights, and student movements. Starting in the second half of the 1960s, proponents of youth voting rights began to formulate the so-called safety-valve argument.[39] Without the right to vote, young people turned to protest; with the vote, they would turn to politics.

"Left without the voice of the vote, the young men and women have recourse only to defiance, civil disobedience and, oftentimes, actual criminal acts as a means of influencing government or informing the people of their position," argued a student in a September 1966 letter to the *Michigan Daily*. To prove his point, Mark E. Glendon referenced recent riots in Black urban neighborhoods. The Los Angeles Watts riot in 1965, the Cleveland Hough and Chicago West Side riots of 1966, and riots closer to home, in Benton Harbor and Lansing, Michigan, showed the "fighting that concerns this country" at home. Of concern, too, was "the fighting and dying that is going on across an ocean" by men subject to the military draft. For a draftee "it really doesn't matter how he feels about it, because, you see, he can't do anything about it; he doesn't even vote."[40] Antiwar activists were trying to do something about it at the time. As protests escalated, they further proved Glendon's point.

The safety-valve argument would gain greater traction as the sixties continued, at least with liberals. But calling attention to youth frustration and protest had disadvantages with conservative Americans. As in the 1950s when juvenile delinquency was used as an argument against youth suffrage, opponents in the 1960s did the same with protest, even peaceful actions by young people. "The public, at the present time, is wary of lowering the franchise because of the recent picketing and increased delinquency," admitted Michigan state legislator Jack Faxon. A former Detroit school teacher and an advocate of youth suffrage, Faxon advised proponents to "wage a convincing campaign of responsibility" to counter the idea and image that all young people were radical or violent.[41]

Local public officials were also wary, as the voting age referendum raised another issue related to youth voting rights. Residency requirements for voters aged 21 and up suppressed "student voting in college towns throughout America," accused an opinion writer in the *Michigan Daily*. They were "an injustice" that required immediate court or legislative action.[42] Like the war on poverty board elections, the Michigan referendum heightened demands for the voice of youth to be heard and listened to in local politics. Apprehension about student voters forming "power blocs" in towns and cities contributed to "overwhelming opposition" to Proposal No. 1 in the Michigan Townships Association.[43] As it turned out, the association's membership reflected the views of most referendum voters.

On November 8, 1966, in what was seen as a test case for the issue at the national level, Michigan voters defeated Proposal No. 1 by a substantial majority. The proposal carried in only 4 of the state's 83 counties.[44] The resounding referendum vote in favor of the status quo and against this political and social change represented a microcosm of the 1966 elections as a whole. The congressional midterms resulted in Democrats losing 47 seats in the House of Representatives and 3 seats in the Senate. Although still maintaining the party's majority in Congress, the election hurt the liberal wing. Characterized as a conservative backlash against LBJ and the Great Society, especially civil rights and the war on poverty, the vote also indicated criticism of the administration's conduct of the American war in Vietnam. The elections of 1966 shook the confidence of youth voting rights proponents, and not just in Michigan. In California Ronald Reagan won the governor's race with a backlash campaign against civil rights legislation and student activism. When the time came he would not look favorably on youth suffrage.

In Georgia a familiar face in favor of the 18-year-old vote tried to make a political comeback. Ellis Arnall declared his second candidacy for governor in July 1965. With the slogan "move Georgia forward into the 21st Century," Arnall revived from 1942 his reform agenda. The Democratic Party primary contest pitted Arnall, at age 59, against an up-and-coming Jimmy Carter and Lester G. Maddox, an unreconstructed racist. Maddox ran a backlash campaign against Arnall, accusing the former governor of being "the granddaddy of forced racial integration" and bringing "the same old dragging and lagging government with more sellouts, SNCC, Great Society, and lawlessness."[45] Maddox, who had closed his restaurant rather than comply with the Civil Rights Act of 1964, won the Democratic primary and then the governorship.

Maddox's success and continuing political support for white supremacy in Georgia in the wake of the Voting Rights Act of 1965 affected not only Arnall but also another advocate of youth voting rights in the state. Congressman Charles Longstreet Weltner withdrew from his own reelection race in 1966 rather than remain in a state party headed by a segregationist. "I cannot compromise with hate," he declared when he stepped down just a month before the election. "I love the Congress. But I will give up my office before I give up my principles."[46] Consistent with Weltner's principles was youth suffrage.

Earlier that year, in the spring of 1966, Weltner had reached out to college newspaper editors to request assistance with advancing his proposal for an amendment to the US Constitution lowering the voting age to 18. Given its success in his own state of Georgia, he sought "to extend this privilege—and responsibility—to all the citizens of the United States." His request to student editors recognized the need for action from the bottom up to balance his top-down initiative. "The response of your fellow students can be quite beneficial."[47] They and their older allies were responding. Undeterred by these political setbacks, proponents at the grassroots and in government readied for action.

8

This Is Democracy?

Due to the Vietnam War youth voting rights rose to the top of the US political agenda in 1967. As the war ground on "old enough to fight, old enough to vote" gained prominence. Two years into full-scale war, draft calls continued to rise, as did popular and political support for lowering the voting age. In April the Gallup Poll recorded the highest public approval rating thus far: 64 percent. The lesson from Michigan, however, was that national polling doesn't always translate into local election results. So more work needed to be done to build support for lowering the voting age. In 1967 young Americans started more organizations and launched more campaigns in more states than ever before. A majority of governors favored either a state or federal constitutional amendment. And US senators, including Democrats Birch Bayh of Indiana and Robert F. Kennedy of New York, backed the latter by a ratio of three to one.

Backing a federal amendment to achieve the 18-year-old vote was a new position for Senator Kennedy. As had his older brother, RFK initially believed the power to set suffrage qualifications belonged to the individual states. "I personally favor lowering the voting age to eighteen," he affirmed in 1966. "As a resident of New York, I would support state legislation to lower the voting age to 18." At the same time he confirmed his opposition to an amendment to the US Constitution. "This is a matter which each state should be free to decide for itself," he concluded, expressing the states' rights position advocated by many political conservatives, particularly southerners.[1]

As a liberal southerner, Representative Charles Weltner held a very different position. "I strongly disagree with his conclusion that a constitutional amendment would be in violation of states' rights," Weltner wrote in the summer of 1966. Seeking RFK's support for his voting age initiative, he urged the senator to reconsider. The "problem of insuring the right to vote to those who have earned it is best solved by a constitutional amendment creating a uniform age for all Americans."[2]

By early 1967 Kennedy had reconsidered. Perhaps he was swayed in the previous year by Weltner, before the Georgia congressman removed himself from his reelection race. Or he may have been won over by the outreach of the Michigan Citizens' Committee for the Vote at 18 during that state's referendum campaign.

Seeing the Michigan referendum "as a test case for the nationwide issue," the Citizens' Committee had organized an action aimed at Kennedy just before the 1966 election.[3] The officers hoped a popular national political figure would bring visibility to their campaign. In advance of RFK's late October one-day swing through the state in support of local congressional campaigns and on the advice of the UAW, they sent him a flurry of telegrams and letters. They all asked Kennedy "to speak out strongly in favor of lowering the voting age on your forthcoming trip to Michigan." He did.[4] Capitalizing on the Kennedy charisma, the Citizens' Committee quoted RFK's endorsement in their advertising. "By the time a person has reached 18 he should be mature enough to assume the responsibility of voting."[5]

But the Michigan Citizens' Committee for the Vote at 18 state coordinator, Michael P. Wood, did not consider Kennedy's maturity argument compelling enough. "Of more importance is the growing alienation of young people from the prevailing social system," he addressed the Senator. "Though the 60's have witnessed an awakening of student political activism, the prominent methodology has been non-electoral and protest orientated." Wood attributed this political method or approach to "the refusal of 'adult' society to extend relevant adult roles to young people." Articulating the safety-valve argument, he promised a change with the 18-year-old vote. "Voting rights—which would enable young people to exercise a fair share of power—would enable them to turn their enthusiasm, their freshness, and their considerable creativity into the arenas of traditional politics."[6] Wood's three-page, tightly argued letter for lowering the voting age in Michigan and nationally may have proved persuasive.

Kennedy could have been further persuaded by the letters he had received from young people in his own state of New York over 1966. Without an exception, these letter writers advanced the foundational argument for lowering the voting age. "Why in our state," asked one male teenager ardently, "can't men who are drafted into service and sometimes killed, vote or take part in the government sending them over there? This is democracy?" A young woman echoed his expression

Senator Robert F. Kennedy, with students at Eastern Michigan
University, October 29, 1966. Published in "Crowd Gives Evidence
of 'Kennedy Magic,'" *Ann Arbor News* (October 31, 1966). Courtesy
of Ann Arbor District Library. Copyright © MLive/Ann Arbor
News. All rights reserved. Used with permission.

of the foundational argument. "I do not think it is right that a boy can
be drafted when he is 18," she exclaimed, "yet he cannot vote. This is
ridiculous! How can a person feel that he plays a meaningful part in the
operating functions of his country?"[7]

Another young New Yorker, soon after being swept up in the Vietnam
War draft, surely brought the issue home to RFK. "I am 19 years old and
just graduated from high school this year," wrote Dennis L. Crofts from
the US Air Force base in Amarillo, Texas. "Quite often, while still in
school, the subject of being able to fight for and to lose one's life for our
country, and yet not having any voting say in the election of the officials
who run the government, came up in discussions," Crofts informed the
senator. "Would you support and possibly introduce a bill into the Sen-

ate enabling all persons who meet requirements other than age to vote in national elections? I am sure the voters of New York State would be proud to see your name on such a bill."[8]

On January 12, 1967, Kennedy cosponsored just such a bill. Under the name of Senate majority leader Mike Mansfield of Montana, Senate Joint Resolution 8 proposed a US constitutional amendment lowering the voting age. Mansfield's remarks on introducing his resolution recounted the usual reasons for youth suffrage, including the foundational argument. "If they are old enough to face a bullet, they are old enough to cast a ballot."[9] Kennedy's fellow senator from New York, Jacob Javits, signed on. Everett Dirksen of Illinois, who had sponsored his own joint resolution back in 1961 and had been so important in the Senate fights for the Civil and Voting Rights Acts, added his name.

Also cosponsoring were familiar figures in favor of youth suffrage, including Jennings Randolph and Birch Bayh. Both men's contributions over the long run would prove crucial. As chair of the Senate Subcommittee on Constitutional Amendments, Bayh had recent experience with amending the Constitution. In the aftermath of President Kennedy's assassination, he had initiated the 25th Amendment providing for succession in the offices of the president and vice president. In 1965 Bayh successfully steered the amendment through Congress, and on January 12, 1967, it was just a month away from being ratified.

Four days later Senator Randolph introduced his own resolution, Senate Joint Resolution 14, with the reminder that it was his eighth. For over two decades he had considered a federal amendment the best way to achieve the 18-year-old vote. He could now feel gratified to have so much agreement on his side. He praised the action of "our majority leader, the distinguished Senator from Montana." "I am," he added, "also delighted to note that his resolution has so many splendid Senators as cosponsors—including my beloved friend, Senator Dirksen."[10]

One of the splendid senators, Robert Kennedy, needed to answer questions about how he justified his change of mind. He explained his new position in support of a federal amendment as still respectful of states' rights due to the ratification process. "This proposed amendment does not take away the traditional role of the States in deciding voter qualifications because it will be put to the States for a vote and must be ratified by the legislatures of three-fourths of the States in order to become operative."[11]

Adopting this position contributed to RFK's rise to prominence as a proponent of youth suffrage over 1967. That year Kennedy's case for lowering the voting age came to include the safety-valve argument. He and advocates in government and at the grassroots also began to reference generational differences between young and older Americans on a range of issues in culture, politics, and society. This so-called gap between the generations started to be used as a reason for both supporting and opposing the 18-year-old vote.

The Generation Gap

In early 1967 public and press attention gravitated to "the generation gap." Editor John Poppy is credited with coining the term in a February 21 article in *Look* magazine to describe a divide between young and older Americans, a divergence in ideas, values, tastes, and aims. "Strong evidence now shows . . . that a 'generation gap' wider than we suspect is opening under us."[12] A slightly varied term, "the generational gap" appeared in *Time* magazine's January 6, 1967, cover story on its annual "Man of the Year." That distinction belonged to "a generation: the man—and woman—of 25 and under." This age cohort encompassed both baby boomers and those born just before, as did the decade's student activism. "This is not just a new generation," stated the article, "but a new kind of generation." *Time* offered "the now generation" to describe this cohort.[13] Later commentators would use the phrase "the sixties generation" and question whether there really was much of a gulf between youth and their parents during the 1960s.

But in 1967 the generation gap was assumed to be real, as shown in an analysis offered by Senator Kennedy in March. In an address before educators RFK emphasized how young Americans were becoming increasingly disillusioned with politics. They felt "no one is listening" about the problems of poverty and racism or their fears of nuclear weapons and the Vietnam War. The "insincerity and the absence of dialogue" in politics were considerably compounded by "the absurdity" of the current political backlash against civil rights. He condemned the fact that the white supremacist who murdered Medgar Evers in 1963 not only avoided conviction but in 1967 could run as a candidate for Mississippi lieutenant governor. For these reasons he believed young people were turning "from politics to passivity."[14]

Kennedy was right to recognize rising frustration and anger among young Americans around a range of contemporary concerns but not to conclude that political passivity resulted. For youth participating in the issues and movements of the day, politics and political change remained important and immediate. Still they questioned how to create that change in the new context of the latter half of the 1960s. Whether involved in civil rights, student, and antiwar activism, the war on poverty, or emerging movements among women, Chicanos, American Indians, and other groups, their answers took them in different strategic directions. For a growing number the 18-year-old vote held the key.

By 1967, after the legislative achievements of the mid-1960s, the freedom movement shifted into a new phase. Activists focused on implementing the Civil Rights and Voting Rights Acts in southern communities and on initiating new campaigns in the South and the North around housing, education, and social welfare. In the process a generational divide opened up in the movement, with many younger members adopting Black power as their approach to the problems plaguing African Americans and their communities.

The leading spokesman and theorist for Black power, Stokely Carmichael, used the phrase for the first time publicly on June 16, 1966, near Greenwood, Mississippi, during the March Against Fear. The 25-year-old activist had participated in the Freedom Rides in 1961 in his first year at Howard University. As a full-time organizer for SNCC in Mississippi and Alabama he worked on Freedom Summer in 1964 and the Selma campaign in 1965. From mid-1966 to mid-1967 Carmichael served as SNCC chairman and started to develop Black power as a stance and strategy for the organization.

His 1967 book, *Black Power*, coauthored with Dr. Charles V. Hamilton, a political science professor at the University of Chicago, defined Black power as "a call for black people in this country to unite, to recognize their heritage, to build a sense of community. It is a call for black people to define their own goals, to lead their own organizations. It is a call to reject the racist institutions and values of this society." At the core of the strategy was "organizing and developing institutions of community power within the black community." With independent bases of political power, African Americans could enter into coalitions from a position of strength, able to shape the political agenda to their own needs and aims.[15]

Describing the MFDP as a frustrating, failed effort at working in coalition, Carmichael and Hamilton discussed the founding of Lowndes County Freedom Organization in 1966 as a way forward. This new, independent political party set out to contest for political power in Alabama. Although unsuccessful, it showed the crucial, continuing importance of electoral politics in the Black freedom struggle. The Lowndes County Freedom Organization and its Black panther symbol inspired additional independent political efforts around the country. The Black Panther Party, founded in Oakland, California, later in 1966, was one.

Carmichael and Hamilton believed that Black power "could speak to the growing militancy of young black people in the urban ghettos and the black-belt South." They clarified how unrelenting white violence against the freedom movement fused with unchanging poverty and inequities of daily life. Together, they created more frustration and more anger, especially among Black youth. "These are the conditions which create dynamite in the ghettos." Published in October, after the "long, hot summer of 1967" with deadly riots in Newark and Detroit, the authors described urban riots as "explosions—explosions of frustration, despair, and hopelessness." And after three years of the war on poverty, there were still no effective "programs to deal with the alienation and the oppressive conditions in the ghettos."[16]

Paul Minarchenko saw this ineffectiveness every day from his office in the Department of Labor in Washington, DC. Brought on board to help reform the US Employment Service toward focusing "its resources on increasing employment opportunities in the impoverished communities of America's large cities," Paul thought he would be contributing to real social and economic change.[17] In 1967, after more than a year in the job, he had to face the facts. When a reporter for the *Wall Street Journal* interviewed him for an article about his experiences in the poverty war, Paul held nothing back—apart from his name. The front-page story painted a portrait of "a lowly 24-year-old who came straight out of college to assist a key Labor Department official, enthusiastic over tasks of 'social significance.' Now he's bitter."[18]

Paul's bitterness stemmed from frustration with President Johnson's war on poverty. Despite many good initiatives, like the food stamp program, the war on poverty fell far short of LBJ's initial aspiration and agenda. Because the poverty war had become a target of conservative political backlash, the Johnson administration discouraged the proper evaluation of new policies and programs. "Word comes down from the White House: 'Show that they work.'" Moreover, the escalation of the war in Vietnam took focus and funding away from domestic programs. "Vietnam leaves little money for such things as a big push on job-training," Paul disclosed. Disillusioned, he and other young colleagues were asking "what are we doing here?"[19] Paul already had his answer. "Actually, this young fellow no longer constitutes a case of depressed Governmental morale," noted the *Wall Street Journal* reporter. "A few days ago, he quit."[20]

"Young people who had come to Washington to fulfil Johnson's promise, to work on the war on poverty, became disillusioned because of the Vietnam War," Paul recalls. "That was my transition from student activist, whether around the war in Vietnam or the war on poverty, to the recognition that without political power, and therefore without the right to vote, your ability to be heard and to influence governmental policies to achieve social justice was limited." His evolving philosophy, strategy, and tactics for social change were taking him in a different direction. He was now convinced that "the way to solve the world's problems was through political engagement and involvement."[21] Paul took a job with the YMCA to set up its first office in Washington, DC, and began to find others interested in lowering the voting age.

As it so happened the New Jersey Student Committee for Undergraduate Education, the student organization he helped found in 1965, had just turned its attention to youth voting rights. Credited with contributing to New Jersey's 1966 commitment to major higher education reforms, CUE showed how the student movement could make a difference—not just on campus but in state politics and policy. On the 18-year-old vote CUE joined with other student groups, such as the Princeton Student Committee for Lowering the Voting Age formed in 1967.

Similar developments were happening with the student movement all across the country. "Youth Keeps Eye on Ballot Box," headlined one newspaper article. At UCLA a student referendum on lowering the voting age passed with a two-thirds majority. The University of Minnesota's student government voted its support and started to organize on the state's other colleges and universities. The Montana Student Presidents Association, representing six public and three private colleges and universities, were already engaged in a statewide push. A group of student governments in Iowa and Nebraska elected a Drake University student, Ken Davis, to lobby for youth suffrage in their region. Davis teamed up with the local Young Democrats, who were also busy building support among the student body at the University of Colorado.[22]

The Young Democrats at Rice University formed a committee to work with the brand new State Organization to Lower the Voting Age to Eighteen. With a snappy acronym, SOLVE constituted "a political action group" for student governments and activists in Houston. When the 18-year-old vote came before the Texas legislature that year, SOLVE representatives testified to show "that the proposal is supported by those who will be most affected by it." There were many ways they could use the franchise to address the issues they cared about, such as providing "food, medicine, and moral support" to farmworkers, mostly Mexican Americans, on strike in Rio Grande City for better pay and working conditions.[23]

Campus newspapers enthusiastically endorsed youth suffrage campaigns, and editors and writers frequently invoked the distinctiveness of their generation. An editorial in the *Daily Tar Heel* at the University of North Carolina at Chapel Hill insisted that students were "more aware of injustices and more questioning of existing institutions than any other age grouping." Even more, "young voters would tend to elect younger candidates, helping to perpetuate the forward thinking demonstrated by much of the youth today."[24] An article in Penn State's *Daily Collegian* agreed. "Most high school and college students are better informed about election issues and candidates than their parents are—if only because they have been forced to learn about them by civics teachers." Young people "wouldn't be duped" into ignoring the real issues by a political candidate's "confession of love for apple pie, mother and the flag."[25]

These student campaigns generally followed the model developed by students in Michigan in 1966—despite their referendum's defeat. "The major reason we lost is because not one politician campaigned actively for us," argued Ed Robinson, the student body president at the University of Michigan. Still he anticipated further action. "The issue of the

18-year-old vote could easily pick up again by election time in 1968." It was already picking up. The Michigan campaign featured in *Moderator* magazine's January 1967 three-part series on "Should an 18-Year-Old Vote?" "Its passage doubtless would have spurred the 18–20 age group in other states. But then its defeat isn't exactly hurting the issue."[26]

The issue continued to be relevant to young Americans because the Vietnam War and the draft continued to be relevant, relentlessly so. By 1967 the United States had a massive military presence and over 500,000 soldiers in Vietnam, yet it had failed to turn the tide. Public support for the war continued but dramatically declined for LBJ's handling of it. The antiwar movement grew in size and visibility. In the spring of 1967 Martin Luther King led his first march against the war and, in a passionate plea, laid out his moral reasoning for opposing it. "If we will make the right choice, we will be able to transform the jangling discords of our world into a beautiful symphony of brotherhood," he profoundly believed.[27] In the fall tens of thousands of protestors marched on the Pentagon in the largest antiwar demonstration to date. On college campuses students organizing for the vote and against the war shared a commitment to keeping the war in Vietnam at the forefront of political action and public attention.

They also considered the Johnson administration's decisions to escalate and extend the war deeply undemocratic, even illegal. The US Congress never voted on a declaration of war, as the Constitution requires. In this way all American citizens were disenfranchised on the issue of the war, but especially unfranchised youth. Under the law young citizens were obligated to carry out a military policy they had no role in making and no say in shaping. Democracy—its denial and its demand—is what gave the foundational argument for youth suffrage such power in the Vietnam era.

Within this context, the more radical arm of the antiwar movement, including SNCC and SDS, adopted draft resistance as a strategy. To stop the war they moved from peaceful marches and demonstrations to militant action and civil disobedience, from protest to resistance. The renewed and renamed Military Selective Service Act of 1967, which did little to reform the discriminatory draft system and, in fact, lowered the draft age from 18 1/2 to 18, intensified resistance. Denying the military—"the war machine"—the men it needed to fight took many forms. Seeking conscientious objector status, refusing induction, picketing or disrupting draft boards and induction centers, and burning draft cards meant young men directly confronted and even defied their government. Declaring "hell no, we won't go" risked induction in the military anyway, jail time, significant fines, and ostracism.

One Chicago student columnist described the dilemma for "The Voice of Youth" in 1967. "Thousands of boys are facing the grim reality of military service with no legal voice in the federal government," he denounced. "What can a boy within this system of draft do? Not much. Without the vote he doesn't have a strong voice in government. His congressman doesn't have to worry about his support, mainly because he doesn't have any to give." The draftee was left with resistance. "Of course there are private avenues of representation. One can burn his draft card, move to Canada, or he can join an organization against the war and be branded a traitor or a radical."[28] The contradiction of a democratic government forcing young men without a voice or a vote into fighting an undemocratic war galvanized members of the sixties generation like this young man as well as those in the youth counterculture.

Caricatured as "hippies" interested only in "drugs, sex, and rock 'n' roll" by the mainstream media, the counterculture seriously challenged and critiqued dominant American culture, politics, and society. Although emerging for several years, the counterculture received national publicity in 1967. During the summer, dubbed the "Summer of Love," thousands of young people made their way to San Francisco to participate in this new way of living and being. They sought authenticity and community rather than conformity and competition in values, lifestyle, and appearance. *Time* magazine described San Francisco's countercultural Haight-Ashbury district as "a state of mindlessness," "the center of a new utopianism, compounded of drugs and dreams, free love and LSD."[29]

Such media images of the counterculture shaped popular and political understandings of the generation gap and its relationship to youth suffrage. For example, when Senator Robert Kennedy expressed his concern that youth had turned "from politics to passivity" in 1967, he also believed they had turned "from hope to nihilism, from S.D.S. to LSD."[30] Timothy Leary's phrase to promote LSD—"tune in, turn on, and drop out"—popularized in 1966 and proclaimed again during the Summer of

Love resounded in this statement. For RFK lowering the voting age was one way to bridge the generation gap.

Not so for opponents like the most powerful Democrat in the House of Representatives, Emanuel Celler. Still chairman of the House Judiciary Committee, and deserving of credit for progressing the recent civil and voting rights legislation, Celler had been a staunch opponent of youth suffrage since World War II. He was not shifting from that stance. For the Brooklyn Democrat, lowering the voting age posed a danger when "we consider how easily the adolescent is inflamed, how passionately he attaches himself to 'causes.'" He again warned of demagogues. "Witness the regimes of Hitler and Mussolini."[31] Kennedy and Celler's opposing views garnered attention as a serious campaign for the 18-year-old vote arose in their state.

State Campaigns

With the news that New York would hold a constitutional convention in 1967, proponents of youth voting rights in the state prepared. It had been nearly 30 years since the last convention, and they didn't want to waste their chance at constitutional change. Jerome Bork, chairman of the New York State College Young Democrats Committee for the 18 Year Old Vote, reached out to Senators Robert Kennedy and Birch Bayh for assistance and put together a useful fact sheet of arguments and statistics. Other advocates formed the Fair Franchise Committee, with a 27-year-old chairman, John Patrick Conroy. Although the committee's founders were adults, they reached across the generation gap to recruit and work with students.

The Fair Franchise Committee had two aims: to get the convention to amend the New York State Constitution to lower the voting age and to then mobilize voters to ratify the new constitution through popular referendum. The Michigan campaign had demonstrated that legislators and delegates were not the same as average voters. Different strategies were needed for each group. In January 1967 committee members began lining up bipartisan backing for their resolution at the convention. "Students Press Drive for Vote" headlined an article about a lobbying effort the Fair Franchise Committee sponsored at the state legislature.[32] At the same time they recruited members in each of New York's 62 counties to sign a Fair Franchise petition "to bring pressure on the constitutional convention" and to build toward statewide ratification.[33]

"American democracy is based upon a social contract: the right to vote in return for meeting adult citizen responsibilities," stated the Fair Franchise Committee's pamphlet. "Those over 18 are meeting their responsibilities. They have earned the franchise." The image of a soldier in Vietnam and the title "Old Enough to Vote" on the pamphlet's cover highlighted the foundational argument. The committee also reminded their fellow New Yorkers "that a majority of state residents between 18 and 21 are married; a majority of the U.S. casualties in Vietnam are below 21 years of age; and most youths between 18 and 21 are employed and pay taxes."[34]

When the New York state constitutional convention of 1967 took up the voting age issue—100 years after the 1867 convention had—the debate lasted four hours. Proponents used old and new arguments. They named youth education and military service as reasons for lowering the voting age. They also advanced the safety-valve argument. Young Americans "feel frustrated, they feel boxed in," declared one delegate. Thus they "turn to demonstrations and picket lines when they are not allowed to participate." Action on youth suffrage would signal trust and ensure youth "are included in this democracy," declared another. Like their senator, Robert Kennedy, advocates argued that "lowering the voting age could help bridge the 'generation gap' by giving the sometimes rebellious youth a sense of belonging, or participation in governmental affairs."[35]

One delegate, Charles S. Desmond, a former judge and a Democrat from Eden, New York, composed his argument for the convention in verse.

> At age 18 he can drive a car,
> Own his home or drink in a bar.
> He can work and pay taxes and go to college,
> High school courses provide the knowledge.
> He can go to war and he can marry,
> Heavy burdens we let him carry.
> Let him pull his oar in the civic boat,
> Let's trust him and give him the right to vote.

Desmond's "plea through poetry" won him laughter and applause but, alas, few votes.[36]

The opposition won the day. Convention delegates resoundingly rejected proposals for voting at 19 and 20 before approving again New York's voting age as 21. The 18-year-old vote never had a chance. It didn't help that the *New York Times* had editorialized against it. "If this change were effected, the voting rolls would be enlarged by nearly a million inexperienced and immature voters."[37] Delegates both for and against the proposals were bipartisan. But a majority of Democrats at the convention favored lowering the voting age and a majority of Republicans did not.

An old, familiar partisan calculation was at work. Despite support from prominent New York Republicans, such as Senator Jacob Javits and Governor Nelson Rockefeller, convention delegates felt that the future youth vote would fall into the Democratic column. One journalist publicized this electoral possibility—rather than democratic principle—as why "Democrats Push Drive for Voting Age of 18."[38] Conspiracy-minded conservatives went further, falsely accusing RFK of building a "new alliance" with "campus agitators" to enfranchise youth and erroneously labeling the Fair Franchise Committee part of "the highly vocal 'new left.'"[39]

Although less overwrought, the opposition at the New York state constitutional convention greatly disappointed proponents, but the defeat had a silver lining. At the convention they pushed to empower the state legislature to lower the voting age through statute, sidestepping the state constitutional amendment process. In its final form Article 2 of the 1967 New York Constitution stated, "The minimum voting age shall be twenty-one years, which the legislature may reduce to not less than eighteen years but may not thereafter increase."[40] Yet it never became law because voters in the Empire State never approved the proposed constitution.

What happened in New York paralleled political developments in other states. Maryland had a constitutional convention in 1967 as well. In contrast to New York and in a celebrated victory, delegates there did lower the voting age to 19. Well-received testimony from US senator and Maryland Democrat Joseph D. Tydings may have contributed. "Although the twenty-one year minimum is traditional in this country, it is not sacred or immutable," Tydings argued.[41] But as in New York,

Duke University students James Hutchens, C. William Lowry Jr., and Steven T.
Corneliussen of the Voting Age Council of North Carolina, 1966. Courtesy of Steven
T. Corneliussen.

Maryland voters did not ratify the proposed constitution the next year,
and the 19-year-old vote there went unrealized.

Youth suffrage also went unrealized in North Carolina in 1967. The Tar
Heel State did not have a constitutional convention that year, so proponents focused on the state legislature. As in other states they needed a bill
passed with a two-thirds majority in both the State Senate and House of
Representatives, followed by a voter referendum. Toward this end C. William "Bill" Lowry, a freshman at Duke University, launched the Voting
Age Council of North Carolina in October 1966. "A significant segment
of the responsible citizenry of North Carolina is currently being deprived
of the right to participate in electoral processes," he explained.[42] Lowry
served as president and recruited two of his friends, Jim Hutchens and
Steve Corneliussen, to be vice president and executive advisor.

"Bill basically instructed Jim and me that we were going to create the Voting Age Council," Steve recalls. At Duke on a Navy ROTC scholarship, Steve felt "if I can be sent to fight, I ought to have the vote." The foundational argument, he says, "made sense to me." He also was interested in politics. "At the time—until I got beaten pretty soundly in freshman class elections at Duke—I fancied myself a future politician." The 18-year-old vote definitely appealed to him. "After all, I was 18, and I already knew everything, so of course the world should eagerly wish for my vote." At the time "lots of people hadn't yet thought about it," Steve remembers. So their campaign "let a few more people see that yes, there was interest in lowering the voting age."[43]

The Voting Age Council took off in early 1967. "This is the year for it," Lowry pronounced.[44] They proceeded with outreach to North Carolina colleges and universities, legislators, and editors of mainstream and campus newspapers. Articles and editorials were running mostly in their favor, although the *Ram's Horn* at Southeastern Community College in Whiteville ran a negative opinion piece. "Personally, I'd rather not have the responsibility. It's the older people (over 25) who have messed this country up," wrote student Tina Ravishhe. "Let them take the blame." She also called attention to the 1966 election backlash in "one state which has a voting age of 18—Georgia. And look what they got—Lester Maddox!"[45]

Still Lowry and his fellow council officers remained confident. Of three voting age bills proposed in the state House of Representatives, two progressed out of committee. "We have talked to about 30 legislators and have gained overwhelming support in the house," reported Lowry. Still they needed to "intensify our campaign in the senate," recognized vice president Hutchens.[46] As the vote in the House came up in May, they coordinated lobbying with student leaders and editors from Duke and UNC–Chapel Hill, and they cooperated with one of the bill's sponsors, representative and Olympic athlete Jim Beatty, "to plot their persuasive strategy." But they lost in a close vote, winning a majority but not a two-thirds majority.[47]

"I'm disappointed that North Carolina has passed up this opportunity to list its name in the roster of at least semi-progressive states," Lowry confessed.[48] He was not alone, especially as last-minute "politicking" prompted a dozen state representatives to change their votes. For young people, seeing up close the "political—nasty word, 'political'—pressure" brought to bear "will make many of them angry and bitter over the defeat," observed the *Daily Tar Heel*. Even so students can't "sit around and gripe about the situation." They needed to "look on the bright side: now there are two more years in which to snow the entire state into making 18 the voting age—and snowing the entire state is exactly what's going to be needed."[49]

The story in New Jersey unfolded along similar lines. In 1967 state legislators proposed amendments to the state constitution to lower the voting age to 18 and 19, which, if passed, would still need to go before the voters in a referendum. Students mobilized in support. They activated their student governments, formed new organizations, like the Princeton Student Committee for Lowering the Voting Age, and collaborated across the state's colleges and universities. Rutgers University students held a debate on the issue, followed by "a series of workshops on how pressure can best be exerted on the legislature."[50]

After Princeton's Undergraduate Student Council unanimously passed a motion in support of the 18-year-old vote in early March, the *Daily Princetonian* printed an endorsement. "In the past such proposals have died quietly with their most vocal public enthusiasm coming from college campuses and other youth groups." Now New Jersey needed an "adjustment of our democratic framework to the shifting role and growing stake of its younger citizens in the nation's future."[51] Later that month the student council chairman and Princeton senior Stephen A. Oxman gave his conditional support at a hearing of the Judiciary Committee of the state General Assembly. "In the absence of any change in the present policy of compulsory military service for 18-, 19-, and 20-year-olds, I would find it most difficult to reconcile the present 21-year-old voting policy with the dictates of democratic theory," he contended.[52]

Also speaking at the hearing was James J. Howard, US representative from New Jersey and a strong proponent of youth suffrage. A former teacher, principal, and leader in his county and state NEA affiliates, Howard introduced his House Joint Resolution 18 to lower the voting age on the very first day the 90th Congress convened. By February 21, more proposals had already come in than in the entire two years of the previous Congress. "It is apparent that enthusiasm and interest for this proposal is high and that support is bipartisan," Howard argued. "The time to act is now. I fervently hope, therefore, that the distinguished chairman of the Judiciary Committee will see his way clear to speed a House vote on this proposal, up or down, during this Congress."[53] Emanuel Celler did not.

Nor did the New Jersey state legislature. By early May, with the legislative session soon coming to a close, Howard admitted that "passage of such legislation is almost impossible this year." In a speech at Rutgers he held out the possibility of progress in 1968. Students now had "time to galvanize campus teams throughout New Jersey to prepare a massive campaign." He suggested a slogan like "Eighteen in '68." Young people throughout the state needed to join together to petition, write letters, and lobby their legislators to lower the voting age. Otherwise it wasn't going to happen.[54]

A positive sign of progress later in 1967 came from the New Jersey Democratic Party. At the party's convention delegates adopted a plank advocating the 18-year-old vote. Governor Richard J. Hughes played a pivotal role, swinging from opposition to support. "I'm not ashamed to change my mind," he stated, after hearing strong appeals from Representative Howard and another proponent.[55] The governor's change of mind inspired the "Question of the Week" for passersby in downtown Princeton. "Governor Hughes says now that he is in favor of lowering the voting age in New Jersey to 18. Are you?" The responses were pretty evenly divided, with students and adults both providing answers of yes and no.

A strong negative response came from a banker at the Princeton Bank and Trust. "People today at 18 aren't mature enough—the so-called hippie generation. If they don't want to get their hair cut, why should they be able to vote?" His response drew an equally strong rebuke from a female student at Sarah Lawrence College. "It seems to me that the length of one's hair should not be the determining factor of his eligibility to vote."[56] This exchange revealed the generation gap in microcosm, with clear implications for youth suffrage.

An event during the 1967 campaign in Connecticut offered a contrast, by showing young and old bridging the generation gap toward achieving the 18-year-old vote. Nine bills to lower the voting age to 18, 19, or 20 were pending in the General Assembly's Constitutional Amendments Committee. Rather than speaking at the committee's public hearing himself, state representative Paul A. LaRosa brought his son's taped testimony—sent from Vietnam. Stationed at the US military base in Da Nang, Peter LaRosa offered a statement of support for youth suffrage. "Peter isn't really talking for himself in this," said his father, "but rather for the fellows he has seen shot or killed in Vietnam."[57]

Along with the LaRosas, Connecticut college and high school students rallied to the cause. Yale students, led by freshman Edward J. Forand Jr., started Let's Vote—the Connecticut Committee for the 18-Year-Old Vote. Let's Vote made numerous arguments for lowering the voting age but emphasized the safety-valve argument. Recent protests reflected not "an irresponsibility or immaturity in our nation's youth," argued Forand and friends, but "a deep-seated frustration of being full-fledged citizens in every sense except the privilege to vote."[58]

Just as Representative Howard advised in New Jersey, young proponents in Connecticut circulated petitions, wrote letters to the editor, and testified before the legislature. For the climax of their campaign they held an 18-hour vigil—from six in the morning to midnight—on April 18 for the 18-year-old vote at the State Capitol in Hartford. They devoted all these activities to showing "the state legislators that there is more support for a lower voting age than they think." To no avail as it turned out. The Constitutional Amendments Committee instead initiated a study committee on the issue, which Edward Forand called "a stalling tactic."[59] Months later he was named to the study committee, with work scheduled to last into 1969.

Forand and Let's Vote would remain at the forefront of Connecticut's voting age campaign as the sixties continued. Yet the earlier VOTES, or Vindication of Twenty-Eighteen Suffrage, had pretty much been forgotten. One reason was that VOTES had become a national organization. Another was a common situation faced by campus organizations: student turnover due to graduation. Continuity would come only when these separate state-level campaigns became a national movement. The turning point was right ahead.

PART III

"It's time that we all made a contribution"

1968–1969

9

Turning Point '68

As the year 1968 began Paul Minarchenko was well into his new job at the YMCA's first Washington, DC, office. Connecting the YMCA's local and national levels, his job included bringing the YMCA into conversations about the direction of federal urban and poverty policy. "Let's make the YMCA relevant to solving the urban crisis."[1] Roz Hester was on track to graduate from Southwest Texas State College that year. Les Francis had already graduated with his teaching credential from San Jose State College. Like Roz in Texas, Les in California had been active in his campus and state student affiliate of NEA. After a brief stint as a substitute teacher he became the youngest person to join the staff of the parent California Teachers Association (CTA). As director of student programs, he collaborated closely with Mel Myler, president of Student CTA. Together, they campaigned for the 18-year-old vote. In 1968 they would take their campaign from California to the country.

For these four young people, 1968 constituted a turning point—personally, professionally, and politically. It set them on the path to building a national movement to lower the voting age to 18. Youth suffrage proponents at the local and state levels continued their campaigns but would now do so within a new context. Inspiration, backing, and staffing came forth from major multi-issue national organizations, starting with NEA. A full-fledged political movement for youth voting rights now felt like a real possibility and a cause for optimism, just as conflict and crisis engulfed the United States and the world.

It's a truism that 1968 was a turning point, globally and nationally. It was for the civil rights movement and the American war in Vietnam, for student activists and the antiwar movement, for the Democratic Party and presidential politics. Globally it was too, with major protests in countries from Czechoslovakia to France, Japan to Mexico. And 1968 definitely brought a change in direction for American proponents of the 18-year-old vote. As is often true with historical turning points, the full consequences of this change would not be clear right away. With hindsight, however, the change proved to be pivotal, and the consequences would be coming into view soon enough.

Upset and Upheaval

In January 1968 Johnson administration officials and the US military commander in Vietnam, General William C. Westmoreland, were still issuing positive assessments of the progress of the war. But the promise of progress—that there "was light at the end of the tunnel"—was proven false on January 30, the Buddhist lunar new year, Tet. On that date North Vietnamese and Vietcong forces launched their most massive military campaign of the war to date in the Tet Offensive. Their coordinated attack on South Vietnam reached the capital of Saigon, and Vietcong soldiers breached the wall of the US embassy compound. With heavy fighting and air strikes lasting into February, American and South Vietnamese troops pushed back the offensive, but at a high cost. Conveyed in shocking photos and news reports, the brutal combat, deaths, and destruction made it clear that the United States was not fighting a moral or just war, nor was it winning.

The most important, incalculable impact of Tet was on the people of Vietnam and American soldiers; the most immediate domestic impact was exposing the truth to the American people about the purpose and progress of the war. The lies of the Johnson administration came to be called euphemistically the "credibility gap." The undeniable divergence between White House pronouncements and the actual fighting in Vietnam changed public opinion on the war. After Tet a majority of Americans polled now opposed the administration's policy in Vietnam, with LBJ's mishandling of it getting even lower marks. The political impact in a presidential election year was far-reaching, starting with an impetus to the antiwar faction within the Democratic Party.

Democrats opposed to the war—the "doves" up against the party's "hawks"—considered anathema nominating President Johnson again. At the forefront of this effort to "Dump Johnson" in 1968 was Allard Lowenstein. At 39 Lowenstein already had a long career in activism and politics, including civil rights and student government. He had held a position on Vice President Hubert Humphrey's staff, and he would succeed in his 1968 bid for Congress from New York. Highly committed to youth participation in politics, he remained connected to student activists, especially the NSA. At his alma mater, UNC–Chapel Hill, he contended that "students are part of a generational change" but cautioned against "making a whole generation grow up cynical about democracy because of the American intervention in Vietnam." To question the war was legitimate, he argued, given that "questioning is the basis of democracy."[2]

Lowenstein set out to draft a challenger to LBJ to raise these questions, sounding out Senators Robert Kennedy and George McGovern, before securing the agreement of Senator Eugene McCarthy of Minnesota. "We all owe a debt to McCarthy, a man doing a difficult thing at a difficult time," Lowenstein believed.[3] A strong liberal with a track record of support for civil rights and the war on poverty, McCarthy stood against Johnson's war policy. "I am not for peace at any price but for an honorable, rational, and political solution to this war," he stated in explaining his presidential candidacy in November 1967. Like Martin Luther King and others McCarthy saw the war as taking necessary funding away from poverty, housing, and education programs and "growing evidence of a deepening moral crisis in America."[4] He sought to address these issues in the primaries.

In 1968 not every state had a primary election, nor did the Democratic Party's presidential nominee have to participate in the primaries. But McCarthy and Lowenstein recognized the primary campaigns as opportunities for political mobilization and education around the war in Vietnam. New Hampshire held the first presidential primary election, and young antiwar activists flooded into the state to help the McCarthy campaign. They came first from colleges and universities on the East Coast and then from as far away as California. Before door knocking and distributing literature, they ditched their countercultural garb and got "clean for Gene." Local citizens in New Hampshire also volunteered for the McCarthy campaign, including a high school sophomore from Hampton, Robert (Renny) Cushing.

"I was a high school kid," Renny says. "I had no idea who Gene McCarthy was. I knew the war sucked, and I didn't want the war. I was a foot soldier because I knew how important it was." Ending the war was his moral purpose and political priority. "I think what changed me is in

1966 my cousin Ralphie came back from Vietnam in a chair with stumps instead of legs. Like everybody else, it made me think about what was happening in our country, what was happening with this crazy war." McCarthy's antiwar stance spoke to Renny. "There weren't a whole lot of us" in his small Republican town, and McCarthy campaigners were red-baited. "A vote for McCarthy is a vote for Hanoi," he remembers hearing.[5]

But they made a difference. LBJ still won the primary on March 12, but McCarthy received 42 percent of the vote, a far stronger finish for a challenger to a sitting president than expected. "Dove bites Hawk," wrote one journalist.[6]

Four days later RFK announced his candidacy for the Democratic nomination for president. Reactions to Kennedy's announcement ranged from appreciation to apprehension to anger. McCarthy supporters looked upon Kennedy as an opportunist, entering the race only after McCarthy, at great political risk, revealed President Johnson's vulnerability on the war. "We woke up after the New Hampshire primary like it was Christmas day," as one campaign worker put it. "And when we went down to the tree, we found Bobby Kennedy had stolen our Christmas presents."[7] Other liberal Democrats welcomed the candidacy of a charismatic Kennedy, who had come far from his days as attorney general. He had committed himself fully to civil rights and allied himself with farmworkers' labor struggles. Just days before he was at César Chávez's side as he came off a hunger strike to win their right to unionize. And just days after he criticized the Johnson administration's course of action in Vietnam.

Kennedy's candidacy put a well-known proponent of youth and the 18-year-old vote into the 1968 race. "In my judgment it is imperative that young people be given both the opportunity and the responsibility of having a voice in the selection of public officials," he stated. "They deserve to be consulted by those who would lead the nation."[8] His book, *To Seek a Newer World*, had recently been published and a portion on the generation gap excerpted in *Ladies' Home Journal*. RFK praised young people's "honest commitment to a better and more decent world for all of us. It is for us now to make the effort, to take their causes as our causes," he urged parents.[9] He also appeared on the cover of *'Teen* magazine with his daughter Kathleen—"Next President's Daughter?"—accompanied by an article about a potential presidential run.

Young letter writers to the senator enthusiastically expressed their support. "When you announced your candidacy for President, we were all glad," wrote an eighth grader from California. "I believe the different points in your book, *To Seek a Newer World*, just might work." "I agree with the majority of teens who feel you should be our next president," noted a *'Teen* reader from Iowa. "I feel Johnson is doing a lousy job, which you could improve. Either as a senator or our next president, would you try to pass legislation to lower the voting age from 21 to 18." Two high school juniors in Minnesota also sent a letter after reading *'Teen* magazine. "The youth of today needs a President who is willing to stand up for the rights of teenagers," including the right to vote. "We as young adults want to take part in the national affairs of our country."[10]

By mid-March Kennedy's announced candidacy combined with McCarthy's upset showing changed the presidential race for President Johnson. With two Democratic rivals, the American public and members of his own party turning against the war, and polls predicting his defeat, the incumbent president made an unexpected decision. On March 31 LBJ withdrew from the race. "I have concluded that I shall not seek and I will not accept the nomination of my party for another term as your president."[11]

Tragedy and Turmoil

Four days later, on April 4, Dr. Martin Luther King Jr. was assassinated by a white supremacist in Memphis, Tennessee. Another leader of the freedom movement felled. King felt it coming. He had come to Memphis to support a months-long strike by the city's Black sanitation workers. At the time he and SCLC were immersed in preparations for the Poor People's Campaign. In May they planned to bring a multiracial movement to Washington, DC, to demand an end to poverty and, King pledged, "stay until America responds."[12] Like the Poor People's Campaign, the Memphis sanitation strike integrated civil and economic rights, racial and social justice. It was his third trip to Memphis, riot and reaction had already arisen in the city, and tensions remained high.

King spoke on the evening of April 3 before the strikers, their families, and community allies. A recipient of harassment and death threats over many years and with increasing intensity, he ended with prescient words. "I've been to the mountaintop," King shared. "I've seen the Promised Land. I may not get there with you. But I want you to know tonight that we as a people will get to the Promised Land." It was his last speech. The most prominent proponent of the philosophy and strategy of nonviolent political protest felled by violence.

News of King's murder spread swiftly and sparked uprisings in at least 120 cities across the nation. In Washington, DC, members of Congress could hear breaking glass and see burning fires. In Chicago, a large swath of the impoverished West Side went up in flames. The US Army was sent in and the National Guard called out to several major cities. The exception was Indianapolis, where Robert Kennedy happened to have a campaign event that evening. "I have bad news for you, for all of our fellow citizens, and people who love peace all over the world, and that is that Martin Luther King was shot and killed tonight." The crowd erupted with gasps and cries and tears as he spoke. Kennedy did not talk long, but he called for "love and wisdom, and compassion toward one another," and the city stayed in peace.[13]

Also peaceful was a Memphis march held in honor of King on April 8. Three days later President Johnson signed the third pillar of America's Second Reconstruction. The Fair Housing Act of 1968 prohibited discrimination based on race, religion, national origin, or sex in the sale, rental, and financing of housing. On April 16 the Memphis strikers won a settlement that included union recognition and better wages and working conditions.

These were important achievements for the freedom movement still reeling from King's assassination. His murder left the movement without its most respected and effective leader in the midst of its current campaign and critical challenge. The hurdle of overcoming economic inequality and achieving economic justice was high enough. It would now be even harder to surmount without King and without the hope he inspired. Civil rights and Black power activists on the local and national levels would continue, as would the Poor People's Campaign. The SCLC's new president, Reverend Ralph Abernathy, confirmed that "we are going to carry through on Dr. King's last great dream."[14]

Within a week of the Memphis sanitation strike settlement radical students, led by SDS and the Student Afro-American Society, began an occupation at Columbia University. The issues at stake included the university's plans for constructing a gym in a nearby neighborhood and removing mostly Black and Puerto Rican residents from their homes to do it. Columbia's research and military ties to the war effort also became a flashpoint. On April 23 a political rally led to occupied buildings, which students held for a week and transformed into a "liberated area." SNCC veteran Stokely Carmichael stopped by and SDS's Tom Hayden sat in. Calling an end to it, Columbia authorities ordered police to enter the buildings and arrest, violently, hundreds of students on April 30. A six-week student strike followed, and the campus remained in turmoil.

Campuses around the world became sites of student demonstrations and strikes in 1968. Hayden called on students to "create two, three, many Columbias." Students were at the forefront of Prague Spring and May '68 in France and took over the Free University of Berlin. In the United States an estimated 40,000 students took part in over 220 actions on 100 campuses, just in the first half of 1968.[15] "The desire for student power," concluded the commission charged with investigating the crisis at Columbia University, "was a powerful element of the explosion." This conclusion had implications beyond Columbia. Ways needed to be found to integrate students into the governance of the institution and to allow them to "meaningfully influence the education afforded them." Although the commission did not address the fact of youth disfranchisement in politics beyond the university, it affirmed a democratic principle. "Participation in self-government is a natural human desire that today's students feel with greater urgency."[16]

Students soon had an opportunity to demonstrate this desire voting at the ballot box rather than protesting at the barricades. On April 24 *Time* magazine sponsored Choice '68, a mock nationwide presidential primary election on college and university campuses. Choice '68 provided a ballot where students could list their first, second, and third choices for president. Campus journalists wondered whether—and which—students would participate. At the University of Wyoming one writer feared radical students would boycott, given that the "American democratic process strikes them as more absurd with each passing day." Another forecast a big win for conservative students because they believed in "power gained and administered through accepted formulas and established structures." Liberal students hoped that after this experience everyone would "channel their considerable energies into the drive to lower the voting age to eighteen."[17] The drive was gaining steam in Wyoming, along with legalizing 3.2 percent beer!

In the end votes were cast from about a fifth of the nation's students, in a turnout charitably considered "light." Meanwhile the International Student Strike against the American war in Vietnam held two days later on April 26 drew an estimated million students and faculty members in the United States and many more worldwide. For the Choice '68 collegiate primary, Eugene McCarthy won the national tally, with 285,988 votes, Robert Kennedy came in second, and the Republican frontrunner, Richard Nixon, came in third.[18]

Not on the Choice '68 ballot but declaring his candidacy three days later was Vice President Hubert H. Humphrey. Putting himself into the race for the Democratic nomination for president, with no intention of participating in any primaries, led to questioning about Humphrey's commitment to democracy within the party. But no one could question his commitment to democracy for youth. The Minnesotan had spent the past 15 years as a public proponent of the 18-year-old vote. The next month Humphrey sent a statement of support to the hearings on lowering the voting age before the Senate Judiciary Committee's Subcommittee on Constitutional Amendments, as did Nixon.

Chaired by Indiana senator Birch Bayh, who was running for reelection himself that year, these Senate hearings were held on May 14, 15, and 16, 1968. They were the first on the voting age since 1961. In one small way they showed a significant change over the course of the decade of the 1960s. Where only one young person participated in the 1961 Senate hearings, the 1968 hearings had six representatives of youth organizations, including two focused solely on lowering the voting age. Proposals on the table included Mike Mansfield's Joint Resolution 8 and Jennings Randolph's Joint Resolution 14, introduced the year before.

In his opening remarks Bayh summed up his subcommittee's consideration of constitutional reforms in several areas: legislative reapportionment, the Electoral College, congressional representation for Washington, DC, presidential and vice presidential succession (which became the 25th Amendment), and now youth suffrage. This recent ac-

Senator Birch Bayh with students at Ball State University, 1968. Courtesy of Ball State University Archives and Special Collections.

tivity followed the achievement of the 23rd and 24th Amendments in the first half of the 1960s. Of this period of remaking the Constitution, Bayh noted, "I believe it is part of the fabric of our time. In almost every aspect of American life today, there is discontent with the status quo. . . . If America is to continue to grow and to prosper and to improve, we must all recognize the need for positive change."

Lowering the voting age was just such a positive change. Like Nixon and Humphrey, Bayh had been a proponent since the 1950s, but his arguments had evolved with the times. In May 1968 he emphasized the safety-valve argument. "The generation of young Americans in the 1960s . . . are deeply involved in the issues of our time, the issues of war and peace, freedom and equality for all Americans, and uncompromising fulfillment of the promise of our Nation." "This force, this energy" that youth embodied "is going to continue to build and grow," he explained. Either it will "dam up and burst and follow less-than-wholesome channels" or will be "utilized by society through the pressure valve of the franchise." For those opponents who already saw the dam bursting, Bayh ensured that the vast majority of young people were responsibly engaged, with only "a few extremists, whether they be the flower children dropouts or the ultramilitant anarchists."[19]

Bayh's fellow proponents picked up on these themes, both advancing the safety-valve argument and offering assurances that only a small minority of young Americans were radical. Senator Jacob Javits, Republican from New York, felt "that in facing the enormous crises before the Nation today, we must provide an effective role within our established system of politics for the idealism, the activism, and the energy of youth." He pointed to the "Clean for Gene" McCarthy campaigners as "a constructive object lesson" for youth's role, while its "negative form [was] campus demonstrations and acts of civil disobedience" at Columbia University and elsewhere. "I am convinced that self-styled student leaders who urge such acts of civil disobedience would find themselves with little or no support if students were given a more meaningful role in the electoral process." Toward this end were "the painstaking research and promotion efforts of many organizations of young people" seeking suffrage, and Javits mentioned the NSA, the young Republicans and Democrats, and even VOTES.

Senator Javits also put forth familiar arguments for lowering the voting age, except one. Young people were well educated and well informed. They were making important contributions to programs like the Peace Corps and VISTA. Youth suffrage worked well where it already existed in Georgia, Kentucky, Alaska, and Hawai'i. "Nothing in the recent political history of these States indicates that the college-age vote is irresponsible, or 'radical.'" Neither was expanding the franchise to include 18- to 20-year-olds. Referring to earlier expansions of suffrage to citizens without property, to African Americans, and to women, Javits reasoned that "in each case the eventual expansion of the electorate brought new ideas and new vigor to our national political life."[20] Tellingly, however, Javits did not reference young soldiers fighting in Vietnam or repeat the foundational argument of "old enough to fight, old enough to vote."

Other speakers did, but very briefly. Two sponsors of the joint resolutions, Senators Mansfield and Randolph, devoted a sentence or two. On the very day voters in his state of Maryland voted on (and rejected) the new constitution that would have lowered the voting age to 19, Joseph D. Tydings stated only that "Maryland boys" were experiencing hardship "in the jungles and on the battlefields of Vietnam." The chairman of the Young Republican National Federation, Jack McDonald, simply listed the foundational argument alongside many others.[21] By 1968, within the context of a disastrous, divisive war, arguing the fairness of matching the voting and draft ages became less of a focus for some proponents at the national level.

The one national-level witness at the 1968 Senate hearings who focused fully on the foundational argument was the president of the Young Democratic Clubs of America and director of the Youth Division of the Democratic National Committee, Spencer Oliver. From a prominent political family of Texas Democrats, Oliver "was a Johnson guy." "I was the one who they were sending out to college campuses to defend the war in Vietnam in '68–'69," he recalls.[22] Not an easy position to be in, but it did make his case for the foundational argument less complicated.

"Of all the adult responsibilities placed upon the 18-year-old, none compares with his obligation to military service," he argued at the Senate hearings. "How can we send men off to die without allowing them to express their opinions through the due process of the ballot?" But the United States was doing just that. Oliver cited a damning statistic: 29 percent of Americans dying in Vietnam were under the age of 21.

> One of those who died there was Pfc. Milton L. Olive III, a Chicago Negro. Olive was only 18 when he fell on an enemy hand grenade to save the lives of four comrades. For his courage, Private Olive . . . was awarded the Congressional Medal of Honor by President Johnson. And Milt Olive was too young to vote?

Just as Jennings Randolph had done 25 years earlier during World War II, Oliver told the story behind the statistics, a story of an individual soldier who lost his life before having the right to vote.

Yet the circumstances of 1968 were far from those of 1943, and Oliver made that clear by prefacing his comments with a caveat. "I do not for one moment believe that the right to vote will immediately cause every young American to abandon the picket lines or the barricades, or prevent demonstrations and protests," he told the senators. "But I do believe that it will ease the frustrations of a generation obviously intent upon having a voice in the determination of their own destinies and that it will open up a legitimate and desirable avenue of participation in the democratic process to them."[23]

Although the majority of speakers at the Senate Judiciary Committee's Subcommittee on Constitutional Amendments hearings supported lowering the voting age—although not always to 18—the few opponents, like Senator Spessard L. Holland, Democrat from Florida, stayed strong. Holland advanced the states' rights argument that Congress cannot take "from the States their right to determine this question for themselves." He then detailed all the states that had rejected lowering the voting age, beginning in the 1950s through Michigan's referendum in 1966 and New York's constitutional convention in 1967 to Maryland's vote just the day before. Holland couldn't help but remind Bayh's subcommittee of the unsuccessful legislative efforts in the "state of Indiana from which your distinguished chairman comes." To his mind the voters of the country in referenda and through their state representatives had spoken.

Senator Holland then quickly dismissed the foundational argument—"I do not subscribe to that theory for the draft age and the voting age are as different as night and day"—and the safety-valve argument. For Holland, like Emanuel Celler, youth suffrage posed "a fertile ground for demagogues." Even if student radicals were few in number, as Senators Bayh and Javits assured, "the greater numbers of students are followers." Citing "student power demonstrations" at Berkeley, Columbia, and elsewhere, he believed "such action was effected by the young and less mature students following leaders of a more militant sort." The ages 18 to 21 were "years of rebellion, as had been indicated on the college campus today, rather than reflection."[24] At that age, American citizens did not deserve voting rights.

Holland's comments reinforced Bayh's concern that campus protests undermined the case for a constitutional amendment: "The chances of getting it passed diminish every time this kind of demonstration takes place."[25] Mail from his Indiana constituents indicated as much. Bayh did hear from young proponents. "Contrary to what political cartoons portray, I am neither a hippie nor a soldier," wrote one young woman, and she was "quite willing to assume the responsibility of voting." "Not everyone my age is responsible, but neither is everyone your age." But he mostly heard from older opponents. Attached to a May 6, 1968, *U.S. News and World Report* news clipping about Columbia titled "Anarchy Spreads to U.S. Colleges" was this note. "Dear Birch, Are these the people you think are mature enough to vote?"[26]

Hollywood wasn't helping. Two weeks after the Senate hearings wrapped up, American International Pictures released *Wild in the Streets* (1968). A teen exploitation film with a hit soundtrack album, *Wild in the Streets* charts the rise to political power of a rock star revolutionary. Performing at a campaign event for a liberal senatorial candidate who supports the 18-year-old vote, the protagonist Max Frost calls for a voting age of "Fourteen or Fight!" Lowering the age to 14 first for voting and then for office holding—after lacing the water supply with LSD—allows Frost to win the presidency and his fellow hippie fascists to take over the government. Adults over 30 are forced to retire. Those over 35 are forced into "Paradise" rehabilitation camps decorated with peace symbols and then dosed with LSD. Whether received by audiences as farce or as the future, the dystopia pictured in *Wild in the Streets* hardly helped youth voting rights in 1968.

Crisis and Change

Americans headed into the second half of a year of compounding crises with more to come. On the evening of June 5, after winning the California and South Dakota Democratic primaries, Robert Kennedy was shot by an assassin. Coming just two months after the murder of Martin Luther King, RFK's killing cut down another national leader too soon and too young. It was less than five years since his older brother too had been assassinated. To many Americans the United States seemed to be coming apart.

In an attempt to address pervasive violence President Johnson established the National Commission on the Causes and Prevention of Violence on June 10, 1968. The commission would investigate and make recommendations on individual acts of violence as well as uprisings such as those that occurred after King's assassination. Earlier in the year

LBJ had received the report of the National Advisory Commission on Civil Disorders, established after the 1967 riots. Called the Kerner Report, after the commission's chair, it indicted white racism as the cause of urban uprisings by African Americans. One of the commissioners was the NAACP's Roy Wilkins. "This is our basic conclusion: our Nation is moving toward two societies, one black, one white—separate and unequal."[27]

The Kerner Report urged solutions to the persistent and pernicious problems of high unemployment, inadequate schools, and poor housing that plagued Black neighborhoods. The Poor People's Campaign did the same for poor Americans of all races, using an "economic bill of rights for the disadvantaged." In mid-May campaigners began coming to Washington, DC, to march and demonstrate to gain these rights. They met regularly with members of Congress in a move spearheaded by Charles Diggs and attended by Jacob Javits. The Poor People's Campaign also constructed a tent city on the mall, named Resurrection City. It lasted until government officials forcibly closed it in late June, just days after 50,000 people joined the campaign for a day of solidarity on June 19. A "restructuring of priorities" in Congress must occur to meet the needs of impoverished Americans of all races, agreed Senator Javits.[28]

A few days after the removal of Resurrection City, President Johnson sought a different restructuring of congressional priorities. On June 27 he sent a special message to Congress proposing action on a constitutional amendment lowering the voting age. "The hour has come to take the next great step in the march of democracy. We should now extend the right to vote to more than ten million citizens unjustly denied that right. They are the young men and women of America between the ages of 18 and 21." Seconding the first president to officially propose such an amendment, LBJ cited the foundational argument. "At the age of eighteen, young Americans are called upon to bear arms." He also expanded on Eisenhower's focused argument. Johnson's case for youth suffrage encompassed their education, civic awareness and participation, and adult responsibilities. Steering away from current conflicts about the war and poverty, class and race inequalities, he did not state the safety-valve argument. But he alluded to it. "The essential stability of our system is not served" by youth's exclusion from the electorate.[29]

"Johnson Speaks Too Late," announced the *Michigan Daily*'s news analysis. Johnson's call for a constitutional amendment came only after he decided to pull out of the presidential race. Just when he no longer needed to fear being "voted out of office if additional millions of young people are given the right to vote." Even with the Senate hearings the president "still waited so late that it is unlikely Congress will have time to act on it this year." Moreover the schedule of Congress and those state legislatures meeting biennially meant the 18-year-old vote was unlikely to become the law of the land until, at the earliest, 1971. This prediction, as it turned out, was right.[30] Other criticism emerged. The *New York Daily News* "facetiously urged that the voting age be raised to 30, or lowered to two."[31]

Yet LBJ's message to Congress mostly received positive attention. Nearly fifteen members of the House of Representatives responded the same day, lauding the president for his "vision and leadership" and "great service to the Nation." "L.B.J.: A President Who Understands Young People," the *Congressional Record* titled these responses, which was not quite how many young people would have characterized the president.[32] The AFL-CIO endorsed the president's "confidence" and "faith" in youth.[33] Positive responses also came from the press. The *New York Times* even reversed its editorial stance. "President Johnson, who once opposed lowering the voting age, has changed his mind—and so have we," wrote the editors.[34] The *New York Times Magazine* also featured an essay by Andrew Hacker exploring the issue and ending with an endorsement. Hacker warned that "the youth-in-politics issue has . . . many emotional and ideological undertones." The adult public needed to be wary of exaggerated portrayals of young people, as "in the current movie, *Wild in the Streets*." In contrast to that movie's "pop politico," most youth were "clean-cut and career-bound."[35]

LBJ's proposal presaged the party platforms for the presidential election in November. For the first time both Democrats and Republicans included a youth suffrage plank, but with a big difference. The Republican Party held that states had the power to set suffrage qualifications and should take action. The Democratic Party's plank—organized and pushed by Spencer Oliver of the Young Democrats—pledged to advance a US constitutional amendment. These positions on process reversed those the parties had held just seven years earlier, as stated at the 1961

Senate hearings by their respective national chairmen. This reversal testified to the profound impact of political events and policy developments over the middle years of the decade, most prominently the Voting Rights Act. Democrats now upheld federal power to determine voter qualifications, while Republicans reasserted the rights of states to do so.

Another political party, the Peace and Freedom Party, supported youth suffrage in 1968. Founded by members of the white new left in 1967, the Peace and Freedom Party allied with the Black Panther Party heading into the 1968 elections. This alliance brought together radical antiwar, antiracist, and antipoverty activists and got the party on the ballot in California and other states. The Peace and Freedom Party allowed 18-year-olds to be members, vote, and participate and advocated for their enfranchisement. In California the Peace and Freedom Party, alongside other groups, worked hard to get a statewide initiative to lower the voting age on the ballot for November. "The initiative would transfer real electoral power to the college age (and draft age) population," argued an organizer for the campaign.[36] But the bar was high, because over half a million signatures were needed. With 100,000 signatures collected, they didn't get close.

Still California's voting age initiative campaign represented an innovative state-level strategy for proponents. A form of direct democracy—along with the referendum and recall—the initiative allows voters to create legislation rather than relying on their representatives. In 1911 California became the 10th state to adopt the initiative. In 1953 the Junior Statesmen of America in the state tried and failed to collect enough signatures to use the initiative process to lower the voting age. Starting in 1968 California advocates of youth suffrage would seriously pursue this strategy, alongside others.

One persuasive proponent in California, Monroe Sweetland, was very familiar with the initiative process. As an Oregon legislator in the 1950s he had worked on lowering the voting age through both legislative and initiative processes. Now in California as NEA's political coordinator for the thirteen western states, Sweetland continued his efforts. He believed that "the 18-year-old vote is the most underestimated political issue in the nation." In 1965 he emphasized that the country would benefit from youth participation in politics. "In four states where the voting age has been lowered to 18, interest in political, social and economic issues has been greatly stimulated," sparking "a higher level of discussion of society's problems."[37] In early 1968 he endorsed the safety-valve argument. The franchise "would de-fuse and de-emphasize direct action and violent conduct."[38] Sweetland made his case in public forums, before the California Assembly, and within NEA and CTA.

He also reached out to leaders and staff of Student CTA, in particular Les Francis and Mel Myler. They agreed "that the best way to address the generational divide in our country was to encourage active participation in the political process," Les recalls. "Prompted, provoked, inspired, counseled and led by NEA lobbyist Monroe Sweetland, we undertook a determined drive to first persuade the student organizations, then CTA, and finally NEA to endorse an amendment to the US Constitution making the voting age 18." "Our pitch for CTA and NEA involvement was that teachers take pride in and support for their products," Les elaborates. "Teachers, by supporting the 18 year old vote, are saying 'we believe we have prepared these young people for citizenship.'"[39] Although this contention had been implicit in NEA's earlier advocacy for youth suffrage beginning in 1943, it was now explicit.

Mel's leadership positions first as president of Student CTA and then of Student NEA facilitated this process. With a teaching credential from California Western University in San Diego, "I was all set to go and be a teacher, but then I got involved in the student association work." These positions required extensive travel around California and the country over 1966, 1967, and 1968. Mel encountered many young people, whether involved in the civil rights, student, or antiwar movements, "really looking for voice and wanting to have an impact on the system." "And how do you impact the system? You impact that system historically by the vote."[40] Getting that vote for youth required NEA's local roots in school districts, associations at the state level, and national reach and relationships.

Their campaign paid off. By mobilizing student educators from the bottom up in California and the country to pass their own resolutions on the 18-year-old vote in 1967 and 1968, they put pressure on the parent state and national associations. The American Federation of Teachers passed similar resolutions in 1966 and 1968.[41] So when the 1968 NEA Representative Assembly met in Dallas in July, it did more than pass a resolution of support. "It directed the NEA staff to work for both state and federal constitutional amendments to lower the voting age," as Sweetland put it.[42]

What this directive meant and how it would be implemented still needed to be worked out. Sweetland took the lead. Together with Student NEA staff, including director Dirck W. Brown and Mel Myler in a new position, they put pressure on NEA leadership. "What the hell are we going to do with this thing? This is an important issue here," Mel remembers thinking. They approached Cecil Hannan, assistant executive director of NEA. "Does this resolution sit on the shelf of indecision, as most resolutions do, or can you help and provide us with some seed money to begin to really do something with this resolution?"[43] In the end NEA established two staff positions, allocated office space, and committed $40,000 in direct funding to get started on a special effort to work for a lower voting age, soon to be called Project 18.

At the same time Paul Minarchenko was grappling with his grief over the assassinations of Martin Luther King and Robert Kennedy. Alongside his YMCA job he'd worked hard on RFK's presidential campaign.

> I saw that everything I had fought for and believed in was . . . beginning to disintegrate in front of my very eyes. I was very upset and I decided that there had to be something that I could do to try to change this and get associated with people who thought the same way.[44]

Soon Paul and the YMCA would connect with Mel, Les, and NEA and many more like-minded contacts in other organizations, such as Spencer Oliver of the Young Democrats. By the middle of 1968 these proponents of the 18-year-old vote were set on a path to come together, even as it felt like the rest of the country was coming apart.

10

We Can Vote Them Out

Further evidence of America's conflict, crisis, and coming apart in 1968 was on display in August. That month attention turned to Chicago, where the Democratic National Convention would be held. The year constituted a turning point, and the Democratic National Convention was the pivot upon which 1968 turned. Emerging in the aftermath of the convention and expanding after the November elections were developments that provided momentum for lowering the voting age. Progress occurred even in the face of recent defeats in several states. These developments happened on both the national and local levels, involved the interaction of bottom-up and top-down political forces, and revealed the range of strategies proponents would use to win the 18-year-old vote. By early 1969 all the elements of a movement for youth voting rights were in place.

Chicago '68

As delegates gathered in Chicago to nominate a candidate for president, so did thousands of antiwar protesters. With the aim of confronting the party of LBJ, the party most responsible for the American war in Vietnam, the protestors demanded the war's end. For doves within the Democratic Party, like convention delegate Allard Lowenstein, the priority was the nomination of Eugene McCarthy. The fundamental problem, however, was the party's undemocratic nomination process. Despite the fact that 80 percent of the votes cast in the 1968 Democratic primaries were for either Robert Kennedy or McCarthy, most of the convention delegates were already pledged to President Johnson's successor: Vice President Hubert Humphrey.

To this problem New Hampshire Youth for McCarthy, including Renny Cushing, directed a pointed political advertisement. "Sen. McIntyre-Gov. King: 'The Eyes of New Hampshire Are on You.'" As members of the Democratic Party and pledged delegates to the Democratic National Convention, Senator Tom McIntyre and Governor John King would be casting their votes for Humphrey. The 42 percent of New Hampshire Democrats who voted for McCarthy in the primary would not be represented at the convention. "When You Cast Your Vote at the Democratic National Convention Next Week in Chicago—We Shall Remember," blasted the ad. "WE **DO** QUESTION: WHY YOU ARE NOT SUPPORTING AND VOTING FOR SENATOR EUGENE J. MCCARTHY."[1] Renny signed the ad to put pressure on his state's convention delegates, as did every member of his family: his six siblings and his parents. His parents had voted for McCarthy in the primary. "There was the vote I could not cast. They did that."[2]

Despite challenges to party rules and procedures inside the convention amphitheater and antiwar protests outside, Humphrey emerged as the Democratic nominee with a platform plank on Vietnam more hawkish than not. This outcome was all too reminiscent of what had happened with the Mississippi Freedom Democrats at the 1964 Democratic National Convention. That injustice had been righted in 1968 with the seating of biracial convention delegations, including Fannie Lou Hamer. Spencer Oliver of the Young Democrats counted that, along with the 18-year-old vote plank, as "two victories" at the convention.[3] On the nomination, however, party rules and party politics again prevailed over democratic process and moral principle.

Renny was too young to travel to Chicago to witness this outcome, but not Jane Greenspun. Janie was "a child of the sixties," as she tells it. "I graduated high school in 1967, jumped into my friend's Volkswagen," and headed to California for the Monterey Pop Festival. "That was the Summer of Love. Then we spent weeks wandering around Haight-Ashbury, going to be-ins in the park, and I was a hippie." "Everything was about peace, love, and understanding," she explains, "but we had this war going on." "Boys I knew were going off to Vietnam." Janie's older brother Brian was enrolled in ROTC at Georgetown University, "so at least he would be an officer and not be cannon fodder." Her younger brother faced the draft.[4]

"The more I learned about it, the more I was against the war. I became a peace activist and I supported Eugene McCarthy for president in '68." She had just finished her first year at California State College at Fullerton. "I announced to my father that I was going to the Chicago convention to work for Eugene McCarthy."[5]

Janie's announcement aligned with her "justice-loving" family. Her father Hank Greenspun was a liberal Republican and publisher and editor of the *Las Vegas Sun*. "He was always trying to fight injustice, and he was one of the first newspapermen in the country to come out against the Vietnam War." In a frank and furious editorial in March 1968, Hank Greenspun argued that recent events exposed not only the administration's credibility gap but "Vietnam as the most bestial, monstrous political war in history. Thousands upon thousands of beautiful young dead Americans are the only thing real about this administration's phony war." "My father was out on a limb being against the war," Janie notes, and supported her going to Chicago, with one requirement. "He said, 'I'll tell you what. I'll get press passes. We'll both go cover it for the newspaper.'"[6]

Another young person who headed to Chicago was Patricia Keefer. Half a decade older than Janie, Pat had spent four years as a mostly apolitical student at the University of Cincinnati before stepping into the job market. "I missed civil rights in the 1960s because I was an apathetic university student."[7] But she didn't miss the Vietnam War. When her younger brother—"a young white guy from a working-class family and a middle-class neighborhood in Cincinnati"—was drafted into fighting there, his letters home opened her eyes. He wrote about "the waste and the insignificance of this war" and that "we have no idea why we're here." Still he assured her, "I'll be home soon," until he wasn't. Just a month before he would finish his tour of duty and come home, David Keefer was killed in Vietnam. "He was dead. And it was a big hole in my life," Pat says.[8]

A week later she testified at the Democratic Party platform hearings for a change in Vietnam policy. By then she was working at the *Cincinnati Enquirer*, serving as a leader in the Ohio Young Democrats, and very active in the antiwar movement. At the hearings she read aloud the Defense Department telegram informing her family of David's death. "I felt that my being here might bring this home to you. I not only dislike this war, I hate it. . . . I just want to plead with you to do everything you can to come out with a strong platform" to bring about an end to the war.[9]

Pat was also very aware of the unfairness of young Americans forced into fighting abroad while "politically powerless at home." "There were a lot of people dying in a war that . . . weren't allowed to vote." Compounding her sense of grief and loss over her brother's death was Kennedy's assassination. "Bobby Kennedy, who was my candidate who I worked for in Indiana, had been killed." "I lost my brother. I lost my politics. And what could I do?"[10]

What she could and did do was attend the Democratic National Convention. Just weeks after her brother's death she came to Chicago as an alternate delegate. Still committed to a change in Vietnam policy, Pat concentrated her efforts on the platform debate. "I spent time on the floor of the convention working on what was the minority plank to the platform, which was to call for an immediate end and defunding of the war in Vietnam." When the "peace plank" failed, she went out and joined the antiwar protests. "I came out of the 1968 convention distraught, a loss of faith in politics as such."[11]

Greenspun v. Nevada

Like Pat Keefer and other young people, Janie Greenspun's experiences at the 1968 Democratic National Convention changed her. When she wasn't allowed into the convention amphitheater with her McCarthy button but was with a Humphrey button, "I knew the nomination was fixed, and I was getting mad." She and her father also joined the antiwar protestors outside and discovered firsthand the police brutality being directed against them. "It was scary because the police were right there. They would charge at any second. My father and I ran. We were chased. We were tear gassed." Hank Greenspun tried to get the Nevada delegation to pay attention to what was going on outside. "Kids are being beaten outside, kids are being beaten," he told them. "He was outraged that this was America."[12]

Janie and her father were not alone in their outrage over the treatment of protestors or the outcome of the convention. On the night of August 28 antiwar delegates and demonstrators came together. "We had a candlelight vigil march through the streets of Chicago, singing 'We Shall Overcome,' and there must have been a thousand of us, and it was just one of the most moving experiences of my life." But she remained outraged. "I was a sweet, loving, peaceful hippie when I got to Chicago." When she left "I was so angry I wanted to blow up the Pentagon. That's all I wanted to do."[13] But a chance meeting on the flight home to Las Vegas sent her in a different direction.

"I was just snarling, I was so angry," Janie maintains, when she met William Treadwell, a lawyer for the Republican presidential nominee, Richard Nixon. Treadwell asked her, "What do you want to do about it? Do you want to do something constructive?" He revealed that they wanted to try a litigation strategy to win the 18-year-old vote. With this strategy a plaintiff under the age of 21 would sue for the right to vote, but they needed a test case. "What do I have to do?" asked Janie. Treadwell explained the plan, and she executed it.

On September 11, 1968, Janie attempted to register to vote in Clark County, Nevada. When the registrar of voters refused to allow her to register, she asked, "Are you denying me the right to vote because of my age?" When the registrar said "yes," she told him she "was going to sue the State of Nevada for the right to vote." And she did. On October 22, attorney Ralph Denton filed a lawsuit on her behalf in federal court. "The suit asks that the court declare Miss Greenspun a full citizen of the United States with the right to vote in federal elections for president and vice president," reported the *Nevada State Journal*. "The outcome could result in a landmark decision on the question of whether 18-year-olds should be allowed to vote in federal elections under guaranteed rights in the US Constitution."[14]

This qualification was important. *Greenspun v. Nevada* focused on national citizenship and federal elections. "She does not contest the laws of Nevada qualifying voters as to 21 years of age in order to vote in Nevada State elections," stated the opening appellant brief.[15] At issue was whether Nevada authorities could prevent a citizen from voting in a national presidential election. Citing several Supreme Court cases, including *Smith v. Allright* (1944) and *Baker v. Carr* (1962), this legal argument held that there was a federal right to vote secured by the federal constitution. Moreover, the US Constitution was "peculiarly silent" on voter qualifications, so youth suffrage existed unevenly.[16] The "national government allows, accepts, and validates the votes of United States citizens in Georgia, Kentucky, Alaska, and Hawaii, who are in the same age classification as the Appellant." To not do the same for Janie Greenspun

Janie Greenspun attempting to register to vote in Clark County, Nevada, with lawyer William Treadwell, September 11, 1968. Courtesy of Jane Greenspun Gale.

was to "invidiously discriminate" and "patently deny equal rights under the law."

The voting age standard of 21 in Nevada constituted "discriminatory treatment" and violated Janie's rights to due process guaranteed by the 5th Amendment as well as her right under the 14th Amendment to equal protection of the laws.[17] Summing up the legal argument, Janie said that "states should not be allowed to restrict people from voting for the president and vice president."[18]

After taking her case to court, she spoke to the press, explaining her motivation and reasoning.

> I began thinking of this during McCarthy's campaign. There were so many young people working for him, but they wouldn't be able to vote. I think 18-year-olds should be able to vote. In the eyes of the court an 18-year-old is tried as an adult. Eighteen-year-olds serve in the military forces and should be able to dictate who sends them to fight. Most 18-year-olds are high school graduates and have taken courses in government.

"And since it is a government of the people in a democracy," she stated, "then everyone should be able to participate."[19]

In this way Janie's case integrated the usual arguments with an innovative strategy. As a supporting fact in the case, her lawyers Treadwell and Denton included a bold restatement of an old argument for lowering the voting age. "The Establishment of 21 Years of Age as the Standard upon Which to Base a Presidential Voter Age Classification is Purely Arbitrary and Without Any Foundation in Fact or Reason."[20] Treadwell's client Richard Nixon made this same point at the same time, although he avoided the legal implications.

In mid-October during the final weeks of the 1968 campaign, the Republican nominee clarified his support for youth suffrage. He first put aside the foundational argument and then put forward other arguments. "The reason the voting age should be lowered is not that 18-year-olds are old enough to fight—it is because they are smart enough to vote," he affirmed. "They are more socially conscious, more politically aware, and much better educated than their parents were at age 18." His conclusion conveyed the changing construction of age categories and their meanings. "Youth today is just not as young as it used to be."[21]

Seventeen magazine addressed this same argument the same month, when it published an article and reader survey (postcard included) titled "Do You Want to Vote at 18?" The article started with President Johnson's recent message to Congress on lowering the voting age and surveyed the history of such proposals. It then summarized proponents' arguments, including changing notions of "maturity." *Seventeen* told its readers that according to scientists, 18-year-olds in 1968 were physically "at least three years ahead of an eighteen-year-old of 1900 because of better food and medical care." With top-down support from a sitting president, the two major political parties and their presidential candidates, and senators like Birch Bayh, "you may be voting sooner than you expect."[22]

Utterly undercutting *Seventeen*'s hopefulness was another magazine article published that October: "Who Killed the 18-Year-Old Vote?" *Look* magazine published this hard-hitting piece by Roger Rapoport, a 22-year-old graduate from the University of Michigan, where he edited the *Michigan Daily*. Rapoport started not with LBJ's recent message but with Private George Jackson, a wounded 19-year-old Vietnam veteran from Buffalo, New York.

> "Ever since I went into the Army, I wished I could vote," says this thin Negro, glancing down at his wheelchair. The lower half of George's left leg was amputated last spring after he was hit by a grenade in Vietnam. Doctors are working to restore full use of his burned right foot, which was also damaged in the explosion. "Most of my buddies felt the same way," he adds. "We feel the Vietnam war is a mistake, and we want to vote to end it."

Rapoport went on to summarize the arguments for enfranchising young Americans like George Jackson and survey the lack of progress in the 90th Congress.

Rather than blaming opponents like Emanuel Celler or Spessard Holland for this lack of progress, Rapoport held proponents responsible. His point of view reflected the frustration and anger at the actions and failures of liberals—for the war in Vietnam, for the persistence of poverty and racism—held by many young activists. He characterized Johnson's endorsement as a "publicity coup" with little consequence, given the late timing. Bayh's subcommittee hearings were similarly too late, letting the resolution languish. "The villains in this case are well-meaning congressional liberals who let the bill die without a fight," criticized Rapoport. "The coroner was Birch Bayh; the funeral arrangements were made by his subcommittee; the services were on Capitol Hill; and the eulogy was delivered by Lyndon Johnson."[23]

The '68 Election and After

Over the fall of 1968 Americans of all political persuasions, liberal and conservative, radical and reactionary, geared up to have their voices heard—or not—in the upcoming election. Proponents and opponents of youth suffrage were no different. For Democrats the developments, disorder, and disunity in Chicago put the party at a disadvantage. So did radical activists who called for voting in the streets rather than at the ballot box, protesting rather than participating in the political system. For Republicans, coming out of a relatively united convention—California governor Ronald Reagan briefly posed a challenge—the chaos and conflict in Chicago demonstrated the need for Nixon's "law and order" platform. Humphrey campaigned hard, but he had an uphill climb and not just due to the convention or disaffected activists.

The Democratic National Convention capped off a series of decisions in the 1960s that transformed the party's electoral base by 1968. Apart from LBJ's Texas, the Democrats lost the South to Republican Richard Nixon and segregationist George Wallace running as a third-party candidate. With the Republicans promising "de-Americanization" of the war in Vietnam and "peace with honor" to end it, the Democrats lost most states outside the South as well. They also lost the youth vote as defined at the time, with only 38 percent of voters aged 18 to 29 casting their ballots for the Democratic ticket.[24] Although the popular vote in the November election was close, the Republican victory in the Electoral College was overwhelming just four years after Johnson's landslide victory in 1964. Democrats kept control of Congress. But the stunning 1968 shift in the Democratic Party's presidential prospects set up Republicans to dominate the White House for decades to come.

The November elections also spelled defeat for youth suffrage proponents. In Hawai'i a complex ballot on the new state constitution went before voters. After seeing voters in New York in 1967 and Maryland in 1968 reject new constitutions after being offered only a straight "yes or no" say, the Hawai'i constitutional convention presented each of the proposed amendments separately as well as together. Of 23 proposals only one failed to pass: lowering the voting age from 20 to 18.[25] In Tennessee the electorate had the opportunity to empower the next state constitutional convention to draft an amendment for the 18-year-old vote. That too went down to defeat. The new state constitution that did pass in Florida omitted, after a long debate, a lower voting age. And North Dakota voters had already rejected a referendum for a voting age of 19 during the state's September primary election.

Another referendum for the 19-year-old vote came up in Nebraska in November. The vote was close—49 percent in favor and 51 percent against—but the referendum lost in both urban Omaha and the state's rural areas. Prior to the election proponents had been positive. "In a year of political uncertainty, Nebraska's proposed constitutional amendment lowering the minimum voting age to 19 looked like a sure winner," wrote a *Wall Street Journal* reporter. "Almost no one campaigned against it. Avowed supporters were numerous and spanned the political spectrum."[26]

"This is the kind of issue where you have people tell you they're for it," declared John Schrekinger, a University of Nebraska student who headed the state campaign. "But then they get in the voting booth and vote against you." Television coverage of the protests in Chicago hindered the campaign in its last months. State legislators backing the referendum started to receive more letters in opposition. "What do you think of your proposal now?" Local red-baiting also hurt. One state senator saw "a world-wide conspiracy" in which students "are being used." "Do you have to wait until it crosses the state line to stop it?" The campaign tried hard to define Nebraska youth as moderates and differentiate them from out-of-state militants. "Don't vote against NEBRASKA young people," pleaded proponents. But voters did. Liberal faith in youth enfranchisement as a constructive action foundered on conservative convictions of young people as a destructive force. "People are afraid of change," Schrekinger concluded.[27]

Where to go from here? Loyal Democrats needed to pick up the pieces of their party's disarray and defeat. For many antiwar activists "the system was broken." For some young Americans radicalism was the answer, while others reacted with cynicism. But there was another response to the events of 1968, even with the state referenda defeats: a new determination to lower the voting age. Neither protest nor persuasion from outside the political system was working. Young people needed real political leverage within the system. They needed the vote.

Pat Keefer "was very disillusioned by what was happening" in the country, but lowering the voting age "seemed like a change in the system that would empower young people."²⁸ She headed home to Ohio and began to work on a "Vote 19" campaign there. To achieve the same end Janie's case wended its way through the federal court system. And Renny knew he needed another way to stop the war. "It was just inexorable, it was just going on and on. So I seized upon the idea, well, if we could only vote." "I just decided that I was going to be involved in the youth franchise movement, although I didn't have that name."²⁹

Others did, however. Paul Minarchenko and Mel Myler were busy in the nation's capital. "There was lots of activity," Paul recalls. "What there wasn't was anybody in Washington, DC who could channel and focus all that energy and apply political pressure."³⁰ That situation was shifting. NEA personnel had begun to work out how Project 18 would proceed and recruited Les Francis to be Project 18's first director. Les felt that the "young men and women who campaigned so vigorously during the last election proved their interest, concern, and judgment."³¹ Paul, Mel, Les, and allies closely followed state actions in Hawai'i, Nebraska, and Tennessee and started to formulate a national approach. All agreed that "an ad hoc youth coalition" and "a national coordinating committee" would be necessary, with young people, Monroe Sweetland ensured, at the forefront.³²

Developments in December 1968 signaled accelerating momentum for youth voting rights. On December 10 a small group representing key organizations—NEA, Student NEA, the NAACP, NSA, Young Democrats, Young Republicans, and others—met in Washington to found the Youth Franchise Coalition. An Interim Steering Committee was selected to organize funding for staff, office space, and supplies. Tom Hipple would take on the role of acting executive director until a permanent person could be appointed. An Indiana native with connections to Senator Birch Bayh, Hipple brought experience from working on the McCarthy campaign in his own state as well as in California, Nebraska, and New York. A formal announcement of the coalition would come in the new year.

Meanwhile the NAACP announced its participation in "a drive to lower the voting age to 18 throughout the nation."[33] Since the achievement of the Voting Rights Act of 1965 the association had focused on ensuring its implementation and registering and mobilizing Black voters. Along with the rest of the Youth Franchise Coalition members, the NAACP wanted Congress to establish a uniform, national voting age of 18. Executive Director Roy Wilkins put this drive in historical context. "Throughout its 60-year history, the NAACP has consistently worked for expansion of the vote." Contemporary conditions also warranted the association's involvement. "Young people, 18 years of age, now have virtually full legal liability in all the states. It is difficult to see how in all justice they can be denied their manifest wish to join in settling the burning issues of the day at the ballot box."[34]

The drive received strong support from Black newspapers. Editors at the *Atlanta Daily World* expressed "agreement with the idea that all youth in our country should have the right to vote when they reach their 18th birthday." They reminded readers of their state's early achievement of youth enfranchisement, although erred on exactly when it took place. "The State of Georgia was foresighted enough to lower the voting age to 18 as far back as 1945." Although the year was actually 1943, the paper's current endorsement was right on target. "The vote is vital to the solving of problems of the people and the advancement of our race."[35]

Along with announcing its drive for the 18-year-old vote in December, the NAACP publicized plans for a National Youth Mobilization in Washington, DC, in 1969. Reverend James G. Blake, vice president for youth affairs, outlined the plans. Delegations from youth organizations across the country would convene in the capital to participate in a conference and lobby Congress to lower the voting age. With its nationwide network of branches, especially its Youth and College Division, and organizing know-how, the NAACP provided inspiration and impetus for youth voting rights at just the right time.

Other developments took place on the local level. In Massachusetts a new organization was founded on December 5. As with earlier youth suffrage groups its name was its goal but with a mathematical twist.

18 × 72 aimed to lower the voting age in Massachusetts to 18 by 1972. The founders were committed to the principle "that the organization, labor, and enthusiasm needed to accomplish our goal must come from those presently below the minimum voting age." They circulated a familiar list of arguments for proponents, including the safety-valve argument. 18 × 72 also subtly echoed the efforts of the Nebraska campaigners to differentiate proponents of youth voting rights from more radical students and activists. "For those who fear the generation gap and believe the involvement of 18-year-olds in government to be either irresponsible or dangerous, it should be pointed out that the interest of young people in obtaining the vote is an expression of faith in the system." Seeking the vote showed "a strong commitment to the democratic process as the best method for seeking change."[36] Such distinctions arose in relation to another December 1968 development. This time across the country, in California.

LUV—Let Us Vote

In late 1968 students at the University of the Pacific in Stockton, California, launched the Let Us Vote campaign after a campus visit and speech from Birch Bayh. Indiana voters had just reelected Bayh to the Senate. He would keep his position as chairman of the Senate Judiciary Committee's Subcommittee on Constitutional Amendments and his commitment to lowering the voting age. At a dinner with student leaders during his visit to UoP he met Dennis Warren, a political science student and national debating champion. They discussed the possibility of achieving youth suffrage in the near future, and Senator Bayh challenged Warren and his fellow students to build a grassroots campaign to help to make this possibility real.

Although a student-led organization in California already existed— Citizens for Lowering the Voting Age—Warren and his fellow UoP students took up the challenge but in a different direction. "Our whole theory behind the campaign was—we had no competency politically, in the sense of actually being skilled at politics—but what we could do is be a public information campaign," recalls Dennis. "We tried to create a campaign that could appeal to almost anybody. We were taking a really constructive advocacy position."[37]

In its focus on education, information, and publicity, Let Us Vote (LUV) overlapped with but also expanded on the work of earlier campaigns. "Our office will serve as an information center," Dennis announced at the time. "The campaign seeks to organize a massive public information program supplying young adults with statistics and documentation for the various arguments favoring lowering of the voting age." These materials could then be used in lobbying and letter writing. At first, given Bayh's influence, LUV focused on a federal amendment. "We want to have college students and their friends and parents to inundate Washington with letters indicating support of the lowering of the voting age to 18 before Congress votes on the issue," Dennis explained.[38]

LUV soon expanded its focus to lowering the voting age either by an amendment to the US Constitution or by individual state action. To this end Dennis offered statements before both Congress and the California Assembly in 1969. He spoke of his generation and sought to convey their principles and priorities. "I suggest to all those charged with governing this nation that our generation will no longer accept as right that which merely exists," he told Bayh's subcommittee. "We cannot adhere to oxcart standards in a space age. We will not accept promises of equity and be served with inequity." With the enfranchisement of youth, "I genuinely believe that the generation gap, which is a reality, can be closed."[39]

"I was motivated because I had already had several friends die in the Vietnam War," Dennis remembers. "So this notion that if you are old enough to die for your country you are old enough to vote for it really meant something." As an experienced competitive debater, he knew how to "construct a persuasive set of evidence and arguments." He also knew that one argument—even one as profound as the foundational argument—wasn't enough.[40]

In his letter to new LUV members, he outlined seven. "Psychologists, educators and sociologists agree that those in this age bracket today are far better emotionally oriented to the problems of our time and are thus capable of making more mature and effective decisions than previous generations." He reminded readers that 18-, 19-, and 20-year-olds were serving in the military, marrying, working, and paying taxes, were well informed about political issues, and wanted to participate in politics and government. They were demonstrating the responsibilities of citizenship and deserved the rights. He added the safety-valve argument. Disfranchisement was a "major cause of young adult unrest on and off college campuses." Dennis concluded that opponents might object to one or two of these arguments but that "the logic and historical significance of these combined arguments" would win them over.[41]

UoP's public relations director R. Doyle Minden played up LUV's campaign in letters to politicians, including Governor Ronald Reagan, and to the press. "With all the turmoil on other California campuses, it is rather refreshing for us to have on our campus students interested in using traditional methods of change," he wrote. "We feel this is a good example of constructive student power, and, naturally, prefer it to what has been taking place in San Francisco State." Minden referenced protests and a long strike by a multiracial student coalition over late 1968 and early 1969 at San Francisco State College. The strike led to the hiring of a new, hardline president, S. I. Hayakawa. With the strong backing of Governor Reagan, Hayakawa forcibly opened the college with a massive police presence, arrests, and brutality. Although the student strikers succeeded in establishing ethnic studies in higher education, Minden touted Let Us Vote as a counterexample that may "help renew students' faith in the system of political change."[42]

Along with some familiar elements of youth suffrage campaigning, Let Us Vote brought a new cultural style and much media visibility. Due to connections to publicists and to Hollywood, LUV had a televised launch on *The Joey Bishop Show* on December 20, 1968, giving the campaign immediate national exposure. As a talk show host, comedian, and member of singer Frank Sinatra's "Rat Pack," Joey Bishop's interest in the voting age issue was initially inspired by his son. When his son turned 18 three years earlier, he asked why he couldn't vote. Bishop couldn't answer but "admired the fact that his son and other college students wanted to be actively involved in their country and its government."[43]

Bishop featured Dennis Warren on his show in December and followed up with an appearance at a LUV rally in Stockton in January. And he agreed to become the national honorary chairman of Let Us Vote. "I have to condone all of this," he said, "because it is in the manner in which I hope that all youth movements will take place. As opposed to rioting or demanding, this is being done constitutionally correct. It is being done by petition and in a peaceful manner."[44] In lauding moderate, vote-seeking youth and lamenting militant activism, Bishop joined Minden, Bayh, and others in making this distinction.

These show business connections got LUV something no other youth voting rights campaign ever had: a theme song. Pop musicians Tommy Boyce and Bobby Hart, who appeared regularly on Bishop's show, wrote and recorded the song. Dennis enjoyed being part of the process and appreciated how "so many people wanted to be helpful."[45] Boyce and Hart's campaign song, "L.U.V.," had a catchy melody and a lively beat. Most importantly, its lyrics made a case for lowering the voting age.

> It's been a long time getting' here
> A change is comin' and it's very near
> A way to change things peacefully
> And live together in harmony
> Let us vote!
> It's time that we all made a contribution
> Come on and let us vote
> It's a solution
> L.U.V., I'm talking 'bout you and me
> And changin' things peacefully
> We're old enough so L.U.V.
> The time is now and the feeling's right
> To look at things in a better light
> We're old enough to lend a helping hand
> Together we can build a better land

The lyrics offered a positive restatement of the safety-valve argument, with no mention of frustration and anger. Enfranchised young people would achieve political change with peace and harmony.

Boyce and Hart were invited to Stockton to perform their song at the Let Us Vote campaign rally in January. They had no idea what to expect. "There was a very different vibe in the air when Tommy and I stepped on the rally stage," Hart recalled. "The faces we saw in this packed auditorium of college-aged kids held expressions of hope, unity, and strength. The response was thunderous when we introduced ourselves and expressed our solidarity with their cause." For Hart this performance was a profound experience. "For the first time, I felt a deep connection to an audience that was based on something bigger than just the music." He and Boyce had not been musician activists like Joan Baez or Phil Ochs. But with this song "we had been given the chance to write music that could actually be an influence for change."[46] He began to personally champion lowering the voting age, and he and Boyce donated the song royalties to the campaign.

As an example of cultural politics, the "L.U.V." song used popular culture to express the political aim of youth enfranchisement. Earlier movements had shown the power of music to build solidarity and support toward achieving aims, and participants in the Let Us Vote campaign hoped for a similar outcome. The song did generate more popular exposure for Let Us Vote and youth voting rights. It got radio play, appeared on the *Billboard* Hot 100 chart, and provided a way into teenage culture. An article in the popular teen fan magazine *Tiger Beat* illustrated how Let Us Vote and the song reached a younger audience. The article noted "the groovy L.U.V. song," where readers could buy it, and how to get involved in the campaign.

"It doesn't matter what age you are—9, 13, 15 or 18—you can help." By writing to LUV headquarters readers could get a useful package of materials. "The best thing about the package is that it contains a list of reasons for lowering the voting age—arguments which you can use to defend your stand whenever someone challenges you. You'll really *know* your facts and will be able to carry on an intelligent debate." *Tiger Beat* cautioned that the campaign was going to take some time. But if they didn't "start right now, here, 18 year olds will *never* vote. Never, never, never." "So, lend a hand. Grab a pen and . . . sock it to 'em!"[47]

Dennis Warren and members of Let Us Vote did not anticipate the size of the audience for their message or the enthusiasm of young people for their movement. Perhaps it was their counterculture-inflected acronym, LUV, or Boyce and Hart's song. But in just six weeks Let Us Vote expanded from its base at the University of the Pacific to be a nationwide organization with chapters at 327 colleges and some 3,000 high schools. LUV's appeal at the high school level in late 1968 and 1969 coincided with the start of the peak years of activism among school students, aided by a major Supreme Court decision, *Tinker v. Des Moines* (1969), upholding their 1st Amendment rights at school.[48] Later television appearances by Dennis on shows like *The Dating Game*—which

LUV Rally, Stockton, California, January 1969. LUV Collection. Courtesy of Holt-Atherton Special Collections Department, University of the Pacific Library.

he won!—further heightened LUV's visibility and impact. "That sounds crazy now," Warren admits, "and I never actually ended up going on the date. But a program like that had a huge viewership. We were literally getting bags of mail as a result of that appearance."[49]

One high school student reached by Let Us Vote was Renny Cushing. "I became networked into the Let Us Vote movement nationally," he recalls. He started to push for youth voting rights at his school and in his state. As a leader of Students for a Better School, he sparked a controversy over his refusal to shave his sideburns as a challenge to the school dress code. Then he ran for student government. "That was my platform—end the war and lower the voting age, so that by the time we graduate we can vote, we can vote them out, and we can end that war."[50] Renny also spoke in favor of voting age proposals before the Constitutional Revision Committee of the New Hampshire House of Representatives. He told legislators that the "arguments used against giving women and the Negro the vote are being used today against youth" and were equally erroneous. The continuing political powerlessness of youth came down to the older generation, given that "those voting on the proposal are the ones holding public office—all persons over 21."[51]

The swift expansion of Let Us Vote among students like Renny caught the attention of the older generation in the mainstream press. In their stories media outlets couldn't resist using love-related clichés. Students at UoP "decided to make LUV," their work is a "labor of LUV," and a "Little LUV has gone a long way."[52] Even *Time* magazine indulged in idiom, with "Can LUV Conquer All?" "More than 20,000 letters inquiring about LUV have flooded into Warren's busy headquarters on the Stockton campus. Only three of these have been critical."

Time's January 1969 story presented youth suffrage proponents to its adult readership as an appealing alternative to the young Americans who "stormed on the national political scene in 1968 with galvanic gusto." Let Us Vote showed young people like Dennis Warren engaging in the political process. "The very antithesis of the stereotype student radical, Warren wears his hair closely cropped, dresses in conservative pinstripe suits and black shoes." *Time* also reported that LUV would be joining a new national coalition of organizations to win youth voting rights. "Though other groups have tried in the past to lower the voting age in individual states, the coalition will mark the first time that students will have merged with other interest groups to achieve the goal on a national basis."[53] The Youth Franchise Coalition had come together.

11

It's About Time

On February 5, 1969, a group of some 50 proponents of youth voting rights gathered in Washington, DC, for the first organizational meeting of the Youth Franchise Coalition. At this meeting they formally approved, established, and elected a board and officers for the Youth Franchise Coalition (YFC). "Never before has anyone tried to do what we are," Paul Minarchenko told a reporter. "That is, to focus national attention on the 18-year-old voting issue."[1] Familiar figures were there on behalf of their organizations—Paul for the YMCA, Mel Myler for Student NEA, Les Francis for Project 18, and Spencer Oliver for the Young Democrats. Prominent organizations such as the NAACP, the NSA, and the AFL-CIO were well represented. With the aim of building a broad and bipartisan coalition, some 470 student, civil rights, voting rights, education, labor, political, and religious organizations had been invited to send representatives. Radical students also were welcomed, including the Students for a Democratic Society. In the midst of disintegrating, SDS never responded.[2]

Senators Birch Bayh and Jennings Randolph attended this meeting and cautioned against any such radical associations. "It must be remembered that the spotlight is . . . on the militant demonstrators and beatniks," Randolph declared, dating himself with use of the term "beatnik." For the cause of lowering the voting age, campus protests "do not help much." Bayh agreed that "student unrest will lead some people to question the wisdom" of the cause. Despite the fact that the group gathered before the two senators could hardly be described as militant or radical, they were charged with the task of overcoming this stereotype of young people popularly portrayed through the media. "It's up to you to illustrate your desire to participate as an elector," Randolph told them. "The burden of proof rests with you—and rightly so."[3]

The NAACP's Roy Wilkins reinforced this message in his newspaper column covering the founding of "a lobby of young people organized as the Youth Franchise Coalition." His column appeared in several news-papers under different titles. In the *Los Angeles Times* the title asked the alarming question, "18s: Vote or Violence?" After relating the latest campus disorders and demonstrations, Wilkins repeated Randolph and Bayh's points. "This kind of thing is not likely to persuade the country to place its elections in the hands of 18-year-olds." Wilkins hoped that "the campaign for lowering the voting age to 18 will succeed in driving home to assorted militant youth, including the campus variety, that molasses, rather than vinegar, attracts flies." But if that didn't happen Congress and the nation may not differentiate, or "split hairs," between militant and moderate students or between liberal and radical youth. And a federal youth suffrage amendment would not be forthcoming.[4]

Senators Bayh and Randolph were more optimistic and spurred on the new YFC. "Never before have youth so embodied the hopes and dreams and promises for the future," contended Randolph in his char-acteristic energetic style. "The time is ripe to achieve success in the 91st Congress for the Constitutional amendment to enfranchise American youth." Liberal and labor forces believed that this new Congress, even with Richard Nixon in the White House, would be "responsive," as the *AFL-CIO News* put it, "to the continuing need for change."[5] Randolph had already introduced his ninth resolution to lower the voting age to 18. For the first time he was able to cite both the Democratic and Re-publican 1968 party platforms in support. He also alluded to the safety-valve argument. "We must channel the spirit of youth in a constructive direction."[6]

For proponents this argument for youth suffrage remained as relevant as ever in the wake of 1968. The premise of the safety-valve argument arose in the interim report of the National Commission on the Causes and Prevention of Violence, presented to President Johnson in January before he left office. "Violent protest . . . has occurred in part because the protestors believe that they cannot make their demands felt effectively thru normal approved channels and that 'the system' for whatever rea-son, has become unresponsive to them."[7] The 18-year-old vote was one way to make the system more responsive. Despite the many challenges ahead, Senator Bayh agreed. "I am confident that we will succeed."[8]

The founding of the YFC certainly was a reason for confidence. With this crucial catalyst the nearly three decades of efforts and campaigns for youth voting rights moved into a third and final phase and became a movement. The seeds of the national coalition planted back in 1943 were now flourishing. Older associations, such as NEA and the NAACP, committed people and resources, while new groups dedicated solely to the 18-year-old vote sprang up and spread. Together they supported and sustained a youth franchise movement in the United States. The years 1969 to 1971 saw unprecedented activity and attention at the local, state, and national levels. It was the movement's moment.

The Youth Franchise Coalition

As momentum for lowering the voting age to 18 transformed into a movement, the YFC grew rapidly. Although membership increased and changed over time, within a few months over 25 organizations were listed on the coalition's letterhead. The NAACP Youth and College Division, the SCLC Citizenship Education Program, the NSA, the YMCA National Student Caucus, NEA, and Student NEA were all member organizations. National, multi-issue organizations, such as Americans for Democratic Action and the United States Youth Council, and local, single-issue groups, like LUV in California and Citizens for Vote 18 in New York, joined.

Raising membership numbers were state affiliates of the Student NEA, including California, Hawai'i, Iowa, Minnesota, North Carolina, and Wisconsin. Later Colorado, Kansas, and New Mexico affiliates signed on, as did many more organizations. The National Student Young Women's Christian Association, the National Association of Social Workers, B'nai B'rith, and the Episcopal Church Executive Council were just a few. Not every allied organization could or did join, but they still offered backing, funding, and lobbying. The AFL-CIO and the League of Women Voters fell into this category. And when the YFC appeared before Congress and in other settings, they could marshal a show of strength and support from an even wider array.

The coalition's first officers and board of directors reflected this breadth, with younger Americans at the forefront, as Monroe Sweetland had assured. The board had twice as many directors representing youth organizations as adult organizations. Paul Minarchenko, YMCA, Mel Myler, Student NEA, Spencer Oliver, Young Democrats, James Blake,

NAACP Youth Affairs, James Graham, NSA, Terry Watson, US Youth Council, Julian Butler, Southern Committee on Political Ethics, Jim Chiswell, Citizens for Vote 18, and Dennis Warren, Let Us Vote served alongside Dirck W. Brown, NEA, Verlin Nelson, Americans for Democratic Action, David Cohen, Committee for Community Affairs, James Brown Jr., NAACP, and David Cato, SCLC Citizenship Education Program. Paul became chairman, James Blake, vice chairman, and Dirck Brown, treasurer, while the position of secretary shifted early on.

Bringing together such a diverse range of organizations under the umbrella of the YFC was their first order of political organization. "The Youth Franchise Coalition was created to provide a rallying point for proponents," stated a 1969 YFC pamphlet. "It unites the common interests of numerous organizations into a single-purpose organization with the means to give the movement the full-time attention it needs."[9] "They were already really, really skilled politically," Dennis Warren recalls about the YFC leaders, especially those who had been "on the frontlines" of the civil rights movement. "So everybody had a role to play, and that was the neat thing about it, and for me an extraordinary education."[10]

Although proponents on the local level later began informal chapters of the YFC in Baltimore and Minnesota, the coalition founders never intended to go out and create or control new groups. Instead, existing organizations would join the coalition and still "do their own thing," as Mel said at the time.[11] At its height the YFC's member organizations encompassed an estimated 8 million individuals. "The beauty of the movement," Paul recalls, "was in its indigenous creation and the fact that these people were doing it because they believed in it and they wanted to do it and it was theirs. We didn't need to control them." "The more the merrier," he felt.[12]

As they strove for inclusion they stressed the YFC's nonprofit, nonpartisan nature. But it could be difficult to overcome differences among coalition members in order to act together. The premise for building coalitions is that participants share and work together on one goal. They don't have to prioritize the shared goal in precisely the same way. They don't have to agree on everything, or even anything, else. In fact, as Paul emphasized at the time, "while few significant issues concerning youth today had broad acceptance, the extension of the franchise was an exception in being a uniting issue."[13] Even so the YFC soon ran into political conflict with the Young Republican National Federation.

The two main political parties were to come into the YFC through their youth divisions. The Young Democratic Clubs of America and its college-based affiliate, with Spencer Oliver's leadership, were founding member organizations of the coalition. Oliver still sees the YFC "as one of the most effective lobbying operations in history."[14] Chairman of the Young Republicans Jack McDonald had tentatively agreed to join the coalition. Cathy Cargle, in charge of Public Relations for the Young Republicans, was appointed as the YFC's first secretary.

McDonald's agreement and Cargle's appointment made sense. The Young Republicans had called for youth suffrage before. McDonald himself had spoken strongly in favor of a constitutional amendment to lower the voting age at the 1968 Senate hearings. But Jack McDonald was also a new kind of Republican. Elected chairman of the Young Republicans in 1967 as a staunch supporter of Barry Goldwater and "ultra-conservatism," McDonald had run on a right-wing platform of anticommunism and anti–civil rights. Ideology and factionalism alienated many liberal and moderate members of the Young Republicans and set up the conflict with the YFC.[15]

In March the Young Republicans met to consider coalition membership. Paul attended to make the case and answer any questions. *Washington Post* columnists Rowland Evans and Robert Novak reported on the contentious meeting. Conflict first emerged over the question of dues. Although the YFC required only $50 for an organization to join, the Young Democrats had been able to offer a donation of $1,200. Insinuating corruption McDonald "suggested some youth organizations were buying their way into the Coalition." Paul quickly countered that suggestion. Then McDonald reversed his position from the year before. Following the lead of President Nixon and the 1968 Republican Party platform, the Young Republicans opposed any plan to progress a federal constitutional amendment and proposed proceeding only through the states. That alone was a major stumbling block given the YFC's goals.

Another arose when Paul listed the founding member organizations of the coalition. "There were snickers when he mentioned the NAACP and the Southern Christian Leadership Conference." Outright objections came when Paul named the US National Student Association and Americans for Democratic Action, which the Young Republicans deemed too liberal. Despite supporting youth voting rights in principle, they voted against joining the YFC. Ideology and partisanship trumped coalition and compromise. Evans and Novak held nothing back in condemning the "GOP Young Fogies." "The Young Republicans have showed again how they enjoy being an inbred little conservative clique by refusing to join a broad-based youth movement to lower the voting age."[16] Their refusal portended the country's future political polarization, although in the short term the Ripon Society provided a centrist Republican member for the YFC.

Their refusal also meant that Cathy Cargle could no longer serve as the YFC's secretary, but James "Jim" Graham, vice president of campus affairs for the NSA, was ready to step in. As state chairman of the Michigan Citizens' Committee for the Vote at 18 in 1966, Graham had experience with a state referendum campaign. Through his position with the NSA he had published a useful pamphlet called "Lowering the Voting Age" in 1968. That year the 21st National Student Congress of the NSA reinforced its commitment to the cause with a mandate "to seek a lower voting age within the states" and "to support a lower voting age on Federal level."[17] In keeping with the mandate Graham could tell student government officers across the country that "the National Student Association played a leading role in the formation of the Youth Franchise Coalition."[18]

The YFC's formation was welcomed by many politicians. "I want to do all I can to help the Youth Franchise Coalition in mounting a nationwide campaign to secure the vote for 18-year-olds," former Vice President Hubert Humphrey wrote Paul. "I agree completely with the importance of this act at this point in our history and I will be making the case for a lower voting age at every opportunity."[19] In addition to Senators Randolph and Bayh, Senator Jacob Javits and six additional senators—both Democrat and Republican—identified early as YFC allies. "The nub of the practical politics," Javits explained, "is that without assurances from organized college-aged groups that 18-to-21 year-olds really want the franchise, the chances of passage are dim."[20] Working closely with the senators and their staffs, the YFC and allies aimed to provide these assurances. Access to the House of Representatives proceeded more slowly. Charles Diggs remained a proponent. But his new roles chairing the Subcommittee on Africa of the House Foreign Affairs Committee and forming what would become the Congressional Black Caucus left little room for leadership on this issue. Digg's colleague from Michigan, John Conyers, and James J. Howard, from Paul's home state of New Jersey, stayed steadfast supporters.

The YFC was also well received in the press. "Despite a woeful record of no wins and umpteen losses last year, the 18-year-old vote is back, like a freshly painted pop-up on the political firing range, ready for another round," wrote the editor of *Moderator* magazine. In a substantive story on the state of play for youth voting rights, he considered "the greatest cause for optimism is that, for the first time ever, a coherent, multifaceted campaign is beginning to be waged at the national level." The YFC and its supporters showed that in 1969 "more people may be taking it more seriously. It's about time."[21]

YFC leaders left no doubt about their serious intentions on the issue of the 18-year-old vote. "For the first time, we're going to go really hard on this issue," Jim Graham stated. "This will be no kiddies' brigade."[22] "For years people have been passing resolutions," Terry Watson of the US Youth Council said. "Now, organizations are determined to put muscle into it."[23] Paul put it more profanely: "We're going to try like hell."[24]

Strategic Developments

Such determination was soon demonstrated. YFC leaders wrote bylaws and put together a budget. Estimating that $50,000 would be needed for a year of activity, they sought donations, large and small. They asked member organizations. Graham solicited student governments, which had worked well in Michigan in 1966. "For this campaign to be successful young people have got to believe in it," Mel noted. "So you'll see the students passing the hat for 50-cents donations."[25] Fortunately they started with funding and in-kind support from NEA and other organizations, such as the League of Women Voters. That year, in addition to Les and his full-time position as director of Project 18, the YFC had a full-time executive director and an administrative staff assistant. This core of professional paid staff coordinated with coalition members working through their own organizations.

During the first few months of 1969 they generated ideas, plans, and strategies about how the coalition would work in practice. Les stated it simply: "Try Everything!" And in fact they did. The primary goal was to secure the 18-year-old vote at the national level. They had differing views on the timeframe. "If it doesn't pass this time, for many of us it will be the last straw," said Graham, who had been working on the issue for more than four years.[26] For Ian MacGowan, fresh to the fight in 1969 in his new position as permanent YFC executive director, "I give it five years; otherwise it is going to fizzle out."[27] Either way, to get started they needed to lobby Congress.

Paul had been honing his lobbying knowledge and experience in his position with the YMCA. "One of the things I had the YMCA join was the Leadership Conference on Civil Rights." He learned from lobbyists with legendary reputations, Clarence Mitchell and Joseph Rauh. "They were indispensable" to the passage of the Civil Rights, Voting Rights, and Fair Housing Acts. A founding member of Americans for Democratic Action, Rauh had also served as general counsel for the United Auto Workers. "They became my mentors," Paul says. Paul benefited from others too, including two members of the YFC's board of directors, Verlin Nelson and David Cohen. He also sought advice from Kenneth Meiklejohn and Ken Young of the AFL-CIO. Paul planned to register with the clerk of the House of Representatives and the secretary of the Senate as an unpaid lobbyist for the YFC.[28]

They all recognized, however, that another important legislative issue demanded attention in early 1969: Electoral College reform. Birch Bayh made this point at the YFC's organizational meeting in February as well as at the University of the Pacific in December. "In his speech at U.O.P., Senator Bayh had predicted that lowering the voting age to 18 would be even more difficult to secure than the abolition of the Electoral College."[29] At first Electoral College reform, which would also require a constitutional amendment, looked very promising with legislation advancing in the House in 1969. "It's a question of staging the issue," David Cohen explained about progressing youth suffrage. "Now people are concerned with electoral reform. Part of lobbying is timing—it cannot occur on this issue until electoral reform is somewhat down the road."[30]

The YFC's national goal still encompassed state-level action. "Separate actions to lower the voting age in all of the states is an unrealistic

goal," stated the 1969 YFC pamphlet. "However, early and favorable action by a limited number of states could provide enough momentum to
gain 2/3's support in Congress for a constitutional amendment." Each
state that lowered the voting age helped to put pressure on the federal
government to enact a uniform national voting age. State campaigns
also helped to identify and increase support. "Congress isn't going to
act unless it feels the heat from home," Les pointed out. It was necessary to get citizens on the ground to "petition, write, visit, or phone"
to put pressure on their representatives in government to act.[31] Finally,
state action could contribute to laying the foundation for winning the 38
states needed for ratification.

The YFC and its member organizations thus worked on "the state
and national levels simultaneously, helping to organize state coalitions
and supporting their efforts while maintaining a presence on Capitol
Hill and keeping the issue before the American public."[32] This last goal
reflected an understanding of the necessity of public education around
youth voting rights as well as NEA's long-standing commitment to civic
education. In a May 1969 interview the newly appointed Ian MacGowan
declared a "massive educational program to make the general public
aware of 'the importance' of lowering the voting age from 21 to 18."
Education would "create a receptive atmosphere for discussion and
debate." Education also preceded politics when Ian summed up YFC's
strategy. To "coordinate a national, broadly based, educational and political campaign to secure the right to vote for all citizens of the United
States who have reached the age of 18 years."[33]

To advance these aims the YFC and its member organizations fostered communication and contact both within and beyond the coalition.
Letters and literature poured forth. Paul thought at the time that one of
the "principal functions of the organization's Washington headquarters
is to keep groups throughout the country in touch with one another."
Early on he estimated mailings to nearly one million Americans.[34] YFC
began to issue a semiregular bulletin to report on federal government
actions, state-level developments, activities of different organizations,
and related news.

The hiring of Ian MacGowan, together with Marcia Stickle as the first
administrative staff assistant, kept the paper flowing. At age 29—close
but not quite yet in the "you can't trust anyone over 30" category—Ian

came to the YFC with experience in Democratic politics at the state level and four years of working in the nation's capital.

> I was seething with anger at the war in Vietnam and feeling a great deal of empathy for the thousands who marched on Washington and knew I needed to do something of value. Because of my background in politics, my concept of change came from within the system rather than protest. Lobbying was what I knew and was good at.

At the time he also liked "the idea of working with young people, they need someone a little older—but still young."[35]

In pamphlets and mass mailings, YFC leaders reached out to young people, the wider public, and their own organizations. They explained their purpose and how they were working to lower the voting age in the United States. All of these communications included a section addressing readers on how they could help. "What Can You Do?" asked an early YFC pamphlet. "What You Can Do" stated NEA's pamphlet. "There are a number of ways you can help," Jim Graham told student government leaders. A core set of such activities emerged. People could express their views to state and national representatives. They could start or take part in an existing campaign at their state or local level. To this end Graham prompted student leaders to organize petitions, pass resolutions, program discussions and debates, and circulate information on campus. NEA encouraged everyone to get "organizations of which you are a member to take a positive position on the issue." Student NEA affiliates hosted teach-ins. And YFC asked that participants "keep us informed of your activities."[36]

Most of all they could educate themselves on the issue. NEA's pamphlet recapped how suffrage laws could be changed at both the national and state levels and restated the main arguments for the 18-year-old vote. That fulfilling citizenship responsibilities should earn one citizenship rights was emphasized, and the safety-valve argument was included. Other organizations provided informational literature to be ordered. "Area of Debate" was available from the YFC and included a "capsule sum of arguments" and useful statistics. How many 18- to 20-year-olds were high school graduates, married, in the labor force, in the armed forces. What were the ages of majority, for driving, drinking alcohol, owning firearms, making a will. These materials did a good job of showing the nationwide "confusion" around what different ages meant in terms of "maturity." The YFC also provided kits for organizing state campaigns and fostering public information.[37]

From the NSA you could get a "completely re-written and brought up-to-date" edition of Graham's pamphlet. "Times have changed, and the events of 1968, both within and without the system, have provided new compelling reasons why 18 to 20 year olds deserve the vote." One of Graham's vital contributions was an entire section on "The Left and the Vote." Although leftist groups counted among proponents in the 1940s, the same could not be said of the left in the late 1960s. Graham explained the conflict. Skeptical of "the importance of the single vote cast at this time, in this society," new left activists saw in the 18-year-old vote "the possibility of co-optation into the system." At the same time some youth suffrage proponents were "playing down the merits and accomplishments of activism." Instead of devolving into "youth divisiveness," Graham called for his fellow proponents to address the left's concerns. The youth vote won't be enough to solve all problems, but at least it will be a start. In such dialogue "exists a real opportunity, based upon some degree of mutual respect and honesty, for unity."[38]

Another opportunity Graham promoted was to "plan on attending the NAACP mobilization day"—the first national event to bring youth voting rights proponents together for two days of training and action in Washington, DC.[39]

NAACP National Youth Mobilization to Lower the Voting Age

In April 1969 proponents came from around the country to participate in the NAACP's National Youth Mobilization to Lower the Voting Age, with the aim of rallying popular support and lobbying Congress. The NAACP began organizing for this national conference shortly after announcing it at the end of 1968. Taking the lead were the two NAACP representatives on the YFC board: James Blake, who held the role of chairman of the Mobilization National Committee, and James Brown Jr., director of the Youth and College Division. As chair of the NAACP's National Youth Work Committee Janice Johnson took charge of much of the organizing. Carolyn Quilloin, a veteran of the Savannah sit-in movement and NAACP youth field director for Tennessee, Mississippi, Alabama, and North Carolina, served as coordinator for the conference. This gender division of labor appeared to repeat that of the civil rights movement—"men led, but women organized"—but everyone worked hard on the event.[40]

The NAACP first mobilized its own membership, including 67,000 students in the Youth and College Division. Roy Wilkins also sent out a letter to all adult branches. "Peal the Bell! The Youth and College Division of the NAACP needs your help." With this mobilization conference they aimed to "demonstrate the importance of the issue and to dramatize the earnestness with which our young people are working." Achieving the 18-year-old vote would allow young people to participate in politics in a "responsible" and "positive" way.

Over the past few years Wilkins had been trying to come to terms with Black power and criticisms of the NAACP as old-fashioned and conservative. Being responsive to youth voting rights could help. He called upon the adult branches to offer "spiritual and financial support." They could provide facilities and resources for local mobilization events and transportation and scholarships to send young people to Washington. "These are indeed troubled times for most of us, but especially for our youth, who are looking up to us for help and direction. Let's stand with them today so that they stand up by themselves and with us tomorrow."[41]

The NAACP made a major outreach effort for the National Youth Mobilization. James Brown Jr. wrote to numerous organizations and individuals, including those in the YFC and allied organizations. Letters were sent to fraternities and sororities, college and university presidents, and churches. He urged church leaders to have a "Youth Mobilization Sunday," with sermons to address youth voting rights. Brown repeated the suggestions that Wilkins sent to branches for hosting local events and helping youth head to the national one. "Let us resolve to do, within reason, that which is asked of us by our youth and be resolute in whatever we are able to do. I believe that when we stoop to help we walk taller."[42]

The organizers also designed materials and a message to specifically reach young people. The leaflets—"Lower the Voting Age 18"—bumper stickers—"Youth Deserve the Vote 18"—and buttons—"Vote 18"—were fairly standard. But the posters and cover for the "Manual of Instructions" for participants had a countercultural, pop psychedelic look. A flower pattern alluded to hippie "flower power." A mod color scheme of blues, red, and purples and a groovy font added to this style. "Do Your Thing!" headed the poster. Radio spot announcements for the mobilization continued this hip theme. "Youth . . . youth . . . prove you are the NOW generation." "Sock it to 'em. Let 'em know how America's youth feels about lowering the voting age from 21 to 18. . . . Say it loud in Washington DC." "Join the action where it's at. Do your own thing to lower America's voting age."[43]

As the National Youth Mobilization grew near, plans accelerated. Organizers finalized locations for events and sessions, including Hotel America, the Hilton Hotel, the Metropolitan African Methodist Episcopalian Church, and the Senate Auditorium. Wilkins invited congressmen to speak—yes, they were all men—and offer their pledges of support. "Because of the importance of the issue and in support of our firm belief in the democratic process, we ask that you join us in our conference." Each letter was personalized to specify the congressman's state and the number of young citizens planning to attend from that state. The intention was to have one congressman from every region of the country. Although that intention wasn't fulfilled, eleven members of the Senate and the House of Representatives accepted Wilkins's invitation.[44]

Just days before the mobilization conference started, Carolyn Quilloin reported a long list of buses hired for the trip to Washington from cities and states. NAACP youth and allies came on buses from the states of South Carolina and Virginia and from the cities of Birmingham, Boston, Hartford, Philadelphia, Cleveland, Detroit, Chicago, Louisville, and New Orleans.[45] In the end over 40 local and national organizations participated and over 2,000 young people from 33 states attended, including Renny Cushing. Still in high school he enjoyed meeting "so many other young leaders from across the country" and discussing strategies for lowering the voting age. "You could go to the meetings and bring your sleeping bag and you could be part of the conversations and how we're going to do that." "It was pretty wild," he recalls.[46]

On April 21, 1969, the NAACP National Youth Mobilization Conference opened with a packed two-day program. Greetings came from Kivie

NAACP National Youth Mobilization Poster, 1969, group IV, box E18, Folder Youth Mobilization Samples, April 21–29, 1969, NAACP Records. Courtesy of the Library of Congress.

Kaplan, the president of the NAACP, and Roy Wilkins. James Blake gave the opening address, and Ian offered the luncheon address. He explained the purpose of the YFC to "provide coordination, planning, ideas, and support" at the national level for what previously had been "a diluted total effort." "This is how victory will be ours. Working as individuals, properly channeled on one campaign, we can speak to the nation."[47] Paul and Clarence Mitchell provided the legislative overview at the afternoon briefing and strategy session. They were able to convey that the executive committee of the Leadership Conference on Civil Rights had just unanimously endorsed the campaign to lower the voting age to 18.

An evening reception and mass meeting followed. Mitchell's son, Clarence Mitchell III, spoke at the mass meeting held at the historic Metropolitan African Methodist Episcopalian Church. Now a state senator from Maryland, he had been 22 when first elected to the Maryland House of Delegates, making him America's youngest Black legislator. He reminded his audience that even without lowering the voting age their political contributions mattered, especially for voter education and registration. In fact NAACP's Youth and College Division members reported registering voters door-to-door, driving voters to the polls, and babysitting. Mitchell said young people had definitely made a difference in local elections in Baltimore.[48]

The second day of the conference program opened on Capitol Hill, with pledges of support from ten congressmen. To demonstrate bipartisanship the politicians came from both the Republican and Democratic parties and represented states from Massachusetts to Missouri, from Maryland to Michigan. Well-known proponents of youth suffrage Birch Bayh and Jacob Javits spoke, as did newer advocates.

A featured speaker was Senator Edward Brooke, Republican from Massachusetts. "I have long been in favor of legislation to lower the voting age to 18." The first African American to serve in the US Senate in the century since Reconstruction and the first to be popularly elected, Senator Brooke represented the racial progress resulting from the freedom movement. The NAACP publicized Brooke's views in press releases and on its Vote 18 leaflet. "Our young people deserve a voice, and a vote, in the counsels of the nation." He believed they "are in a position to inject new ideas and a new spirit of participation in our government and economy."[49]

The mobilization conference attendees then split into state delegations and set out for several hours of visiting and lobbying their respective members of Congress. Their task was twofold: to find out and record support and opposition for youth suffrage and to present arguments to persuade the opponents. James Brown Jr. reported that these "congressional visits were indeed fruitful. Many congressmen who had been hedging on the lowering the voting age issue came off the fence and offered their pledges of support."[50] These results were forwarded to the YFC, providing "not only its first tally of Congress but also a basis for developing legislative strategy."[51]

Brown and Quilloin chaired the closing session on "Where Do We Go from Here," and Representative Louis Stokes, Democrat from Ohio, offered the final address. Another pathbreaking politician, Stokes was the first African American from Ohio to be elected to Congress. As a lawyer and member of the Cleveland chapter of the NAACP, Stokes had also helped to win a voting rights case around legislative apportionment in Ohio. In offering his concluding remarks on the successful conference, Stokes "took the news media to task" for failing to cover it. Apart from a short advance notice in the *Washington Post*, only the Black press covered the National Youth Mobilization. "There must be something wrong with America," Stokes argued, "when hundreds of youth who are pursuing their aims through the democratic process go unnoticed by the news media." Instead "all the attention must go to young people who threaten to burn down buildings."[52] He was right.

Overshadowing the NAACP's event in the media was a dramatic SDS-led uprising at Harvard University starting on April 9 and lasting until just days before attendees gathered in Washington, DC. Few there—whether protestors, politicians, or the press—would have been paying attention to the NAACP's mobilization conference in April, despite its historic importance in uniting and unleashing the national youth franchise movement. Coalition building and lobbying Congress lacked the drama of campus conflict, but it also lacked the divisiveness, and organizers hoped the strategy would prove effective. As it turned out, the movement, or at least its aims, did not go unnoticed at Harvard. The next month a group of 275 Harvard students sent a letter to the editor of the *New York Times* calling for the 18-year-old vote in "view of the growing radicalism on college campuses."[53]

James Brown Jr. and the other organizers agreed that their National Youth Mobilization was "highly successful in every aspect except press attention." Brown also affirmed that those in attendance challenged the press stereotype of young Americans spurred by uprisings like those at Columbia, San Francisco State, and Harvard. "I am more than pleased to report that not one major incident marred the good name of NAACP or disrupted our conference."[54] Carolyn Quilloin knew where the credit belonged. "Many organizations do a lot of rabble-rousing about the issues. But when it comes down to getting something done, the NAACP is always on the front line seeking meaningful results." She added, "This was only the beginning." In addition to the NAACP's work at the national level, Youth and College Division members "will follow through on local and state levels to insure the passage of Vote 18 bills at those levels."[55]

Turning to the States

The NAACP's 1969 mobilization conference demonstrated the new youth voting rights coalition in action. "Never before in the history of this country has so much power been massed in support of the 18-year-old vote," Ian noted.[56] On the second day of the conference, April 22, he highlighted additional achievements when the YFC board of directors met. They had incorporated the YFC and a second entity, the Youth Citizenship Fund. While the YFC was explicitly political in order to lobby for the 18-year-old vote, the Youth Citizenship Fund would raise money for programs to educate and register the soon-to-be enfranchised young voters. Already in early 1969 "we were so cocky that we were going to be successful," Paul says.[57] Ian reported another early accomplishment. "We have done something in every state even if it is just defined interested individuals" in those states.[58]

The states at the time were sites of unprecedented action on the voting age. New organizations dedicated to the issue were popping up everywhere, and legislation was pending in 38 states. Since June 1968 every state except Mississippi had taken up or studied the issue. In contrast, over the previous six years nearly half the states hadn't even considered it. Ohio and New Jersey approved referenda to go before the voters in November. Ohio's proposed constitutional amendment would lower the voting age to 19, while New Jersey's would go to 18. And many more states had moved or were moving to put similar measures before voters in 1970. Alaska and Hawaiʻi were looking at lowering their ages for voting to 18, while Wyoming and Montana had already approved referenda for a 19-year-old vote.

Proponents who had worked on earlier state-level efforts and campaigns had good news to report. Connecticut's Interim Commission to Study the Qualifications of Electors, set up in 1967, issued its report and recommended a voting age of 18. Along with being a member of the study committee, Edward J. Forand of Yale University and Let's Vote—the Connecticut Committee for the 18-Year-old Vote (or Let's Vote 18)—helped to draft the legislation. His prognosis was good for positive action in 1969.[59]

North Carolina state representative Jim Beatty offered a similar forecast. "The public is more conscious of the issue and there is increasing sentiment for it," he observed. In his opinion circumstances had changed since his bill failed in 1967 when he had collaborated with Duke University students in the Voting Age Council of North Carolina.[60] One major change was the Vote 18 campaigning coming from NAACP college chapters. The UNC–Chapel Hill chapter circulated a petition calling for North Carolina's representatives in Congress to support a US constitutional amendment. A uniform national voting age would address problems that "arise when a person leaves a state with a lower voting age and comes to a state where the age is 21," commented chapter president Kelly Alexander. "I know at least three students here from Georgia who have voted in elections down there. But when they come up here and find out they can't vote, they feel like they are cut off from the entire political process." "18–21 year olds want to vote and to participate in the political process," Alexander confirmed.[61]

"There has been more state action in 1969 than ever before," Paul Minarchenko told a reporter in April. The YFC "can't take credit for that happening. But it does indicate a climate of receptiveness that we can build on."[62]

12

Where It's At!

Many Americans agreed that the political climate at the end of the 1960s was receptive to lowering the voting age. One challenge was moving elected officials at the federal and state levels from receptive to responsive to results. Another challenge was winning over state referendum voters. As young proponents had discovered in earlier state campaigns, politicians more often offered support than took action, and the adult electorate more often rejected than approved referenda. "There's a disfranchised group of people frozen out, and no one inside to let them in," commented the chief counsel for Birch Bayh's Senate subcommittee.[1] Proponents understood that the way to change this situation was by demonstrating the deservingness and desire of young Americans for the right to vote and to do so through political organization and action.

What was needed was a movement "mobilizing the youth of this country into a powerful force seeking the right to vote," as Youth Franchise Coalition executive director Ian MacGowan put it in May 1969.[2] The YFC was doing its part at the national level, and many, many young Americans were doing their parts at the local and state levels. Around the country, from coast to coast, campus and community groups were organized and energized to achieve the 18-year-old vote. These groups, together with the affiliates and chapters of the YFC and its member organizations, like NEA and the NAACP, created a movement. Like all movements this one encompassed a multiplicity of groups and organizations pursuing the same goal but with their own strategies within their state and local contexts. This multiplicity gave the youth franchise movement visibility and vitality—even if few immediate victories—in this final phase leading up to success.

The Case of California

"I think the time is right for the 18-year-old vote and California is the cutting-edge," stated Tom Hipple, YFC's acting executive director before

Ian MacGowan was hired. Over the 1960s California became the state with the largest population in the nation, surpassing New York. If the state acted to lower the voting age to 18, over a million Californians would gain the right to vote and America's youth vote might matter. Signs were improving for such action. Californians had lagged behind the nation in support for youth suffrage. In 1967 when 64 percent of Americans supported the 18-year-old vote, 53 percent of Californians wanted to keep the voting age at 21. Between 1967 and 1969 public opinion in the state changed to majority support for a lower voting age, although 20 was more popular than 19 or 18.[3]

Hipple's statement also owed much to the swift expansion of Let Us Vote from the University of the Pacific in Stockton. Ian described it as "sensational."[4] "L.U.V. is where you find it," trumpeted UoP's newspaper in early 1969. "And where it's at!"[5] LUV was only one of many single-issue groups working in California to lower the voting age, alongside multi-issue organizations like the Young Democrats, Student CTA, and the YWCA. Citizens for Lowering the Voting Age had been active for several years before LUV arrived on the scene.

State chairman Dennis King discovered the voting age issue in his first year at Foothill College in the Los Altos Hills. It was the fall of 1966, and a chance meeting with the president of his freshman class got him interested in the issue. He'd already felt "a direct emotional connection to civil rights and the pursuit of justice." Later he would take part in the consumer grape boycott in support of Filipino American and Mexican American farmworkers in the United Farm Workers and meet César Chávez. He also was an early opponent of the Vietnam War. "I was still in high school but all of a sudden the war didn't make any sense; it didn't seem to add up right." Strengthening his opposition was the death of a very close friend in the war. At Foothill College Dennis volunteered to head up a student committee on lowering the voting age, which started him on a journey lasting over half a decade. He never looked back.[6]

"Technically I was a student, but I was very, very involved in the Vote 18 movement." He became a student government officer and eventually served as student body president, which "tended to become an extension of my lowering the voting age efforts." With the support of the college administration and advisers he hosted a youth suffrage conference that drew some 600 students. He also visited over 80 colleges in the state, and those contacts "became the backbone of the Vote 18 campaign when we kicked it into gear." He then took a year off from college to work full-time on the California campaign. Giving speeches raised public awareness and much-needed funding. As happened elsewhere, student governments and clubs, civic organizations, and unions donated. More uniquely to California, local bands, like Santana, donated proceeds from concerts, and *Rolling Stone* magazine helped get the word out. Dennis's commitment to the campaign reflected his dedication to democratic decision making. "One of the first questions in any kind of democratic decision making is who is entitled to be participating? Who's in, who's not in?"[7]

Dennis and Citizens for Lowering the Voting Age seized every opportunity to get young Californians in, pursuing a flexible, multifaceted strategy over time. To start they sought to "influence the influencers" in government and at the grassroots. "We'd talk with and try to understand where key people were on this issue," Dennis explains, "and understand if they weren't in a supportive position what did we need to do to move them to be in support, and if they were supportive how do we move them to commit to action."[8] At the same time they worked on legislation—lobbying and speaking at hearings—to lower the voting age in the state constitution. From 1947 to 1969 such legislation had been proposed in California some 30 times, with little progress.

They collaborated with several "influencers" like Monroe Sweetland who were committed, consistent proponents of youth suffrage. State Senator George Moscone from San Francisco and Assemblyman John Vasconcellos from San Jose proposed multiple bills to enfranchise California's youth, although at what age—18 or 19—varied. In 1969 Vasconcellos identified the contradiction inherent in opponents' position that youth protests were a reason to reject voting age proposals. "We condemn their civil disobedience, and tell them to change the laws instead. Yet we deny them access to the voting booth, the law-changer, the foundation of democracy."[9] "Giving them the right to vote is one of the most singularly important things we can do," Moscone said the same year. "It would be a clear admission on our part, on the part of the Establishment, that we realize times have changed."[10] Falling short of the required two-thirds majority for a constitutional amendment, Moscone's third Senate proposal ended in defeat on April 9, 1969.

That same day, the West Coast version of the NAACP National Mobilization to Lower the Voting Age took place. The national organizers recognized that not everyone could make the long trek to Washington, DC, and encouraged local mobilizations in state capitals. The West Coast region of the NAACP hosted one in Sacramento, which drew 200 young participants from California and Nevada. NAACP youth members spoke and presented a petition at an Assembly committee hearing. They lobbied legislators and held briefing sessions with state officials and a rally at the State Capitol building. A banner headline with a photo of the rally appeared in the *Sacramento Observer*, heralding the "Lower Voting Age Drive." The *Sacramento Union* provided good coverage as well, indicating that local events drew local media more easily than the equivalent at the national level. NAACP organizers deemed the event an overall success.[11]

Monroe Sweetland also spoke at the Assembly hearing on April 9, something he had done the year before and would do again. Picking up on a point put forward in 1968, Sweetland differentiated young proponents of lowering the voting age from their more radical peers. Youth suffrage would "help defuse the nihilists and direct actionists" and support those who believed in "orderly processes of decision-making."[12] Out of these efforts and campaigning, California's Assembly legislated a study of the voting age as part of lowering the state's age of majority, with a report and recommendations expected in 1970.

Given the slow pace of the legislative process and the difficulty of winning a two-thirds majority in both the Assembly and the Senate, the initiative remained another important strategy for proponents in California. Attempted four times before, the initiative got another big push in 1969–1970. Independent Voters for Vote Extension (INVOLVE) needed 520,276 signatures by April 6, 1970, to put the 18-year-old vote on the ballot. Given the size of the state and the number of signatures, they needed to recruit an estimated 40,000 people to circulate the petitions. Proponents worked in coalition across California to achieve this challenging goal.[13]

In the process INVOLVE and Citizens for Lowering the Voting Age encountered a major problem with their initiative plan. "You have to be a voter in order to ask voters to sign petitions," Dennis King points out. "Here we are trying to get people to sign a petition to lower the voting age to 18, and you have to be at least be 21 at the time and a registered voter" to both sign and circulate a petition. They launched a lawsuit in federal court contesting these qualifications for petition circulators. Denise Puishes and Sharon Guerrero sued the Santa Clara County registrar, asserting a "personal political right" to circulate petitions to obtain the vote. After all it was the signatures that mattered, and they would be from registered voters. California proponents also tried a second route. As Dennis says ironically, "I now need to introduce legislation to lower the petition age on petitions to lower the voting age." With the crucial help of Moscone and Vasconcellos, the legislation "passed, barely, but it passed."[14]

"We had another hurdle. It also had to get signed by the governor, who was Ronald Reagan. And he'd already been vigorously against lowering the voting age." Vigorous was one way to characterize Reagan's opposition; vehement was another. On lowering the age of petition circulators he agreed to give young people a chance and signed the legislation. But his opposition to youth voting rights would last, and last longer than most public officeholders. To understand why is to know Reagan's political purpose. His candidacy, election in 1966, and governance constituted a conservative backlash against liberalism and many of the decade's developments.

Topping Reagan's agenda was taking a hard line against militant student activists, but he also undermined young moderates. In 1969 he disparaged mostly liberal student government officers as not "representative of their respective student bodies," given low voter turnout on college campuses. And "he couldn't imagine apathetic students suddenly rushing out and voting in national elections."[15] Both assertions undercut California's voting age campaign. Proponents in student government needn't be listened to, and 18- to 20-year-olds didn't use the franchise they already had, so why expand it?

Monroe Sweetland criticized the governor for this stance. In a 1969 letter to the editor he objected to Reagan's reasons for opposing youth suffrage. If the problem was militant student protest on California's campuses, then "democratic American methods should be the way these issues are solved. Our governor aids the anarchist elements by this unreasoned hostility to ballots of young adults." Cutting off constructive political action would only catalyze the destructive kind. "His vehemence and contrived rationale lead to the suspicion that he really fears how they might vote on him."[16]

How young Californians might vote still seemed like a long way off when proponents got started on the fourth and final facet of their campaign in the state: litigation. Alongside the lawsuit challenging the age of petition circulators they filed a voting age lawsuit. Again Denise Puishes was the plaintiff, and the Santa Clara County registrar the defendant. Attorney John Cosgrove prepared both cases pro bono. "He was volunteering his energy and his talent to help us," Dennis recalls. These cases were in the name of the plaintiffs and on behalf of a larger "class of persons." To advance the litigation process research help from Stanford University students was sought on 19 different topics, from the history of draft laws to statistics on young people's participation in VISTA and the Peace Corps.[17]

The goal was to bring a voting age case of such national significance that it would get to the Supreme Court. "Although we knew it was a long-shot," Dennis admits, "we wanted to start that process." They were inspired by the freedom movement. "How do you make change in this country?" Looking at cases like *Brown v. Board of Education* (1954), it was clear that major successes had come through the courts, particularly with the 14th Amendment. "In that spirit, if it worked in the civil rights movement and the Vote 18 campaign is an extension of the civil rights movement, let's see if we can apply that here."[18]

Like the lawyers in Jane Greenspun's case, Cosgrove crafted an argument based on the Equal Protection Clause in the 14th Amendment. He did not cite Janie's case, which was heard, dismissed, and now on appeal in 1969. But Cosgrove did cite two additional legal precedents. In *Carrington v. Rash* (1965) and *Kramer v. Union Free School District No. 15* (1969), the Supreme Court held the Equal Protection Clause—in the absence of "compelling state interest"—applicable to state and local suffrage laws. "Elaborate qualifications for voters are incompatible with our nation's commitment to full and equal participation in political life," Cosgrove argued. Californians, aged 18, 19, and 20, "are not entitled to less equal protection than others." Puishes's case was dismissed in District Court without a hearing as "frivolous and insubstantial" in late 1969.[19] But John Cosgrove soon had an appeal in the works, and similar litigation was in process across the country in New York.

The States of New York and Connecticut

Attention gravitated to New York as much as to California. With New York's large population, achieving the 18-year-old vote would mean an estimated 900,000 new voters. After the defeat of youth suffrage at the state's 1967 constitutional convention, new single-issue organizations emerged. The biggest and best known was Citizens for Vote 18, which affiliated with the Youth Franchise Coalition. Working for a voting age of 18 both for New York and for the nation, Citizens for Vote 18 maintained a Washington legislative bureau, directed by Jim Chiswell. He emphasized that their "ultimate goal is lowering voting ages across the country so that 18 year olds can vote for all elective offices; but I recognize that the process of legislation is one of compromise." Executive Director Bruce J. Marsh, just 21, expressed more hope for victory in New York as "it is highly unlikely there will ever be a national groundswell for national action."[20]

Jim Pugash, 18, youth director of Citizens for Vote 18, explained their state campaign strategy in a 1969 interview. Their primary focus was legislative, so they were lobbying the state legislature. Like the Youth Franchise Coalition and especially NEA they also pursued a program of public education. They wrote to high school history and English departments suggesting classroom discussions and debates around youth voting rights and sought to sponsor a statewide essay contest in cooperation with popular radio stations. "We're going to have to do a tremendous selling job to prove . . . that the average eighteen-year-old is deserving of the right to vote," Pugash stated. "And the best way we can do this is by running an orderly campaign."[21]

Based in Buffalo, as Marsh and others attended the State University of New York there, Citizens for Vote 18 worked hard to encompass the entire state. In 1969 they held a New York state strategy conference at Syracuse University and invited all groups participating in the campaign. They planned a series of rallies in support of the 18-year-old vote, starting with one in Rochester. The mayor of Rochester issued a proclamation for "Vote 18 Day." In speeches a state senator and a city councilman told young people in the audience that success "depends entirely on your ability to convince the rest of us" they deserved the vote and "keeping the pressure on." Governor Nelson Rockefeller sent a statement of support.[22]

Rockefeller's support set New York apart from California. Like Reagan Rockefeller was a Republican, but he was a liberal not a conservative Republican. He had long supported lowering the voting age to 18, and his statements featured in NAACP and Project 18 publicity. In February 1969, for the first time, he did more than state his support. He proposed a state constitutional amendment and pressed for its passage "to bring our young people into a positive participation in the democratic process."[23] Rockefeller's effort had the backing of the *New York Times*, expressed in an extended water-inspired metaphor. The "good of the nation as well as its youth will be served if extension of the franchise channels this potent reservoir of fresh perception and idealism into the often stagnant mainstream of American political life."[24] As with other states New York required constitutional amendments to be approved by two different legislatures and by referendum voters, so this channeling would take some time.

Over the next months proponents focused on lobbying the state legislature in Albany. The Consolidated Association to Lower the Voting Age (CALVA) featured in a *New Yorker* article in April 1969. "These rules make altruists of the present members of CALVA" because they would be enfranchised anyway by the time any constitutional amendment took effect, a description that fit many in the youth franchise movement. One 19-year-old altruist, CALVA chairman Larry Douglas, postponed his sophomore year at Long Island University to work as a legislative aide that year. Asked how long he'd been in politics, Douglas responded. "'Let's see, I coordinated my public school for John Kennedy in 1960, when I was eleven,' he said. 'I guess I've been in politics eight years now. I hate to say it.' He sighed deeply, apparently feeling his age."[25]

Despite the lobbying of CALVA, Citizens for Vote 18, and other organizations, Rockefeller's proposal did not progress. "I deeply regret that the Legislature did not see fit to enact it." He remained hopeful for action in 1970, but the Republican leader of the Senate quickly rebuffed the governor. "I don't think its chances look too favorable." And he would not be supporting it himself for a "whole cafeteria of reasons," including "irritation" at the attitudes and actions of youthful protestors.[26]

With the legislative strategy stymied, proponents in New York turned to litigation. Aware of the *Puishes* case in California, they advanced a similar legal argument based on the 14th Amendment. Taking the lead on litigation in New York was another local group, the WMCA Vote at 18 Club. WMCA was New York City's most influential and innovative radio station at the time. Independently owned by Straus Communications and headed by R. Peter Straus, WMCA played rock and roll and became prominent for promoting the Beatles. A longtime Democrat, Straus added a public service role for the station, airing editorials and establishing the Vote at 18 Club. "We want to be broadcasters, but we want to make a difference," he later said. He, WMCA, and others had already made a difference. In 1961 they filed a reapportionment lawsuit in federal court to provide fairer representation for cities in New York. The case fostered the "one person, one vote" doctrine to come in *Reynolds v. Sims* (1964).[27]

The *WMCA Vote at 18 Club* case constituted a class action, as did the California petition and voting age cases. Directed against several New York state and local officials, including the attorney general, the complaint makes a clear argument highlighting intentional discrimination. "By purposeful plan, embodied in the State Constitution and implemented by statute, to discriminate against those citizens 18 years of age but not yet 21 years of age, and to deny them the Equal Protection of the laws, plaintiffs are denied rights guaranteed them by the Federal Constitution." The fact that citizens under 21 years of age could vote for president in other states also led to potential violations of recent "one person, one vote" decisions.[28] This injustice caught the attention of proponents in 1969. "A new argument is that under the recent one man-one vote ruling by the Supreme Court, 18-to-21-year-olds in states not permitting them to vote are being deprived of rights their counterparts in Kentucky, Georgia, Alaska and Hawaii have," reported the College Press Service.[29]

Litigation proceeded slowly but no more slowly than the legislative process, even when pushed by active campaigners as the case of Connecticut showed. From the work of VOTES starting in the first half of the 1960s to Let's Vote 18 in the second half, young people in the state had kept the pressure on. Real progress came in 1969. At the forefront Edward J. Forand still chaired Let's Vote 18 and also organized a new group. The Caucus of Connecticut Democrats, formed by supporters of the McCarthy campaign, established a youth suffrage committee, which he headed.

Like other state-level proponents, Forand, Let's Vote, and their allies used every political tactic and tool available. For example, at the six public hearings held by the Interim Commission to Study the Qualifications of Electors starting in 1967 Let's Vote set up a telephone network to get students to the hearings. When "there were over 200 at some of the hearings," Forand said, "the leadership in Connecticut figured we were too big to ignore anymore." Similarly, on February 5, 1969, the Constitutional Amendments Committee held its final public hearing before voting to send the proposed amendment to the General Assembly. About 500 students crowded into the Capitol to cheer on Forand and others. "In some sense this was the culmination of our whole two years of work," he said.[30]

But then the proposed amendment sat in committee without a vote for five and a half weeks. "Needless to say we're pretty worried," Forand told the *Moderator*. To get the process moving again Let's Vote 18 planned to put pressure on individual committee members and then, if needed, organize a letter-writing campaign. Finally they had a way to "put the local legislators on the spot." In the lead-up to the November 1968 election Let's Vote 18, together with the Connecticut League of Women Voters, had polled 242 candidates for both houses of the General Assembly. They found that three-fourths favored the 18-year-old vote. The day before the election they took out a full-page ad, listed all those candidates by name, and thanked them for their support. "We plan to make sure they stick to their word," Forand promised.[31]

They did stick to their word, as it turned out. In the spring of 1969, by massive bipartisan majorities, the Connecticut House of Representatives (153 to 17) and then the Senate (29 to 1) passed the proposed amendment. The state's referendum voters still needed to have their say in November 1970. And not all "yea" votes meant approval. A Republican senator voted for the proposal "just to place it before the people. But I hope it will be defeated, and it will be no great loss!" A Democratic senator voted for it "with great reluctance" because of the "conduct" of some young people. "They will have to prove to the people in the next two years that they deserve this right."[32]

Proponents didn't let these attitudes take away from their achievement. "I am tremendously pleased," exclaimed Forand. The proposal's passage was "the only way to begin creating a sense of trust between generations." Looking ahead, Forand laid out the plan to pass the referendum. "We are now going to be organizing an extensive grassroots campaign, a youth lobby to the people, to persuade the public in the next year and a half to vote for the proposal."[33] They formed the Connecticut Citizen Coalition to campaign for the referendum. Sharing the coalition leadership with Forand were two of the state's foremost politicians, Secretary of State Ella Grasso, a Democrat, and John Alsop of the Republican National Committee.[34] They opened offices in Hartford and New Haven and aimed for outreach to 160 towns. Forand hoped to have young people in every town going door to door talking up the issue. Winning would mean their voices had been heard. "Where they will go from there—who knows? The sky's the limit."[35]

The Connecticut campaign provided "a good case study," contended the *Moderator's* reporter in April 1969. It definitely provided a good case study of patience and persistence on the part of proponents. They demonstrated flexibility and a willingness to "try everything," as Les Francis had urged. Of course it wasn't over yet, and even if successful Connecticut was only one state. Still "it could be crucial to the success of the national campaign," Forand remarked. "I'd like to see a national campaign succeed, but I think a couple of other states are going to have to go first as a kind of catalyst."[36] With referenda in November, the states set to go first were New Jersey and Ohio.

Vote 18 New Jersey and Vote 19 Ohio

In the spring of 1969 the state legislatures in New Jersey and Ohio approved amendments to their state constitutions, which would now go before the voters. The votes in the Ohio Senate and House of Representatives and the New Jersey Senate were strongly in favor, but drama arose in the New Jersey Assembly. After initially pledging their support members of the Republican Assembly caucus abstained or voted against the proposed amendment in an early vote. "It was very disappointing after trusting all these people to have them turn around and lie to you," stated Chris Muzikar, a student at Paul Minarchenko's alma mater, Newark State College, and local chairman of the Voting Age Coalition of New Jersey. This sudden turn of events infuriated Muzikar. "The defeat of the 18-year-old vote creates dissent and downright frustration among young people against the so-called system of American Democracy," he fumed.[37] Less than two weeks later the Republican caucus switched back to support, giving the proposed amendment the votes needed.

At issue among Assembly Republicans in New Jersey was not the question of lowering the voting age but to what age—18 or 19? This question stirred discussion and debate across the country, with different results depending on the state. The Ohio General Assembly went with 19, as did others. By age 19, advocates argued, young people now had a year of experience in the world beyond high school, either in college or in the workforce, and had grown more independent. National proponents in the Youth Franchise Coalition and its member organizations disagreed. The voting age had to be 18.

Les Francis made this argument as director of NEA's Project 18. In March 1969, just as legislative proponents in his own state of California and elsewhere were proposing the 19-year-old vote, Les wrote a letter to the editor of the *Los Angeles Times* and other newspapers around the country. "It is therefore essential to restate the case for the 18-year-old vote, to point out that 18 is the only logical turning point." By that age the majority of Americans have graduated from high school and, as had been argued earlier, that three-year gap until voting "is a devastating one." Even more, 18 "is the year for three most decisive adult responsibilities—marriage, responsibility under criminal law, and military service." Granting that age markers and their meanings were mutable, the voting age line had to be drawn somewhere and justified. "While the age 19 may seem attractive to some as a political compromise," Les concluded, "it cannot be supported by logical argument."[38]

As it turned out Les did have to make the case for the 19-year-old vote. When Project 18 and the YFC decided to contribute to the two state campaigns ongoing in 1969, he went to help Vote 19 in Ohio, while Ian MacGowan aided Vote 18 in New Jersey. "So in addition to work on the federal piece, we were commuting to those two states to help organize."[39] Despite seeking different voting ages the New Jersey and Ohio referendum campaigns shared a lot of features, including, in the end, failure.

Student-led coalitions were at the forefront of both campaigns. Ohio Volunteers for Vote 19 (Vote 19) and the Voting Age Coalition of New Jersey (VAC) were grassroots groups with local leadership. Clark W.

Wideman, an Ohio State University student and former leader of the Ohio Young Republicans, and Pat Keefer directed Vote 19. "We had been involved in state campaigns in our respective political parties," Pat recalls, so they provided bipartisan leadership.[40] David DuPell, Stuart Goldstein, and Ken Norbe, students at Rider, Trenton State, and Glassboro State colleges, respectively, founded and led VAC. For Stuart the 18-year-old vote movement was a logical extension of the work he'd been doing with CUE, the student activist group from Paul's college days. "We would go to class in the morning, change into suits in the afternoon and go down to Trenton to lobby the legislators," he remembers. They gained respect for being able "to work with great effectiveness within the political system," editorialized the *Trenton Times*.[41]

The YFC did what it could. Charles Koppelman, who had just graduated from high school, volunteered with the YFC that summer. "Whether it was pressure or support with their congressional delegation or giving those states materials for a national perspective which helped their cause, we would do all of that."[42] YFC staff also held organizational meetings in both states to foster contact and cooperation among local proponents. They encouraged the formation of adult "citizens committees" to advise and augment student leadership. Reliable proponents, like Representative James J. Howard, participated in these committees. Through the *YFC Bulletin* and letters, they kept YFC member organizations updated and asked for assistance. "The future of the 18-year-old vote issue in many other states and in the U.S. Congress depends, to a great extent, on the outcome," Paul wrote to the YMCA–National Student Caucus coordinator. Any support—financial, staffing, or in-kind services like printing—would help.[43]

Organizing for Ohio and New Jersey state campaigns was widely shared, with student and adult proponents collaborating. Cities, counties, high schools, and college campuses had their own Vote 19 and VAC committees and allied organizations. The aim in New Jersey, according to Stuart, was to have a VAC chair in each of the 21 counties and 535 municipalities and recruit young people to lobby in their localities.[44] Invaluable and innovative local leadership had a statewide impact. As just one example, Terry Lee, a social studies teacher at Tippecanoe High School in Tipp City, Ohio, advised the local committee, led by 17-year-old Susan Robinson. In 1968 Lee's students started working on a class project to lower the voting age. They conducted research, wrote letters, secured tens of thousands of signatures for a petition, put together information packets, issued press releases, and spoke before the Ohio Senate Election Committee. After pressing for the referendum they now sought to get it passed, with crucial funding from the local Jaycees.[45] Proponents, including educators and the founders of VAC, had long believed youth suffrage would spur curriculum changes; Lee changed the curriculum to spur youth suffrage.

In these ways the Ohio and New Jersey referendum campaigns had all the hallmarks of the youth franchise movement as a whole. Ohio's Vote 19 and New Jersey's VAC had support from multiple organizations, including those in the YFC. The Ohio Education Association, the New Jersey Education Association, and their student affiliates greatly contributed, as did groups like the Coalition for Action to Save Education in Ohio and CUE in New Jersey. The AFL-CIO made a difference, particularly in Ohio. According to Pat Keefer, "the labor unions saw that having 18 to 21-year-olds able to vote was something that was necessary for their constituency of working families."[46] The campaigns successfully solicited endorsements from Democrats and Republicans at every level of government, including their governors. The New Jersey State Youth Commission endorsed, as did the Campus Ministry Association at Ohio State. At Ohio University in Athens, student and Vote 19 campus coordinator Rita Coriell convinced the Interfraternity Government to endorse as part of starting "to take a more meaningful stand on relevant issues today."[47]

Proponents also used a variety of strategies. They held rallies and circulated posters and pamphlets, buttons and bumper stickers. Stuart wrote and designed VAC's brochure, which featured six presidents on the cover, from FDR to Nixon. With this presidential iconography VAC aimed to convey "credibility and continuity." "The leaders of our country have all thought that young people should be involved and full participants in the democracy. We thought that approach would be more effective than us talking for ourselves," he explained. Campaigners made phone calls and went door-to-door to poll opinions and persuade any undecided voters. Students raised money at bake sales and football games. VAC gained $10,000 in funding from a one-dollar membership fee. They pressed for favorable media coverage and wrote opinion pieces and letters to the editors of mainstream and campus newspapers. "The dailies didn't always print it but the weeklies ate it up," Stuart remarks.[48] VAC planned an Election Day "strike force" to get out voters and help with transportation and babysitting.

And throughout this organizing they made arguments. They offered all the usual arguments about the maturity, education, political awareness, civic participation, military service, wage earning, tax paying, and adult legal status of Americans aged 18, 19, and 20. Expanding and ensuring American democracy was another reason. "We had a shared vision that young Americans be allowed to fully participate in our society, our economy, and public decision making," Stuart recalls. Voting rights was one of many "rights we felt were being denied young people."[49] Although it was losing favor at the national level the foundational argument remained prominent in these campaigns. Back in February Birch Bayh had told YFC members, "I personally don't think the strongest intellectual argument is 'If you're old enough to fight, you're old enough to vote.'" One reporter referred to it as a "hack" argument.[50]

Several factors had contributed to this development. Les Francis remembers that Project 18 and the YFC "didn't use it as a campaign message because we didn't want the 18 year old vote to be a referendum on the war—to be a proxy of approval or disapproval of the war."[51] The fairness of matching the voting and draft ages also had never justified the right to vote for all young people. This was even truer in 1969, with the vast majority of young Americans, male and female, not serving in the military, a vocal minority actively opposing the war, and women not drafted in any case. Finally the Nixon administration was in the midst of reforming the draft. The long-term goal was an all-volunteer military. But in the short run a national lottery system, instituted later in the year, would make the draft a somewhat fairer process. President Nixon hoped this reform would lessen antiwar protests.

Of course the slogan "old enough to fight, old enough to vote" was never the complete statement of the foundational argument, which focused on balancing citizenship rights and responsibilities. That balance is what the Ohio and New Jersey referendum campaigns sought. "They have earned the right and responsibility," stated a Vote 19 pamphlet. Stuart's pamphlet from the New Jersey campaign quoted President Abraham Lincoln: "I go for all sharing the privileges of the government who assist in bearing its

New Jersey Vote 18 and Ohio Vote 19 campaign pamphlets, 1969. © 2020, Rutgers, The State University of New Jersey, and courtesy of Patricia Keefer.

burdens."[52] This balance encompassed all the many citizenship responsibilities young American bore, with military service the most momentous.

For citizens in New Jersey and Ohio the foundational argument still proved poignant and persuasive. In New Jersey a UAW leader reminded listeners at a State Senate hearing that the majority of Americans who had died in the "foolhardy war" in Vietnam were under 21.[53] Susan Burchfield, cochair of the Ohio State Vote 19 Committee, similarly reminded her readers. "Keep in mind that of all the Ohio boys killed in Viet Nam, 51% were under 21. Isn't it about time we give their peers the vote?"[54] Of seven high school students interviewed by the *Cincinnati Enquirer* a few weeks before the November 4 election, five cited the foundational argument in support of the Vote 19 referendum. Like all male high school seniors 17-year-old John Nortman was facing the draft. "I can't help but think about the poor guys in Vietnam fighting for a country they don't even have the right to vote in," Nortman said. "People think it would be a disaster to let all 19-year-olds vote, but the 19-year-olds don't start the wars."[55]

In addition to older arguments, a new argument came from Jerry Springer, the future tabloid talk show host. The 25-year-old Springer, "a dynamo of nervous energy," had taken time off from his legal career to coordinate the Vote 19 campaign in Cincinnati. He rejected the safety-valve argument in the process of distinguishing militant from moderate young people. Instead of the vote providing an outlet for youth protest, it would offer a means of expression for the non-protestors. The "2% that protest and riot—it is only they who have a political voice. The time has come to offer the young silent American, the 98%, a political voice also."[56] Springer's use of "silent" anticipated by a few weeks President Nixon's famous call to the conservative "silent majority" of Americans. Springer's argument may have been expected to play well in Ohio, a state that fell into the Republican column in 1968 and where over 10 percent of voters favored the racial reactionary George Wallace.

"In conservative Ohio, it is going to be a close race," Susan Burchfield predicted, and she was right.[57] State Issue 1 lost by only 1 percent in Ohio, although Public Question No. 2 lost overwhelmingly by 18 percent in New Jersey. For proponents at the state and national levels these defeats were not just disappointing but demoralizing. "Don't adults have faith in young people?" asked local Vote 19 leader Susan Robinson.[58] More accusing of adults were the cochairmen of VAC at Newark State College. "I have lost a great amount of respect for the 'older generation,'" asserted Dave Lichtenstein. "I feel that those over twenty-one have widened the generation gap by their outright refusal to give the vote to their own children," argued Tony Levi. Both warned of the consequences. "Right or wrong, for many students, this was the last attempt to work within the system."[59]

Vote 18 and Vote 19 campaign leaders presented a more positive front. "The resolve is there," VAC's Dave DuPell contended. "It's just a matter of time until we can convince the voters of our cause. We are not pessimistic." In Ohio Clark Wideman concurred. "We can only go up, and we're just about one percent away from victory." A reporter for the College Press Service observed that "in traditional good-loser political style, organizers of the campaigns refuse to admit discouragement."[60]

But they did begin to analyze the failure, together with Project 18 and YFC. Some reasons for failure could have happened in any political campaign. They didn't have enough money to campaign effectively. Their prominent political supporters, like the governors, didn't help with fundraising or actively campaign for the referenda. New Jersey officials in both parties conceded these points but "emphasized that the drive primarily benefited young people, and that it was up to them to make it succeed."[61] Low voter turnout among key constituencies was also a factor. In Hamilton County, Ohio, for example, over 70 percent of African American voters supported the Vote 19 referendum, but turnout was low in this off-year election.[62] Proponents believed residency requirements—a suffrage qualification just then at the Supreme Court in *Hall v. Beals* (1969)—suppressed voter turnout among college students aged 21 and up.

Other reasons for failure were specific to youth franchise campaigns. The voting age question got confused and complicated with the age of majority, as was happening in California's current study of the two issues. It was for this reason that the *Columbus Dispatch* came out against Vote 19: "The matter should have been submitted in better form, clearly defining the other rights it would grant to 19-year-olds."[63] Partisanship may have motivated Republicans to vote against the referenda. Polling in New Jersey by the Federation of Republican Women found Democrats outnumbering Republicans among college and high school students, buttressing the idea that the future youth vote would benefit Democrats.[64]

An editorial in Ohio University's campus newspaper offered another familiar reason for failure. Voters "feared a political takeover by the radical left."[65] As in the 1968 Nebraska campaign the effort to convince referendum voters they had nothing to fear from the vast majority of young adults in New Jersey and Ohio appeared to have fallen flat. Making this effort more difficult had been the disintegration of SDS into two revolutionary factions in June 1969. These minority factions excluded most SDS members, the majority of the new left, and of course everyone else. But calls for revolution grabbed attention and gave opponents of youth suffrage another counterargument. Even nonviolent protest against the war—if it led to acts of violence—could do the same. This threat posed a dilemma for proponents, given their own antiwar positions and politics. And concurrent with the Vote 18 and Vote 19 campaigns was the largest and most significant demonstration of the war.

The Moratorium to End the War in Vietnam on October 15, 1969, drew an estimated two million participants into nonviolent protests across the country. The unremitting American war in Vietnam had recorded another 10,000 Americans and many more Vietnamese dead, despite a new president who'd promised a change in policy. The Moratorium showed a vast antiwar sentiment among a diversity of Americans. "It couldn't be at a worse time," Clark Wideman feared. "I am personally opposed to the Moratorium because publicity from it may be bad," and then "Vote 19 is dead." His codirector Pat Keefer felt very differently, and she took part. "These were not left-wing radicals. They were students, veterans, mothers and fathers."[66] But concern was real that violence could hijack the day's and subsequent events. VAC also asked New Jersey students "not to cause any trouble" and hoped the Vietnam Moratorium "will pass without any incidents of violence that could antagonize the voters."[67]

Whether or not such antagonism toward activism and protest motivated voters to reject the 1969 referenda is hard to ascertain. Still addressing such antagonism while holding true to their antiwar convictions would remain a high priority going forward. Proponents in Ohio, New Jersey, and other states as well as Project 18 and YFC were not giving in or giving up. "Although we lost the elections on Tuesday," Ian MacGowan told the YFC membership, "we gained valuable experience."[68] They would be employing that experience at the national and state levels in the first year of the new decade, the youth franchise movement's most consequential year.

PART IV

"Come on and let us vote—it's a solution"

1970–1971

13

The Hour Is Striking

At the turn of the decade, as 1969 became 1970, there were promising signs for youth voting rights. Admittedly the defeats in New Jersey and Ohio led to pessimism. That "was a real down time," Ian MacGowan recalls. "You realized, after all the work and all the young people that were committed and they worked their tails off, that there was still a barrier."[1] Such barriers existed in other states with organizations and campaigns, including California, New York, North Carolina, Wisconsin, Iowa, and Senator Birch Bayh's Indiana. Neighboring Illinois had no progress, but proponents saw a possibility with the state's constitutional convention opening in December. In the states of Delaware and Jane Greenspun's Nevada the legislatures approved measures, although needed to do so again in their next sessions. There also were a number of close losing votes, as in Maryland's General Assembly. One of the biggest letdowns of 1969, apart from the votes in Ohio and New Jersey, occurred in New Mexico.

Campaigners sought the 18-year-old vote at New Mexico's 1969 constitutional convention. They got the 20-year-old vote but lost when voters—like those in New York and Maryland—did not ratify the new constitution in December. Charles Gonzales, a student at the College of Santa Fe and president of the Student New Mexico Education Association, had helped to build the campaign before becoming regional president of the Rocky Mountain Student NEA. From there Charlie became national president of Student NEA. Now a national spokesman, he explained why NEA and Student NEA were at the forefront of the youth franchise movement. It was not only that "the cause is right. Through our leadership in the movement, we are saying that we believe in the system, that we believe in the democratic process, and that we will not copout." In his new position over 1969–1970, Charlie was able to bring his local and state experience to the national level. "I was out in the country urging people to get involved."[2]

Timing helped. With the majority of state legislatures meeting biennially in odd-numbered years, 1969 had provided an opening for action. A sweeping number of state legislatures plus the Legislative Assembly of the Commonwealth of Puerto Rico passed proposals. The US Virgin Islands petitioned Congress to put the 18-year-old vote before its electorate. As a territory of the United States, the Virgin Islands required congressional approval through an amendment, which came in 1970. A few more states moved on voting age measures in the new year, setting up 1970 as a remarkable referendum year.

The list of possibilities was the longest ever, with the odds for success better than ever. "If one state goes, we'll be in business," Ian MacGowan believed at the time. "What Congress is waiting for is some signal from the states."[3] The first referendum was in May for the 19-year-old vote in Oregon, followed in August by Alaska's to lower the voting age from 19 to 18. The rest would come up for a vote in the November election. Voters had another chance in Michigan, Hawai'i, Nebraska, New Jersey, and, for the third time, South Dakota. Proposals also were put forward to voters in Colorado, Florida, Maine, Massachusetts, Minnesota, Montana, Washington, Wyoming, in addition to Connecticut, Puerto Rico, and the US Virgin Islands. In December the 18-year-old vote would indeed go before the Illinois electorate as part of the new state constitution.

Not all of these possibilities would lower the voting age to 18. In fact the majority didn't. The most popular voting age was 19. Proponents were trying again in New Jersey and South Dakota with this higher age and in Nebraska with an even higher age of 20. In several cases multiple proposals came before state legislators, each with a different voting age, and they had to choose among them. Falling between 18 and 20, 19 was seen as a compromise, as Les Francis had commented. In New Jersey, right after the defeat of Vote 18, VAC leaders set to work on 19. They had to wait two years before putting a defeated measure before the voters again, so 18 was a no go. Plus perhaps 19 would stand a better chance of passing. Of course it didn't in Ohio, but the vote was closer. And evidence for optimism on the 19-year-old vote was support in Ohio's rural areas, unsurprising given the history of rural youth taking on adult responsibilities, like driving, earlier than their urban peers.[4]

Despite seeking different voting ages the 1970 state campaigns shared a common characteristic: gubernatorial backing. A governor's endorsement did not necessarily spell success, as Governor Nelson Rockefeller of New York showed. Without it, as in California, campaigns slowed. Kentucky's successful 1955 referendum—without the state's highest official in support—was the exception that proved the rule. Governors inspired. "It is time to quit preaching at the young to become interested while blocking them from becoming involved," proclaimed Minnesota governor Harold E. LeVander. "Let us let them in."[5] They could influence, helping to overcome opposition among legislators.

Some of the opposition at the time could be outrageous—and unconstitutional. In Wyoming a rogue state senator, J. W. Myers, proposed an amendment to the 19-year-old vote requiring all voters to meet military grooming standards. "If we're going to give these youngsters voting privileges, they should look like citizens," Myers insisted. Their hair should be "at a length and grooming to meet standards prescribed by the military service." A Montana state senator, Joseph B. Reber, made the same claim. If young people are going to vote, "they should get a shave and a haircut and be like the rest of us."[6]

Although Myers's amendment may have started as a joke, the Wyoming Senate initially passed it before finally removing it. "Young people in Wyoming were not laughing. They were embarrassed. They were shocked," wrote Philip White, the editor of the *Branding Iron*, the student newspaper at the University of Wyoming. Making appearance a qualification for suffrage was unconstitutional, and Myers knew it. Neither hair, clothing, nor skin color could be taken into consideration for determining voting rights, White explained. Young people wanted the vote. "But we will not stand to be judged by the length of our hair."[7] In the end the controversy subsided, and the Vote 19 referendum would go before the state's electorate in November 1970. "I'd take my chances with the 18-year-olds in the political saddle today instead of their parents," expressed longtime proponent Gale McGee, one of Wyoming's US senators.[8] Meanwhile he and his colleagues were busy in Washington, DC.

The National Scene

Over 1969 and 1970 the 91st Congress had many resolutions to lower the voting age come forward and many speeches from the floor. Jennings Randolph secured a supermajority of sponsors for his Senate Joint

Resolution 147 and statements of support from over 70 senators. The required two-thirds majority for a constitutional amendment had been achieved in the Senate. In his telegram to Ohio Volunteers for Vote 19 right before Election Day in 1969, Randolph conveyed this information as well as his congratulations for Vote 19 and their "vital endeavors to secure a lower voting age." He made it clear that state and local organizing, "together with that of the Youth Franchise Coalition, is a critical element in the national campaign to broaden the base of our democracy."[9] Although Randolph focused on top-down federal action, he recognized the importance of bottom-up pressure.

Bottom-up pressure of a different kind came together with a push for federal action on youth voting rights in December 1969, when the National Commission on the Causes and Prevention of Violence released its final report. *To Establish Justice, to Insure Domestic Tranquility* had an entire section on "Youth and the Political Process." The disfranchisement and alienation of young Americans from the political system drove "them into a search for alternative, sometimes violent, means to express their frustrations over the gap between the nation's ideals and actions." After highlighting the adult responsibilities already fulfilled by young Americans, including military service, the commission called for the 18-year-old vote.

> Their way of life—and, for some, even the duration of life itself—is dictated by laws made and enforced by men they do not elect. This is fundamentally unjust. Accordingly: We recommend that the Constitution of the United States be amended to lower the voting age for all state and federal elections to eighteen.[10]

Earlier commissions had recognized the vital importance of Black voting rights as part of a solution for civil disorders, but this one was the first to do the same for young adults.

The same recommendation came from the June 1969 Brock Report, presented by Representative W. E. Brock of Tennessee, after a congressional tour of college campuses to investigate student uprisings and unrest. On the tour Brock and his colleagues, including Representative Tom Railsback, Republican from Illinois, heard about student concerns and came back to Congress convinced to lower the voting age to 18. "We feel that active involvement in the political process can constructively focus idealism on the most effective means of change in a free society." The right to vote also would "engender in our youth (and future leadership) an awareness of the full meaning of democracy."[11]

A college poll of students at over 100 campuses later in the year confirmed the Brock Report's findings. "Nine out of 10 of America's college students believe that the 18-year-old vote is a right which should be given America's youth." The poll also revealed "a deep-seated resentment by most students in being denied the right to participate in this civic exercise." The timing of its release—just after the referenda defeats in New Jersey and Ohio—contributed to those failures being "viewed by collegians as another evidence of the lag in the democratic process." This democratic lag added further to their "sense of frustration and resentment toward the political process itself."[12] That top-down action on the 18-year-old vote could ease bottom-up pressure—the conclusion of the National Commission on the Causes and Prevention of Violence—had a receptive audience in December 1969.

The Youth Franchise Coalition immediately issued a press release. The violence commission's findings and recommendations reinforced what proponents had been arguing since the mid-1960s. Providing a safety valve was a reason to give 18-, 19-, and 20-year-olds the right to vote. As Ian MacGowan asserted, "So long as this right is denied them we feed the frustrations that are the source of unrest in our society." A quote from Senator Mansfield relayed his "sorrow" that young people "do not help to make policy. They can only protest." Now change appeared to be coming. "The violence commission report may well be the vehicle to turn the momentum into the necessary decisive action," Ian acknowledged.[13]

A driver was conspicuously absent, however. "We are anxiously awaiting word from the President to see if he will support a constitutional amendment to extend the franchise," Ian admitted.[14] A full year into his presidency, Richard Nixon had remained noncommittal on the question. Early in 1969, he asked his attorney general, John Mitchell, to advise him on the best strategy to lower the voting age. Should he spur the states to act or support a constitutional amendment? The former was in keeping with the 1968 Republican Party platform. As for the latter, Nixon sought information for lowering the voting age for federal elections only.[15]

"Nixon has declined to publicly throw his support to lowering the voting age to 18," wrote reporter John Zeh in an angry article for the College Press Service. Instead, "Nixon has carried his law 'n order campaign to the campus," with help from Mitchell. With help from his secretary of state, Henry Kissinger, Nixon continued the American war in Vietnam, sacrificing many more young lives in pursuit of "peace with honor," an unachievable end for an illegal and immoral war, argued antiwar activists, and Zeh agreed. "His promise of a 'new road' for young people in the 'Great Generation' (part of his campaign rhetoric), has turned out to be paved, as predicted, in bullshit."[16] Without a stated commitment from Nixon, confidence in the chances of a constitutional amendment lessened for some proponents, with Jennings Randolph the notable exception.

Within this context proponents at the national level began to formulate a new strategy. The groundwork had already been laid with a 1966 *Harvard Law Review* article by professor of law Archibald Cox. Cox had served as the solicitor general of the United States during the Kennedy and early Johnson administrations and later would gain fame as the first hired—and soon fired—special prosecutor of the Watergate scandal in 1973. Reflecting on the Supreme Court's recent decisions, Cox reiterated the importance of the enforcement clause of the 14th Amendment.[17] Section 5 of the amendment states that "the Congress shall have power to enforce, by appropriate legislation, the provisions of this article." Although slightly reworded, this clause was included in the 15th, 19th, and 24th Amendments and would also be in the 26th Amendment. For supporters, it had been the enforcement clause in the 15th Amendment that justified the Voting Rights Act of 1965.

Among other cases Cox highlighted the key voting rights decisions of the Court's just completed term. Over 1965 and 1966, using the 14th and 15th Amendments, the Court again decided in favor of expanded federal intervention in state voting practices.[18] *South Carolina v. Katzenbach* (1966) validated the preclearance provisions of the Voting Rights Act. *Katzenbach v. Morgan* (1966) did the same for the act's prohibition of English literacy tests for citizens literate in Spanish with a sixth-grade education. *Harper v. Virginia State Board of Elections* (1966) declared state and local poll taxes unconstitutional, after the 24th Amendment had abolished them for federal elections. This legal reasoning later shaped the arguments in the *Greenspun, Puishes,* and *WMCA Vote* cases that youth disfranchisement constituted discrimination that violated the Equal Protection Clause. Those cases were trying to get the courts to act; Cox was thinking about Congress.

"The decisions call attention to a vast untapped reservoir of federal legislative power to define and promote the constitutional rights of individuals in relation to state government," contended Cox. The enforcement clause in the 14th Amendment especially gave Congress the power and responsibility to ensure equal protection and "the promotion of human rights." *Katzenbach v. Morgan* meant Congress could use appropriate legislation to achieve the end of equal protection in a number of areas, including youth suffrage. "Congress would seem to have power to make a similar finding about state laws denying the franchise to eighteen, nineteen, and twenty year-olds even though they work, pay taxes, raise families, and are subject to military service."[19] Lowering the voting age could happen without amending the US Constitution.

Cox's article and argument came to the attention of members of the Youth Franchise Coalition and Congress, including Paul Minarchenko and Senator Ted Kennedy. In 1970 they would collaborate to take these ideas and implement an innovative, even audacious, strategy for achieving youth voting rights. Their vehicle was the extension of the Voting Rights Act of 1965. With some of the key provisions like preclearance set to expire, Congress needed to reauthorize the act. This process opened up the opportunity for amendments, which proponents eyed as a way to propose and pass the 18-year-old vote.

By then Paul felt pessimistic about the prospects for a constitutional amendment. "It was never going to happen."

> So I set about finding a way that I could generate support for an amendment to the Voting Rights Act. That's how I spent my time, that's what I was lobbying for. Birch Bayh was agreeable to help. We utilized all the activity that was going on in the country, the support that was developing locally. I would go around and talk.

"I had a good beginning because I was already lobbying for civil rights so I knew all the players."[20]

He and others backing this new strategy faced a major challenge, however. They needed to convince civil rights leaders and lobbyists, like the NAACP's Clarence Mitchell and Joseph Rauh of the Leadership Conference on Civil Rights. "We had some very tense conversations," Paul says. "They had taught me so much." But by adding the 18-year-old vote, "I was running the risk of jeopardizing the extension of the Voting Rights Act." Similarly, Ian remembers that the situation "really produced anxiety" because "no one wanted to jeopardize the Voting Rights Act for the 18-year-old vote." "We had to prove at that point that it wasn't going to be that controversial," Charlie Gonzales recalls. "That there was enough momentum for that to happen. It just needed legislation."[21] Convincing the civil rights lobby would take time and effort.

Doing this work alongside Paul, Ian, and Charlie was a new leadership team in the YFC and Project 18. In fact Paul himself had changed his role, stepping down as YFC chairman but keeping a position on the board of directors. He made this move in tandem with taking up a new job with the American Federation of State, County and Municipal Employees, the fastest-growing union in the United States. "I actually backed a little bit away from the Youth Franchise Coalition at that point, because I was wearing a very different hat than when I was with the YMCA."[22]

Then for family reasons Les Francis returned to California. He soon had a job at his alma mater, San Jose State College, and served as faculty adviser for Students for Vote Extension there. He also saw a future career in politics. "The place to make the change, to have the greatest impact on the things you cared about, was in elective office." He entered the 1970 Democratic primary for a seat in the California State Assembly. "One of my issues as a candidate was the 18 year old vote." In a campaign statement at the time Les pointed out that "students have many good ideas concerning ecological problems, racism, and other situations which affect them. The problem is, they have no representatives on a state level to air their grievances or views."[23] Although Les lost the primary he promoted Vote 18 in the process.

Les and Paul left open the Project 18 directorship and the YFC chairmanship, and both positions would be filled by Roz Hester. After graduating from Southwest Texas State College Roz devoted a year to a graduate program in political science before deciding it wasn't for her.

She did enjoy the teaching part though, until she came face-to-face with the reality of the war in Vietnam.

> One of my students tracked me down, because I had given him a C or D or something like that and he was going to be drafted because the grade that I had given him was not going to allow him to stay in college. So I changed his grade! I was not going to be responsible for sending somebody to war.

That experience hit home for Roz. She started looking for ways to oppose the war, and the foundational argument made absolute sense to her. "The rally cry was if somebody can be sent to war to fight and die for the country they ought to be able to vote for the blankety-blank who sent them there."[24] In fall 1969 she joined the NEA staff in Washington, DC. When Les left later that year, she became director of Project 18 and then YFC chair in early 1970.

Roz found herself in a team with Charlie, Student NEA president, Mel Myler, now in a Student NEA staff position, Ian MacGowan, still YFC executive director, and a new YFC assistant director, Pat Keefer. Les recruited Pat after their work on Vote 19 in Ohio. With Roz and Pat in leadership positions the youth franchise movement had significant female leadership for the first time. Young women had been involved in earlier efforts and campaigns and took part as the movement took off. But consistent with the period of time and politics more generally these were all male-dominated. In 1969 one woman expressed frustration at being seen "as a member of the male sex." She wrote a YFC member that "all the letters have been addressed to Mr. Sandy McConnell and I thought someone should know!"[25] Against the backdrop of a flourishing feminist movement, 1970 marked a new moment for proponents of youth voting rights. And in more ways than one.

1970 Senate Hearings on Lowering the Voting Age

In February and March 1970 the Subcommittee on Constitutional Amendments of the Senate Judiciary Committee, chaired by Senator Birch Bayh, held four days of hearings on lowering the voting age. Young proponents appealed in advance to Bayh. Seniors at one Indiana high school filled a massive sheet of paper with messages. "I feel that any person who is old enough to fight for his country's freedom deserves the right to vote," wrote one young man. "Good luck with your legislation and thanks for listening to me." A young woman from Missouri, who cut her letter into the shape of the number 18, asked "Is there anything I can do to help?" Jay Berman, staff director of Bayh's subcommittee, was helping by putting the hearings together. The witness list and testimony, as he puts it, "needed to establish legitimacy for the issue, develop support outside of Congress, and start to put pressure on lawmakers." They set about doing that.[26]

In a departure from the 1968 hearings Bayh's subcommittee focused as much on how to establish a uniform national voting age as why. With near unanimity on why—no witnesses and only two submitted statements expressed opposition—the major disagreement was on how to proceed. Senator Ted Kennedy and others spoke in favor of Congress taking action by legislative statute rather than constitutional amendment. To justify this new strategy Kennedy submitted Archibald Cox's article as a supporting document for the hearings.

In another departure the 1970 hearings quadrupled the number of speakers and statements from youth organizations focused solely on lowering the voting age. The Youth Franchise Coalition made the difference. Ian MacGowan had written to member organizations urging them to send a representative to ensure the hearings "establish a complete record."[27] He and researcher Alan DiScuillo from the YFC, Clark Wideman and Jerry Springer from Ohio's Vote 19, and Earl Blumenauer from Oregon's Go-19 campaign testified. Bruce Marsh and Jim Chiswell of New York's Citizens for Vote 18 submitted statements. A supporting document came from Bruce K. Chapman of the Ripon Society, the YFC's one Republican organization.[28] Adding their voices later were the NAACP's James Brown Jr. and Philomena Queen and Student NEA's Charlie Gonzales. Bayh heralded this participation. "What has so far been the missing ingredient in our efforts to lower the voting age is missing no longer."[29]

After testimony from the YFC and state campaigners on the first day of hearings, Bayh's subcommittee colleague, Senator Marlow Cook, Republican from Kentucky, observed that before him were "four extremely fine, articulate young men." But their words and actions did not win the attention of the press, which had already packed up and left the hearing. The fact that the media image of young Americans focused on political and cultural radicals rather than more mainstream liberals and moderates irked Cook as well as Bayh. Both believed that adult backlash against the so-called media kid had hurt state referenda and hindered their own efforts to lower the voting age. Cook commented that if these witnesses had caused a disturbance at the Senate hearing, "you would have been on every national television program in the United States tonight."[30] The audience greeted his comment with applause.

Attuned to matters of sex, or gender, equity due to the Equal Rights Amendment (ERA) also on the subcommittee's agenda, Cook offered an observation about the all-male group representing the YFC and the state campaigns. "I would hope that you all have an enthusiastic group of women who are working in your organization." Bayh interjected: "I notice some young ladies in the room that I know were active in the Ohio campaign."[31] He was referring to Pat Keefer. Although Pat didn't speak at the hearings, she was there and visible. Philomena Queen would provide one young woman's voice at the proceedings, and it was a powerful one. "We see in our society wrongs which we want to make right," she said with passion and purpose, "conditions that we want to change, but cannot. You have disarmed us of the most constructive and potent weapon of a democratic system—the vote."[32] Queen and other witnesses made the compelling case for why and how to enact youth suffrage.

Why Enact Youth Suffrage?

Over 30 witnesses, including YFC members, testified at the 1970 Senate hearings. Jennings Randolph once again took the lead. "I am excited about this subject in February 1970, just as I was excited about this subject in 1942," Randolph declared. Like Martin Luther King insisting "now is the time" at the March on Washington, Randolph issued the same message, even if in a much less momentous setting. "I believe that now is the time, and I think the hour is striking now for 18-year-old voting."[33] Together with Randolph, speakers made all the arguments for youth suffrage. "The traditional arguments for and against a lower voting age are well known and often repeated," noted Deputy Attorney General Richard Kleindienst. "They have been stated and restated until they are almost incapable of novel recitation."[34] Although he was certainly correct, witnesses did update their arguments to reflect the contemporary context.

Young adults had earned the franchise, first and foremost, because they were fulfilling citizenship responsibilities. They were working, paying taxes, volunteering, and serving in the military. Ted Kennedy alone felt the foundational argument "deserves special mention," but all agreed young Americans were meeting the challenges of citizenship.[35] Without the vote they unjustly lacked political representation. "If taxation without representation was tyranny, then conscription without representation is slavery," argued Ted Sorensen, former special counsel to JFK. With the Nixon administration cutting back on poverty programs, Charlie Gonzales asked about the impact on disfranchised young adults. "Consider a VISTA worker under 21 whose program is decelerated because of increased defense spending. What recourse does he have?"[36]

Young Americans also had the education and information necessary to exercise the right to vote. "We believe," NEA's spokesman asserted, "that this generation is probably the most knowledgeable generation and the more interested in government than any generation we have had." Ramsey Clark, former attorney general for LBJ, assured that a "constant bombardment of TV, radio, newspapers, magazines and books make our young the most informed people in history." The spokesman for the American Federation of Teachers affirmed that the average 18-year-old "has typically completed a school curriculum designed and taught to prepare him for active participation in a representative democracy." But then there's a three-year wait to vote. "At that age we should not immediately close the doors to them," Jerry Springer argued, "we should say, take your interest and become a part."[37]

Several speakers spoke to the maturity of young adults. "In the age in which we live, in this fast age, men arrive to maturity both in body and mind at a great deal earlier period than formerly," Birch Bayh quoted at the opening of the hearings. Of this observation from Marcus Bickford at the 1867 New York State constitutional convention, Bayh commented, "there can be no doubt about the wisdom of this statement as we sit here today, more than 100 years later." Young adults were considered mature enough to marry, start families, and vote in four states and two territories. They also were treated as adults in criminal proceedings, which Randolph documented with a three-page summary of state laws. The most respected witness on youth maturity was acclaimed anthropologist and public intellectual Margaret Mead. With her monthly column in *Redbook* magazine, Mead had an audience of millions for her views. Both mentally and physically, she confirmed, "they are more mature than young people in the past."[38]

Mead also contributed to the argument about the social construction of age and such connotations for maturity. Based on her first book, *Coming of Age in Samoa* (1928), Mead understood how age categories can and do change over time, place, and culture. She criticized using the term "teenagers" to describe 18- and 19-year-olds in 1970. When "classified with 13-year-olds and so treated," these young adults are "made dependent and not given the political responsibility they deserve." Under common law age 21 was "the hallmark of maturity and adulthood," noted Kleindienst. "Significantly, England, the origin of this tradition, only recently abandoned it." (Eighteen became the age of majority, accompanied by the right to vote, at the start of 1969 in Great Britain.) Other witnesses testified to the mutability of age markers and their meanings for maturity as well. "There is nothing magic about age 21 as the dividing line between childhood and adulthood," Randolph quoted from a West Virginia newspaper editorial. "Chronological age bears little relationship to maturity beyond an early point," noted Allard Lowenstein, now a member of the House of Representatives.[39]

In full agreement was Philomena Queen, youth chair for the NAACP's Mid-Atlantic region and not yet 21. Queen called the voting age of 21 "arbitrary and hypocritical." Arbitrary because "it is not based on any educational or scientific fact." Hypocritical because reaching that age hardly "confers instant electoral wisdom on a voter." To prove her point Queen referred to a recent white mob attack on a bus of Black schoolchildren in South Carolina. The students were traveling to a newly desegregated school, which the racist rioters violently resisted. One spokesman believed white backlash had the support of the White House. "I definitely feel there's been a change since the Nixon Administration took over." That "an angry mob of blood-thirsty adults" had the right to vote when responsible young citizens did not was "a grave injustice," Queen believed.[40]

To correct this injustice would expand American democracy and "make government more responsive and more representative," Lowenstein avowed. He and others put this democratic expansion in historical context. "We have extended the vote to the non-propertied, to blacks, to women, to those who do not speak English—all in the hope and to the purpose of strengthening democracy." Ian MacGowan agreed. "The American democracy has survived for nearly two centuries. A major reason for its durability has been . . . to broaden the franchise so as to continue to be truly representative." Realizing and strengthening American democracy had been one of Randolph's arguments for the 18-year-old vote for nearly three decades. "The future in large part belongs to young people. It is imperative that they have the opportunity to help set the course for that future." The "franchise of freedom" would let them do that.[41]

In addition to advancing these long-standing arguments for lowering the voting age, witnesses at the 1970 Senate hearings addressed the new arguments that arose in the context of the sixties. Margaret Mead emphasized enfranchisement as a way to bridge the generation gap. In her just published book, *Culture and Commitment: A Study of the Communication Gap* (1970), Mead made the case that the generation gap was real due to dramatic social and technological change. What was needed to bridge the gap was "a continuing dialogue in which the young, free to act on their own initiative, can lead their elders in the direction of the unknown." Adults needed to listen to young adults, and lowering the voting age would foster this communication.[42]

Another witness, renowned psychiatrist Walter G. Menninger, argued that youth suffrage would shrink the generation gap. Menninger had been a member of the National Commission on the Causes and Prevention of Violence, and he repeated the commission's recommendation on the 18-year-old vote. He insisted that adults try "tuning in" to young people, including through rock music. "While often the noise level of the electric guitars and organs, and the distortion of the sound systems make it hard to decipher the words, the lyrics are worth noting." He quoted Jefferson Airplane's "Crown of Creation" on the older generation—"In loyalty to their kind, they cannot tolerate our minds"—and the Beatles' "Revolution" on the younger generation's desire for social change—"We all want to change the world." Young adults "want to be heard, and now," Menninger argued.[43]

Last but not least proponents put forward the safety-valve argument. Menninger conveyed "the sense of helplessness and hopelessness which many students have expressed in reaction to the apparent unresponsiveness of the 'establishment' to issues affecting the survival of the human race." With the first Earth Day just two and a half months away environmental pollution topped Menninger's list, followed by global population growth and the nuclear arms race. Unresponsiveness to racism, poverty, and the Vietnam War further fed "frustration and disillusionment," attested Charlie Gonzales. The answer was for "Congress to give the vote and allow evolution to proceed. By denying the vote you are encouraging a revolution." S. I. Hayakwaka had implemented a safety valve in microcosm at San Francisco State College through "inclusion of students into the decision-making processes" following the previous year's protests. Inclusion in the electorate was also needed "so that they have decisions to make that count in the world."[44]

Based on the witness testimony and submitted statements, the Senate Subcommittee on Constitutional Amendments could conclude that there was a strong consensus for Congress to act to lower the voting age to 18. "We can find no moral, legal or political reason to justify keeping these young people on the outside of the decision-making arena of this country," declared the NAACP's James Brown with reference to Roy Wilkins.[45] Although state campaigns were in progress, the requirement for both state legislative action and voter referenda was too slow a process. Moreover, the differing ages proposed by the various states confused matters further, making a uniform national voting age even more compelling. For Bayh's subcommittee hearings to have reached this consensus was a major accomplishment since 1968.

How to Enact Youth Suffrage?

But major conflict remained on how Congress should act to enact youth voting rights. The majority of participants in the hearings sought a constitutional amendment to encompass local, state, and national elections. The Nixon administration wanted an amendment only for federal elections. If asked about the new strategy of lowering the voting age through legislative statute, most witnesses approved. Jennings Randolph was less enamored, although he would soon come around. Assistant Attorney

General William H. Rehnquist, speaking for the administration, wholly opposed. The "constitutional validity of such a statute would be open to the most serious doubt," Rehnquist argued, requiring "the widest possible judicial review." He took particular issue with the idea that setting age qualifications for voting constituted discrimination and a violation of equal protection. A later witness, Louis Pollack, dean of the Yale Law School, backed up Rehnquist. A voting age of 21 was "not remotely vulnerable on equal protection grounds."[46]

Although the weight of the White House was against the statute strategy, prominent speakers supported it. In his statement Kennedy made a bold case for the new strategy. "I believe not only that the reduction of the voting age to 18 is desirable, but also that Federal action is the best route to accomplish the change, and that the preferred method of Federal change should be by statute, rather than by constitutional amendment." He admitted that, like his brothers, he had initially "leaned toward placing the initiative on the States in this important area." Now, for reasons of speed and uniformity, Congress should act. Recent court decisions showed Congress had the power to act. "The historic decision by the Supreme Court in the case of *Katzenbach v. Morgan* in June 1966 provides a solid constitutional basis for legislation by Congress in this area."[47]

Support for the so-called Morgan approach came from opposite ends of the ideological spectrum. Senator Barry Goldwater provided conservative Republican backing. After his unsuccessful presidential run in 1964, Goldwater won reelection to the Senate from Arizona in 1968. "The voting age should be lowered and lowered at once across the entire Nation. To my mind, the change can validly be achieved by either a constitutional amendment or statute." For this statement to come from Goldwater, who opposed the Civil Rights Act of 1964 on states' rights grounds was significant, to the say the least. "Since I happen to like the idea of 18-year-olds voting, I feel it is entirely appropriate to use the Morgan approach."[48]

From a liberal perspective Lawrence Speiser, director of the American Civil Liberties Union's Washington office, agreed alongside Senator Kennedy. He found Archibald Cox "persuasive in his argument that it can be done by statute. It is not necessary to do it by constitutional amendment." In contrast to Rehnquist and Pollack, Speiser held that the

Senator Edward M. Kennedy and Ian MacGowan, Youth Franchise Coalition
executive director, Washington, DC, 1970. Bill W. Kuniholm, photographer.
Courtesy of Ian MacGowan.

denial of the vote to Americans aged 18 to 20 would "be an 'invidious'
discrimination itself in violation of the Fourteenth Amendment" if Congress found it so. And "Congress can pass legislation to enlarge liberties
of American citizens," including "the liberties of 18-year-olds to vote."[49]

The Morgan approach also occupied the attention of another subcommittee of the Senate Judiciary Committee. Concurrent with the hearings
of Bayh's Subcommittee on Constitutional Amendments were those of
the Subcommittee on Constitutional Rights. Chaired by North Carolina
senator Sam Ervin, hearings started in 1969 on extending and amending
the Voting Rights Act of 1965 and continued in February 1970. Ervin had
opposed the Voting Rights Act in 1965, and he still did. He considered
the act "contrary to the Constitution" and contended it should not be
extended. Most senators disagreed, so work in the Senate continued.

Work in the House of Representatives had already wrapped up. In December 1969 the House approved a version proposed by the Nixon administration. This version replaced HR 4249 as reported out of Emanuel Celler's Judiciary Committee. Back in July 1969 Celler's committee had voted to extend the Voting Rights Act of 1965 for five more years with no amendments. But riding the wave of white backlash the Nixon administration sought only a three-year extension. It also sought to undermine the "coverage" and "preclearance" provisions in the act that they said unfairly singled out the southern states. The *Los Angeles Times* declared that Nixon's proposal "gutted" the 1965 act; the *New York Times* dubbed it a "repeal."[50] "The whole thing is an approach toward Republicanizing the South," contended Representative John Conyers. The NAACP's Clarence Mitchell called it "appeasement" and "nothing other than a destructive and politically divisive intent." Instead of "regional legislation," as Attorney General Mitchell put it, the administration wanted the law to operate "on a nationwide basis." Celler felt national coverage was "like trying to stem a flood in Mississippi by building a dam in Idaho."[51]

The House bill came over to the Senate to be taken up in 1970, the second session of the 91st Congress. To ensure prompt consideration of the voting rights bill, a bipartisan coalition of pro–civil rights senators held up a Supreme Court nomination. The Subcommittee on Constitutional Rights held additional hearings in February, and HR 4249 came to the Senate floor in March. Another reversal happened. Spearheaded by Senate minority leader Hugh Scott, Republican from Pennsylvania, and Philip Hart, Democrat from Michigan, the senators significantly revised the House version, retaining or removing provisions as they saw fit. They ended up with a five-year extension, a regional focus on the South as well as new coverage of jurisdictions outside the South, a national ban on literacy tests, and uniform registration, absentee voting, and residency requirements for presidential elections.

Most importantly for proponents of youth voting rights the Senate version included the 18-year-old vote. On March 4, even before Bayh had finished holding all of his subcommittee hearings, majority leader Mike Mansfield introduced Senate Amendment No. 545 to Scott and Hart's revised version of HR 4249. "The issue is perhaps more pertinent in 1970 than at any time in the past," Mansfield argued. After steadily working on the strategy, Kennedy recalled how it was Mansfield who became the sponsor. "We suddenly held back . . . fearing it might jeopardize passage of the overall Voting Rights Act. Mike saw it differently. He felt so strongly about the basic fairness of the idea that he proposed it himself as an amendment to the bill." "I've been advocating this for a decade, but nothing ever happens," Mansfield affirmed. "I thought this was a way to have the Senate face up to its responsibilities in this area."[52]

Still, in recognition of Kennedy's work in promoting the statute strategy, many referred to it as the "Kennedy-Mansfield Amendment." Originally cosponsoring with the Senate majority leader were Kennedy and Warren Magnuson, a long-serving Democrat from Washington State. Immediately upon Mansfield's introduction of Senate Amendment No. 545 more senators joined, including Jacob Javits and Joseph Tydings. Agreeing with the strategy but not with attaching the voting age to the extension of the Voting Rights Act of 1965, Goldwater and Cook introduced their own separate youth suffrage bill. But Mansfield, Kennedy, and the many cosponsors stayed on track. "This is the only chance we have to get the vote for the 18-year-olds," Mansfield told a fellow senator.[53]

For opponents, like Senator Ervin, the Kennedy-Mansfield Amendment once again was "usurping for the Congress the powers reserved to the States to prescribe the qualifications for voting."[54] During several days of Senate debate, Ervin and his southern colleagues attempted a rearguard action against the entire voting rights bill. They were unsuccessful. In a stunningly strong vote of 64 to 17 the US Senate passed Amendment No. 545 on March 12, 1970. By a similarly strong margin the Senate approved HR 4249 with the Scott-Hart revisions and sent it back to the House the next day.

The Nixon administration had engineered a backlash against the extension and amendment of the Voting Rights Act of 1965. It had backfired and spectacularly so. The House of Representatives now had a substantially stronger bill to consider with the voting age lowered to 18 for federal, state, and local elections. Of the 18-year-old vote, powerful opponent Emanuel Celler promised "to fight it tooth and nail. There'll be no voting-rights bill unless I can knock that out."[55]

14

Enfranchised?

If Jennings Randolph could declare his enthusiasm for youth suffrage as strong in 1970 as it had been in 1942, then Emanuel Celler could say the same about his opposition. In mid-March, when the Senate's bill to extend and amend the Voting Rights Act of 1965 came back to the House of Representatives with the 18-year-old vote, Celler held his own. "Come hell or high water I'm not going to accede to it, and I'm sure that my fellow conferees from the House agree."[1]

The opposition of Celler, nearly 82 years old and in his 48th year in Congress, to lowering the voting age was legendary. Any proposed constitutional amendment needed to come to the House Judiciary Committee he chaired. Despite the many calls and campaigns for youth voting rights over the decades, Celler continued to resist this political and social change. He refused to hold public hearings on the issue or report any resolution out of his committee. For these reasons Senator Marlow Cook characterized Celler's committee as "a real buzz saw." "18-Yr. Old Vote Won't Pass This Year" was the definitive, disappointed March 25, 1970, headline in the *Independent*, Paul Minarchenko's old college newspaper.[2] John Zeh of the College Press Service put Celler's "bitter" opposition down to fear. "A main reason is fear of change itself, and the threat old politicians at the federal, state, and local levels see in an electorate expanded by 12 million young people." Introducing a new, younger constituency into an established political system could make elections more competitive for older, incumbent politicians like Celler. Zeh couldn't resist pointing out that Celler had been 18 back in 1906.[3]

"Enfranchised?" asked the editors of the campus newspaper at Wellesley College after the Senate approved the 18-year-old vote.[4] Not if Emanuel Celler could help it. Celler considered the Senate's statute strategy "unconstitutional and unwise." "Let's assume we lower the voting age and a Governor or even a President is elected by the teen-age vote," he said. "Then, just suppose the Supreme Court decides this law is unconstitutional. This could be catastrophic." Any change in the voting age needed to be through constitutional amendment. Celler now promised he would hold hearings this time if such a proposal came to his committee. But he also stood by his staunch opposition. He remarked that many states in the past ten years, including his own New York, had rejected moves to lower the voting age. And he restated his argument about the immaturity of those he still labeled "teenagers." "Their minds are too malleable, too subject to the emotional appeals of demagogues."[5]

The *Wellesley News* objected to Celler's opposition and his arguments. They "are themselves emotional appeals, geared to evoke images of a nationally irrational and irresponsible youth." Also emotional was his claim of catastrophe should youth suffrage via legislative statute be overturned. Especially when the Senate sought swift judicial review and, to allow for it, an effective date of January 1, 1971, for the new voting age. Apart from Celler, the *Wellesley News* editors knew that considerable obstacles to youth enfranchisement—whether through statute or amendment—still existed. The Supreme Court could overturn the statute. States' rights forces could hold up an amendment. Even so the editors believed this turn of events in Congress "represents an increase in the political influence of youth."[6]

Overcoming the Opposition

"The Age of Aquarius appears to be overtaking the Constitution," joked *New York Times* legal affairs reporter Fred P. Graham in late March. This reference to the opening song of *Hair*, the popular "American Tribal Love-Rock Musical" performing since late 1967, was apt even if in jest. "This is the dawning of the Age of Aquarius" went the song lyrics about an astrological age encompassing the expansion of human consciousness. For Graham, using this phrase reinforced his argument that the 18-year-old vote was "an idea whose time has come." A former lawyer, he credited Professor Archibald Cox's legislative statute argument and Senator Ted Kennedy's use of it to lower the voting age. "This remarkable political spasm," Graham argued, "was an impressive tribute to the occasional impact of scholarly work on public policy."

Graham also reported that the House leadership had decided to clear the way for a vote on the Senate's entire bill. They wanted to avoid any amendments or, even more threatening, a Senate-House conference where opponents could block the bill.[7] To save his beloved voting rights bill Emanuel Celler had come around. Rumor had it that the 78-year-old Speaker of the House, John McCormack, Democrat from Massachusetts, had done the convincing, channeling Bob Dylan. "Manny," McCormack told Celler, "the times are changing and we have got to change with them."[8] Celler preferred the Senate's stronger provisions to ensure African American voting rights over the weaker House bill anyway, and he didn't want to put those at risk. So much so that he could live with the 18-year-old vote—for now. A court challenge still remained.

But Celler's change of mind did not quell the opposition. In early April, Louis Pollack marshaled four of his Yale Law School colleagues to write a letter to the editor of the *New York Times* outlining why the legislative statute strategy was unconstitutional. They did not believe that unfranchised 18-, 19-, and 20-year-old Americans were being denied the 14th Amendment's equal protection and thus Congress did not need to enforce it. They buttressed this belief with "the long-ignored" Section 2 of the 14th Amendment. Designed to punish states that practiced racial disenfranchisement by reducing their representation in Congress, Section 2 defined the electorate as "male inhabitants of such State, being twenty-one years of age." Never enforced in over 100 years—despite appeals from Black voting rights advocates such as Charles Diggs—Section 2 became a way to undercut youth voting rights via statute in 1970.

Pollack had recently testified along the same lines at the Senate subcommittee hearings chaired by Birch Bayh. Given that men aged 21 were entitled to vote, according to the 14th Amendment's Section 2, the converse was also true. If "you were not yet 21 then there was no constitutional infirmity in denying your right to vote." This condition could be changed, Pollack and his colleagues wrote. In the past when a national consensus emerged to expand the electorate and enfranchise African Americans and women, it "was embodied, in permanent and unchallengeable form, in a constitutional amendment." If now there was a new consensus for enfranchising young adults, the same process was necessary. "As constitutional lawyers" they called for Congress to, "in fidelity to our constitutional traditions, submit to the states for ratification a new constitutional amendment embodying that consensus."[9]

Senator Ted Kennedy and Harvard law professors Archibald Cox and Paul A. Freund fired back the same day with their own letters to the editor. Their letters restated the rationale for the statute strategy and rebutted the Yale professors' claims. "Congress has broad power," Kennedy asserted, "to weigh the facts and make its own determination of discrimination under the equal protection clause." Three weeks ago by a vote of 64 to 17 the "Senate held that laws setting the voting age at 21 unfairly discriminate against millions of 18, 19, and 20-year-old Americans." Moreover, "Section 2 of the Fourteenth Amendment says only that if a state denies the vote to male citizens over 21, the state's representation in Congress must be reduced."[10] It did not limit the franchise only to citizens aged 21 years and older or to men for that matter. Cox and Freund agreed. "The sanction was directed at restriction of the franchise; it has nothing to do with enlargement." "Congress," they argued, "should exercise its responsibility for the fairness of electoral processes under contemporary constitutional decisions."[11]

While this debate played out in the pages of the *New York Times,* President Nixon prepared his own position after consulting constitutional scholars, including those at Yale. On April 27 he sent a four-page letter to House leaders objecting to the voting age provision.[12] "I believe that it represents an unconstitutional assertion of Congressional authority in an area specifically reserved to the States, and that it therefore would not stand the test of a challenge in the Courts." Article 1, Section 2 of the US Constitution gave the power to set suffrage qualifications to the states. The only limitations on that power were to be found in the suffrage amendments. According to the 15th, 19th, and 24th Amendments citizens could not be barred from the ballot on the basis of race, sex, or failure to pay poll tax. Because of the 14th Amendment "nor can States impose voting qualifications so arbitrary, invidious or irrational as to constitute a denial of equal protection of the laws."

The 14th Amendment's equal protection and enforcement clauses did not justify congressional action on the voting age, Nixon argued. The *Katzenbach v. Morgan* decision upheld the prohibition on English literacy tests for Spanish-literate citizens because such literacy tests constituted "discriminatory treatment." Setting an age qualification for voting did not. "A 21-year-old voting age treats all alike, working no invidious distinction among groups or classes." That age "may be no longer justified, but it certainly is neither capricious nor irrational." It was the traditional and still the standard age of enfranchisement. And "it is explicitly recognized by Section 2 of the Fourteenth Amendment itself as the voting age." Nixon felt the Senate had acted out of "expediency" because legislative statute appeared "easier and quicker."

But the consequences would be great. "There are no constitutional corners that may be safely cut in the service of a good cause," the president warned. If the statute was overturned, "it will have immense and possibly disastrous effects." At the very least time toward amending the Constitution would have been lost. Worse, millions of young Americans would be left "frustrated, embittered and voteless." At the very worst election results could be thrown in doubt, as Celler had initially feared. Although the Senate included a quick judicial test, "there can be no guarantee that such a test would actually be completed before elections took place. And the risk of chaos, if it were not completed, is real."

Nixon concluded by calling for "The Path of Reason." What he derogatorily deemed "the 18-year-old vote-rider"—implying it had no connection to the original voting rights bill—should be separated out, the latter passed, and the former enacted through a constitutional amendment. The president did not specify whether such an amendment would encompass local and state as well as federal elections. Given his emphasis on Article 1, Section 2, however, the implication was no, it would not. "Nixon Sees Peril in Voting Age Bill" headlined the *New York Times*. "Mr. Nixon's letter may cause the House to remove the rider from the bill."[13] It certainly caused consternation among proponents and greater confidence among opponents.

Recent Gallup polling did the same. In early April 1970 George Gallup reported that a clear majority, 58 percent of Americans polled, supported lowering the voting age to 18. "If the House of Representatives follows the lead of the Senate and approves of lowering the voting age to 18, it will be in accord with the wishes of the American people as recorded in surveys over the last 17 years." Yet this result represented an 8 percent fall in support from the Gallup poll in 1968, which registered 66 percent in favor of the 18-year-old vote. Those opposed increased by 7 percent. Over the past two years of greater attention to the issue and public information campaigns, proponents had lost support. A further finding showed a widening gap between Democratic (60 percent) and Republican (51 percent) support; a nonpartisan issue had become decidedly partisan.[14] Proponents on the ground and in government attributed these numbers to campus and civil disorders turning off older and more conservative adults.

This concern preoccupied leaders of Oregon's Go-19 campaign as they geared up for the May 26 election. Most prominent was Earl Blumenauer, a senior at Lewis and Clark College and the Go-19 campaign director, who had testified before the Senate subcommittee hearings in February. Started by high school students, the Oregon campaign first reached out to college students and civic organizations, like the NAACP. From there they formed a coalition with adults in the labor movement, business, politics, and the professions. Together they engaged in lobbying and "arm-twisting" state legislators to get the 19-year-old vote on the ballot. Since then the campaign had focused on outreach to voters to pass the referendum. "In Oregon, the campaign to lower the voting age has created the broad sort of coalition that transcends racial and generational and political barriers," Blumenauer stated. The Go-19 coalition prefigured the political coalition needed to "deal with the tremendous environmental and social problems that confront us."[15]

Early on the Oregon campaign had "impressive support" from voters. The referendum would enfranchise 70,000 Oregonians, making up about 7 percent of the electorate. A month out from the election, polling showed 52 percent in favor and 43 percent against.[16] Still, for the first time a state campaign had an organized opposition. The Committee for Realistic Voting Age Limits was chaired by a Portland lawyer who sounded a lot like early Emanuel Celler. He feared 19- and 20-year-olds "might be swayed by a demagogue" and that "democracy could thus be destroyed."[17] Typical of opponents, his take on the issue was "primarily an emotional response against young people," Blumenauer argued. Adults weren't listening to reasoned arguments about young people attaining education and responsibly "assuming the burden of citizenship." Instead, "what they consider irresponsibility on college campuses is a reason to oppose the lower voting age."[18]

It was reason enough for over 60 percent of Oregon referendum voters, as the 19-year-old vote lost by a margin of three to one. This result came despite recent government reports, including one just out of New York on campus unrest, recommending youth electoral participation to preclude militant political protest. The safety-valve argument wasn't working because referendum voters didn't want to enfranchise potential militants—much less reward current ones. For more conservative Americans, the answer to youth dissidence was repression and the restoration of order, not political inclusion and representation. Letters to proponent governor Tom McCall "foretold the defeat," which he tried to hold off by assuring the public that "most leaders in campus dissent were already old enough to vote and were a tiny minority anyway."[19] "Backlash Blamed," headlined the *Capital Journal* in Salem.[20] Most immediately Oregon voters were reacting to student antiwar protests sparked by the US invasion of Cambodia.

On April 30, 1970, just three days after President Nixon sent his voting age letter to House leaders, he sent American alongside South Vietnamese troops into neighboring Cambodia to destroy North Vietnamese military bases, infrastructure, and supplies. What Nixon claimed was not an invasion of Cambodia widened the war just when Americans were expecting a final end to it. College and university campuses exploded at the news. Demonstrations and strikes flared up across the country. Devastating were events at Kent State University in Ohio. After the first day of protest on May 1, the governor called in the Ohio National Guard to occupy the campus. A series of confrontations, arrests, and tear-gas attacks led on May 4 to the guardsmen opening fire and killing four students.

The invasion of Cambodia and the killings at Kent State intensified protest and political divisions in Oregon. "American is in travail," announced Governor McCall. Protests at Portland State University led to police taking violent action on May 11. "There is very little doubt the student-police violence of the past month influenced the vote against the measure," Blumenauer declared right after the Go-19 defeat. "I have to admit that bitterness is my gut reaction. I will try to chart a more realistic course."[21] The Go-19 forces in Oregon did regroup, but they faced the same challenges as the national youth franchise movement. As the war in Vietnam wore on and even widened, antiwar protests would too with adult voters reacting negatively. "The same backlash that we experienced will be felt in Congress," Blumenauer was certain.[22]

Over to the House

In June the House of Representatives returned to the Senate-revised HR 4249, with a new Title III lowering the voting age. On June 4, in an unusual move, the House Rules Committee approved a resolution to bypass the usual process of sending the bill to a House-Senate conference committee to work out the differences. Instead the House would have the chance to vote up or down on whether or not to accept the Senate's bill as it was. The vote was scheduled for June 17. "Despite evidence of a public backlash against anti-establishment youths, Congress may well approve a bill this week that would cut the minimum voting age to 18 years old," reported the *Wall Street Journal*. "Celler is Confident Despite Opposition," led the *New York Times*.[23]

Emanuel Celler and the ranking Republican on the House Judiciary Committee, William McCulloch of Ohio, managed the legislation on the floor. Their bipartisan partnership had helped to win civil rights legislation in the past. Celler was certain it would again. "I'm confident we have the votes," he said. "I want the voting rights bill."[24] So did a majority of his colleagues. They agreed that the Voting Rights Act of 1965 was "the most effective civil rights law in our nation's history," as McCulloch contended.[25] It had enabled an estimated 800,000 to 900,000 African Americans in the South to regain their voting rights in the past few years. More still needed to be done, and House members started to commit their support to HR 4249. The risky strategy of tying youth to Black voting rights seemed closer to paying off.

Organizations for both concerns and constituencies were lobbying intensely. Clarence Mitchell arranged a Leadership Conference on Civil Rights "emergency assembly" in Washington, DC. Several hundred Black southerners came to make the vital case for the extension of the Voting Rights Act, including the 18-year-old vote. A delegation from Mississippi detailed the deadly events at Jackson State College the prior month. In the early hours of May 15 state and local police fired on students, killing two. "The Voting Rights Act is the only hope for Black people in Mississippi," proclaimed the delegation, "because the only power we have against the bullet is the ballot!" One student in the delegation, Farries Adams, laid it on the line for both Black and youth voting rights. Protection for Black "voting power" was needed, and "if a cat is old enough to go off to war, he is old enough to vote."[26]

Lobbying alongside the Leadership Conference on Civil Rights was the Youth Franchise Coalition. "We've been doing the hard lobbying," Project 18 director and YFC board chair Roz Hester recounted. "We've been effective, too." At one point they organized some 40 students from 12 states to lobby on Capitol Hill, where they encountered little backlash. "It's much easier to wage a campaign in Congress than it is to overcome all of the popular fears at the local level," Roz realized.[27] She liked lobbying. "Being involved in something that could really make a difference, meeting a lot of interesting and powerful people, and using my communications skills, I guess I was always a bit of a political junkie." Pat Keefer found it a "rather intimidating process, going to a meeting with a congressman." But "the gratifying, satisfying part of this work for me was that I was learning about lobbying and congressional relations and rules of the House of Representatives from some of the very best in Washington." Mitchell, Joe Rauh, the AFL-CIO's Ken Young, and others continued to serve as mentors.[28]

As effective as they were they still ran into patronizing adults. The *Washington Post* labeled the YFC a "'kids' lobby" and members as "non-rebels with a cause." Roz remembers her local congressman from Texas telling her "if I really wanted to learn how things worked I could be a secretary in his DC office. Of course I was totally offended!"[29] But they learned a lot. They kept track of the headcount of House members in favor, opposed, and undecided. Up in the air especially were representatives from New Jersey, Ohio, and Oregon given the recent voter referendum rejections in those states.

To put pressure on, the YFC called on member and participating organizations to mobilize and write, telephone, or wire their local representatives urging them to vote yes. These organizations, in turn, got word out to their own memberships. "Suffrage for 10 million youths hangs by a thin thread this month as the House prepares to accept or reject a Senate-approved bill to give 18-year-olds the right to vote," stated a *NEA News* press release. Roz was quoted as Project 18 director. "Students and student teachers throughout the country are finally tuned in and turned on to the political picture."[30] The National Council of the YMCA explained that the 18-year-old vote "is presently at a very strategic place in the legislative process." A sample letter was included to encourage letter writing to Congress.[31]

The YFC also tapped state campaign organizations. "We've never been this close to having the voting age lowered. If the young people want to get the vote, then they are going to have to help us work for it," Pat advised.[32] One key aspect of how the YFC operated was a division of labor between Pat as assistant director and Ian MacGowan as executive director. "All my political life, I have been very good at organizing," Pat acknowledges, so she focused on aiding the state campaigns and mobilizing grassroots pressure on members of Congress. "Ian was a professional lobbyist. He knew how to approach congressional offices." Ian adds, "We had convinced the powerful people, Kennedy, Magnuson, Mansfield, Birch Bayh. . . . And that made the difference." Grassroots campaigning and political lobbying came together. Over time they grew more confident in success. "We think we've got it this time."[33]

Clarence Mitchell and other allies were starting to think the same. Mitchell admitted that he had "originally resisted" the addition of the 18-year-old vote because "it would complicate final passage" of the voting rights bill. But he changed his mind with pressure and persuasion from the NAACP's Youth and College Division and youth suffrage proponents like Carolyn Quilloin. He also believed that "the young people unearthed a lot of good will for the 18-year-old vote that people didn't know was there." Youth enfranchisement gave some foes of the Voting Rights Act another reason to fight its extension. At the same time it gained some supporters too.[34]

The strategy was unquestionably a gamble. Paul Myer (formerly Minarchenko) remains convinced it was the only way to put pressure on proponents in Congress. "We needed to find a mechanism to force them to take a stand and not just make speeches and put out statements." Ian made the same point in 1970. "Only by attaching the amendment to the Voting Rights Act can the political obstacle that has prevented consideration of the issue . . . be overcome." Ian further observed that "there is a difference between 'talking the talk' and 'walking the walk.'"[35] The Voting Rights Act extension propelled politicians to back up their words with action.

Warren Magnuson and Ted Kennedy had already done their part in the Senate, but they both paid attention to developments in the House, including the arrival of President Nixon's voting age letter. Magnuson responded right away with a press release, criticizing Nixon for withholding his support. "The President, not the Congress, will be responsible for a new disillusionment of our young people if this measure is defeated."[36] Kennedy issued a quick rejoinder as well. "Contrary to the Administration's suggestion, I believe the Senate acted responsibly on this issue." The arguments of the Nixon administration had already been relayed to the Senate, first at Birch Bayh's subcommittee hearings and then in floor debate. The Senate, Kennedy reminded the president, "rejected the Administration's arguments." He also disagreed with Nixon's assertion that because all Americans were subject to age qualifications no discrimination existed. Again, he reminded, "the Senate found that such discrimination does exist."[37]

At the time the term "discrimination" was gaining traction among proponents. They utilized the term where variations on "fairness" had been used earlier. The Ripon Society's Bruce Chapman reflected this change in an early 1970 article. "The law discriminates against youth—particularly against those aged 18 to 21. Adult demands are made on them, but adult rights and privileges are often denied." Of all the forms of discrimination faced by young adults in the United States, disfranchisement was the utmost. "The principal discrimination, however, is the exclusion of otherwise adult young people from legitimate participation in the democratic process." Although the Ripon Society had a good relationship with President Nixon, Chapman saw age discrimination against 18- to 20-year-olds where his party's president did not.[38]

The House Decides

As it turned out Nixon's intervention in House deliberations over the voting rights bill and the 18-year-old vote had less impact than expected. It empowered some opponents, such as House minority leader Gerald Ford. He supported state action—as in his own state of Michigan—combined with a constitutional amendment to enfranchise youth at the local, state, and federal levels. Ford spoke on June 17, 1970, when the House of Representatives debated the resolution to accept in its entirety the Senate's version of HR 4249. "I am deeply concerned about the constitutionality of a statute." He wondered "whether or not the President could in good conscience sign this proposal if and when it should come to his desk," implying a possible Nixon veto.[39]

Fewer dissents could be heard, however, because House leaders had limited the first House debate on the 18-year-old vote in US history to just one hour. Several House members objected. William Colmer of Mississippi, already outvoted once with this legislation in his role as chairman of the House Rules Committee, declared that "one of the great tragedies of what we are going through here today is that very limitation on time."[40] To compensate, representatives were given five days to revise and extend their remarks and insert additional materials into the *Congressional Record*.

As recorded, opponents advanced all the standard arguments against lowering the voting age. Young people were immature and irresponsible in spite of their education. Revising the voting age now could lead to even lower voting ages later. And "old enough to fight, old enough to vote" failed to persuade in 1970. The "screaming mob espousing this slogan," John Rarick of Louisiana derided, "are not veterans nor fighting men but rather draft dodgers, draft card burners, and revolutionary vandals who have no intention whatsoever of fighting—at least not for the United States."[41] Rarick was wrong, but he revealed how conservatives were reinterpreting and rejecting the foundational argument within the context of antiwar activism and draft resistance.

Opponents in the House also condemned the process. On states' rights grounds argued Alabama's George Andrews. He asserted that "the Senate amendment lowering the voting age to 18 shares a common evil with the 1965 Voting Rights Act, to which it is attached; both trample on the rights of the States."[42] Opponents, and not just southerners, attacked the legislative statute strategy. Clark MacGregor of Minnesota inserted pages and pages of letters from constitutional scholars to President Nixon on the issue. Still others believed accepting the resolution and thus the Senate's version of HR 4249 subordinated the House in the legislative process. It betrayed the bicameral structure of Congress.

But proponents carried the day. Celler made the pragmatic case for the resolution. A "vote against is tantamount to a vote against the extension of the Voting Rights Act" because the bill would go to conference where southern Senators would kill it. "If this bill goes back to the other body, then this bill is as dead as that flightless bird called the dodo."

Celler also made the principled case for the voting rights bill, referencing both past and present circumstances in his statement. "The Voting Rights Act is finally making the promise of the 15th amendment of the Constitution . . . a reality. It avails us little to cleanse our rivers and the air if we allow racism and bigotry to pollute our political atmosphere."[43]

Representative Abner Mikva, Democrat from Illinois and an important ally of the YFC, addressed the accusation that the 18-year-old vote was "some kind of 'ungermane' rider." It was not. In fact, "age, like race, residence, and reading, has a history of being used as an excuse to keep people from participating in the choosing process." These were equivalent qualifications and equally discriminatory and disfranchising. Mikva, a lawyer and political reformer, future judge and mentor to Barack Obama, captured what was at stake in the House vote. He entreated his colleagues: "We have the obligations to remove all impediments that deny people the most fundamental blessing of liberty, and that keep the Union from being more perfect."[44]

Mikva's reliable colleague among Republicans and another representative from Illinois, Tom Railsback, spoke to the motivations and frustrations of disfranchised young Americans. After serving as a member of the Brock congressional campus tour and report of the year before, he came away "convinced that the overwhelming majority of our students and our young people were sincerely motivated about their concerns. They were also very frustrated." Railsback considered a voice for youth in the political decision-making process to be absolutely vital.[45]

The most passionate plea came from Speaker of the House John McCormack, who had chosen to retire that year rather than run for reelection in November. "What the young people of this country want is to be part of our democracy. They want in. They want to be responsible citizens." YFC leaders spoke "fondly of that craggy political elder" for this reason and more. "In the closing seconds of the time allotted to me— and I shall not be back here next year—might I make a personal observation. Nothing would make John McCormack happier than to see this resolution adopted."[46] On this stirring note he got a standing ovation.

With a vote of 224 to 183 the House of Representatives passed the resolution to accept the Senate's version of HR 4249. Then, by an even bigger margin of 272 to 132 the House approved the final voting rights bill. Representatives who voted against the resolution, like Gerald Ford, switched to support on the final bill. Although more Democrats than Republicans voted for the resolution and the bill, they both had unassailable bipartisan support. Filled with youth franchise proponents, the gallery erupted in applause at the closing vote. "We were ecstatic," Ian remembers. "Hundreds of meetings, thousands of letters. Young people meeting on the Hill, meeting in their districts, meeting with the congressmen. And they finally culminated in success." "It was a good feeling, a very good feeling."[47]

Now the voting rights bill with the 18-year-old vote went to the president. Such strong support in Congress made a presidential veto less likely, but Nixon still had a decision to make. He could in fact veto the bill. He could sign it. Or he could decide to wait it out, whereby the bill would go into effect after ten legislative days. On June 22, 1970, Nixon signed reluctantly and released a statement explaining his decision. "Although I strongly favor the eighteen-year-old-vote, I believe—along with most of the Nation's leading constitutional scholars—that Congress has no power to enact it by simple statute, but rather it requires a constitutional amendment." He issued instructions to Attorney General John Mitchell "to cooperate fully expediting a swift court test of the constitutionality of the 18-year-old provision."[48] Nixon signed because to veto would have meant rejecting the entire voting rights bill. The urgency of extending the Voting Rights Act of 1965 compelled the new act's passage and signing in 1970.

Proponents of voting rights for African and young Americans applauded the president's action, but Nixon did not emerge unscathed. "Congress, Nixon Sacrificed Constitution for Vote at 18," accused James J. Kilpatrick, prominent conservative commentator and defender of segregation. "By signing this bill, our law-and-order President subverts law and order." A constitutional amendment was the correct path to youth suffrage. "This is the lawful, the orderly way to proceed in the matter at hand." Kilpatrick held out hope that the Supreme Court "will say as much in rebuking the impatience of Congress and the expediency of a President."[49] While Kilpatrick lamented, the Voting Rights Act of 1970 became the law of the land.

Many in the media emphasized the simple but significant fact that Black and youth voting rights had progressed in tandem. "Two big battles were won in a single bill—the Voting Rights Act of 1970," trumpeted the *AFL-CIO News*. "Votes for Blacks and Youths," topped the *Los Angeles Times*. An article in *Time* magazine presented the legislative process that produced the new Voting Rights Act as unparalleled. "Parliamentary historians may someday marvel at what the Democrats wrought." Progressing the political rights of two key constituencies simultaneously was equally unprecedented. "The maneuver turned two minorities into a majority."[50]

What a contrast from the Senate in 1954 when progress for African Americans with *Brown v. Board of Education* and school desegregation had set back progress for young Americans and their voting rights. Revealed then was how the future of the 18-year-old vote would be bound up in the fate of civil and voting rights for African Americans. In the subsequent decade and a half civil rights organizing, legislation, and successes provided and paved the way for the youth franchise. The Voting Rights Act of 1970, designed to ensure the continued enfranchisement of African Americans, had enacted the national enfranchisement of 18-, 19-, and 20-year-olds.

It didn't escape political, press, or popular attention that 1970 marked the 100th anniversary of the 15th Amendment. Black and youth suffrage had another connection. Even more 1970 celebrated the 50th anniversary of the 19th Amendment and the achievement of women's suffrage. These dates of 1870, 1920, and 1970 could be put aside as chronological coincidence. But for proponents and pundits Title III of the Voting Rights Act of 1970 symbolized the progress of American democracy and another step toward universal suffrage.

Yet only two branches of government had signed off on the enfranchisement of youth. Attention now turned to the Supreme Court and to the states. Attorney General Mitchell asked the states "to pledge full compliance" with the new law by August 3, 1970. He also affirmed that the Justice Department "would be defending the law when the court test came."[51] On August 25 Chief Justice Warren E. Burger announced the Supreme Court would hear arguments in two months. With the 1972 election soon approaching the case moved quickly.

Meanwhile, voting age referenda were pending in fifteen states, plus Puerto Rico and the US Virgin Islands. Alaska's referendum to lower the voting age to 18 occurred on the same day as Chief Justice Burger's announcement. For proponents those campaigns needed to succeed.

"We've got to work now, hopefully with administration support, to win approval," Pat Keefer said. "We feel it's vital to win as many of those referendum votes as possible, because we believe this will influence the courts in the constitutional tests" to come.[52] State action still very much mattered because no one knew how the Supreme Court would rule.

15

A Step Forward

Responses on the state and local levels to Title III of the Voting Rights Act of 1970 were as widely varied as those at the national level. The new legislation did not and could not instantly forge a consensus of opinion on the 18-year-old vote, especially with a judicial review pending. What Americans did agree on was that the issue topped the US political agenda and demanded attention and action now. This immediate situation could be seen in small and large ways among government officials, local journalists, and citizens at the grassroots.

One small indication of public interest in the issue was the response to media inquiries about youth voting rights. When *Ladies' Home Journal* ran a questionnaire in June 1970, within days they received over 8,000 responses to the question "Should 18-year-olds be allowed to vote?" Editor John Mack Carter called this "towering evidence of interest in the subject." In the midst of a feminist challenge to the stereotypical content and male-dominated staff of the most important women's magazine in the country, Carter contextualized youth suffrage with the history of women's suffrage. "*Females* voting? Only 50 years ago, this just didn't happen in America. Now the hot question isn't the sex of the balloter, but the age."

Reader responses divided evenly, 50–50, on the question. The geographical distribution of answers showed readers from the New England and Middle Atlantic states more in favor than those from the South Atlantic, Central, Mountain, and Pacific states. The age of the respondent mattered, perhaps unsurprisingly, with those older less in favor than the younger ones.

Readers of *Ladies' Home Journal* raised the usual arguments both for and against lowering the voting age to 18. Young people were responsible and mature enough to vote or they were not. "I was one of the first of the 18-year-olds to vote in 1943 in Georgia," wrote one woman. "We now have two sons of 19 and 23—responsible voters. The nation is long overdue giving the 18-year-olds the vote." They advanced the foundational argument. A Wisconsin woman with seven of her nine sons in the armed forces felt "it is outrageous that 18-year-olds have no voice in the government while 'old men' vote for war and profits at their expense." Opponents also reflected the backlash among adult voters. "Last year I would have voted yes. This year, after the destruction of property, drugs, and demonstrations on college campuses everywhere, I have less confidence."

Carter ended up editorializing in favor. "An 18-year-old vote probably won't change things, but it could encourage our most capable young leaders to stay and work within our democratic system." It also could foster connections between youth and their parents' generation. One young woman from Illinois, not yet a voter, noted, "I know just as much about politics as my mother does. She even agrees with me." "That's closing the generation gap," Carter concluded.[1]

A reporter for the *Los Angeles Times* conducted her own survey on the "new voting age" right after President Nixon signed the Voting Rights Act and with similar findings. Now that the youth vote was a reality and not just an idea, the younger respondents especially emphasized the impact they thought it would have on US politics. They believed the youth vote would make a difference. "Kids want to do some good for the country," stated one 18-year-old. "If I could vote in an election today, I would make the most sincere choice I could." "A lot of 18-year-olds are more aware of what's going on than a lot of adults," stated another. "I think there is going to be a bigger movement toward peace and that young people will help elect candidates who are for peace." "I do think that young people should help elect better qualified and younger candidates," said a third. A 22-year-old agreed. "I think it will mean younger people elected to government with younger ideas."[2]

The question of the youth vote's impact appeared in much local news coverage, revealing positive, negative, and neutral perspectives. An editorial on the new Voting Rights Act in the *Honolulu Advertiser* noted all three. "The potential impact of the 18-year-old vote can be exaggerated." Although over ten million young Americans would gain the franchise, their distribution across the country meant they could contribute to voting majorities but would rarely constitute one. "The danger in this country is not from young people becoming interested in the political process," as some opponents feared. "The danger is if they are not stimulated to take part." Given this concern, and while waiting for the Supreme Court test of the Voting Rights Act, the editors endorsed Hawaiʻi's proposed constitutional amendment lowering the voting age to 18 in a November referendum.[3]

Very positive perspectives on the local impact of the youth vote were also expressed. "Lowered Voting Age Brings Opportunities" headed a column in the Baltimore *Afro-American*. One was the opportunity to replace the political old guard and "aged political thinking." "This could be the start of a revolutionary era for black America in politics—in a whole lot of places. Young, more progressive thinking is given opportunity for meaningful expression."[4] Civil rights leader John Lewis, now head of the Voter Education Project in Atlanta, believed African Americans would make good use of the lowered voting age. In the midst of transforming the Voter Education Project from a funding to an activist organization, Lewis pointed out that "in some Georgia counties the 18 to 21 age group gives blacks a voting majority which is already showing results as blacks are beginning to win political offices."[5]

The aims of the Voter Education Project—voter registration and education among African Americans—were equally applicable to young Americans of all races. In an opinion piece in the *Boston Globe* in early July 1970, John S. Saloma, a founder of the Ripon Society and Harvard political scientist, explained. "The real political test for the 18-year-old vote will not be in the courts. It will be between the political ingenuity and determination of young Americans and the legal devices that will be used to disenfranchise them." Local and varied voter registration systems posed the greatest barrier to youth political participation, argued Saloma. "America is the only major democracy in the Western world that places the burden of voter registration on the individual instead of the state." Due to their high residential mobility, young people "are among the groups most severely hurt by restrictive registration." Saloma supported the so-called Princeton Plan of annual nationwide registration drives on college and high school campuses. He also encouraged the YFC to turn its attention to voter registration, which its companion organization, the Youth Citizenship Fund, was already prepared to do.

Saloma concluded with a mix of determination and inspiration. "A lot of hard grimy work is ahead. But, if the new political generation succeeds in cracking the registration barrier, it could be just the begin-ning of the most far reaching changes our encrusted political system has seen."[6] Saloma's opinion piece was prescient in every way. As with the freedom movement, every legislative achievement in Washington, DC, needed to be implemented on the ground and safeguarded by local people. The youth franchise movement couldn't rest, especially as the Voting Rights Act of 1970 still faced a court test.

The States Respond

Government officials in the 50 states began to respond to the Voting Rights Act of 1970. The states needed to decide whether or not they would comply with the new act and its different provisions. A pend-ing voting age referendum complicated the decision-making process, which was the case in fifteen states. In very few states was that process straightforward anyway. Still officials had to inform Attorney General John Mitchell of their intentions and soon.

Nearly half the states were "proceeding on the assumption that voting for 18-year-olds is the law of the land, and plan to set registration machin-ery in motion for them." New York was one. Pennsylvania's governor set Title III's effective date of January 1, 1971, as the state's youth registration start date. "I think we would be perfectly willing to comply with all terms of the voting rights act," said a legal adviser for the governor of Illinois. It helped that the state's recent constitutional convention included a voting age of 18, although Illinois voters still needed to approve the new constitu-tion in a December referendum. The governor of North Dakota sent the same message. "I would assume that we would have to follow federal law just like any state." After all, the Tennessee attorney general noted, "the legal presumption is that the act is constitutional until it is proven otherwise."

Other states were waiting for a Supreme Court ruling. South Carolina would take action "after we understand exactly what the law says," an-nounced the governor. In some states there was disagreement between state and local officials. New Mexico's governor pledged to "cooperate to the fullest in seeing New Mexico implement these provisions." But coop-eration would not be forthcoming from the city of Albuquerque, whose assistant district attorney believed that Title III was unconstitutional. A court ruling was needed to resolve such conflicts.

Finally, a group of states were "unable to pledge compliance because of specific restrictions in their state constitutions." "Under our constitution, the voting age is 21," explained a Wisconsin spokesman. "The governor couldn't arbitrarily indicate the state will abandon its constitutional requirements." California also refused. In these cases where the new Voting Rights Act conflicted with state law, the next step would be to "seek judicial relief in the courts," as North Carolina's board of elections executive secretary put it.[7]

Complicating this situation even further state voting restrictions not only pertained to age qualifications but other requirements, including those banned or changed by the new law. Arizona, for example, had a minimum voting age of 21 and an English literacy test. Idaho had a 21-year-old vote law, a literacy test, and a 60-day residency requirement. State officials stated they would be upholding these laws until a federal court ruled otherwise. With the Voting Rights Act of 1970 banning all literacy tests, requiring only a 30-day residency for presidential elections, and lowering the voting age to 18, Attorney General Mitchell would be taking both Arizona and Idaho to court. "The Justice Department picked the two states they figured would be the easiest to push around," Idaho's attorney general declared, "but they've got a fight on their hands."[8]

Adding to the complexity of the situation Oregon and Texas officials who had conveyed their cooperation in late July had changed their minds by mid-August. At first Governor Tom McCall of Oregon affirmed that the state would comply with Title III "provided it's adjudicated to be constitutional." He took this stance despite that fact that only two months before Oregon referendum voters had rejected the state's voting age amendment. In the meantime Oregon would "develop machinery to preregister young people" to be ready for January 1. Similarly, the Texas Secretary of State asserted voter applications for 18-, 19-, and 20-year-olds would be accepted starting on October 1. Voter certificates, however, would not be issued until a legal decision declared Title III constitutional.[9] Just three weeks later Oregon and Texas were suing the US government, with Attorney General Mitchell as defendant. "Both states said that their constitutions had set the voting age at 21, and charged that Congress lacked the constitutional authority to change this by statute."[10]

Responses also varied among states with an upcoming voting age referendum. If Nebraska's voters decided in the November referendum to lower the voting age to 20, the state constitution would again need to be revised to comply with the new federal law, assuming the Supreme Court upheld it. Maine voters also were weighing in on the 20-year-old vote in November. Yet in July the governor "said he had ordered that local voter registration boards be notified of the change in the voting age." Other Maine officials objected, saying the state constitution still needed to be changed to match Title III's 18-year-old vote.[11] The phrasing for New Jersey's referendum encompassed these various possibilities. "This State Constitutional amendment would extend all voting privileges to all properly registered voters 19 years of age and over. However, if the United States Supreme Court upholds the amendments to the Federal Voting Rights Act the voting age will be 18 years."

As proponents in the state campaigns planned and prepared for the upcoming elections, similar uncertainty and confusion affected them. Connecticut secretary of state Ella Grasso was in the unique position of combining her official role with cochairing the Connecticut Citizen Coalition "Let's Vote 18." She also was running for her first term in Congress. In July Grasso appealed to the state's attorney general for a ruling on whether or not to start registering 18-, 19-, and 20-year-olds in preparation for voting in 1971. One month after President Nixon signed the new voting rights act young people were inquiring about how to proceed. "I don't want to have to wait until Connecticut approves the 18-year-old vote before I can vote," said one former high school student council president.[12]

Edward J. Forand tried to clarify the confusing situation. At a July press conference to mark the opening of the Connecticut Citizen Coalition's statewide office in Hartford, Forand expressed how serious it was not to allow the new federal law to sidetrack their state campaign. "We must advise the electorate that the Voting Rights Act passed by Congress and signed by the President allowing 18-year-olds to vote in 1971 will in all likelihood be deemed unconstitutional by the Supreme Court and therefore won't go into effect." Another coalition and campaign leader, Elaine Orfanos, a senior at Yale, put it more concisely. "We are totally ignoring the bill which passed the US Senate. 99 percent of the people in our organization feel that it will be ruled as unconstitutional."[13] The problem was voters in the referendum states were unsure, undermining campaigns nearly everywhere.

Campaign Success and Failure

There were a few exceptions. Alaska had a very straightforward situation. Both the substance—the 18-year-old vote—and the timing—August—of the referendum aided success there. The voting age matched the new federal law, and the timing came early, only two months after its signing. Smoothing the process too was the fact that Alaska already had a voting age of 19. To all observers youth suffrage in the state had worked well since statehood in 1959. Familiarity with a voting age under the traditional 21 removed the resistance found elsewhere to rethinking this age marker and its significant social and political meanings.

The bipartisan political establishment of Alaska supported lowering the voting age to 18. At the national level, Senator Ted Stevens, a Republican, had signed on as a cosponsor to Mike Mansfield's Title III amendment back in March. At the local level, Henry Boucher, the mayor of Fairbanks, strongly endorsed the vote for 18-year-olds. "I feel that their involvement in our city and our State is vital to the future of Alaska as a pioneering state." Boucher also felt young voters would equally benefit "those States that are not privileged to have it."[14] Young Alaskans valued this privilege. Jacqueline Carr, the daughter of a Democratic gubernatorial candidate that year, participated as a defendant with the Youth Franchise Coalition in an upcoming court case pertaining to Title III. In the end 54 percent of referendum voters approved the voting age change for Alaska.

A similar political dynamic operated in the three states that approved a voting age change to 19 in November 1970. Massachusetts, Minnesota, and Montana had the support of their governors from both parties and endorsements from local leaders. All three states had prominent political figures pushing for youth suffrage at the national level. Ted Kennedy and Mike Mansfield were already in the Senate, and former vice president Hubert Humphrey was just then making a successful bid to return. Student-led organizations in each state worked to lower the voting age, and all were founded in late 1968. Proponents initially set their sights on the 18-year-old vote but settled for 19. 18 × 72 in Massachusetts revised its name to 19 × 70, 18 × 72 to fit this new aim. The Montana Student

Presidents Association started Project 19. The University of Minnesota Student Association, Young Republicans, Teenage Republicans, and the Minnesota Young Democratic-Farmer-Labor Party formed the Minnesota Coalition to Lower the Voting Age, bringing together an estimated 60,000 young Minnesotans.

Within the youth franchise movement the Minnesota Coalition to Lower the Voting Age (MCLVA) was recognized as running a highly effective campaign. The Student Minnesota Education Association was central and called upon its parent organization for legislative and lobbying assistance. The Minnesota Education Association, in turn, kept its 40,000 members informed about the campaign. By the time of the state referendum the governor, both US senators, all eight of the state's US representatives, and a majority of citizens in opinion polls favored the 19-year-old vote, Amendment No. 2. So did a diverse range of civic and professional organizations. The AFL-CIO, League of Women Voters, Minnesota Jaycees, Minnesota Association of Commerce and Industry, and the American Legion joined the statewide movement.

These supporters plus the MCLVA's membership numbered about 40 organizations. They provided volunteers, funding, publicity, and advice. Governor Harold LeVander met with coalition leaders and mentored them, especially on handling backlash attitudes among older adults. He told them, "You're going to have this psychological argument and you might as well face up to it."[15] They emphasized that the vast majority of young Minnesotans already acted as responsible citizens and would continue to do so after enfranchisement.

The MCLVA also needed to face up to voter confusion over state versus federal action on youth voting rights. In a newspaper advertisement published the day before Election Day, the coalition directly addressed this question. "Why, you might ask, is it necessary for Minnesota citizens to vote on this amendment following President Nixon's approval of the federal Voting Rights Act, which gives 18-year-olds the right to vote in national elections?" Since suffrage qualifications "have traditionally been considered a states' rights issue," uncertainty existed over "whether it is a proper matter for Federal control." "Amendment 2 will clarify the situation for Minnesota voters." "Don't let your apathy kill youth's responsible alternative," urged the MCLVA's ad. "Vote on November 3!"[16] Minnesotans did, and the Vote 19 amendment passed.

Voting age campaign buttons, ca. 1970. Courtesy of Division of Political and Military History, National Museum of American History, Smithsonian Institution.

Voting age amendments also passed in other states and territories in November. Puerto Rico lowered the voting age to 18, and Maine and Nebraska to 20. Given that just two years ago Nebraskans had rejected the 19-year-old vote, proponents there appreciated this success. An explanation emerged for the change of heart. "In Nebraska, voters kept one eye on the ballot and the other on their wallets. Which offers one possible reason that the lower voting age amendment was approved. It doesn't cost anything."[17]

Referenda results in the US Virgin Islands and Wyoming required court decisions. In both cases not every voter taking part in the election marked their ballot on the suffrage age measure. In the Virgin Islands a voting age of 18 won the most votes, as did 19 in Wyoming. Project 19 at the University of Wyoming, chaired by Nena Roncco, had convinced referendum voters of their motto: "Responsible action by responsible youth."[18] But the question arose of whether a majority of the total votes cast was necessary to secure victory. Following the intervention of the Legislature of the Virgin Islands and two petitions to the Wyoming Supreme Court, 18-year-olds won enfranchisement in the Virgin Islands, but 19 and 20-year-olds did not in Wyoming. "I accept the decision of the court," announced Wyoming's governor Stanley Hathaway, "and hope the legislature will focus its attention on the amendment process." He sought a simple majority for amendment approval.[19] For proponents of youth voting rights in Wyoming, though, democracy had been thwarted by a technicality.

Democracy in eight other states went against proponents in November 1970. For the second time the 18-year-old vote was defeated in Hawai'i and Michigan. New Jersey and South Dakota voters rejected the 19-year-old vote, the second and third time they chose not to lower the voting age. Colorado and Florida's first Vote 18 referenda ended in losses. But the most heartbreaking loss had to be in Connecticut, followed by the defeat in Washington State.

For four long years Let's Vote 18 in Connecticut had been consistently working to achieve youth voting rights. Organizing, strategizing, lobbying, and testifying from 1967 to 1969 culminated in what Edward Forand called "an unrelenting campaign" in 1970. "The strategy is that of a professional political campaign in which the issue is the candidate," explained Elaine Orfanos.[20] An estimated 3,000 volunteers took part in politicking in the months before the 18-year-old vote referendum. They sent speakers out to schools, community organizations, and service clubs. They raised money through car washes and bake sales. "By leafletting, telephoning and person-to-person discussion, we hope to show . . . voters the positive, constructive results that a lowering of the voting age would bring," stated one local chapter chairman.[21]

Just as in Minnesota, Wyoming, and everywhere else proponents in Connecticut concentrated on correcting the negative media stereotype of young Americans. "We have to demonstrate to adults in Connecticut that the great majority of young people are deeply concerned with and involved in the issues of Vietnam, the inner cities, environmental control, the tax structure, and other state and local issues," contended Forand at the start of the referendum campaign, "without resorting to violence and disorder." "I'm not condemning anyone—not cutting down what the radical students and SDS are doing—but I think it's important."[22] In Forand's final analysis, the campaign's failure to counter the "media kid" predominated.

After a referendum loss the *Hartford Courant* called "a squeaker"—a difference of 20,000 votes out of over 600,000 cast—Forand dissected the disappointing results. He attributed the loss mainly to the fact that "not one of the major candidates went to bat for us. I don't think it showed very much leadership on the part of any of them." It hadn't helped that days before the election there had been "an egg-throwing incident near President Nixon's car" in California. He also wondered if perhaps "we might have been too organized." By stationing Let's Vote 18 volunteers outside polling stations, they may have not only won supporters for the 18-year-old vote but "reminded opposed persons to vote against it." Tellingly, 60,000 more voters marked their ballot on the suffrage age measure than did on another, passing measure. "If nothing else, we convinced the people to vote," Forand concluded disconcertedly.[23]

A similarly diligent campaign with similarly discouraging results occurred in the state of Washington. "History will not record this as a well organized, well executed, or well financed campaign," observed Mark Brown—actually the YFC disagreed on that point—"but it will show that a true coalition of young and old people worked very hard today for our future." Campaign coordinator for Vote 19 and a 20-year-old student at the University of Washington, Mark estimated they had 10,000 young people working through local committees in the state's 39 counties. Mike Lowry of the Young Democrats and Sam Reed of the Young Republicans served as cochairs for the bipartisan Vote 19. They got Governor Dan Evans, a Republican, to declare "Vote 19 Day" on October 19, the same day, it turned out, that the Supreme Court heard arguments on the constitutionality of the new Voting Rights Act. Although "virtually broke," the Vote 19 campaign benefited from "student manpower," the support of civic organizations, and positive local news coverage. "This is the only advertisement we have," Mark admitted at the time.[24]

As elsewhere, Vote 19 campaigners and state officials in Washington confronted questions about state versus federal action on youth voting rights and the pending Supreme Court decision. "At this point the vast majority of people are very confused," secretary of state Ludlow Kramer believed.[25] "People assume that because the federal act has been passed, there is no reason to support this state movement," Mark commented. The opposite was true. "We can't just wait for the ruling, because it comes after the election, and we have no guarantee that they will rule favorably. So, we have to keep campaigning."[26]

Vote 19 proponents in Washington joined other state campaigns in trying to change the "media kid" image of young Americans. "Our biggest task is to convince adults not to condemn an entire entity—the 19 and 20 year olds—because of the actions of a few," Mark told the press. "The vast majority of that age group are concerned and involved citizens." But "every time a building is bombed, we lose votes." Garnering much media attention at the time was the Seattle Liberation Front and allied antiwar activists, of which seven were on trial for street demonstrations and disruptions earlier in the year. The date of October 31 also had been set for another Vietnam Moratorium in the state. "If the demonstrations get out of the rational bounds of protest, it will hurt its chances of passage," Governor Evans conceded.[27]

Not only was backlash a big concern for Vote 19. Mark worried the radical left would intentionally aim to discredit the campaign. "The radicals do not want this bill to pass," he argued, "because they operate on the premise that the system does not work. Every time something like Vote 19 succeeds or a liberal candidate is elected, it is a setback for the radicals, because it shows that the system does work."[28]

Student proponents elsewhere made points along similar lines. Why weren't members of the new left involved in campaigns to lower the voting age? Since they prioritize "involvement of self in social action and reforms, their silence on this very important issue is perplexing to some." Perhaps they want "to increase student alienation, not student participation," editorialized a student newspaper in North Carolina.[29] At the same time Young Americans for Freedom now overtly opposed lowering the voting age. YAF allied with older conservatives, dividing and disparaging their own generation. "Young people, having had few experiences in day-to-day life, tend to have a theoretical approach to government and to embrace extreme positions," explained one spokesman. "Witness the fact that Hitler attributed much of his electoral success to young people."[30] The early sixties student movements of the left and the right were not in the fight for youth voting rights in 1970.

When the referendum returns came in, the 19-year-old vote had lost handily in Washington State, with 44 percent in favor and 53 percent opposed. "At the end of the day, we had our asses handed to us," Mark recalls. "I was surprised and disappointed. You had broad bipartisan support, you had little or no active opposition. I thought we had a real shot at winning."[31] So did the Youth Franchise Coalition, which had helped with campaigning there and elsewhere. The "Vote 19 effort of Washington State could not overcome the irrational voter backlash against youth," reported Rosalyn Hester and Ian MacGowan to YFC board and member organizations.[32] Of course this was the story for most campaigns that year.

Of 19 referenda in the greater United States in 1970—including the December referendum on the 18-year-old vote provision in the proposed Illinois constitution—only eight voting age amendments passed. Commentators concluded that a combination of factors—some applicable nationally, others local in nature—defeated voting age measures on Election Day. Major factors were the old "voter resentment over campus unrest" and the new one in 1970 of "apathy stemming from this year's approval of a federal 18-year-old voting law." In Illinois, low youth voter turnout in Georgia and neighboring Kentucky became a factor. "These returns," a Project 18 organizer in Chicago wrote, "are one of the facts they are holding against us."[33]

Reports out of Louisville registration and voting projects that election year proved relevant. They showed that college and university students aged 18 and up did participate regularly. "But their question very often is, 'what will it profit me?'" Reverend Arthur Smith of the NAACP felt that "you have to be sure and show them what they'll personally get out of voting." Significantly, Smith found "some enthusiasm in the primaries" among young African American voters, "because of the black slate we had." When there was something or someone meaningful to vote for, they did. Of young people not enrolled in higher education, the turnout was much lower. "The tragedy is they don't vote," expressed a spokeswoman for the Louisville League of Women Voters.[34]

Of the varied voting age developments across the nation in the fall of 1970, one place was singular: Washington, DC. That September the District of Columbia gained a minor measure of representation in Congress. After decades of proposals and petitions, DC citizens won the right to elect one nonvoting delegate to the House of Representatives. Like Puerto Rico's resident commissioner and the soon-to-be delegates from American Samoa, Guam, the Northern Mariana Islands, and the US Virgin Islands, the District of Columbia delegate could introduce but not vote on legislation. Still the District of Columbia Delegate Act (1970) expanded on the 23rd Amendment giving DC citizens votes in the Electoral College.

Because DC is not a state the Voting Rights Act of 1970 with its Title III became immediately effective there. The Youth Citizenship Fund, now activated with Ian MacGowan as executive director, began assisting with registration. The DC board of elections held a special youth registration event on Saturday, October 17. "Above all, the point of today's hoopla is that this colony is serious in its desire to win the human and civil rights enjoyed by the rest of the nation," editorialized the *Washington Post*. The editors also recognized that "we will have to turn out in droves for this small beginning at political self-expression."[35] The 18-, 19-, and 20-year-old voters were seen as vital to this expression. For proponents of youth voting rights the courts were now the place to make this case.

Challenge in the Courts

On Monday, October 19, 1970, the US Supreme Court heard arguments in four cases concerning the constitutionality of the Voting Rights Act of 1970. *Oregon v. Mitchell, Texas v. Mitchell, US v. Arizona,* and *US v. Idaho* sought to determine whether the literacy test ban, 30-day residency requirements for presidential elections, and 18-year-old vote were constitutional. Each of the states had counsel, and US Solicitor General Edwin N. Griswold represented Attorney General Mitchell and the United States. The YFC, its allies, and additional states submitted amicus curiae, or "friend of the court," briefs. Some also asked to participate in oral arguments, but to no avail.

Citizens for Lowering the Voting Age in California also participated in this process. Their lawyer, Jack Cosgrove, had been offering legal advice to Senator Birch Bayh and other proponents along the way and submitted an amicus brief. According to Dennis King it was important for a state-based voting age organization like theirs to contribute to these important national developments. They were especially concerned about Mitchell's commitment to the case. "Why would he do a good job defending legislation that he didn't want?" Senators Bayh and Ted Kennedy harbored similar doubts and even suggested a special "Senate counsel" to represent them and their arguments before the court. "There has been no criticism on these grounds of the government's briefs," assured a reporter for the *Washington Post.*[36]

In fact the US government's brief defending the Voting Rights Act of 1970 in *Christopher v. Mitchell*, an earlier case in federal district court, drew on the arguments of Senate proponents. The three-judge panel issued two opinions that unanimously upheld the constitutionality of the Voting Rights Act on October 2, 1970. The decision in *Christopher v. Mitchell* bolstered youth voting rights proponents and boded well for forthcoming arguments before the Supreme Court.

Still everyone knew the outcome was uncertain. "If the Supreme Court rules against this bill," Roz Hester stated in September, "we will launch a more massive campaign than last year's to get this bill passed by Constitutional amendment." More hopefully, if "the Court's ruling is in our favor, we will launch a nationwide voter registration campaign to bring all 11 million American youths into the voting booths."[37] Representative Richard H. Poff, Republican from Virginia who objected to Title III and rejected the Voting Rights Act as a result, saw the Supreme Court in a "no-win" situation. "If it sustains the provision, it will bring down severe criticism on itself for having amended the Constitution via judicial fiat. And if it fails to sustain it, it will have contributed to a new divisiveness in our society."[38]

Out of this situation came an extraordinary Supreme Court ruling on December 21, 1970. In *Oregon v. Mitchell* the nine justices issued five separate opinions totaling 184 pages. William J. Brennan Jr. wrote one, which Thurgood Marshall and Byron R. White signed onto. Potter Stewart's opinion was joined by Chief Justice Warren Burger and Harry A. Blackmun. William O. Douglas, John Marshall Harlan, and Hugo L. Black each penned their own. Taken together these opinions upheld unanimously the literacy test ban and affirmed eight to one the 30-day residency requirement in the Voting Rights Act of 1970.

But on the power of Congress to lower the voting age to 18 for local, state, and federal elections, they sharply divided. At stake once again was the relationship between states' rights and federal authority. An issue that originated with the nation's founding arose time and again with Americans' struggles over suffrage. In 1970 the states of Oregon, Texas, Arizona, and Idaho argued that they had the right to determine the minimum age for voting in their states, not Congress. Eight of the nine Supreme Court justices divided evenly on this question, although their four opinions laid out different legal reasoning for these conclusions. Four—Stewart, Burger, Blackmun, and Harlan—were in favor of the states determining suffrage qualifications and thus striking down Title III. Four—Brennan, Marshall, White, and Douglas—were in favor of Congress taking action on youth voting rights and thus upholding Title III.

Differing interpretations of the 14th Amendment were at the heart of this disagreement between the so-called conservative and liberal justices. The conservatives interpreted the 14th Amendment narrowly. For Harlan it concerned civil not political rights, which was why the 15th Amendment was needed later. For Stewart, Burger, and Blackmun, Congress could not define the scope of the Equal Protection Clause, find a violation, and then provide a remedy. This conclusion constituted a major change from *Katzenbach v. Morgan* (1966), the result of two new Nixon-nominated justices on the court, Burger and Blackmun. All four conservatives agreed that state sovereignty over suffrage qualifications was guaranteed under Article 1 of the US Constitution. The four liberal justices reversed each of these arguments with their broad interpretation of the 14th Amendment. It did concern political rights, and Congress did have the power to use the equal protection and enforcement clauses to set the voting age for local, state, and federal elections. The eight justices were at an impasse.

In a surprising development the ninth, Justice Hugo Black, split the difference both ways, forming a majority of one. Black issued the Supreme Court's judgment that Congress could set the voting age for federal but not for state and local elections. Importantly, he concluded that the 14th Amendment did concern political rights and that Congress had wide scope to apply equal protection in matters of race—but not age. The 14th along with the 13th and 15th Amendments "were unquestionably designed to condemn and forbid every distinction, however trifling, on account of race." But neither the equal protection nor the enforcement clauses were "intended to permit Congress to prohibit every discrimination between groups of people." The 14th Amendment thus did not give Congress the authority to set the voting age.

Instead Black located the authority to set a federal voting age in Article 1, Section 4. "The Times, Places and Manner of holding Elections for Senators and Representatives, shall be prescribed in each State by the Legislature thereof; but the Congress may at any time by Law make or alter such Regulations." For Justice Black 1970 was one such time, and the 18-year-old vote was one such regulation. "It cannot be doubted that these comprehensive words embrace authority . . . to enact the numerous requirements as to procedure and safeguards which experience shows are necessary in order to enforce the fundamental right involved."[39] For the first time in US history the Supreme Court had judged voting in federal elections a "fundamental right" for young Americans.

It could be said that Black crafted a "win-win" decision. Everyone got something they wanted, and no one got everything. The decision supported state sovereignty over suffrage qualifications but provided a role for Congress in expanding voting rights. Both were priorities of Justice Black. At 84 he had been serving on the Supreme Court since his 1937 nomination by President Franklin Roosevelt. Considered a southern progressive, Black contributed to the court upholding rather than striking down New Deal legislation, and he was a staunch believer in civil liberties. Yet he'd been a member of the Ku Klux Klan in Alabama in the 1920s, leading to a bitter joke upon his nomination. "Hugo won't have to buy a robe. He can dye his white one black." With regard to key civil and voting rights decisions over the decades, he was mostly in the majority, as with *Katzenbach v. Morgan*, but not always.

Black's careful crafting of two majorities in *Oregon v. Mitchell*—five to four rejecting the 18-year-old vote for state and local elections and five to four upholding it for federal ones—meant he bore the brunt of criticism. Supporters of states' rights and opponents of youth voting rights (and these categories tended to overlap) didn't see any wins for their positions. A "shabby sequel to a shabby gesture in Congress," pronounced a *Washington Post* commentator. The "American people are being ruled by a judicial oligarchy," proclaimed Senator Sam Ervin.[40] Newspaper editorials could be scathing. "Ruling on Vote Law Nibbles at Dwindling Rights of States." "The Damage It Has Done." "A Dreadful Error on 18-Year-Old Voting." "A Sad Day for Justice Black." Condemnatory letters filled the justice's mailbox. The most vituperative came by telegram from St. Louis. "This conservative condemns your decision yesterday as illegal, unconstitutional, immoral, aberrated, hideous, evil, and despicable."[41]

Of course proponents of youth voting rights were not completely happy with the outcome either. The *Oregon* decision was obviously contradictory. As Paul Myer recalls it would "allow 18-year-old men and women to vote for President of the United States and Congressmen, but they could not vote for the mayor or the dog catcher." After the decision *Newsweek* suggested "a new refrain took shape: 'If he's old enough to vote for President, he's old enough to vote for county clerk.'"[42] A cartoon in the *Christian Science Monitor* captured this contradiction well. Captioned "Gift wrapped," the December 24 cartoon pictured a crate under a Christmas tree labeled "The 18-Year-Old-Vote." But it was bound up with ropes called "Tie-Ups," "State Laws," and "Registration."[43] This situation, which would require a dual-age voting system in most of the country, was untenable.

Proponents at the local, state, and national levels quickly pointed out the problems and proposed solutions. The day after the *Oregon* decision, Los Angeles councilman and future mayor Tom Bradley called on California governor Ronald Reagan and the state legislature to act immediately to lower the voting age to 18. "The Supreme Court decision, albeit the right one, has left us with a chaotic and illogical situation," Bradley argued.

> Unless the situation is remedied by an amendment of our election laws, we shall have to furnish separate ballots for those between the ages of 18 and 21, for those 21 and over; also separate registration lists. The consequence will be increased costs for all elections, as well as justifiable criticism of the arbitrary distinctions made.[44]

Similarly speedy actions occurred at the national level. "Minutes after the ruling was announced Sen. Edward M. Kennedy (D-Mass.) said he would move for the quick adoption of a constitutional amendment to lower the voting age to 18 in state and local elections."[45]

An amendment to the US Constitution setting a uniform national voting age had become necessary. "This would eliminate the pandemonium that would be caused at the polls by conflicting state and federal laws," noted the *AFL-CIO News*.[46] Proponents of youth voting rights had long seen a constitutional amendment as needed. They were now joined by others, even former opponents. "The clean and proper way to lower the voting age to 18 was, and is, a constitutional amendment," observed one legal scholar.[47] The daunting prospect of two different sets of voting regulations and procedures drove the push for the 26th Amendment.

Just two days after *Oregon v. Mitchell* came down, Roz Hester wrote the board of the Youth Franchise Coalition. "Securing a lowered voting age for national elections is a step forward, but it's just the beginning. The task now is twofold: to translate the franchise into meaningful political participation and to give young people the right to vote on all levels of government."[48] They had their work cut out for them.

16

On Account of Age

The Youth Franchise Coalition's leadership team lost no time in getting back to work. Through the Youth Citizenship Fund, Project 18, and their membership organizations, they were already working to ensure that young Americans used their new voting rights to take part in the political process. Voter registration was the logical place to start. "Let's go register those 18 year olds. Let's not lose this moment," Pat Keefer recalls thinking at the time. "Let's use the National Education Association and the American Federation of Teachers and these youth groups that are part of the coalition to start registration. Let's go!"

And they did. In addition to the Youth Citizenship Fund assisting youth registration in Washington, DC, the Student California Teachers Association began registering 18-, 19-, and 20-year-olds in California. "Their members are becoming deputy registrars and are actively soliciting potential youth voters," Roz Hester and Ian MacGowan reported. Oregon's Go-19 reorganized as the Vote 18 Coalition and reached out to student groups, churches, the League of Women Voters, and the secretary of state to publicize and facilitate registration for young Oregonians.[1] Director of the NAACP's Youth and College Division James Brown Jr. announced a nationwide drive to register newly enfranchised young people, with a campaign kickoff early in the new year. "It is high time that we realize that black people, poor people, and young people, regardless of color, have been the victims of scorn by those who make our laws," argued the NAACP field director in South Carolina. "This situation will not be alleviated until all are given full franchise."[2]

The YFC and Project 18 were also working to extend youth suffrage from the national level to the state and local levels. Following the decision in *Oregon v. Mitchell*, they consulted with a handful of state and local officials. Included were Ludlow Kramer, secretary of state for Ian's home state of Washington, and the board of elections director for Hamilton County, Ohio, where Pat Keefer hailed from. On January 5, 1971, they

Patricia Keefer urging 18-year-olds to use their newly won political power and vote, 1971. Bettmann Archive via Getty Images.

began to hold a series of meetings on Capitol Hill. They met with key members of Congress, their administrative or legislative assistants, and legal counsel for Senator Birch Bayh's Subcommittee on Constitutional Amendments. Out of these discussions came two clear conclusions. Maintaining dual-age voting systems would cost state and local governments millions of dollars. As a consequence, a quick constitutional amendment lowering the voting age to 18 was definitely possible.

Meanwhile, the NAACP hadn't given up on a more favorable Supreme Court ruling on Title III of the Voting Rights Act of 1970. In early January 1971 NAACP attorneys, including Clarence Mitchell, sought a decision that covered state and local as well as federal elections. They filed motions for a rehearing and for leave to intervene, that is, to have a 19-year-old petitioner, Dawn P. German, become party to the proceedings alongside the states and the US government. The attorneys contended that their amicus brief had not been raised in court by Attorney General John Mitchell. Their brief also had not been addressed in any of the justices' opinions in the case. Former NAACP chief counsel and now justice Thurgood Marshall may have done so, but he did not write his own opinion. The argument in the NAACP brief focused on Congress's war powers as defined in Article 1 of the US Constitution. "The national defense needs and conditions that exist in the nation can reasonably be held to warrant the exercise of congressional power to grant the vote to 18-year-olds." The Justice Department declined the NAACP motions as "unwarranted."[3]

Despite this disappointment, the NAACP's Youth Work Committee soon called upon all youth councils, college divisions, and adult branches to advance the 18-year-old vote in their states. "Now that the Supreme Court of the land has taken the lead in the issue for federal elections, the state and local authorities should immediately take the necessary legal steps to secure the vote for 18-year-olds at the sub-national level."[4]

Similar developments occurred among other youth voting rights proponents. After the Vote 19 victory in November and *Oregon v. Mitchell* in December, the Minnesota Coalition to Lower the Voting Age reorganized as the Minnesota Youth Franchise Coalition. The new organization set to work on voter information and registration for "all newly enfranchised young Minnesotans" and on "obtaining consistent voting age of 18 in all elections." They had no preference whether consistency was obtained through a state or federal amendment. They just wanted "the most expedient route."[5]

State actions to register young voters and make the voting age consistent across all levels of government were also in progress. The YFC polled the states in January and found that 33 states had started to register citizens aged 18 and up to vote in federal elections. Thirty-seven states had introduced legislation to lower the voting age to 18. In Massachusetts Governor Francis W. Sargent issued a proclamation declaring January to be "Youth Voter Registration Month." It began a "concerted effort to register to vote all eligible young citizens of the Commonwealth." And Sargent sought another constitutional amendment to further lower the voting age to 18, although voters had just approved the 19-year-old vote in November.[6]

Of course most states required a constitutional amendment and voter referendum to change the voting age. Kansas, Nevada, and New York were on track to hold Vote 18 referenda in April, June, and November 1971. A few—Indiana, Tennessee, Utah, West Virginia, and Wisconsin— would seek to change the voting age by legislative statute.[7] State officials were exploring other strategies too. One strategy was to pass a resolution or "memorial" requesting Congress to initiate an amendment to the US Constitution. Legislators in Connecticut and Michigan pursued this strategy. To prompt their state legislature, the Minnesota Youth Franchise Coalition worked with the secretary of state's office to draft and introduce a "resolution memorializing Congress to submit to the states a federal 'vote at 18' constitutional amendment."[8]

In many of these states, officials, legislators, and proponents acted within the context of recent referenda results, successful or not. In February the Wyoming House of Representatives and the Senate again approved a state constitutional amendment to lower the voting age—this time to 18. The proposed amendment would again go before Wyoming voters. There were two catches, however. After the 1970 referendum, when Vote 19 passed but not by a large enough majority, the governor had called for a change to the state's amendment process. That change hadn't happened yet, so a simple majority still would not succeed. In addition, the new referendum would not be held until 1972, meaning Wyoming would have to provide for dual-age voting in that election. This last catch affected over 20 other states as well.

Citizens in the various states recognized the contradiction and challenge of the youth suffrage situation. A Chicago high school student offered her opinion for "The Voice of Youth" column in the *Chicago Tribune*. "The Supreme Court ruling on the lowering of the Federal voting age and the subsequent action of Illinois retaining 21 as the voting age in state elections clearly points to a difference in attitudes that could be smoothed out with common sense." Coming much too late for the current circumstances, her compromise was a voting age of 19. But she raised an important reason: "Since 19 is the draft age, 19 also should be the voting age." In fact, the draft lottery held in July 1970 effectively raised the draft age to 19 by limiting selection to men born in 1951. The August 1971 lottery would be limited to men born in 1952. In her mind the 19-year-old draft no longer justified the 18-year-old vote.[9]

Such a compromise was no longer pragmatic or principled in 1971. It would not solve the problems of dual-age voting, and the federal voting age of 18 now set the ideal and practical standard for suffrage. In January President Nixon joined the effort to encourage young Americans to use their new voting rights. Addressing students at the University of Nebraska, Nixon harkened back to early proponents like Jennings Randolph and Harley Kilgore and placed youth suffrage within a larger national story.

> The whole history of democracy in this country is a chronicle of the constant broadening of the power to participate. Each new group receiving the franchise has had a beneficial effect on the course of America. Each new group has given freshness and vitality to the purposes of government. And now it's your turn to do the same.[10]

The president didn't discuss whether young Americans would have a turn at the state and local levels or, if so, how national leadership could help to bring about such an opportunity. To find out all eyes turned to Congress.

Youth Will Be Served

In late January and early February 1971 the House of Representatives and the Senate of the 92nd Congress initiated the amendment process to lower the voting age to 18 for the final—and finally fruitful—time. The Youth Franchise Coalition was there every step of the way. On January 25 Roz Hester reported to YFC member organizations and allies that the leadership in both political parties and in both houses of Congress had committed support. Even more they "assured success for an amendment if an intensive lobbying effort is begun immediately." She called upon the coalition for a letter-writing campaign to each member of Congress and outreach to specific legislators. "Time is of the essence," Roz wrote. "This demands immediate action!"[11]

Yet an unavoidable limit to taking action existed, as Roz and Ian MacGowan explained to the YFC board of directors a few days earlier. The YFC had the knowledge, experience, connections, and membership to undertake this massive lobbying effort. Combined with "the absence of any other group to do so, the leadership of the Youth Franchise Coalition must coordinate." But they were in dire financial straits. A debt of $25,000 led to "their inability to financially support the Coalition."[12]

Coming to the rescue was a new mass-membership lobbying organization, Common Cause. John W. Gardner, a Republican and former

Secretary of Health, Education, and Welfare in the Johnson administration, launched Common Cause in August 1970. Gardner strongly believed that there were "many, many Americans who would like to help rebuild this nation but don't know where to begin" and "the things that unite us as a people are more important than the things that divide us." A citizens' lobby devoted to the public interest could make a difference, because real reform was "the common cause."[13] Youth suffrage via a US constitutional amendment was one such reform because it would benefit every constituency in the country. "Common Cause has agreed to fund the lobbying effort," Roz and Ian told the YFC board, and hired Ian and Pat as consultants for the next four months.[14]

"We need to get this thing out to the states by April," Pat said, after getting hired by Common Cause. "That way the states will have time to ratify it before the end of January, 1972."[15] Since the schedule for legislative sessions varied across the states, the timing was tricky. It was fortunate that 1971 was an odd-numbered year, meaning a majority of state legislatures would meet. Some already were, and the length of their sessions varied. Others not scheduled to meet in 1971 could hold special sessions. "But, we are working against time."[16]

So were congressional proponents. For the eleventh time, Jennings Randolph introduced an amendment to the US Constitution lowering the voting age to 18. On January 25 he proposed Senate Joint Resolution 7, ultimately cosponsored by 86 senators. Randolph had secured more cosponsors than the two-thirds majority needed for the passage of a constitutional amendment. He kept his comments relatively brief, starting with the many "cumbersome" and "costly" difficulties arising from dual-age voting. Still he didn't let his fellow senators forget the fundamental reason for action. "That persons who have attained the age of 18 should have the right to vote is the overriding issue."[17] Four days later Emanuel Celler introduced House Joint Resolution 223. Both resolutions went straight to their respective judiciary committees.

House Joint Resolution 223 raced through the House Judiciary Committee. Instead of his decades-long obstruction, Celler smoothed the way. As chair he submitted a report to accompany the resolution. It covered the recent history of Title III, *Oregon v. Mitchell,* and the dual-age voting that resulted. The problems of dual-age voting and of each state trying to adopt the 18-year-old vote separately were outlined. This information helped to make the case for a uniform national voting age achieved through constitutional amendment. The House report included supporting letters from Paul A. Freund and Louis H. Pollack. After disagreeing on the legislative statute strategy used by Congress in 1970, these legal scholars concurred on the constitutionality of the amendment strategy in 1971. Given "the need for expeditious action," the report concluded, "additional hearings at this time would be undesirable." After all, the merits of the 18-year-old vote had been well demonstrated by the Senate subcommittee hearings held by Senator Birch Bayh the year before.[18] By a 32 to 2 vote the committee approved the resolution on March 2.

At the same time Senate Joint Resolution 7 advanced through Bayh's Subcommittee on Constitutional Amendments and then the full Senate Judiciary Committee. As in the House new hearings were deemed unnecessary, given those held just a year ago. The subcommittee also issued a report, a survey of the 50 states on the impact of dual-age voting, which it found "illogical and morally indefensible." The report went over much of the same ground as the House report, although at greater length and in more detail. Summaries of each state's situation—the number of voters aged 18, 19, and 20 affected, the costs and problems of dual-age voting, and the process of lowering the voting age in that state—were included. It turned out that some individual states could not take action until 1973, 1974, or even, in the case of Tennessee, 1977. The YFC facilitated this information-gathering and, along with Common Cause and Ludlow Kramer, were thanked for their "valuable assistance."[19] On March 4 the Senate Judiciary Committee unanimously passed the resolution.

On March 8 and 9 Birch Bayh and Emanuel Celler reported these resolutions favorably to the Senate and the House of Representatives. Rules for proceeding had already been decided, and dates for floor action were set. During this crucial time YFC staff, members, and allies worked both wings of the Capitol building. Debate was limited to just one day in both legislative chambers. And on March 10 and 23, senators and representatives had their say on the Senate and House joint resolutions, with permission to revise and extend their remarks for the record.

Even with the critical consequences posed by dual-age voting, there were opponents in Congress, at least in the House of Representatives.

Wiley Mayne, Republican from Iowa, and Charles E. Wiggins, Republican from California, were the two House Judiciary Committee members who opposed House Joint Resolution 223. Their dissenting views were included in the House report submitted by Celler and again in the *Congressional Record* as part of the March 23 debate. Maintaining state sovereignty over suffrage qualifications motivated their opposition. Mayne criticized proponents of youth suffrage. "They have renewed their attack upon the federal system, and I protest that they do so with unseemly and unnecessary haste." He took issue with the lack of House Judiciary Committee hearings in the current Congress or in "any preceding Congress since 1943." Wiggins also blamed the liberalizing American culture of the sixties. With young people, "we lack the collective will to say 'no' to them. In this we sadly mirror the permissiveness of society as a whole."[20]

Other representatives felt they couldn't vote for youth enfranchisement when referendum voters in their states had recently refused it. Edith Green, Democrat from Oregon, was one. "I think it is seldom that any constituency gives such a clear-cut mandate on any legislative issue as my State did on the 19-year-old vote when they voted better than 2 to 1 in defeating that proposal last year when it was on the Oregon ballot." She also expressed concern about the "very special problems for small college towns" posed by large numbers of student voters if residency requirements were minimal. Despite the failure of the 1966 and 1970 referenda in Michigan, Gerald Ford departed from Green's stance. "We must move to bring order out of chaos by quickly—and overwhelmingly—approving a constitutional amendment lowering the voting age to 18 in all elections."[21]

The Senate was filled with supporters. Antagonists of the inclusion of Title III in the Voting Rights Act of 1970, like Senator Sam Ervin, had been persuaded. "Usually it is said that there are two sides to every question; but, apparently, there is only one side to the issue now before the Senate," contended James Allen, Democrat from Alabama, "and that is the matter of granting the vote to young people of the age of 18 years or older." Still he reminded his colleagues of his stance the previous year. "I am proud that I opposed 18-year-old voting authorization by statute and insisted that it be authorized by constitutional amendment." Virginia Republican Richard Poff did the same with his House colleagues. "Today, we have the opportunity to correct the mistake of last year."[22]

Proponents and supporters of youth voting rights dominated the debate in both the House and the Senate. "Democracy draws its strength and assures its survival through the exercise of the vote," Celler proclaimed. He presented principled and pragmatic reasons for action and pointed out "that there is a great ground swell for the 18-year-old voting amendment. This movement for voting by youths cannot be squashed." "Youth will be served," he promised.[23] Randolph praised the young people watching from the Senate gallery and raised the importance of extending to their generation "the franchise of freedom," to which he now added "and responsibility."[24] Tom Railsback specifically recognized "the Youth Franchise Coalition, which is a group of young people who have really tirelessly lobbied on behalf of this proposition which they believe in very strongly." His fellow representative from Illinois Abner Mikva also spoke in favor of "what we hope will be the 26th amendment to the Constitution of the United States."[25]

Familiar advocates offered their approval. A new representative from Connecticut, Ella Grasso, expressed her well-founded endorsement. "I have watched with great pride the development of the 18-year-old vote issue through the continuing efforts of many young people in my State as well as throughout the country." New Jersey's James J. Howard was overjoyed. "I am very, very happy that this legislation concerning a constitutional amendment for the 18-year-old vote is before the House of Representatives today."[26]

Howard also introduced an amendment to the proposed resolution that slowed down proceedings in the House, while Ted Kennedy did the same over in the Senate. Both amendments had merit, and Kennedy's was particularly meaningful. Howard sought to lower the age of majority to 18, alongside the age of suffrage, while Kennedy wanted full congressional representation for the District of Columbia. US citizens in Washington, DC, would finally have two senators and representatives in proportion to the population, just like the 50 states. The District of Columbia had a larger population than ten states and had more residents die in Vietnam than 14 states. Kennedy had more allies than Howard did. But even advocates like Birch

Bayh and Jennings Randolph—who recalled his early efforts for DC democracy—believed this wasn't the right time. And neither proposal progressed.

The debate included tributes to Senator Randolph for his foresight and fortitude over the past 29 years and to Senators Mike Mansfield and Birch Bayh and Representative Celler for their historic leadership. Several speakers noted that this was the fourth amendment to the US Constitution in just the past decade. Bayh would later earn the title "a modern father of our Constitution" because he was the only American since the Founding Fathers responsible for multiple amendments to the US Constitution.[27]

Following debate the full House and Senate each voted on the proposed amendment with its enforcement clause.

Section 1: The right of citizens of the United States, who are eighteen years of age or older, to vote shall not be denied or abridged by the United States or by any State on account of age.

Section 2: The Congress shall have power to enforce this article by appropriate legislation.

The few dissenters were drowned out by unanimous approval in the Senate and a 401 to 19 vote in the House of Representatives.

Within two months the 92nd Congress had proposed and passed a constitutional amendment. Many in Congress who played their part over the years voted yes, from Charles Diggs to Hubert Humphrey, Edward Brooke to Barry Goldwater, Warren Magnuson to Lester Wolff, John Conyers to Gale McGee. This accomplishment and the speed with which it took place set it strikingly apart from some 8,000 previous congressional attempts to amend the Constitution. Indeed, six months earlier the Senate had to shelve Electoral College reform in the face of insurmountable opposition. The Equal Rights Amendment, introduced by Senator Marlow Cook on January 25—the same day Randolph introduced Senate Joint Resolution 7—would take another year to pass Congress. On March 23, 1971, Congress sent the amendment out to the 50 states for ratification. It was only the 29th time to have happened in the history of the United States. Now it was up to the states.

The Bandwagon's Already Rolling

After "a record vote" Congress "overwhelmingly passed the 18-year-old vote Amendment," cheered the Youth Franchise Coalition. "Your help is needed to secure immediate action on ratification by the state legislatures in your region."[28] Given the proposed amendment's swift, smooth passage through Congress, the YFC leadership feared complacency among proponents. Two proponents whose dedication to the cause of youth voting rights could never be in doubt reflected this complacency later on. "After the Court ruled in Oregon v. Mitchell," Paul Myer recalls, "the following adoption of the constitutional amendment was anti-climactic from my perspective." For Dennis King in California, with the court ruling and even before that with the Voting Rights Act of 1970, "we recognized that politically it was done. The 26th Amendment was wrap up and the ratification was the wrap up of the wrap up."[29]

At the time ratification didn't appear to be wrapped up. "Positive action by your legislature cannot be taken for granted," urged the YFC. "Many do not understand the immediacy of the issue or the need for prompt attention."[30] The NAACP did. "Time is of the essence," explained Gloster B. Current, national director of branches. "Many state legislatures are holding short sessions and will be adjourning soon. Write, wire, visit the members of your state legislatures. Urge immediate action on the Vote 18 Amendment." With the 1972 election soon approaching, ratification needed to move quickly. "Prompt action is imperative!"[31]

By acting together with coalition member organizations, affiliates, and allies in states and localities, the YFC aided the nationwide ratification campaign. State voting age campaign organizations and networks turned their attention to ratification and kept in communication with one another and the YFC. Three-quarters of the states, so 38 in total, needed to ratify the amendment for it to become part of the US Constitution. Opinion polling at the time showed strong public support, with 60 percent in favor of youth suffrage for all elections. An impressive 84 percent of 18- to 20-year-olds favored their own enfranchisement.[32] As it turned out the speed of the 26th Amendment's ratification was unprecedented. The cascade of support for youth voting rights halved the record set by the ratification of the 12th Amendment in 1803–1804. In large and small ways the youth franchise movement contributed to this ratification process.

Five states—Connecticut, Delaware, Minnesota, Tennessee, and Washington—ratified the 26th Amendment the same day the House of Representatives approved it. "The bandwagon's already rolling," exclaimed Emanuel Celler. Although certified copies of the proposed amendment would be sent out to all the states, legislators could act before receiving the papers. They were paying attention after the Senate approved on March 10 and as the House vote neared on March 23. "Even before the House vote had been tallied, telephone calls began pouring in from officials of a number of state legislatures anxious to be the first to ratify the amendment."[33]

To earn the first spot the Minnesota state legislature voted even before the House of Representatives did. Spurred by the supporters and the success of the youth franchise movement in Minnesota, legislators ratified the amendment about 20 minutes before it passed and thus was officially proposed by Congress. Delaware also sought the first slot, in keeping with its tradition as the first state to ratify the US Constitution in 1787. As in Minnesota, the Delaware House of Representatives prematurely started the ratification process, but a member halted the proceedings. "The procedure is not proper because we are not fully informed about whether it has passed the Congress or not."[34] Worried about putting ratification in jeopardy, they briefly tabled the resolution and then picked it up again later, passing it overwhelmingly for a second-place finish. "Did Minnesota Jump the Gun? State Cries 'Foul' in Ratifying Race," blasted the front-page of the Delaware *Evening Journal*.[35]

Following in quick succession and within the hour were Tennessee, Washington, and Connecticut. State legislators took pride in their part of the process. "I think it is only proper that Connecticut, who is known as the Constitution State, should or may be the first to ratify," commented one. "I think this is a historic day," confirmed another, citing that "Connecticut has been in the lead in fighting for the 18 year-old vote." Tennessee legislators, whose predecessors cast the decisive ratification vote on the 19th Amendment in 1920, understood such historical significance. Even in these states ratification did not proceed without objection. One Connecticut legislator spoke out because citizens had just rejected the Vote 18 referendum. "I don't want to run over them with a bulldozer. And let them think that we ignored what they have told us in clear tones. I couldn't support this, at this time, today with no proper consideration by us or by the people."[36] The idea of putting ratification before the voters in a referendum was popular among opponents.

Other interruptions occurred. "The legislature wanted desperately to make Washington the first state in the nation to ratify the change, but wound up in a political scrap instead," reported the *Seattle Post-Intelligencer*. The political scrap was over the correct form for advising Congress of the state's ratification. The rival parties each controlled one body in the bicameral state legislature, and House Republicans and Senate Democrats differed over whether a joint memorial or joint resolution was needed. "In the two-hour delay that followed, Minnesota and Delaware . . . beat Washington to the punch."[37] Tennessee's situation—shared by Florida—was a state constitutional requirement prohibiting action on ratification until the next election. Tennessee legislators chose to ignore it and ratify, but Florida didn't. "Florida bandwagon shows signs of heading for a few flat tires before it gets out the Capitol door," the *Tampa Times* later observed.[38]

Ratification votes flowed in over the next three months. Proponents overcame all sorts of obstacles and often in very different ways. For example, officials in the three states with scheduled referenda in 1971 faced a conundrum. Should a state still hold its referendum, ratify the proposed federal amendment, or do both? Kansas did both. Voters approved Vote 18 in the April 6 referendum, and the state legislature ratified on April 7. Nevada held a Vote 18 referendum in June, which passed, but didn't ratify the federal amendment. New York legislators ratified the federal amendment on June 2 and then withdrew the state amendment, which would have gone before voters in November. Just in case ratification failed proponents in some states floated the idea of initiating 18-year-old vote amendments to avoid dual-age voting.

Concern grew as the cascade of support for ratification slowed. Half of the 38 states needed for ratification came in three weeks, with Vermont's action on April 16. It took twice that long to get the next 19 states to ratify. This slowdown occurred at the same time as dramatic demonstrations by Vietnam Veterans Against the War, although few claimed any causal connection. During this period the media amplified the voices of ratification opponents, and some were quite prominent. California governor

Ronald Reagan updated his arguments against youth voting rights to oppose ratification. "It's just another one of those instances where the federal government has imposed on what I think is a state's right, the right to determine its own voting qualifications."[39] Reagan took a states' rights stance that even southern Dixiecrats in the Senate and Governor George Wallace of Alabama didn't. Wallace "burned the late night oil" to ensure his state ratified the federal amendment in a timely fashion.[40] Fortunately governors have no formal role in the ratification process, and California legislators proceeded to ratify.

Opponents in Illinois, Oregon, and New Jersey stalled the ratification process in their states. They called for further study and referenda, saying they were simply representing their constituencies who had recently rejected youth suffrage. "And as a portent of tougher opposition to come, conservatives here marshalled the first major obstacle to ratification since the measure was first offered to the nation's Legislatures in March," noted the *New York Times* of the New Jersey Assembly.[41]

Proponents pressed for action. James W. Shue of the Voting Age Coalition of New Jersey testified at a State Senate Judiciary Committee hearing. Speaking for 5,000 VAC members, Shue argued against overemphasizing the defeats of the Vote 18 and Vote 19 measures in 1969 and 1970. "Public opinion has grown more positive since these two referenda." And circumstances had changed. "The present inconsistency of permitting the vote for 18, 19, and 20 year olds in federal elections but not in state and local elections is absurd and will also cause a great expense to administer."[42] In Oregon Earl Blumenauer directly addressed the adversarial Speaker of the House on principled grounds. "It hardly seems as though Speaker Smith and his cronies are protecting 'representative democracy.'" Blumenauer added a pragmatic point. "It seems odd that the fiscally conservative speaker is willing to invest anywhere from a quarter of a million dollars on up on a system of dual registration and election."[43] These states did ratify in the end, with Illinois taking the 35th slot on June 29.

In a series of maneuvers and machinations the states of Alabama, Ohio, Oklahoma, and North Carolina vied for the 38th spot. Just as with the first place position this last stage of the race for ratification received much press and popular attention. On June 30, 1971, three states had final votes on ratification. During the day Alabama and North Carolina ratified, and then the Ohio House of Representatives met that evening.

"An atmosphere of near-panic attended Ohio's climactic vote," reported R. W. Apple of the *New York Times*.[44] What a change from six weeks earlier when Pat Keefer headed to Ohio to lobby for ratification at the statehouse. "Ohio Solons Not Likely to Ratify 'Vote 18,'" headlined the *Cincinnati Enquirer* in a story about Pat and her work with Common Cause. "She was told her efforts may be in vain." Pat hit back, arguing that if the General Assembly didn't take action Ohio would be known as one of the "regressive" states.[45]

Ohio state representatives avoided the regressive label. After hearing that the Oklahoma legislature was going into special session that night of June 30, the floor manager in the Ohio House stopped the speeches. "The time for debate and discussion is over. The time for action is here." They voted 81 to 9 in favor, joining the Ohio Senate's approval the day before. "It was a race for the history books, and Ohio won."[46] President Nixon immediately issued a statement. "Tonight, Ohio's Legislature ratified the 26th Amendment to the Constitution." With 38 states ratifying, "the Amendment will now become a part of the law of the land."[47] Oklahoma the next day, Virginia and Wyoming the next week, and Georgia in October brought the number up to 42 by the end of 1971.

Two developments the following day dealt blows to Ohio's accomplishment and the overall achievement of the 26th Amendment. Although North Carolina legislators ratified the amendment on June 30, officials there delayed in signing the enrolled bill until the next day. With North Carolina's paperwork finished on July 1, the Tar Heel State won the final slot, and July 1, 1971, is the official ratification date for the 26th Amendment. Then stealing that day's newspaper headlines was the Supreme Court's landmark free speech ruling in the Pentagon Papers case. Upholding the freedom of the press to publish classified government documents, in this case about the American war in Vietnam, was certainly a cause for celebration. But bold banner headlines pushed the historic achievement of youth voting rights to below the fold on the front page of the *New York Times*. And "HIGH COURT UPHOLDS NEWSPAPERS' STAND" overshadowed "Nation's 18-Year-Olds Get Vote" on the front page of the *Michigan Daily*.[48]

The certification of the 26th Amendment on July 5, just one day after Independence Day, brought back attention, but that ceremony too was bittersweet. The president has no constitutional role in the

President Richard Nixon ceremoniously signs the 26th Amendment, July 1971.
AP photo. Courtesy of Richard Nixon Presidential Library and Museum.

amendment process—congressional leadership does—but Nixon
sought the spotlight. Moreover, instead of inviting leaders of the Youth
Franchise Coalition to witness the certification, the White House used
an appearance by the Young Americans in Concert, a touring musical
group. After General Services Administrator Robert Kunzig certified
the amendment's adoption, Nixon and three of the young musicians
added their signatures. No presidential recognition came for all the
proponents in the YFC, Project 18, the NAACP, NEA, and so many
other organizations that had worked so hard over the years. "We
weren't all invited," Pat Keefer recalls, but "we were out celebrating
someplace."[49]

Youth Power

Celebration as well as concern greeted the newest amendment to the
US Constitution. "Youth Power," "Youthlash," "Youthquake" were just
some of the headlines foretelling what would happen when young adults

had the right to vote in the United States. Time would tell, but meanwhile the 26th Amendment needed to be implemented. Ongoing youth voter registration projects and drives were expanded to now encompass state and local as well as federal elections, and new initiatives got off the ground. Yet the forces of progress and reaction were in contest in 1971 and after. Even as many were pressing for young voters to fully participate in American democracy, others were pushing back. And hard.

During a five-day period in May white assailants murdered five African Americans in Mississippi. Among these tragic killings was 18-year-old Jo Etha Collier, slain on the night of her high school graduation. For some observers her drive-by shooting by three drunk white men seemed senseless. But John Lewis, Archie E. Allen, and Julian Bond of the Voter Education Project understood these murders as "acts of political assassination." That spring, as ratification of the 26th Amendment proceeded, voter registration workers in Mississippi were victimized by harassment, intimidation, and threats of violence. The aim, as Julian Bond put it, was to "strike fear into the hearts of black people and make them hesitant about attempting to register to vote."[50] Although voter suppression efforts elsewhere didn't take this murderous form, they were still used to disenfranchise voters of all ages.

Against young people, especially college and university students, residency requirements had been and continued to be the main form of voter suppression. Take New York State law at the time. "Where the presence of an elector within a district is solely because of his attendance as a student in an institution of learning, whatever his intention may be, he is not a resident there."[51] No residency, no voter registration. City and county residents in many regions of the country favored such laws because they feared being overwhelmed by the number of resident college students casting ballots. Amherst, Massachusetts, a city of 13,000 residents, had three campuses nearby—Amherst College, Hampshire College, and the University of Massachusetts—with a total of 21,035 students. When the Massachusetts attorney general said that students may register to vote where they attend school, Amherst residents responded. "I just don't think they should vote here—they're only part-time residents." "The feeling around here is, it's time to move."[52]

Students and their supporters fought back against voter suppression through legislation and litigation. The NAACP took a stance against "efforts in state legislatures to disenfranchise students by passage of restrictive residency laws" and sought "provisions which allow students to designate their legal residence for voting purposes."[53] At the same time, in a series of state Supreme Court cases in California, Michigan, New Jersey, and elsewhere, local election officials were ordered to register bona fide resident students. Veterans of the state voting age campaigns, like Stuart Goldstein of the Voting Age Coalition, enabled these efforts to ensure that young people could exercise the right of franchise they'd earned. "Those kids are living away from home," he says. "There's a better shot trying to motivate them to participate and vote if they could register at their college address."[54] These cases culminated in the Supreme Court case *Symm v. United States* (1979), which held that students have the right to vote where they attend college or university.

Shoring up youth voting rights were innovative voter registration initiatives. The Youth Citizenship Fund was just one. The NAACP Youth Council, the YMCA, the National Movement for the Student Vote, the Student Organization for Black Unity, and Frontlash, to name just a few, were all actively registering new voters on campuses and in communities. They used all sorts of new strategies—getting members deputized as registrars, setting up registration tables at supermarkets, and providing mobile services like "votervans."[55] Radical activists, assumed to be alienated from the political system, also got involved. The Black Panther Party decided to run two leaders, Bobby Seale and Elaine Brown, for mayor and city council in Oakland, California, in 1972. "Register to Vote," "Vote for Survival," "Let the Power of the People Shine!"[56]

As these groups found, the challenges for voter registration were many. Registration dates, times, and locations were limited. Nobody made it easy, but then that was the point. Registration began as a reform to counter voter fraud in the nineteenth century, but its disenfranchising consequences were always clear and not just in the southern United States. When Charlie Gonzales took up a position with the Youth Citizenship Fund, he recalls a direct action in Chicago against a member of the board of elections who also was a bank president. They held up business at his bank by asking again and again for pennies in change for dollar bills and then painstakingly counting out the pennies received. "We wanted to draw attention to the bank president having the authority and the ability to change voter registration if he wanted to."[57] The "count-in" worked. And over the 1970s, through legislation and litigation, voter registration processes and systems opened up.

In the lead-up to the 1972 presidential election, popular culture became an important vehicle for voter information and registration. The magazine and fashion industries took part. "The youth vote can be the lifeline to America's future. Make sure your voice and choice are heard at the ballot box," urged a notice in *Seventeen* magazine. "Register to Vote—Now!"[58] Fashion companies advertised and issued "political information kits." Jeans West stores in Los Angeles had registrars on site. In return for registering, the new voter received a dollar-off coupon. "We'll buy your vote," the company joked, and "put a pair of pants on every bottom. Democrat, Republican, or otherwise."[59]

The music industry also made a big push for youth participation in politics. Building on Tommy Boyce and Bobby Hart's 1969 song "L.U.V. (Let Us Vote)," musicians, songwriters, record companies, and *Billboard* magazine teamed up to deliver voter registration information "via the media of popular music." "The music industry has a unique social responsibility to help bring to the polls the greatest possible number of new 18–20-year-old voters," editorialized *Billboard*. "Rock music is the art form that today clearly has the strongest empathy with young Americans." In March 1972 *Billboard* published a special supplement on voter registration to summarize and spur music industry efforts.[60]

Credit for kicking these efforts off belonged to members of the band Chicago. After meeting with proponents in Washington, DC, in May 1971, they decided to do what they could. To start they included as an insert with their 1971 live album, *Chicago at Carnegie Hall*, the Youth Citizenship Fund's guide to "Registration and Voting Laws of the 50 States," along with a note to fans to register to vote. "And since The System would like to make it difficult for you to register, we're going to make it a lot easier."[61] Radio spots, the singles "Use the Power, 18" and "Register and Vote," notices in print ads and on billboards, and record jackets promoted voter registration. Concerts by Blood, Sweat, and Tears, Chicago, and other bands prompted or provided registration opportunities. The Beach Boys estimated their concerts garnered 80,000 new registrations. Radio stations also offered on-site registration days.

As the 1972 election drew near *Billboard* reminded the music industry of this "chance to do something so worthwhile for its audience and for the entire USA."[62] Bobby Hart continued to appreciate the chance he and Tommy Boyce had to musically contribute to the movement for youth voting rights back in 1969. Their contribution certainly had "a happy ending," Hart recalled. "On the wall of my study hangs a framed copy of the Twenty-Sixth Amendment to the United States Constitution."[63]

Conclusion

"Talking 'bout you and me changin' things peacefully"

As the 1972 presidential election neared, the youth vote was a topic of great interest and speculation. Democratic and Republican parties keenly courted the youth vote, as President Richard Nixon sought reelection against his Democratic challenger, Senator George McGovern of South Dakota. What impact young voters would have preoccupied political partisans, the media, and youth franchise proponents. There were wide differences of opinion. Although the familiar partisan assumption aired that Democrats would get the youth vote, many didn't agree. In back-to-back annual public opinion polls Samuel Lubell found that young voters were frustrated and unhappy about Nixon's Vietnam policy. That gradual US withdrawal or "peace with honor" included invasions of Cambodia in 1970 and then Laos in 1971 angered many, and McGovern ran on a platform calling for immediate withdrawal from Vietnam. Even so only one-tenth of young adult respondents held political beliefs drastically different from their parents. "The so-called generation gap," pointed out one commentator, "is surely one of the most over-inflated myths of our time."[1]

The Vietnam War topped young voters' list of priorities, but what impact the war would have on the larger electorate was open to question. Young Americans held Nixon most responsible for the war continuing, even as draft calls lessened. New groups like Young Voters for Peace and the National Youth Caucus set out to channel this sentiment. "This is something the peace movement hasn't had—a massive show of voters who want the United States to get out now," argued Robert Parsons, the 21-year-old founder of Young Voters for Peace. "Many students objected to working within the system in the past because it had no impact. It can, now that we have the vote."[2] But prominent Democrats worried the war would prove divisive in the election. "We simply cannot allow a love affair

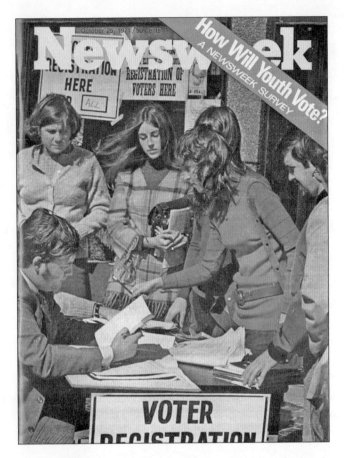

Newsweek cover, October 25, 1971. Courtesy of Division of Political and Military History, National Museum of American History, Smithsonian Institution.

with campus youth on the issue of the war to weaken or obscure the close tie the party has always had with the labor movement and the working man," Ted Kennedy told Democratic insiders. "We have become so preoccupied with the generation gap that we have failed to see the class gap."[3]

Other factors contributed to questions about how or even if the newly enfranchised Americans would vote. The sixties generation was markedly independent from traditional party loyalties. The challenges of registering to vote and going to the polls remained despite the many drives and initiatives. In some places low registration numbers were attributed to apathy or antipathy toward politics among young voters. Those who expressed "a basic hope in the present political/economic structure and the power of the people to vote a change" could encounter cynicism or radical analysis among their peers. Some questioned "whether a violent government can be changed by any other than violent tactics."[4] Perhaps most damning for Democrats was another of pollster Samuel Lubell's findings. "None of the possible Democratic Presidential hopefuls has stirred any surge of enthusiasm among high school and college students."[5] George McGovern emerged battered and bruised from the nomination fight and stumbled during the campaign. Plus presidential incumbents are notoriously difficult to defeat.

In the first presidential political test of the 18-year-old vote, Nixon and his campaign's efforts to win the "sons and daughters of the Silent Majority" paid off. The Republican incumbent won in a landslide, with 60.7 percent of the popular vote and 49 states in the Electoral College. Nixon did lose new voters under 24 and college students—but barely—and he won 52 percent of the youth vote, defined as voters under 30.[6] Overall voter turnout was lower in 1972 than in 1968 for every age group, except among the youngest voters aged 18 to 20, which rose 15 percent. Close to 50 percent of 18- to 24-year-olds voted. Together with 25- to 29-year-olds, youth voter turnout in 1972 reached 55 percent.[7] The 26th Amendment had definitely made a difference with the 18 to 20 age category, but this level of turnout was still far less than proponents had hoped for.

The election result was not what many youth suffrage proponents had hoped for either. For those who were first-time voters, the elation of finally being able to cast a ballot crashed into disappointment and even despair. "My first election was in 1972 when I was 20 years old," recalls Catherine Kieffer Gervase, who participated in Citizens for Vote 18 in New York as a high school student. "I voted for McGovern who sadly lost the election to Nixon." Even so she could say looking back, "I am proud of my involvement in the movement to make this happen."[8]

"It's very cool when I, in '72, cast my first vote for McGovern," Renny Cushing remembers. "Growing up I never thought I would be able to vote till I was twenty-one. And even though I fought for it, it didn't seem like it was going to come. But to actually be able to cast a vote, you know, that was pretty amazing." Since 1968, Renny had spent the intervening years immersed in antiwar activism. But then "the candidate that I cast my ballot for doesn't win and after the election the f***ing president is carpet bombing Hanoi." Designed to put pressure on the parties negotiating at the Paris peace talks, Nixon and Kissinger's Christmas bombings killed thousands of North Vietnamese as well as US airmen. "And the war is continuing."[9] The 26th Amendment had made no difference on the crucial issue Renny cared most about.

Critics of what they saw as the overblown promises of the 26th Amendment soon weighed in. The education editor of the *New York Times* Fred Hechinger enjoyed embellishing the projected impact of the new amendment. "The youth vote would turn the country around. The new ballots would, on election day, emancipate America from insensitivity, reaction and squaredom."[10] Although exaggerated by Hechinger, the expectation or hope that young Americans would turn out in huge numbers to vote and inject US politics with new idealism and energy did exist among proponents. To many the 1972 presidential election indicated otherwise.

The impact of youth voting rights on turnout, parties, and policy remained a subject of popular and scholarly interest after 1972. Although there were ups and downs in voter turnout and changes in partisanship among young Americans over the rest of the twentieth century, two trends were obvious. Youth turnout declined from 1972 and stayed down, and young voters largely mirrored the partisan views of the rest of the electorate. The twenty-first century brought something of a turnaround. From a low in the 2000 presidential election, turnout and support for the Democratic Party began to rise. The 2008 election stands out, with a 52 percent turnout favoring the Democratic winner Barack Obama by two to one over his Republican opponent, John McCain.[11] The youth vote similarly delivered in turnout and for the Democrats in the 2020 election. Still the voting rates of young Americans lag behind those of other age groups.

How to get and keep young people engaged in electoral politics is a perennial puzzle. Tackling voter suppression aimed at the youth vote is still important. Removing barriers to access and opportunity would contribute most to young people voting. Connecting electoral politics to political activism and social movements would also help. Young people's disproportionate participation in community organizing and street protests shows they are engaged in politics broadly conceived. Translating that energy into elections, running for office, and voting are key.[12] Over the years participants in the youth franchise movement have reflected on how to do this. "I don't think it's a failure of young people," Paul Myer says. "I think it's a failure of political leadership."[13] They all agree that greater civic education in school and society is vital to growing civic and voter participation in our democracy. Earl Blumenauer, now a US congressman from Oregon, has cosponsored legislation to strengthen civics education across the country.

Analysis and answers on this important issue matter very much going forward but also for how we look back on the 26th Amendment. Due to lower turnout among young voters, scholars and commentators often assess the impact of youth suffrage on US politics as negligible or even negative—negligible in that the youth vote has rarely made a difference for national campaign outcomes, negative in that overall voter turnout has declined. Young people have been added to the electorate yet vote less than other age groups, bringing down the overall turnout rate.[14] Pat Keefer pushes back against this assessment. For her, and other participants agree, "the fulfillment of providing voting rights to young people in our country is not if and how they vote, but the fact that they have the constitutional right to vote."[15]

Assessing the impact and importance of the 26th Amendment must indeed start with this fact. The US Constitution is exceedingly hard to amend. The National Archives and Research Administration's compiled data on nearly 12,000 proposed amendments from 1787 to 2014 provide a comparative context.[16] The number of failed attempts to amend the constitution puts the achievement of the 26th Amendment in high relief. "Constitutional amendments do not happen by themselves," comments Dennis King.[17] Moreover, enabling the right to vote—the fundamental tool of people in a democracy—to tens of millions of young Americans cannot be taken for granted. This most recent of the suffrage amendments represents a centuries-long, even if altogether incomplete, project to transform the United States into a truly inclusive democracy.

The legal implications of the 26th Amendment also have not been fully explored or utilized. The amendment does more than establish a national voting age of 18. Legal scholars and practicing attorneys have argued against this narrow interpretation.[18] Properly interpreted, the 26th Amendment establishes a broad constitutional prohibition against age discrimination in voting rights. The enforcement clause also grants Congress extensive powers to ensure state compliance with that prohibition. These powers allow Congress to take bold action to protect the rights of students, senior citizens, and any other group whose members suffer discrimination in voting on account of their age. In voting rights litigation leading up to the 2020 election, Supreme Court justice Sonia Sotomayor noted that a Texas case challenging age requirements for absentee voting "raises weighty but seemingly novel questions regarding the Twenty-Sixth Amendment." As Sotomayor indicates, the potential protection for citizens' voting rights offered by the amendment remains untapped.[19]

The political, legal, and constitutional processes that led to the 26th Amendment further reveal profound change in the US system of government during the 1960s. Constitutional change comes through not just formal amendment but also legislation and court rulings aided by mobilized popular support.[20] Youth suffrage involved all four. Before amending the Constitution, politicians legislated Title III of the Voting Rights Act of 1970, and Supreme Court justices ruled in *Oregon v. Mitchell* (1970). Debates over lowering the voting age to 18 raised fundamental questions about the constitutional relationship between Congress and the states. Only at the very end of nearly 30 years of advocacy did proponents prevail in their interpretation of congressional power over states' rights. Followed by affirmation—even if only in part—by the Supreme Court. Then confirmed through constitutional amendment by more than two-thirds of Congress and more than three-quarters of the states, with support from a majority of Americans.

What created the conditions to change the US Constitution in 1971 in contrast to 1942 or 1954 or 1968 were the struggles and successes of African Americans in the freedom movement. Political activism and pressure spurred federal voting rights legislation as well as the 23rd and 24th Amendments. Legal cases, strategy, and argument yielded court decisions affirming expanded voting rights. With Title III as the catalyst, youth voting rights came directly out of civil and voting rights legislation and litigation. In contrast, many scholars see the 26th Amendment as only an expedient solution to the problems and costs of dual-age voting. It avoided "further administrative messiness," was an "afterthought to the federal statute," and was "a side issue, engendered by the Supreme Court's decision in *Oregon v. Mitchell*."[21] These conclusions miss or

Senator Jennings Randolph with former vice president Hubert
Humphrey receiving plaque from West Virginia University Young
Democrats for being the "Father of the Twenty-Sixth Amend-
ment." Jennings Randolph Collection. Courtesy of the West
Virginia State Archives.

minimize the significant shift the statute especially and the decision
signified. Without the civil and voting rights achievements of African
Americans, no 18-year-old vote.

And no 18-year-old vote without liberal proponents in Congress and
in the youth franchise movement ready to use and build upon African
American achievements. Stalwart advocates, starting with Jennings
Randolph, hailed as the "Father of the 26th Amendment," persisted,
persuaded, and finally prevailed. "I have been patient," Randolph told his

Senate colleagues in 1970.[22] His colleagues, Birch Bayh, Ted Kennedy, and many other Democrats and Republicans in Congress, were less patient. They seized on the new legislative statute strategy and ran with it, as did members of the Youth Franchise Coalition. The presence and pressure of young people in the YFC, member organizations, and state campaigns contributed to progressing youth voting rights at every level of government both before and after the passage of the 26th Amendment.

As part of the sixties generation, their contributions were spurred by the era's events and movements as well as their commitment to the US system of politics and government. They worked within the system to change the system. Victory in 1971 validated that commitment and verified that "the system works." "We've all gone our different ways, but we've all stayed involved in doing something to impact the system," Ian MacGowan comments. Of his colleagues in the cause, "the type of people who get involved in issues of any kind have a passion for the system, respect for the system, and a desire to change the system. It lasts all your life." The achievement of youth suffrage signaled that change can and does happen. "Despite all the apparent difficulties we have in this country, we still live in the most alive and creative democratic experiment on the planet," Dennis Warren believes.[23]

This change toward a more inclusive democracy confirms the 1960s as a transformative era. Out of the conflict and contest over fundamental aspects of American life came many changes, among them a commitment to expanding the voting rights and ensuring the first-class citizenship of all Americans. In the case of African and young Americans this commitment has never been fully upheld, but it also cannot be taken for granted. We tend to emphasize the failures of the sixties, faulting liberals especially. But they were responsible for real successes too. The 26th Amendment is one. It demonstrates the same "politics and policies of liberal engagement" that Devin Fergus found in relation to Black power, a finding that "challenges the scholarly view—reflected in broad currents of popular thought—that modern liberalism has failed."[24]

For all these reasons the 26th Amendment needs to be integrated into our histories of the "long sixties," both to bring attention to this historic accomplishment and to add to our understanding of those years. Moreover, the politicians who aided this constitutional change are generally well known (although usually for other accomplishments), but younger proponents are not. They should be. Not only would that correct the misinterpretation of the 26th Amendment as a top-down development. It would recognize their hard work and creativity, their planning, organizing, and lobbying, their youth franchise movement. It would appreciate their strategy for social change—building a coalition, educating the wider public on the issue, working closely with politicians at every level of government—and value their effectiveness and success.

Remembering this history would also put paid to claims that this achievement was inevitable. As one scholar argued, "by the time Congress sent the Twenty-sixth Amendment to the states, it was already a foregone conclusion that eighteen-year-olds would soon be voting in all elections."[25] This book has told a different story, a story Jane Eisner wonderfully summed up as "farsighted individuals stubborn enough to ride into uncharted territory to reach a destination that seems inevitable only in retrospect."[26]

For those individuals I had the opportunity to interview, that ride had an impact, both personal and political. "It really framed what I wanted to do," Rosalyn Hester Baker says, "for the rest of my political career." Like Roz, those involved in the YFC and state campaigns went on to careers in politics, as elected officials, legislators, lobbyists, or organizers. "It was the beginning of my political education," Paul Myer states. "I learned that I had a talent and a passion for getting things done in Washington, DC. Everything that happened afterwards was building on that experience." Mark Brown in Washington State tells a similar story. "Everything I've done professionally goes back to the Vote 19 campaign and the people that I met on the campaign trail."[27]

They also have continued to advocate for expanding and ensuring voting rights, especially those of young people. "I remember my experience and I try to mentor. I try to lift up," Renny shares. "Every time I'm involved in an election," Pat Keefer notes, "I concentrate on working with young people, speaking at high schools, encouraging young people to take advantage of their right to vote." Jane Greenspun Gale does too. "I've had a really long time to think about this and I have lots of causes. One of my causes is getting 18-year-olds to vote." "If we could just get the kids to vote," she still holds, "we could change this world."[28]

As a consequence, those who took part in what Mae C. Quinn has called "the first wave youth suffrage movement" are paying attention to the current "second wave."[29] Across the United States as well as the world young people are working to lower the voting age to sixteen. Earl Blumenauer recently made the case. "Sixteen-year-olds are legally permitted to work, required to pay income tax on their earnings, permitted to drive motor vehicles on their own, and can be tried as adults in the criminal justice system," he wrote. "It stands to reason that they should be able to shape their future by participating in the political process as well."[30]

Calls and campaigns for the 16-year-old vote multiply within the context of climate crisis, gun violence, and police brutality—all of which affect young people disproportionately. "Young people are grasping the speed at which change needs to occur and is occurring. They're more sophisticated and they are more educated," Stuart Goldstein contends. "What can they teach us so that we are better at responding to the nature of change that's going on?"[31]

Yet young Americans today operate in a vastly different political context than did the sixties generation. With the Republican Party now led by those seeking to limit and suppress voting rights, expanding youth voting rights is no longer a bipartisan aim. The political polarization pushed by current conservatives prevents the kind of bipartisanship and coalition building the first wave youth suffrage movement could count on. "What a special political moment it was and how far we've come away from those sort of bipartisan, non-strident political debates and outcomes," Charles Koppelman recalls.[32] They saw signs of this day coming though, when the leadership of the Young Republicans refused to join the Youth Franchise Coalition back in 1969.

That today's youth voting rights movement faces tremendous challenges doesn't discourage their predecessors. "Don't let anybody tell you, you can't do it," Renny urges. Their own experiences demonstrated as much. "The movement for youth voting rights was a reaffirmation of the system and an act of faith in the future," Les Francis feels.[33] With the 50th anniversary of the 26th Amendment upon us, the words of President Barack Obama on the 40th anniversary still ring true. "Young adults have been a driving force for change in the last century, bringing new ideas and high hopes to our national dialogue. Today, we remember the efforts of those who fought for their seat at the table, and we encourage coming generations to claim their place in our democracy."[34]

ACKNOWLEDGMENTS

I've dedicated this book to my students, past, present, and future. Not only did the idea for this book emerge in the process of teaching my course on the history of the 1960s. The excitement and encouragement of my students inspired me throughout the process of researching and writing about youth voting rights and the 26th Amendment.

Students also contributed to my finishing the book in time for the 50th anniversary. Funded by the University of Auckland and the Faculty of Arts, my summer scholars—Tom Atkins, Hebe Kearney, and KDee Ma'ia'i—gave me and this project the benefit of their intelligence, diligence, and creativity. Their research and thinking advanced and shaped every aspect of this book, but I most appreciate how they pushed me on aspects of law (Tom), culture (Hebe), territory and empire (KDee). My graduate students also aided the book's progress. Katie Cammell conducted research at the Lyndon Baines Johnson Presidential Library in Austin, Texas, and Tessa Mazey-Richardson shared her research on *Seventeen* magazine. Ryan Anderson's study of Young Americans for Freedom and Hannah Smith's on Mississippi Freedom Summer informed my discussion here.

Sabbatical and School of Humanities research funding allowed me to travel in 2017 and 2018 to the United States to conduct research in libraries and archives. The knowledge and expertise of archivists and librarians at the John F. Kennedy Presidential Library, the Richard Nixon Presidential Library, the Library of Congress, and the National Archives made my visits there productive and enjoyable.

When I couldn't travel, particularly in 2020 due to the COVID-19 pandemic, the expert research assistance of many made the difference. Sydney Soderberg at the Dwight D. Eisenhower Presidential Library again assisted with one my books. Scot Wilson, guided by archivist Kate Cruikshank, located key materials in the Birch Bayh Congressional Papers in the Modern Political Papers Collections of the Indiana University

Libraries. Ryan Bean, reference and outreach archivist, Kautz Family YMCA Archives, University of Minnesota Libraries, and Nicole Grady, librarian in Special Collections & Archives at the University of the Pacific, helped me access key documents. Erin Schultz at the Minnesota Historical Society and Scott Daniels at the Oregon Historical Society also facilitated my research. Araceli Bareng, US District Court, District of Nevada, and Pamela J. Anderson, National Archives at Kansas City, sourced court filings for me, and Kenneth Johnson, Courtney Matthews, and Mutahara Mobashar at the Library of Congress got me the relevant file from the papers of Justice Hugo Black.

Again and again what struck me about this process of researching from afar—especially during the pandemic—was how friendly, kind, and quick to help were these archivists, librarians, research specialists, and assistants. This wonderful experience repeated when I went looking for photographs and images for the book. Thank you to Becky Marangelli, University Libraries, Ball State University; Jocelyn K. Wilk, Columbia University Rare Book & Manuscript Library; Angela Kepler, Mauldin Project, Pritzker Military Museum & Library; James B. Hill, John F. Kennedy Presidential Library; Ryan Pettigrew, Richard Nixon Presidential Library; Kristine L. Toma, Texas State University Archives; Richard Fauss and Aaron Parsons, West Virginia State Archives; Adam Lyon, Library Services, Museum of History & Industry in Seattle; the Office of Art and Archives, US House of Representatives; Kay Peterson, Archives Center, National Museum of American History, Smithsonian Institution; and again Nicole Grady. These professionals and their institutions helped to make the history presented in this book more accessible and appealing.

Making this book possible were the sheer number of digitized, accessible primary sources for historical research. This book, more than any of my other publications, necessitated and benefited from our digital age. Although the mainstream and local newspapers I used required a subscription, many more of the sources I used were freely available. Colleges and universities have digitized campus newspapers and yearbooks. The American Presidency Project, the Eleanor Roosevelt Papers Project, and the presidential libraries offer political documents, press statements, and publications. Digitized collections and online exhibits from a range of other institutions allowed me to complete and contextualize this history.

More than ever, I appreciate the work of archives, libraries, and other nonprofit organizations to democratize our access to materials from the past.

I also greatly appreciate the generosity of the seventeen participants in the youth suffrage movement who gave their time, thoughts, and materials to help me tell this story. Contacting participants wasn't easy from New Zealand, so I feel so fortunate that they responded to my emails, letters, and messages. Paul Myer was the first to do so, and that first interview confirmed at just the right time my commitment to this project. Interviews with Rosalyn Hester Baker, Jay Berman, Mark Brown, Steve Corneliussen, Renny Cushing, Les Francis, Jane Greenspun Gale, Stuart Goldstein, Charles Gonzales, Patricia Keefer, Dennis King, Charles Koppelman, Ian MacGowan, Mel Myler, Spencer Oliver, Dennis Warren, as well as Paul Myer enriched this book immensely. As did the writings, news clippings, and photographs they sent me.

I am grateful to New York University Press for once again publishing a book of mine. The staff there have been so easy and pleasant to work with. Clara Platter, Eric Zinner, and Veronica Knutson sped this process along, as did the two anonymous readers for NYU Press. Their feedback very much shaped the book and sharpened my argument, and I thank them for that.

Colleagues in New Zealand and the United States supported this book in so many ways. The University of Auckland Libraries interloan staff, especially Ramachandra Radha, located and delivered published and unpublished documents, even during the pandemic. Tim Page, Digital Media Support Specialist in the Faculty of Arts, formatted the photographs and designed the images for the book. Eric S. Fish shared all of his hard-to-get materials on the ratification of the 26th Amendment. William G. Robbins got me a copy of his biography of Monroe Sweetland, facilitated by Marty Brown at Oregon State University Press. Devin Fergus, Mae C. Quinn, and Ellen Schrecker offered insights on key topics. Paula Morris and Helen Sword inspired me by example and instruction on writing style and structure, and Susan Carter and Manuel Vallee jumpstarted my writing process.

Friends and family spurred me on. Maria Armoudian, Lynne Baca, Sara Buttsworth, Janet Davis, Kathy Feeley, Millicent Frost, Alison Kibler, Lon Kurashige, Kate Marsh, Cealagh Taillon, and Luc Taillon, thank you. Cealagh and Luc even served as inexpensive research assistants. Joyce Taillon facilitated my long-distance research assistance. Paul Taillon, my longtime collaborator in teaching and thinking about the sixties, listened to my ideas, pushed my analysis, and edited my writing.

Researching and writing this book against the backdrop of one of the greatest challenges to democracy in US history reminded me again and again of the significance of youth voting rights and the 26th Amendment. In a historic turnout despite so many obstacles, young Americans used their voices and votes to engage in our democracy and effect political change. So, too, in 2020 did young New Zealanders. My daughter, a first-time voter, and my students were among them. To them, thank you for persisting and participating in shaping the world we are trying to create, the world you will inherit.

APPENDIX

Youth Suffrage in States and Territories, 1943–1971

Year	State or Territory	Voting Age
1943	Georgia	18
1954	Guam	18
1955	Kentucky	18
1956	Alaska	19
1958	Hawaiʻi	20
1960	American Samoa	20
1965	American Samoa	18
1965	Micronesia	18
1970	Alaska	18
1970	Puerto Rico	18
1970	US Virgin Islands	18
1970	Massachusetts	19
1970	Minnesota	19
1970	Montana	19
1970	Maine	20
1970	Nebraska	20
1971	Kansas	18
1971	Nevada	18

NOTE ON SOURCES

Without a doubt, more scholarship is needed on the history of youth voting rights in the United States. Much more could be written about every aspect of the story told in this book. The role of individual proponents, national-level efforts, state campaigns, campus-based activism, organizational support, and the opposition all deserve further study. My hope is that this book will encourage others to research and write about these important topics.

In part, the lack of scholarly attention to this historic achievement can be attributed to a lack of archival and library primary source collections. The primary sources for such historical study are voluminous, but they are scattered. With the exception of Project 18 papers in the National Education Association Archives at George Washington University, there is no other dedicated collection. This situation should be changing, as participants in the Youth Franchise Coalition have been gathering and readying materials, including oral interviews, for deposit soon in an archive or library.

With the NEA Archives closed to researchers for most of 2020 due to the COVID-19 pandemic, I was fortunate to locate Project 18, Youth Franchise Coalition, and state campaign materials elsewhere. The Records of the NAACP, Manuscript Division, Library of Congress, Washington, DC, and the Kautz Family YMCA Archives, University of Minnesota Libraries, proved invaluable, as did the Let Us Vote materials, University Archives, Holt-Atherton Special Collections, University of the Pacific Library and the Birch Bayh Congressional Papers in the Modern Political Papers Collections of the Indiana University Libraries.

Research in the presidential libraries of Dwight D. Eisenhower, Lyndon B. Johnson, Richard M. Nixon, and John F. Kennedy—which included the senatorial papers of his brothers Robert F. and Edward M. Kennedy—also yielded helpful materials. Online materials from the Kennedy and Nixon libraries augmented my initial research at both libraries.

Government, legislative, legal, and court documents were another crucial category of primary sources. The *Congressional Record*, US House of Representatives and Senate hearings, as well as studies and reports from states and commissions are available both in libraries and online. The American Presidency Project at the University of California, Santa Barbara has digitized a vast array of presidential speeches and statements as well as political party platforms. The Hugo LaFayette Black Papers at the Library of Congress, and legal briefs and court decisions allowed me to examine youth voting rights litigation.

National, local, and campus newspapers—all digitized—were consistently useful. Mostly freely available or with an affordable subscription, these sources allowed me to find and name proponents of youth voting rights from across the country over a period of 30 years. Best of all, the campus newspapers provided evidence of students advocating and organizing for the right to vote, demonstrating the bottom-up activism that built the youth franchise movement. Other periodicals and magazines over the same period of time illuminated the opinions and perspectives of a wide range of Americans. Some articles were harder to locate, but Eleanor Roosevelt's informative "My Day" columns have been digitized by the Eleanor Roosevelt Papers Project at George Washington University.

Essential to this study were the memories shared by participants in the youth suffrage movement. Interviews conducted by Rebecca Login, Patricia Keefer, Charles Koppelman, and myself clarified their political actions and organizing and conveyed their perspectives and motivations. I made use of interviews with Rosalyn Hester Baker, Jay Berman, Mark O. Brown, Steve T. Corneliussen, Robert Renny Cushing, Leslie C. Francis, Jane Greenspun Gale, Stuart Z. Goldstein, Charles Gonzales, Patricia Keefer, Dennis King, Charles Koppelman, Ian MacGowan, Paul J. Myer, Mel Myler, Spencer Oliver, and Dennis M. Warren. Follow-up correspondence via email occurred in some cases. Participants also shared materials from their personal collections as well as written reflections and analyses.

These primary sources made up the bulk of the research for this book. I relied less on secondary sources, given how few exist on this topic. Still key secondary sources offered guidance and aided my analysis.

The pioneering work of Wendell W. Cultice provided a great starting point. *Youth's Battle for the Ballot: A History of the Voting Age in America*

(Westport, CT: Greenwood, 1992) reflected Cultice's commitment to this topic going back to the 1960s. An educator, Cultice recognized the historical importance of the 18-year-old vote and the role of young people in its achievement from the very start. He conducted research, collected sources, and wrote while the enfranchisement effort was still in process. For valid reasons his book wasn't well received 30 years ago. But his heart was in the right place, and he deserves our appreciation for producing the first historical study of this topic.

I found indispensable Jenny Diamond Cheng's PhD dissertation, "Uncovering the Twenty-Sixth Amendment" (University of Michigan, 2008). A legal and political scholar, Cheng comprehensively examined congressional debates over youth suffrage beginning in the 1940s. Although I seek to balance top-down with bottom-up perspectives, I came back again and again to Cheng's dissertation. By documenting, analyzing, and contextualizing the arguments of proponents and opponents in Congress, she laid the foundation for my and all further study.

Other very helpful secondary sources were Alexander Keyssar's magisterial *The Right to Vote: The Contested History of Democracy in the United States* (New York: Basic Books, 2000) and Jane Eisner's engaging *Taking Back the Vote: Getting American Youth Involved in Our Democracy* (Boston: Beacon, 2004). By detailing the entire history of US voting rights and defining the broad themes, Keyssar's book allowed me to quickly identify what was most important about the history of youth suffrage. Eisner showed me the drama inherent in this history and how undeniably relevant it is to the youth vote today. Both Keyssar (briefly) and Eisner (in more detail) provide useful overviews of the achievement of youth suffrage.

Published after I'd drafted the early chapters of this book, Melanie Jean Springer's "Why Georgia? A Curious and Unappreciated Pioneer on the Road to Early Youth Enfranchisement in the United States," *Journal of Policy History* 32, no. 3 (2020): 273–324, is a major scholarly achievement. Because I had just gone over the same ground, I could appreciate her thorough research, interdisciplinary methods, and thoughtful analysis. Springer's article is a model for future work on the achievement of youth enfranchisement in other states.

Historical works on the construction and changing definitions of age opened my eyes to this fascinating field of study. Howard P. Chudacoff's

How Old Are You? Age Consciousness in American Culture (Princeton, NJ: Princeton University Press, 1989) showed how changing norms around age contributed to the 18-year-old vote. Corinne T. Field and Nicholas L. Syrett's *Age in America: The Colonial Era to the Present* (New York: New York University Press, 2015) rewards with information and insight, not least because it contains a chapter by Rebecca de Schweinitz. "'The Proper Age for Suffrage': Vote 18 and the Politics of Age from World War II to the Age of Aquarius" presents in a microcosm the entire history of the movement to lower the voting age to 18, highlighting the redefinition of that age marker and meaning by 1971. Her own book on this topic is forthcoming.

Finally, I couldn't have written this book without the extant legal scholarship, starting with Eric S. Fish's "The Twenty-Sixth Amendment Enforcement Power," *Yale Law Journal* 121, no. 5 (2012): 1168–1235. Even as I understood the broad outlines, I had a lot to learn about the specificities of constitutional change and voting rights law. Fish's work taught me much, confirmed by two recent articles on youth suffrage and the 26th Amendment: Yael Bromberg, "Youth Voting Rights and the Unfulfilled Promise of the Twenty-Sixth Amendment," *University of Pennsylvania Journal of Constitutional Law* 21, no. 5 (2019): 1105–1166 and Mae C. Quinn et al., "Youth Suffrage: In Support of the Second Wave," *Akron Law Review* 53, no. 2 (2019): 445–479.

NOTES

INTRODUCTION

1 Wendell W. Cultice, *Youth's Battle for the Ballot: A History of the Voting Age in America* (Westport, CT: Greenwood, 1992). Rebecca de Schweinitz usefully summarizes the historiography in "'The Proper Age for Suffrage': Vote 18 and the Politics of Age from World War II to the Age of Aquarius," in *Age in America: The Colonial Era to the Present*, ed. Corinne T. Field and Nicholas L. Syrett (New York: New York University Press, 2015), 209–210, 231n2. See also my Note on Sources.

2 Randolph, quoted in Martin Weil, "Former Sen. Jennings Randolph Dies," *Washington Post* (May 9, 1998), B06.

3 Judith N. Shklar, *American Citizenship: The Quest for Inclusion* (Cambridge, MA: Harvard University Press, 1991), 18. Cultice, *Youth's Battle for the Ballot*, and de Schweinitz, "'Proper Age for Suffrage,'" take issue with this interpretation as well; Cultice's title says as much.

4 Bernice J. Reagon, "A Borning Struggle," *New Directions* 7 (April 1980), 1.

5 Paul J. Myer, interview with author, August 10, 2019.

6 Maurice Isserman and Michael Kazin, *America Divided: The Civil War of the 1960s* (New York: Oxford University Press, 2000), 281.

7 Arthur Marwick, "The Cultural Revolution of the Long Sixties: Voices of Reaction, Protest, and Permeation," *International History Review* 27 (December 2005), 798.

8 "Brief Chronology," in David Farber and Beth Bailey, *The Columbia Guide to America in the 1960s* (New York: Columbia University Press, 2001), 437–444.

9 Gael Graham, *Young Activists: American High School Students in the Age of Protest* (DeKalb: Northern Illinois University Press, 2006), 5.

10 John D'Emilio, "Placing Gay in the Sixties," in *Long Time Gone: Sixties America Then and Now*, ed. Alexander Bloom (Oxford: Oxford University Press, 2001), 209–229; Winifred Breines, "Whose New Left?," *Journal of American History* 75 (September 1988), 528–545; Andrew Hunt, "'When Did the Sixties Happen?' Searching for New Directions," *Journal of Social History* 33 (Autumn 1999), 147–161. Russell James Henderson advances this argument in "The Twenty-Sixth Amendment" (PhD diss., University of Mississippi, 2016), 272.

11 Breines, "Whose New Left?"; William O'Neill, *Coming Apart: An Informal History of America in the 1960s* (New York: Times Books, 1971); Allen J. Matusow, *The Unraveling of America: A History of Liberalism in the 1960s* (New York: Harper & Row, 1984); Todd Gitlin, *The Sixties: Years of Hope, Days of Rage* (New York: Bantam, 1987).

12 Mary C. Brennan, *Turning Right in the 1960s: The Conservative Capture of the GOP* (Chapel Hill: University of North Carolina Press, 1995).

13 Matusow, *Unraveling of America*, xiv.

14 Kevin Mattson, *When America Was Great: The Fighting Faith of Postwar Liberalism* (New York: Routledge, 2004), 6–7.

15 Edward J. Forand, quoted in Joey Williams, "Looking for a Battle Plan?," *Moderator* (April 1969), 13.

16 Terry H. Anderson, *The Sixties* (New York: Longman, 1999), 222.

17 Warren, quoted in Jan Ferris Heenan, "Warren Remembers His Time Fondly on National Stage," *Pacific Law* (Fall 2009), 33.

1. FRANCHISE OF FREEDOM

1 Roosevelt, Report on the Home Front, October 12, 1942, Radio Address of the President transcription, Franklin Delano Roosevelt Presidential Library and Museum, http://docs.fdrlibrary.marist.edu/101242.html.

2 Jennings Randolph, quoted in "Pro: Should the Legal Voting Age Be Reduced to 18 Years?," *Congressional Digest* (August–September 1944), 204.

3 "Rep. Randolph Pledges Action if U.S. Asks It," *Washington Post* (March 18, 1942), 17.

4 Jane Eisner conveys this compelling anecdote in *Taking Back the Vote: Getting American Youth Involved in Our Democracy* (Boston: Beacon, 2004), 13.

5 Vandenberg, paraphrased and quoted in "Vote for Men 18 Asked in Senate by Vandenberg," *Chicago Tribune* (October 20, 1942), 3.

6 Randolph, quoted in House Judiciary Committee, Subcommittee No. 1, *A Joint Resolution Proposing an Amendment to the Constitution of the United States; Extending the Right to Vote to Citizens Eighteen Years of Age or Older*, 78th Cong., 1st sess., October 20, 1943 (hereafter 1943 House Hearing), 3–4.

7 Harley M. Kilgore, "Old Enough to Vote," *The Spotlight* (December 1943), 6.

8 Bickford, quoted in Henrik N. Dullea, *Charter Revision in the Empire State: The Politics of New York's 1967 Constitutional Convention* (Albany: State University of New York Press, 1997), 186.

9 "Vote for Men 18 Asked in Senate by Vandenberg," *Chicago Tribune* (October 20, 1942), 3.

10 Kilgore, "Old Enough to Vote," 6, 18.

11 Jenny Diamond Cheng makes this same point in "Uncovering the Twenty-Sixth Amendment" (PhD diss., University of Michigan, 2008), 6.

12 Kilgore, "Old Enough to Vote," 18; Randolph, "Pro," 204.

13 Randolph, "Pro," 202.

14 Kilgore, "Old Enough to Vote," 18; Randolph, "Pro," 202.

15 Randolph, quoted in 1943 House Hearing, 3.

16 Corinne T. Field and Nicholas L. Syrett, "Introduction," in *Age in America: The Colonial Era to the Present*, ed. Field and Syrett (New York: New York University Press, 2015), 1. Rebecca de Schweinitz's essay in the same collection, "'The

Proper Age for Suffrage,'" applies this theoretical concept to the 18-year-old vote specifically.

17 Bickford, quoted in Eisner, *Taking Back the Vote*, 11.

18 Susan J. Pearson, "'Age Ought to Be a Fact': The Campaign against Child Labor and the Rise of the Birth Certificate," *Journal of American History* 100 (March 2014), 1144–1165.

19 Jon Grinspan, "A Birthday Like None Other: Turning Twenty-One in the Age of Popular Politics," in Field and Syrett, *Age in America*, 86.

20 Kilgore, "Old Enough to Vote," 18, 6.

21 Randolph, quoted in 1943 House Hearing, 2.

22 John J. Cornwell to Jennings Randolph, n.d., inserted into Randolph statement, 1943 House Hearing, 2.

23 Randolph, "Pro," 204, 202; Kilgore, "Old Enough to Vote," 6.

24 John H. Tolan and Celler, quoted in 1943 House Hearing, 5.

25 Vandenberg, quoted in C. David Tompkins, *Senator Arthur H. Vandenberg: The Evolution of a Modern Republican, 1884–1945* (East Lansing: Michigan State University Press, 1970), 56.

26 For an excellent discussion of the framing of the US Constitution and the understanding of the Founding Fathers on the relationship between the federal and state governments with respect to voting, see Alexander Keyssar, *The Right to Vote: The Contested History of Democracy in the United States* (New York: Basic Books, 2000), 18–20.

27 Max Farrand, ed., *The Records of the Federal Convention of 1787*, vol. 1 (New Haven, CT: Yale University Press, 1911).

28 George Gallup, "Sentiment for Lowering Voting Age Gaining," *Washington Post* (September 5, 1943), B7.

29 Randolph, quoted in 1943 House Hearing, 4–5.

30 Gallup, "Sentiment for Lowering Voting Age Gaining," B7.

31 Ellis Arnall, quoted in 1943 House Hearing, 8. For a comprehensive analysis, see Melanie Jean Springer, "Why Georgia? A Curious and Unappreciated Pioneer on the Road to Early Youth Enfranchisement in the United States," *Journal of Policy History* 32, no. 3 (2020), 273–324.

32 *Augusta Chronicle* (August 1, 1942), A4, and (April 7, 1942), A2, cited in Patrick Novotny, *This Georgia Rising: Education, Civil Rights, and the Politics of Change in Georgia in the 1940s* (Macon, GA: Mercer University Press, 2007), 107–108n249, 111.

33 Luke Greene, "Georgia's 12,000 'Joe Colleges' Seen as Major Political Factor," *Atlanta Constitution* (October 26, 1941), 2B.

34 "Better Voters," *Atlanta Constitution* (March 5, 1943), 10.

35 "CIO Official Praises Youth Ballot Measure," *Atlanta Constitution* (March 8, 1943), 18.

36 Arnall, quoted in "Constitutional Changes Piling Up Big Majorities," *Atlanta Constitution* (August 4, 1943), 5.

37 GST, "The Political Pot Brews," *The Technique* (March 23, 1946), 6; "Constitutional Changes Piling Up Big Majorities," *Atlanta Constitution* (August 4, 1943), 5. On Arnall, youth suffrage, and race in Georgia, see Springer, "Why Georgia?," 309–310.

38 "Vote at 18," *Newsweek* (August 16, 1943), 59.

39 "18-Year-Old Vote Measure to Be Pushed," *Berkshire Evening Eagle* (August 9, 1943), 5; "Georgia Started Something," *Atlanta Constitution* (August 14, 1943), 4.

40 Thomas M. Law, "Lower the Voting Age Now," reprinted in *Appendix to the Congressional Record*, 79th Cong., 1st sess. (January 3, 1945), A18.

41 Norman Thomas, "No Magic in 21," *Parents' Magazine* (December 1943), 20.

42 "Dust Off Your Dreams: The Story of American Youth for Democracy," American Left Ephemera Collection, University of Pittsburgh, https://digital.library.pitt.edu.

43 Kilgore, "Old Enough to Vote," 6, 18.

44 Howard P. Chudacoff, *How Old Are You? Age Consciousness in American Culture* (Princeton, NJ: Princeton University Press, 1989), 68.

45 Edith B. Joynes, "No One Knows Why 21," *Parents' Magazine* (December 1943), 18.

46 Joy Elmer Morgan, statement, "Wake Up, America!," May 22, 1944, reprinted as "Pro: Should The Legal Voting Age Be Reduced to 18 Years?," *Congressional Digest* (August–September 1944), 212.

47 "Weaver Debaters Want Voting Age Lowered; Advance Good Reasons," *Hartford Courant* (December 12, 1943), D1.

48 Eleanor Roosevelt, "My Day, January 21, 1943," Eleanor Roosevelt Papers Digital Edition (2017), www2.gwu.edu.

49 Associated Press, "Mrs. Roosevelt Asks a Voting Age of 18," *New York Times* (January 22, 1943), 14.

50 Roger Baldwin, "Old Enough to Fight, Why Not to Vote?," *Parents' Magazine* (December 1943), 20.

51 Clark Foreman, "Georgia Kills the Poll Tax," *New Republic* (February 26, 1945), 291.

52 M. L. King Jr., "Kick Up Dust," *Atlanta Constitution* (August 6, 1946), 6.

53 Foreman, "Georgia Kills the Poll Tax," 292.

2. YOUTH'S OWN FUTURE

1 Ellis Arnall, quoted in 1943 House Hearing, 13.

2 AYD Statement, quoted in Wendell W. Cultice, *Youth's Battle for the Ballot: A History of the Voting Age in America* (Westport, CT: Greenwood, 1992), 28.

3 Emanuel Celler, quoted in 1943 House Hearing, 5.

4 Emanuel Celler, quoted in "Con: Should the Legal Voting Age Be Reduced to 18 Years?," *Congressional Digest* (August–September 1944), 205.

5 Celler, quoted in 1943 House Hearing, 3.

6 Russell and Arnall, quoted in 1943 House Hearing, 10.

7 Russell and Arnall, quoted in 1943 House Hearing, 10–11.

8 Celler, quoted in 1943 House Hearing, 4.

9   Hatton W. Sumners and Russell, quoted in 1943 House Hearing, 5.

10 Arnall, quoted in 1943 House Hearing, 13.

11 Celler, "Con," 205.

12 Joseph E. Harvey and George E. Brown, quoted in "Con: Should The Legal Voting Age Be Reduced to 18 Years?," *Congressional Digest* (August–September 1944), 211.

13 "Is Eighteen Too Young to Vote?," *Woman's Home Companion* 70 (December 1943), 14.

14 New York Bar Association, Committee on State Legislation, "We Vote No," *Parents' Magazine* (December 1943), 20.

15 Alfred P. Haake, statement, *Wake Up, America!* (May 22, 1944), reprinted in "Con: Should the Legal Voting Age Be Reduced to 18 Years?," *Congressional Digest* (August–September 1944), 215.

16 "Is Eighteen Too Young to Vote?," *Woman's Home Companion* 70 (December 1943), 14.

17 Sidney Silvian, statement, *America's Town Hall Meeting of the Air* (April 15, 1943), reprinted in "Con: Should the Legal Voting Age Be Reduced to 18 Years?," *Congressional Digest* (August–September 1944), 221.

18 George Gallup, "Sentiment for Lowering Voting Age Gaining," *Washington Post* (September 5, 1943), B7.

19 Jenny Diamond Cheng, "Uncovering the Twenty-Sixth Amendment" (PhD diss., University of Michigan, 2008), 15; Cultice, *Youth's Battle for the Ballot*, 30.

20 Truman, paraphrased in Carl Wiegman, "Keep U.S. Mighty," *Chicago Daily Tribune* (April 7, 1946), 1.

21 United Press, "Should Youth Vote? Democrats Poll Nation; Answer Is Yes, No," *Washington Post* (May 28, 1946), 10.

22 James H. Smith, "Red-Baiting Senator Harley Kilgore in the Election of 1952: The Limits of McCarthyism during the Second Red Scare," *West Virginia History*, n.s., 1 (Spring 2007), 55–74.

23 "To Secure These Rights," Report of the President's Committee on Civil Rights, 162, Harry S. Truman Presidential Library, www.trumanlibrary.gov.

24 "The Case for 18-Year-Olds," *Newsweek* (January 22, 1951), 20.

25 Carroll D. Kearns, "Lowering Voting Age to 18," *Congressional Record* 91 (January 15, 1951), 266; "Give Youth the Right to Vote!," *Redbook* (November 1950), 21.

26 Eleanor Roosevelt, "My Day, June 23, 1951," Eleanor Roosevelt Papers Digital Edition (2017), www2.gwu.edu.

27 Moody, quoted in "Constitutional Amendments," *Hearings Before a Subcommittee of the Committee on the Judiciary, United States Senate*, 82nd Cong., 2nd sess., June 27, 1952, (hereafter 1952 Senate Hearings), 60, 62.

28 Arnall, Moody, and Kilgore, quoted in 1952 Senate Hearings, 67, 60.

29 Eisenhower, Detroit Press Conference, June 15, 1952, quoted in Eisenhower Quotes, January 1–August 22, 1952, Maxwell M. Rabb Papers, 1938–1958, 1989, box 5, Dwight D. Eisenhower Presidential Library (hereafter DDE Library).

30 "65% of 18–21 Year-Olds Favor Ike, Says Survey," *Wall Street Journal* (October 31, 1952), 1.

31 Humphrey, quoted in "Granting Citizens Who Have Attained the Age of Eighteen the Right to Vote," *Hearings Before a Subcommittee of the Committee on the Judiciary, United States Senate*, 83rd Cong., 1st sess., June 2, 1953, 3–4; Humphrey, "Full Citizenship for Youth," *Redbook* (September 1953), 21.

32 Eisenhower, Annual Message to the Congress on the State of the Union, January 7, 1954, Online by Gerhard Peters and John T. Woolley, American Presidency Project, University of California, Santa Barbara (hereafter Presidency Project), www.presidency.ucsb.edu.

33 Leonard Hall, quoted in "Eisenhower Favors 18-Year Voting Age," *New York Times* (May 26, 1953), 21.

34 George Gallup, "Adults Approve Teen Vote By Majority of Almost 2 to 1," *Washington Post* (March 6, 1954), A; "You and the 18-Year-Old Vote," *Seventeen* (June 1954), 93.

35 "Should the Voting Age Be Lowered to 18?," *Parents' Magazine* (March 1954), 44–45, 134–137; White, quoted on 136.

36 "The Vote on the Voting Age," *New York Post* (May 24, 1954), Republican National Committee, News Clippings, box 635, DDE Library (hereafter RNC clippings); "Eighteen Is Too Young," *New York Times* (May 23, 1954), E10.

37 "18-Year Vote Age Opposed by Truman," *Hartford Courant* (January 9, 1954), 7B.

38 Celler, "Constitutional Amendment Introduced Providing That No Citizen under 21 May Have the Right to Vote," *Congressional Record* 100 (March 10, 1954), 3050.

39 Langer, quoted in "Extension of Voting Rights to Citizens at Age of 18," *Congressional Record* 100 (May 21, 1954), 6956–6957.

40 Russell, quoted in "Extension of Voting Rights to Citizens at Age of 18," 6957, 6963–6964.

41 Kennedy, quoted in "Extension of Voting Rights to Citizens at Age of 18," 6978.

42 Russell, quoted in "Extension of Voting Rights to Citizens at Age of 18," 6963–6964.

43 "Not for 18-Year-Olds," *Newsweek* (May 31, 1954), 24.

44 "An Amendment Deferred," *New York Herald Tribune* (May 23, 1954), RNC clippings.

45 Russell, quoted in "18-Year-Old Vote," *CQ Almanac 1954*, 10th ed., 08–417 (Washington, DC: Congressional Quarterly, 1955), http://library.cqpress.com.

3. MAKE DEMOCRACY LIVE

1 Diggs, quoted in Carolyn P. DuBose, *The Untold Story of Charles Diggs: The Public Figure, the Private Man* (Arlington, VA: Barton, 1998), 23.

2 Diggs, "Death of Walter White Is Mourned by World," *Congressional Record* 101 (March 30, 1955), 4118.

3 Diggs, paraphrased and quoted in "Michigan Congressman Urges Negroes to Vote," *Washington Post* (March 27, 1956), 13.

4 Charles C. Diggs, "Should the Voting Age Be Lowered to 18? Yes," *American Legion Magazine* (November 1966), 8.

5 White, quoted in "Should the Voting Age Be Lowered to 18?," *Parents' Magazine* (March 1954), 136.

6 Diggs, "A Report to Constituents of Accomplishments of the 84th Congress," *Congressional Record* 102 (July 27, 1956), 15777.

7 "Nine Demand Action on Rights Bills," *Washington Post* (June 20, 1955), 2.

8 Diggs, "Death of Walter White Is Mourned by World," 4118–4119.

9 Gladys Johnson, "Gaddings: The Right Not to Vote," *Chicago Defender* (September 25, 1965), 22.

10 "Rep. Diggs Rouses Mississippi Rally," *Chicago Defender* (May 14, 1955), 1.

11 Charles C. Diggs, "Record of Progress in Civil Rights," *Negro History Bulletin* (October 1, 1962), 14.

12 Robert E. Baker, "Manifesto Hit by 3 Speakers in Congress," *Washington Post* (March 16, 1956), 1.

13 Steven F. Lawson, *Running for Freedom: Civil Rights and Black Politics in America since 1941* (New York: Wiley, 2014), 32.

14 "Cong. Diggs Maps Civil Action Plan," *Chicago Defender* (October 15, 1955), 19; Damon Stetson, "Democrats Seek Plank on Rights," *New York Times* (June 3, 1956), 67.

15 Charles C. Diggs Jr., quoted in Mattie Smith Colin, "Till's Mom, Diggs Both Disappointed," *Chicago Defender* (October 1, 1955), 1.

16 Diggs, "Death of Walter White Is Mourned by World," 4119.

17 "Diggs Defeated Incumbent Who Held Office 15 Years," *Ebony* (April 1955), 108, 107.

18 Walden Bradley and Betty Adkins, "A Plea for Lowering State Voting Age," *Courier-Journal* (October 29, 1955), 6; Wetherby quoted in his letter to LaVerne Chapanian, December 7, 1955, in *The Public Papers of Governor Lawrence W. Wetherby, 1950–1955*, ed. John E. Kleber (Lexington: University Press of Kentucky, 2015), 72.

19 Johnson Kanady, "House Rejects Referendum on Voting Age Cut," *Chicago Tribune* (April 27, 1955), A2.

20 Mrs. A.S., Richmond, IN, "Why Not Let Them Vote?," *Redbook* (January 1951), 20.

21 Bayh, quoted in "A Modern Father of Our Constitution: An Interview with Former Senator Birch Bayh," *Fordham Law Review* 79 (December 2010), 785.

22 Eisenhower, quoted in the President's News Conference, June 2, 1954, Presidency Project, www.presidency.ucsb.edu.

23 Eisenhower, quoted in the President's News Conference, October 11, 1956, Presidency Project, www.presidency.ucsb.edu.

24 Wilkins, quoted in Lawson, *Running for Freedom*, 54.

25 "Asks Ike to Halt Little Rock Tension," *Chicago Defender* (December 26, 1959), 21; Diggs, paraphrased and quoted in "'Goodwill Trip' to Little Rock Urged on Ike," *Washington Post* (December 17, 1959), B19.

26 Eisenhower, quoted in Lawson, *Running for Freedom*, 60.
27 Wilkins, quoted in Manfred Berg, *"The Ticket to Freedom": The NAACP and the Struggle for Black Political Integration* (Gainesville: University Press of Florida, 2005), 197.
28 Eleanor Roosevelt, "My Day, August 7, 1957," Eleanor Roosevelt Papers Digital Edition (2017), www2.gwu.edu.
29 "Tribune Gives Teen Writers Opportunity," *Chicago Tribune* (December 1, 1957), N16.
30 Howard P. Chudacoff, *How Old Are You? Age Consciousness in American Culture* (Princeton, NJ: Princeton University Press, 1989), 5.
31 Grace Palladino, *Teenagers: An American History* (New York: Basic Books, 1996).
32 Paulette Hoornaert, "Help, I'm Growing Up," *Chicago Tribune* (December 30, 1962), SW1.
33 Fawn Bifoss, "Adolescence—Definition," *Chicago Tribune* (May 14, 1961), S5.
34 Joan Giancola, "Problems of the Young," *Chicago Daily Tribune* (March 26, 1961), S3.
35 Edwin Stout Jr., "That Often Posed Question," *Chicago Tribune* (April 12, 1964), S5.
36 Mary Forquer, "What Is a Teen?," *Chicago Tribune* (January 17, 1960), W5.
37 Susan Levinson, "How Teen-Agers Think," *Chicago Tribune* (March 9, 1958), W5.
38 Kenneth Hoedl, "Juvenile Delinquency," *Chicago Tribune* (January 26, 1964), SW11.
39 Jack Tockstein, "The Space Age," *Chicago Tribune* (December 13, 1959), W4.
40 Sandra Sciacchitano, "The 'Beat' Generation," *Chicago Tribune* (February 9, 1958), W4.
41 Ruth Selke, "The Name—Teen-Ager," *Chicago Tribune* (December 21, 1958), N12.
42 James Kozicki, "What about Rock 'n' Roll?," *Chicago Tribune* (March 22, 1959), S1.
43 Sharon Vasile, "Delinquents?," *Chicago Tribune* (January 14, 1962), SW11.
44 Jack Tockstein, "The Space Age," *Chicago Tribune* (December 13, 1959), W4.
45 Dick Fontera, quoted in "Columbia's SDA Postpones Discussion to Disaffiliate from Its National Body," *Columbia Daily Spectator* (November 2, 1955), 1.
46 Evan E. Evans, "Making a Difference in Citizenship," *NEA Journal* (February 1950), 102.
47 Margaret Daunora, "United States History Is Important," *Chicago Tribune* (May 13, 1962), S5.
48 Claude Caddell, "A School of Sheep," *Chicago Tribune* (April 1, 1962), S12.
49 Ira Silverman, "Education + Experience = 1 Citizen," pt. 1, *Columbia Daily Spectator* (January 7, 1954), 2, and pt. 2 (February 8, 1954), 2.
50 Humphrey, "Full Citizenship for Youth," *Redbook* (September 1953), 21.
51 "Political Battles Interest Young Blood," *The Blackbird* (November 13, 1956), 2.
52 Dan Zimsen, "Reader Backs Voting Age Registration," *The Spectator* (February 1, 1956), 3.
53 "Youth Gets Out the Vote," *Senior Scholastic* (November 1956), 9.

54 Eleanor Roosevelt, "My Day, October 15, 1956," Eleanor Roosevelt Papers Digital Edition (2017), www2.gwu.edu.

55 Thomas C. Desmond, "Seedbed for Leadership," *Liberty*, condensed and reprinted in *Reader's Digest* 52 (April 1948), 31–33.

56 Natalie Gittelson, "You and the 18-Year-Old Vote," *Seventeen* (June 1954), 64–65, 90, 93, 95–96.

57 Laura Voorhies, "You and That Best American Custom," *Seventeen* (September 1952), 168; "It's All Yours," *Seventeen* (September 1952), 128–129, 192–193, 202; "Democracy, Teen Size," *Seventeen* (February 1945), 64.

58 Quoted in "Should 18-Year-Olds Be Given Vote?," *Los Angeles Times* (April 12, 1953), I1.

59 Quoted in "Should 18-Year-Olds Be Given Vote?," I1.

60 Dot Tillman, "Eighteen-Year Old Vote Causes Disagreement from Grammar Schools to College Campuses," *The Whitworthian* (February 2, 1954), 1.

61 Quoted in "Should 18-Year-Olds Be Given Vote?," I1.

62 James T. Patterson, *Grand Expectations: The United States, 1945–1974* (New York: Oxford University Press, 1996), 361.

63 Lou Griffin, quoted in Marie Edwards, "Inquiring Reporter," *The Twig* (January 19, 1951), 2.

64 Andrew D. Kopkind, "An Age of Political Reason," *Cornell Daily Sun* (December 16, 1955), 4.

65 Nancy Levy, "Definition of an Adult," *Chicago Tribune* (April 26, 1959), N1.

4. CHANGE IS IN THE AIR

1 Kennedy, Remarks, Young People for Kennedy rally, Portland, Oregon, May 15, 1960 folder, Speeches and the Press box 909, Senate Files, Pre-Presidential Papers, Papers of President Kennedy, JFK Library (hereafter JFK Senate Files).

2 Kennedy, The New Frontier, acceptance speech, Democratic National Convention, July 15, 1960, Speeches and the Press box 910, JFK Senate Files.

3 Selection from the first Kennedy v. Nixon presidential debate, September 26, 1960, http://www.youtube.com/watch?v=QazmVHAOoos.

4 Eleanor Roosevelt, "My Day, September 28, 1960," Eleanor Roosevelt Papers Digital Edition (2017), www2.gwu.edu.

5 Kennedy, quoted in Pepe Ferrer, "Hear Your Heroes: Senator John F. Kennedy," *Seventeen* (January 1960), 92.

6 Kennedy, Remarks, Young People for Kennedy rally.

7 Allida Black, *Casting Her Own Shadow: Eleanor Roosevelt and the Shaping of Postwar Liberalism* (New York: Columbia University Press, 1996), 172–173.

8 Kennedy, quoted in William M. Beecher, "Teenage Vote," *Harvard Crimson* (April 23, 1954), 3.

9 RA, Ayer, Mass., to JFK, March 13, 1954 and JFK to RA, March 23, 1954, Voting Age folder, Legislation Files 1953–1960 box 658, JFK Senate Files.

10 RAG, USNA, Annapolis, Maryland, to JFK, November 15, 1955 and Theodore C. Sorensen to RAG, November 23, 1955, Voting Age folder, Legislation Files 1953–1960 box 658, JFK Senate Files.

11 Robert C. Albright, "Southern Hacking Continues," *Washington Post* (April 4, 1960), A1.

12 1960 Democratic Party Platform, Presidency Project, www.presidency.ucsb.edu.

13 "Hail Demo Plank as Step Forward," *Chicago Defender* (July 23, 1960), 1.

14 Carroll Kilpatrick, "Distressed Area Study Ordered," *Washington Post* (December 5, 1960), A1.

15 1960 Democratic Party Platform.

16 King, quoted in "In Newly Unearthed Recordings, MLK Credits Blacks for Helping to Elect John Kennedy," *Stanford Report* (August 10, 2004), https://news .stanford.edu.

17 Jennings Randolph, quoted in "Shipley Talk Assailed," *Washington Post* (March 21, 1961), B3.

18 Diggs, quoted in Carolyn P. DuBose, *The Untold Story of Charles Diggs: The Public Figure, the Private Man* (Arlington, VA: Barton, 1998), 68–69.

19 1960 Democratic Party Platform.

20 John F. Kennedy, Annual Message to Congress on the State of the Union, January 11, 1962, Presidency Project, www.presidency.ucsb.edu.

21 Kefauver, quoted in "Nomination and Election of President and Vice President and Qualifications for Voting," *Hearings Before the Subcommittee on Constitutional Amendments of the Committee of the Judiciary, United States Senate*, 87th Cong., 1st sess. (hereafter 1961 Senate Hearings), May 23, 1961, 1.

22 Kennedy, Report to the American People on Civil Rights, June 11, 1963, JFK Library, www.jfklibrary.org.

23 Katzenbach, quoted in 1961 Senate Hearings, 370.

24 Randolph, quoted in 1961 Senate Hearings, 180, 186–187.

25 Randolph, quoted in 1961 Senate Hearings, 187.

26 "Senator Byrd Favors South Version of Democracy," *Charleston Gazette* (February 8, 1960), reprinted in *Congressional Record* 106 (February 29, 1960), 3874.

27 Randolph, quoted in 1961 Senate Hearings, 189–190.

28 Spencer Oliver, interview with author, August 24, 2020 (hereafter Oliver interview).

29 John M. Bailey, quoted in 1961 Senate Hearings, 542 and William E. Miller, quoted in 1961 Senate Hearings, 553.

30 Leo V. Savage, quoted in 1961 Senate Hearings, 344–345.

31 Savage, quoted in 1961 Senate Hearings, 345.

32 Kennedy, Remarks to the President's Commission on Registration and Voting Participation, 8 May 1963, Speech Files, President's Office Files, Presidential Papers, Papers of John F. Kennedy, JFK Library, www.jfklibrary.org.

33 Kennedy, Executive Order 11100—Establishing the President's Commission on Registration and Voting Participation," March 30, 1963, Presidency Project, www.presidency.ucsb.edu.

34 Astrid Merget, quoted in "Portrait of Victoria Schuck Unveiled," *Political Science & Politics* 36 (January 2003), 121.

35 *Report of the President's Commission on Registration and Voting Participation* (Washington, DC: Government Printing Office, 1963), 49, 43–44.

36 *Report of the President's Commission,* 9.

37 Johnson, "Remarks of the President upon Acceptance of the Report of the Commission on Registration and Voting Participation," December 20, 1963, Commission on Registration and Voting Participation, 23 April 1963–30 March 1964, General File, 1954–1964, White House Staff Files of Lee C. White, Presidential Papers, Papers of John F. Kennedy, JFK Library, www.jfklibrary.org (hereafter LBJ Commission Remarks).

38 Dolan, quoted in Charles Corden, "Students Start Organization to Lower State's Voting Age," *Connecticut Daily Campus* (October 31, 1962), 1.

5. AGENDA FOR A GENERATION

1 Breton, paraphrased in "18-Year Vote Rally Draws Small Audience," *Hartford Courant* (August 26, 1962), 16A.

2 Dolan, quoted and paraphrased in Charles Corden, "Students Start Organization to Lower State's Voting Age," *Connecticut Daily Campus* (October 31, 1962), 1.

3 Keith Schonrock, "Delinquency Hurts Plan to Lower Voting Age to 18," *Hartford Courant* (May 23, 1954), 8.

4 Keith Schonrock, "State Slow to Lower Voting Age," *Hartford Courant* (January 27, 1954), 7.

5 Estes Kefauver and John M. Bailey, 1961 Senate Hearings, July 13, 1961, 542.

6 "Youth Vote Rally Draws Attention of Other Groups," *Hartford Courant* (August 23, 1962), 20.

7 John A. Berman, quoted and paraphrased in Corden, "Students Start Organization," 1; Berman, quoted in "18-Year Vote Rally Draws Small Audience," 16A.

8 Fournier, Kerlin, and DiFazio, quoted in "18-Year Vote Rally Draws Small Audience," 16A.

9 Breton, paraphrased in "18-Year Vote Rally Draws Small Audience," 16A.

10 "18-Year Vote Rally Draws Small Audience," 16A.

11 Dolan, quoted in Corden, "Students Start Organization," 1; Gall Mathews, "Is an 18-Year-Old Ready to Vote?," *Christian Science Monitor* (July 23, 1965), reprinted in *Congressional Record* (January 16, 1967), 515.

12 Joseph S. Dolan, "Report to the President's Commission on Registration and Voting Participation on Lowering the Voting Age to 18 and the Commission's Recommendations: The Results of a 3-Year Study on 18-Year-Old Suffrage" (University of Connecticut, Storrs, January 1, 1964), 1.

13 Dolan, paraphrased in Corden, "Students Start Organization," 1; Dolan, "Report to the President's Commission," 33, 2.

14 Dolan, "Report to the President's Commission," 33.

15 Dolan, "Report to the President's Commission," 33.

16 SNCC's "Statement of Purpose," prepared by Rev. J. M. Lawson and published in *Student Voice* (June 1960), 2, www.crmvet.org; "The Sharon Statement, 1960," reprinted in Gregory L. Schneider, ed., *Conservatism in American since 1930* (New York: New York University Press, 2003), 229–230; "The Port Huron Statement" (New York: Students for a Democratic Society, 1964).

17 Joan Giancola, "Problems of the Young," *Chicago Tribune* (March 26, 1961), S3.

18 Stephen Cohen, "The Value of Boredom," *Chicago Tribune* (January 5, 1964), N_A6.

19 Marilou Cerveny, "Courage in Teen-Age Living," *Chicago Tribune* (February 9, 1964), E11.

20 Paul J. Myer, "Music v. College," "Lost and Found," and "College Life Recollections," in author's possession.

21 Paul J. Myer, "College Life Recollections," 2, in author's possession.

22 Paul Minarchenko, quoted in "Special Election Edition," *Independent* (March 22, 1963), 1.

23 Carl J. Marinelli, "Vote Minarchenko," *Independent* (March 22, 1963), 2.

24 Paul J. Myer, interview with author, August 10, 2019 (hereafter Myer August interview), and email correspondence with author, March 12, 2020.

25 "Next September," *Independent* (April 22, 1965), 2.

26 "Students Rally Better Education through Taxation," *Independent* (May 20, 1965), 1; "Students Stage 22 Hour Vigil at State House," *Independent* (April 14, 1966), 1.

27 Philip Lee, "The Case of Dixon v. Alabama: From Civil Rights to Students' Rights and Back Again," *Teachers College Record* (December 2014), 1–18.

28 Paul J. Myer, interview with author, July 3, 2019 (hereafter Myer July interview), and "College Life Recollections," 2, in author's possession.

29 "Courage: The Most Admirable," *Independent* (May 3, 1966), 2.

30 Hilary Gay Kliver, "What I Can Do for My Country," *Chicago Tribune* (May 26, 1963), S4.

31 Coleman, quoted in Dash Coleman, "Heroes of Savannah's Fight to Desegregate Honored with New Marker," *Savannah Now—Savannah Morning News* (September 23, 2016), www.savannahnow.com.

32 "Students March for Civil Rights," *Student Voice* (suppl., November 1960), 1.

33 "Students Demonstrate throughout the Country," *Stanford Daily* (November 9, 1960), 3.

34 "District of Columbia," *Student Voice* (November 1960), 6.

35 Todd Gitlin, *Sixties: Years of Hope, Days of Rage* (Toronto: Bantam Books, 1987), 129.

36 Tom Hayden, *Revolution in Mississippi* (New York: Students for a Democratic Society, 1962), 21.

37 Les Francis, "Recollections: The 1960s and Personal Awakening," in author's possession, 4; Leslie C. Francis, interview with author, July 8, 2020 (hereafter Francis interview).

38 Pat Caraher, "Blackwell Makes His Mark," *Washington State Magazine* (Fall 2002), http://wsm.wsu.edu.

39 Les Francis, "Recollections: The 1960s and Personal Awakening," in author's pos-
    session, 5.
40 Diggs, quoted in Carolyn P. DuBose, *The Untold Story of Charles Diggs: The Public
    Figure, the Private Man* (Arlington, VA: Barton, 1998), 72–73.
41 Mario Savio, quoted in interview with Bret Eynon in 1985, Reminiscences of
    Mario Savio, Columbia University Oral History Office, Columbia University,
    New York, 44–45.
42 Weinberg, quoted in Joan Morrison and Robert K. Morrison, *From Camelot to
    Kent State: The Sixties Experience in the Words of Those Who Lived It* (New York:
    Times Books, 1987), 226.
43 Savio, quoted in Robert Cohen, ed., *The Essential Mario Savio: Speeches and
    Writings that Changed America* (Berkeley: University of California Press, 2014),
    185–189.
44 Seymour Martin Lipset, *Rebellion in the University: A History of Student Activ-
    ism in America* (London: Routledge & Kegan Paul, 1972), xviii; Ellen and William
    Sewell, quoted in transcribed interview with Lisa Rubens in 2000, Free Speech
    Movement Oral History Project, Regional Oral History Office, Bancroft Library,
    University of California, Berkeley, 2014, 20–21, http://vm136.lib.berkeley.edu.

6. CONSENT OF THE GOVERNED

 1 Roy Wilkins, *Standing Fast: The Autobiography of Roy Wilkins* (New York: Da
    Capo Press, 1994), 300.
 2 Martin Luther King Jr., "I Have a Dream" (1963), in Josh Gottheimer, ed., *Ripples
    of Hope: Great American Civil Rights Speeches* (New York: Basic Books, 2003), 236.
 3 King, "I Have a Dream" (1963), 234–235.
 4 LBJ Commission Remarks.
 5 "Voting Age at 18 Was Johnson Aim," *New York Times* (March 21, 1965), 72.
 6 Martin Luther King Jr., "In a Word—Now," *New York Times Magazine* (September
    29, 1963), 247.
 7 Diggs, quoted in Bob Hunter, "Negroes to Use Acts if Words Fail, Diggs Warns,"
    Chicago Defender (June 3, 1963), 2.
 8 Johnson and aides, quoted in Robert A. Caro, *The Passage of Power: The Years of
    Lyndon Johnson* (New York: Knopf, 2012), xv.
 9 Everett Dirksen, quoted in Clay Risen, *The Bill of the Century: The Epic Battle for
    the Civil Rights Act* (New York: Bloomsbury, 2014), 227.
10 "Negro Summit Meeting Needed, Congressman Diggs Declares," *Chicago De-
    fender* (July 2, 1963), 6.
11 Wilkins, *Standing Fast*, 300.
12 Diggs, quoted in Bob Hunter, "Negroes to Use Acts if Words Fail, Diggs Warns,"
    Chicago Defender (June 3, 1963), 2.
13 William Bruce Wheeler and Susan D. Becker, "Separate But Equal?," in *Discover-
    ing the Past: A Look at the Evidence*, 4th ed. (Boston: Houghton Mifflin, 1994), 255.
14 Diggs, quoted in Bob Hunter, "Negroes to Use Acts if Words Fail, Diggs Warns," 2.

15 Wilkins, *Standing Fast*, 306.

16 Martin Luther King Jr., "In a Word—Now," *New York Times Magazine* (September 29, 1963), 247.

17 Diggs, quoted in Hunter, "Negroes to Use Acts if Words Fail, Diggs Warns," 2.

18 Wilkins, *Standing Fast*, 302.

19 Robert Moses, quoted in Sally Belfrage, *Freedom Summer*, reprint ed. (Charlottesville: University of Virginia Press, 1990), 25–26.

20 Kenney, quoted in Linda Weiner, "Civil Rights Trainees React," *Daily Iowan* (June 26, 1964), 1.

21 "Mississippi Freedom Democratic Party," 6, 1, Council of Federated Organizations Panola County Office, Mississippi Freedom Democratic Party General State Papers, 1964–1965, Freedom Summer Digital Collection, Wisconsin State Historical Society, http://content.wisconsinhistory.org.

22 Dunbar and unnamed white resident, quoted in Claude Sitton, "Negro Queue in Mississippi Is Symbol of Frustration in Voter Registration Drive," *New York Times* (March 2, 1964), 20.

23 Baker, quoted in Barbara Ransby, *Ella Baker & the Black Freedom Movement: A Radical Democratic Vision* (Chapel Hill: University of North Carolina Press, 2003), 337.

24 Hamer, quoted in Chana Kai Lee, *For Freedom's Sake: The Life of Fannie Lou Hamer* (Urbana: University of Illinois Press, 2000), 89, 99.

25 Telegram, quoted in Lisa Anderson Todd, *For a Voice and the Vote: My Journey with the Mississippi Freedom Democratic Party* (Lexington: University Press of Kentucky, 2014), 75.

26 Bob Ross, quoted in Jennifer Frost, *"An Interracial Movement of the Poor": Community Organizing and the New Left in the 1960s* (New York: New York University Press, 2001), 122.

27 Nelson W. Polsby and Aaron B. Wildavsky with David A. Hopkins, *Presidential Elections: Strategies and Structures of American Politics*, 12th ed. (Lanham, MD: Rowman & Littlefield, 2008), 32.

28 Bayh at fundraiser, quoted in John V. Wilson Jr., *Meridian Street: A Memoir* (Denver: Outskirts Press, 2006), 142.

29 Johnson, quoted in Risen, *Bill of the Century*, 254.

30 Johnson, quoted in Gary May, *Bending toward Justice: The Voting Rights Act and the Transformation of American Democracy* (New York: Basic Books, 2013), 48.

31 King, quoted in May, *Bending toward Justice*, 53–55.

32 "A Letter from Martin Luther King from a Selma, Alabama Jail," *New York Times* (February 5, 1965), 15.

33 "Protests Spread Over the Nation," *New York Times* (March 15, 1965), 23.

34 Johnson, "The American Promise," March 15, 1965, in *Public Papers of the Presidents of the United States: Lyndon B. Johnson*, 1965, vol. 1, entry 107 (Washington, DC: Government Printing Office, 1966), 281–287, www.lbjlibrary.org.

35 "Comment, with Civil Rights," *The Independent* (April 22, 1965), 4.

36 King, quoted in May, *Bending toward Justice*, 122.

37 King, quoted in Roy Reed, "25,000 Go to Alabama's Capitol," *New York Times* (March 26, 1965), 1.

38 Johnson, quoted in Michael R. Beschloss, ed., *Reaching for Glory: Lyndon Johnson's Secret White House Tapes, 1964–1965* (New York: Touchstone, 2002), 242.

39 Ervin, quoted in May, *Bending toward Justice*, 155.

40 Rosemarie Tyler Brooks, "15 Solons Urge New Voting Laws," *Chicago Defender* (February 11, 1965), 4.

41 Earnestyne Evans, "Report from Mississippi," *Seventeen* (January 1966), 90, 134.

42 Ardyth Broadrick, "A Plea for the Polls," *Chicago Tribune* (February 28, 1965), S2.

43 Conrad Herula, "Why 18 Year Olds Should Vote," *Chicago Tribune* (October 24, 1965), SCL2.

44 Wendell W. Cultice, *Youth's Battle for the Ballot: A History of the Voting Age in America* (Westport, CT: Greenwood, 1992), 86.

45 "Hartford Rejects Bid to Lower Age for Voters to 18," *New York Times* (October 14, 1965), 49.

46 Lester Wolff, "The Right to Vote," *Congressional Record* 111 (October 8, 1965), 26429.

7. CHALLENGE OF CITIZENSHIP

1 Wolff, quoted in Ross Barkan, "Long Island's 98-Year-Old Former Congressman Eats Dumplings, Hates Trump, Makes Tweets," *The Village Voice* (May 30, 2017), www.villagevoice.com.

2 Lyndon B. Johnson, Remarks in Athens at Ohio University, Presidency Project, www.presidency.ucsb.edu.

3 Lester Wolff, "The Right to Vote," *Congressional Record* 111 (October 8, 1965), 26429.

4 "Challenge and Response," *The Independent* (April 22, 1965), 2.

5 Paul Myer, NEA interview with Rebecca Login, 2011, in author's possession (hereafter Myer NEA interview).

6 "March on Washington Organizing Manual #2," 4, available at www.crmvet.org.

7 "War on Poverty Is Aided by Newark State Students," *The Independent* (March 11, 1965), 5.

8 Johnson, quoted in "Signing of the Higher Education Act," in *Connections: Lyndon B. Johnson in San Marcos* (San Marcos: Texas State University, April 2009), 37.

9 Johnson, quoted in "Signing of the Higher Education Act," 38.

10 Rosalyn Hester Baker, interview with author, March 5, 2020 (hereafter Hester Baker interview).

11 "TSEA Largest Campus Club," *Pedagog 1965* (Southwest Texas State College), 239, https://exhibits.library.txstate.edu.

12 Paul Minarchenko, quoted in "VISTA," *The Independent* (February 25, 1965), 5; "VISTA to Recruit College Volunteers," *The Independent* (February 25, 1965), 1.

13 King, "Why Are You Here?," address at SCOPE orientation, June 15, 1965, and "Summer Community Organization and Political Education Project of the Southern Christian Leadership Conference," n.d., https://kinginstitute.stanford.edu.

14 Jennifer Frost, *"An Interracial Movement of the Poor": Community Organizing and the New Left in the 1960s* (New York: New York University Press, 2001).

15 Tom Hayden, *Reunion: A Memoir* (New York: Random House, 1988), 125; ERAP advertisement, *SDS Bulletin* 3, no. 6 (March 1965), n.p.

16 Economic Opportunity Act, quoted in Allen J. Matusow, *The Unraveling of America: A History of Liberalism in the 1960s* (New York: Harper & Row, 1984), 245.

17 David Zarefsky, *President Johnson's War on Poverty: Rhetoric and History* (University: University of Alabama Press, 1986), 131–133.

18 "1966 Amendments to the Economic Opportunity Act of 1964," *Hearings before the Subcommittee on the War on Poverty Program, Committee on Education and Labor, House of Representatives*, 89th Cong., 2nd sess., March 8–10, 15–16, 1966 (Washington, DC: Government Printing Office, 1966), 486.

19 Myer August interview.

20 Paul J. Myer, "Dreams Do Come True," April 6, 2020, in author's possession; Myer August interview.

21 Paul's commitment, June 21, 1966, in author's possession.

22 Christian G. Appy, *Working-Class War: American Combat Soldiers and Vietnam* (Chapel Hill: University of North Carolina Press, 1993), 6.

23 Myer, "Dreams Do Come True."

24 Robert Postma, "Viet Nam," Letter to the Editor, *The Independent* (April 22, 1965), 2.

25 "Viet Nam," *The Independent* (May 20, 1965), 2.

26 Rosenthal, "Constitutional Amendment on the Voting Age," *Congressional Record* 111 (May 3, 1965), 9194.

27 Fulton, "Voter Discrimination Against Young Adults," *Congressional Record* 111 (August 12, 1965), 20367.

28 Ford, "Resolution to Lower Voting Age," *Congressional Record* 112 (March 17, 1966), 6185.

29 Charles C. Diggs, "Should the Voting Age Be Lowered to 18? Yes," *American Legion Magazine* (November 1966), 8.

30 Graham, quoted in Dan Okrent, "Signs Point Success for Vote at 18," *Michigan Daily* (October 9, 1966), 4.

31 Edward Robinson, quoted in "Plan Action to Push Vote Referendum," *Michigan Daily* (September 3, 1966), 1.

32 Michael P. Wood, State Coordinator, Michigan Citizens' Committee for the Vote at 18, to Senator Robert K. Kennedy, October 26, 1966, folder Civil Liberties: Voting Age at 18, Senate Correspondence: Subject File, 1966, box 9, Robert F. Kennedy Papers, JFK Library (hereafter 1966 Voting Age Correspondence).

33 Dan Okrent, "Signs Point Success for Vote at 18," *Michigan Daily* (October 9, 1966), 4.

34 Bill Mauldin cartoon, *Michigan Daily* (October 9, 1966), 4.

35 "Vote Yes on Proposal No. 1," *Michigan Daily* (November 6, 1966), 10.

36 Spokesman, quoted in Dan Okrent, "Signs Point Success for Vote at 18," *Michigan Daily* (October 9, 1966), 4.

37 "Vote Yes on Proposal No. 1," *Michigan Daily* (November 6, 1966), 10.

38 "Vote Yes on Proposal No. 1," *Michigan Daily* (November 6, 1966), 10.

39 Jenny Diamond Cheng identified "the 'channeling' or 'safety valve' rationale" in "Uncovering the Twenty-Sixth Amendment" (PhD diss., University of Michigan, 2008), 8.

40 Mark E. Glendon, "In Support of the 18-Year-Old Vote," *Michigan Daily* (September 22, 1966), 4.

41 Faxon, quoted in Patricia O'Donohue, "Plan Action to Push Vote Referendum," *Michigan Daily* (September 3, 1966), 1.

42 Neal Bruss, "Students Are Losing on Voter Requirements," *Michigan Daily* (February 20, 1966), 4.

43 "The Michigan Daily Newswire," *Michigan Daily* (November 1, 1966), 1; Neal Bruss, "Students Must Prove Residence to Meet Voting Requirements," *Michigan Daily* (February 18, 1966), 1.

44 Wendell W. Cultice, *Youth's Battle for the Ballot: A History of the Voting Age in America* (Westport, CT: Greenwood, 1992), 87.

45 Arnall and Maddox, quoted in Harold Paulk Henderson, *The Politics of Change in Georgia: A Political Biography of Ellis Arnall* (Athens: University of Georgia Press, 1991), 230, 236.

46 Charles Weltner, Resignation Speech, October 1, 1966, The John F. Kennedy Profile in Courage Award, JFK Library, www.jfklibrary.org.

47 Charles Longstreet Weltner, Letters to the Editor, *Daily Pennsylvanian* (April 6, 1966), 2.

8. THIS IS DEMOCRACY?

1 RFK to FJ, March 1, 1966, 1966 Voting Age Correspondence.

2 Charles Longstreet Weltner to Mary Joe Kopechne, July 25, 1966, 1966 Voting Age Correspondence.

3 "Should Voters Be Younger?," *Daily Tar Heel* (November 2, 1966), 3.

4 See telegrams and letters in 1966 Voting Age Correspondence.

5 "Vote Yes on Proposal No. 1," *Michigan Daily* (November 6, 1966), 10.

6 Michael P. Wood, State Coordinator, Michigan Citizens' Committee for the Vote at 18, to Senator Robert K. Kennedy, October 26, 1966, 1966 Voting Age Correspondence.

7 FJ, New Hyde Park, NY, to RFK, [1966], and BN to RFK, October 31, 1966, 1966 Voting Age Correspondence.

8 DLC, Amarillo Air Force Base, Texas, to RFK, September 25, 1966, 1966 Voting Age Correspondence.

9 Mike Mansfield, "Joint Resolution to Lower the Voting Age," *Congressional Record* 113 (January 12, 1967), 295.

10 Randolph Jennings, "Randolph Introduces His Eighth Joint Resolution for Constitutional Amendment to Extend Franchise to 18-Year-Old Citizens in Federal Elections," *Congressional Record* 113 (January 16, 1967), 512.

11 RFK to MJH, Pleasanton, Texas, January 15, 1968, Civil Liberties: Voting Age at 18, 1/68–4/68 folder, Senate Correspondence: Subject File, 1968, box 5, Robert F. Kennedy Papers, JFK Library.

12 John Poppy, "The Generation Gap," *Look* (February 21, 1967), 27.

13 "The Inheritor," *Time* (January 6, 1967), 18–23.

14 Kennedy, quoted in "Javits and Kennedy View Youth And Some of Its Main Problems," *New York Times* (March 7, 1967), 37.

15 Stokely Carmichael and Charles V. Hamilton, *Black Power: The Politics of Liberation in America* (New York: Vintage, 1967), 44, 78.

16 Carmichael and Hamilton, *Black Power*, 50, 160–161.

17 Paul J. Myer, "Dreams Do Come True," April 6, 2020, 2, in author's possession.

18 Henry Gemmill, "Capital Malaise," *Wall Street Journal* (November 8, 1967), 1.

19 Paul J. Myer, quoted anonymously in Gemmill, "Capital Malaise," 1.

20 Gemmill, "Capital Malaise," 1.

21 Myer July interview.

22 "Youth Keeps Eye on Ballot Box," first of three-part series, *Odessa America* (January 14, 1967), 6; "An Issue That's Not an Issue," third of three-part series, *Public Opinion* (January 13, 1967), 4.

23 "New Group Aims to Lower Vote-Age Limits to Eighteen," and Barry Kaplan, "Movement to Aid Migrant Workers Seeks Rice's Aid," *Rice Thresher* (February 16, 1967), 1.

24 "A Magic Number," *Daily Tar Heel* (February 5, 1967), 2.

25 Jackie Snyder, "Reply to Rothman: Youth Requires Vote," *Daily Collegian*, reprinted in *Daily Tar Heel* (February 15, 1967), 3.

26 Ed Robinson, quoted in "Youth Keeps Eye on Ballot Box," 6; "An Issue That's Not an Issue," 4.

27 King, "Beyond Vietnam," address before Clergy and Laymen Concerned about Vietnam, April 4, 1967, https://kinginstitute.stanford.edu.

28 David Thiel, "Draft without Representation," *Chicago Tribune* (May 21, 1967), IND2.

29 "San Francisco: Love on Haight," *Time* (March 17, 1967), 27.

30 Kennedy, quoted in "Javits and Kennedy View Youth," 37.

31 Celler, "Should the Voting Age Be Lowered to 18? No," *American Legion Magazine* (November 1966), 9.

32 "Students Press Drive for Vote," *Times Record* (February 15, 1967), 13.

33 Clayton Knowles, "Lower Voting Age Sought for State," *New York Times* (January 15, 1967), 39.

34 Knowles, "Lower Voting Age Sought for State," 39; "Students Press Drive for Vote," 13.

35 Richard L. Madden, "Convention Keeps Voting Age at 21: Proposals for Suffrage at 19 and 20 Lose in Albany," *New York Times* (July 18, 1967), 27, and "Voting Age: Conflict over Lowering It," *New York Times* (July 23, 1967), 134.

36 Desmond, quoted in Madden, "Convention Keeps Voting Age at 21," 27.

37 "The Right Voting Age," *New York Times* (July 7, 1967), 32.

38 Thomas J. Foley, "Democrats Push Drive for Voting Age of 18," *Los Angeles Times* (March 26, 1967), G7.

39 Robert S. Allen and Paul Scott, "Inside Washington," *El Paso Times* (April 21, 1967), 4.

40 Official text of proposed constitution of the State of New York, to be submitted to the electors of the State on November 7, 1967, 7, http://nysl.cloudapp.net.

41 Tydings, "Maryland Constitutional Convention Testimony, October 3, 1967," reprinted in *Congressional Record* 113 (December 15, 1967), 37056.

42 Lowry, quoted in Bob Ashley, "Future Seems Doubtful for Lower Voting Age," *Duke Chronicle* (February 2, 1967), 13.

43 Steve T. Corneliussen, email correspondence with author, March 3 and 4, 2020.

44 Lowry, quoted in Ashley, "Future Seems Doubtful for Lower Voting Age," 13.

45 Tina Ravishhe, "Should Teenagers Be Allowed to Vote?," *The Ram's Horn* (February 1, 1967), 4.

46 Lowry and Hutchens, quoted in David Little, "Voting Age Bill Is Debated in Legislature," *Duke Chronicle* (May 9, 1957), 1.

47 Bill Amlong, "Lowering of Voting Age Stopped by Narrow Vote," *Daily Tar Heel* (May 11, 1967), 1.

48 Lowry, quoted in "House Votes Down Change," *Duke Chronicle* (May 11, 1967), 1.

49 "Two Ways of Looking at Voting Age Bill's Defeat," *Daily Tar Heel* (May 12, 1967), 2.

50 Marc Beem, "Committee Urges Passage of Bill Lowering N.J. Voting Age to 18," (February 12, 1969), 1.

51 Chuck Ragan, "UGC Endorses Reform Referendum," *Daily Princetonian* (March 7, 1967), 1; "Lower the Voting Age," *Daily Princetonian* (March 8, 1967), 2.

52 Oxman, quoted in "UGC's Oxman Urges Voting Age Reform," *Daily Princetonian* (March 21, 1967), 1, and in "The Voting Age Bill," *Daily Princetonian* (March 21, 1967), 2.

53 Howard, "Extending Voting Privileges to Citizens Under the Age of 21," *Congressional Record* 113 (February 21, 1967), 4181.

54 Howard, Speech, "Lowering the Voting Age to 18 in the United States, Rutgers University, New Brunswick, May 2, 1967," reprinted in the *Congressional Record* 113 (May 4, 1967), 11684.

55 Ronald Sullivan, "Voting at 18 Gets Support in Jersey," *New York Times* (October 5, 1967), 39.

56 Marguerite Waino, "Maturity v. Appearance," *Daily Princetonian* (October 12, 1967), 35.

57 "Navy Youth Sends Tape to Support Voting Age Cut," *Bridgeport Telegram* (February 15, 1967), 6.

58 "Open Letter on Voting Age," *Yale Daily News* (February 13, 1967), 2.

59 Forand, quoted in Jeffrey Stern, "18-Hour Capitol Vigil Climaxes Student Drive for Vote at 18," *Yale Daily News* (April 18, 1967), 1.

9. TURNING POINT '68

1 Myer August interview.

2 Lowenstein, quoted in "CIA-NSA Ties Hit Students' Integrity Lowenstein Claims," *Daily Tar Heel* (March 4, 1967), 1, 6.

3 Lowenstein, quoted in "LBJ 'Not Inevitable,'" *Daily Tar Heel* (February 13, 1968), 1.

4 McCarthy, "Declaration of Candidacy for the Democratic Nomination for President," November 30, 1967, www.csus.edu.

5 Robert Renny Cushing, interview with author, August 8, 2020 (hereafter Cushing interview).

6 Journalist, quoted in Terry Anderson, *The Sixties* (New York: Longman, 1999), 106.

7 Campaign worker, quoted in Douglas T. Miller, *On Our Own: Americans in the 1960s* (Boston: Cengage, 1995), 220–223.

8 "Eighteen-Year Old Vote," folder National Headquarters' Research Division, Subject File: Youth, 1968 Presidential Campaign: National Headquarters Files, box 69, Robert F. Kennedy Papers.

9 Kennedy, "What Our Young People Are Really Saying," *Ladies' Home Journal* (January 1968), 35, 94–96.

10 See letters in folder Civil Liberties: Voting Age at 18, Senate Correspondence: Subject File, 1968, box 5, Robert F. Kennedy Papers, JFK Library.

11 Johnson, quoted in Maurice Isserman and Michael Kazin, *America Divided: The Civil War of the 1960s* (New York: Oxford University Press, 2000), 225.

12 King, quoted in Gordon Mantler, "Black, Brown, and Poor: Civil Rights and the Making of the Chicano Movement," in *The Struggle in Black and Brown: African American and Mexican American Relations during the Civil Rights Era*, ed. Brian D. Behnken (Lincoln: University of Nebraska Press, 2011), 180.

13 Kennedy, Statement on Assassination of Martin Luther King Jr., Indianapolis, Indiana, April 4, 1968, JFK Library, www.jfklibrary.org.

14 Ralph Abernathy, quoted in Mantler, "Black, Brown, and Poor," 185.

15 Anderson, *The Sixties*, 114.

16 *Crisis at Columbia: Report of the Fact-Finding Commission Appointed to Investigate the Disturbances at Columbia University in April and May, 1968* (New York: Vintage, 1968), 194, 198.

17 "The Radical Left and Choice 68" and "Conservatives and Choice 68," *Branding Iron* (April 19, 1968), 6.

18 "McCarthy Wins in Choice 68 at University; Kennedy 2nd," *Daily Iowan* (May 10, 1968), 3.

19 Bayh, quoted in "Lowering the Voting Age," *Hearings Before the Subcommittee on Constitutional Amendments of the Committee of the Judiciary, United States Senate*, 90th Cong., 2nd sess., May 14, 15, and 16, 1968 (hereafter 1968 Senate Hearings), 2–3.

20 Javits, quoted in 1968 Senate Hearings, 11–14.

21 Tydings statement, quoted in 1968 Senate Hearings, 11; Jack McDonald, quoted in 1968 Senate Hearings, 44.

23 R. Spencer Oliver, quoted in 1968 Senate Hearings, 19–23.

24 Holland, quoted in 1968 Senate Hearings, 29–35.

25 Bayh, quoted in 1968 Senate Hearings, 51.

26 DJE, Gary, Indiana to Birch Bayh, July 11, 1968, and LHH to Birch Bayh, May 1968, folder Mail, Feb–Jul 1968, box CA 4, Eighteen-Year-Old Vote, 1963–1972, Subcommittee on Constitutional Amendments and Subcommittee on the Constitution, Birch Bayh Congressional Papers, Modern Political Papers Collection, Indiana University Libraries, Bloomington, Indiana (hereafter Bayh Papers).

27 *Report of the National Advisory Commission on Civil Disorders* (Washington, DC: Government Printing Office, 1968), 1.

28 Javits, quoted in Robert C. Albright, "Congress Plans Liaison with Poor," *Los Angeles Times* (May 16, 1968), 21.

29 President Lyndon B. Johnson, "Special Message to the Congress: To Vote at Eighteen—Democracy Fulfilled and Enriched," June 27, 1968, Presidency Project, www.presidency.ucsb.edu.

30 "18 Year Old Vote: Johnson Speaks Too Late," *Michigan Daily* (July 2, 1968), 2.

31 *New York Daily News*, quoted in "Youth Movement," *Time* (July 5, 1968), 20.

32 "L.B.J.: A President Who Understands Young People," *Congressional Record* 114 (June 27, 1968), 19079–19082; "Support for Lyndon Johnson's Proposal to Lower the Voting Age," *Congressional Record* 114 (June 27, 1968), 19070.

33 "A Vote for 18-year-Olds," *AFL-CIO News* (July 6, 1968), 4.

34 "Harnessing the Youth Tide," *New York Times* (June 30, 1968), E12.

35 Andrew Hacker, "If the Eighteen-Year-Olds Get the Vote," *New York Times Magazine* (July 7, 1968), 6.

36 Karl Simpson, quoted in "Peace Party Backs Lower Voting Age," *Stanford Daily* (May 4, 1968), 5.

37 Sweetland, quoted and paraphrased in Arthur L. Wood, "Probation Officer Calls Youth of Today Superior," *Fresno Bee* (November 13, 1965), 7.

38 Sweetland, quoted in William G. Robbins, *A Man for All Seasons: Monroe Sweetland and the Liberal Paradox* (Corvallis: Oregon State University Press, 2015), 207.

39 Les Francis, "Recollections: The 1960s and Personal Awakening," in author's possession, 12; Francis interview.

40 Mel Myler, interview with author, July 3, 2020 (hereafter Myler interview).

41 "AFT Urges Lowering of Voting Age," *American Teacher* (October 1968), 18.

42 Sweetland, "Why Does NEA Support a Lowered Voting Age?," *Today's Education* (December 1969), 35.

44 Myer NEA interview.

10. WE CAN VOTE THEM OUT

1 "Sen. McIntyre-Gov. King," advertisement, *Portsmouth Herald* (August 22, 1968), 8.

2 Cushing interview.

3 Oliver interview.

4 Jane Greenspun Gale, interview with author, April 16, 2020 (hereafter Greenspun Gale interview).

5 An Interview with Jane Greenspun Gale, conducted by Barbara Tabach, January 31, 2018, Southern Nevada Jewish Heritage Project, Oral History Research Center, University of Nevada Las Vegas (hereafter UNLV interview), 13.

6 Greenspun Gale interview; Hank Greenspun, "Where I Stand," reprinted in "Other Editors," *Mason Valley News* (March 8, 1968), 2; UNLV interview, 13.

7 Patricia Keefer, quoted in Karen Heller, "The Lady Is a Lobbyist," *Cincinnati Magazine* (November 1973), 11–15.

8 Pat Keefer, interview with Charles Koppelman, 2020, in author's possession (hereafter Keefer interview).

9 Pat Keefer, quoted in "Adopt Reforms, Democrats Urged," *Cincinnati Enquirer* (August 14, 1968), 9.

10 Keefer interview.

11 Keefer interview.

12 Greenspun Gale interview; UNLV interview, 13.

13 Greenspun Gale interview.

14 "Denton Supports 18-Year-Old Vote in Las Vegas Federal Court Suit," *Nevada State Journal* (November 4, 1968), 4.

15 "Opening Brief of the Appellant," in *Janey T. Greenspun v. State of Nevada*, US Court of Appeals for the Ninth District, 1–2, included in 9th Circuit Appellate Case File 24087, National Archives at Kansas City, Missouri.

16 Denton, quoted in "Denton Supports," 4.

17 "Opening Brief of the Appellant," in *Janey T. Greenspun v. State of Nevada*, 12, 16.

18 Jane Greenspun, quoted in "Vegan, 19, Sues to Vote for President," *Reno Gazette-Journal* (October 23, 1968), 25.

19 Jane Greenspun, quoted in "Denton Supports," 4.

20 "Opening Brief of the Appellant," in *Janey T. Greenspun v. State of Nevada*, ii.

21 Richard M. Nixon, "Remarks on the NBC Radio Network: 'Today's Youth: The Great Generation,'" October 16, 1968, Presidency Project, www.presidency.ucsb.edu.

22 "Do You Want to Vote at 18?," *Seventeen* (September 1968), 155.

23 Roger Rapoport, "Who Killed the 18-Year-Old Vote?," *Look* (October 29, 1968), 22.

24 Nelson W. Polsby and Aaron B. Wildavsky with David A. Hopkins, *Presidential Elections: Strategies and Structures of American Politics*, 12th ed. (Lanham, MD: Rowman & Littlefield, 2008), 32.

25 Gerry Keir, "22 Con-Con Proposals Win; Teen Voting Loses," *Honolulu Advertiser* (November 6, 1968), A-1C.

26 Dennis Farney, "A Lower Voting Age? Not for a While," *Wall Street Journal* (November 15, 1968), 20.

27 Schrekinger, Eugene Mahoney, and Terry Carpenter, quoted in Farney, "Lower Voting Age?," 20.

28 Keefer interview.

29 Cushing interview.

30 Myer NEA interview.

31 Francis, quoted in "Voting Rights, Congressional Action Concern Youth," *Fond Du Lac Commonwealth Reporter* (December 1, 1969), 2.

32 Meeting notes, quoted in Dennis King, MA thesis draft, in author's possession; William G. Robbins, *A Man for All Seasons: Monroe Sweetland and the Liberal Paradox* (Corvallis: Oregon State University Press, 2015), 208.

33 "Drive on to Drop Vote Age to 18," *Chicago Daily Defender* (December 21, 1968), 16.

34 Wilkins, quoted in "NAACP Supports Lower Voting Age," *Afro-American* (April 5, 1969), 17.

35 *Atlanta Daily World*, quoted in "2,500 Youth to Attend Conference on Voting Age," *Chicago Daily Defender* (April 5, 1969), 35.

36 18 × 72, Statement of Description and Purpose, folder Mc 1969–1970, box E13, Group IV: Youth File, 1966–1973, Records of the NAACP, Manuscript Division, Library of Congress, Washington, DC (hereafter NAACP Records).

37 Dennis M. Warren, interview with author, October 16, 2020 (hereafter Warren interview).

38 Warren, quoted in UoP Press Release, December 20, 1968 and LUV General Information, University Archives, box 5.4.1.2.1, Holt-Atherton Special Collections, University of the Pacific Library (hereafter LUV Collection).

39 Dennis Warren, Statement on Electoral College Abolition, February 11, 1969, 2–3, LUV Collection.

40 Warren interview.

41 Dennis Warren to Dear Friend, L.U.V. form letter [1969], LUV Collection.

42 R. Doyle Minden to Peter Janssen, January 2, 1969, LUV Collection.

43 "All You Need Is L.U.V.," *Pacifican* (January 15, 1969), 1, LUV Collection.

44 Bishop, quoted in UoP Press Release, January 13, 1969, LUV Collection.

45 Dennis M. Warren, Class of '70, UoP video interview, 2020, in author's possession.

46 Bobby Hart with Glenn Ballantyne, *Psychedelic Bubble Gum: Boyce & Hart, The Monkees, and Turning Mayhem into Miracles* (New York: SelectBooks, 2015), 180–181.

47 "L.U.V. Let Us Vote," *Tiger Beat* (May 1969), 31, news clipping, LUV Collection.

48 Gael Graham, *Young Activists: American High School Students in the Age of Protest* (DeKalb: Northern Illinois University Press, 2006), 5.

49 Warren interview.

50 Cushing interview.

51 Cushing, quoted and paraphrased in "Approval Voiced for Young Vote," *Portsmouth Herald* (March 20, 1969), 12.

52 Carol Botwin, "Young World," *Baltimore Morning Sun* (May 11, 1969), news clipping, LUV Collection.

53 "Can LUV Conquer All?," *Time* (January 31, 1969), 12.

11. IT'S ABOUT TIME

1 Minarchenko, quoted in Lyn Shepard, "Novices Asking Vote at 18 Attract Attention," *Christian Science Monitor* (April 2, 1969), 10.

2 Richard Cohen, "'Image' Called Key to Voting Age," *Washington Post* (February 6, 1969), A7.

3 Randolph, quoted in Cohen, "'Image' Called Key to Voting Age," A7; Randolph and Bayh, quoted in "Young Lobby Group Chided on Militancy," *New York Times* (February 6, 1969), 49.

4 Roy Wilkins, "18s: Vote or Violence?," *Los Angeles Times* (February 17, 1969), B9.

5 Randolph, quoted in Dennis King, MA thesis draft, in author's possession; "For a Responsive Congress," *AFL-CIO News* (January 11, 1969), 4.

6 Randolph, quoted in "Senator Randolph Introduces His Ninth Joint Resolution for Constitutional Amendment to Extend Voting to 18-Year-Olds," *Congressional Record* 115 (January 15, 1969), 318.

7 Russell Freeburg, "Report Links Violence to Youth, 'System,'" *Chicago Tribune* (January 31, 1969), 3.

8 Bayh, quoted in Cohen, "'Image' Called Key to Voting Age," A7.

9 YFC pamphlet, 1969, Paul J. Myer personal collection, in author's possession.

10 Warren interview.

11 Shepard, "Novices Asking Vote at 18 Attract Attention," 10.

12 Myer July interview.

13 Paul Minarchenko, paraphrased in K. A. Beavan, "Voteless Casualties: Removing the Anomaly," *Times Educational Supplement* (August 1, 1969), 14.

14 Oliver interview.

15 Boisfeuillet Jones, "The Young Republican Plight," *Harvard Crimson* (July 11, 1969), www.thecrimson.com.

16 Rowland Evans and Robert Novak, "Peru's Marxist Judge," *Washington Post* (March 23, 1969), 51.

17 James M. Graham, *Lowering the Voting Age* (US National Student Association, 1969), 25.

18 Jim Graham to Dear Friend, April 10, 1969, folder Student Work—Youth Franchise Coalition, 1969, box 216, Kautz Family YMCA Archives, University of Minnesota Libraries (hereafter YFC 1969).

19 Hubert H. Humphrey to Paul Minarchenko, April 9, 1969, Paul J. Myer personal collection, in author's possession.

20 Javits, quoted in John Zeh, "18-Year-Old Vote Fight Continues," *Michigan Daily* (February 6, 1969), 3.

21 Howard A. Coffin, "The 18-Year-Old Vote," *Moderator* (April 1969), 8–9.

22 Graham, quoted in John Zeh, "Resurrecting the 18-Year-Old Vote," *Advocate* (February 6, 1969), n.p.

23 Watson, quoted in Dennis King, MA thesis draft, in author's possession (hereafter King thesis draft).

24 "Youth Lobby Launches Drive for Vote at 18," *Afro-American* (February 15, 1969), 17.

25 Myler, quoted in Shepard, "Novices Asking Vote at 18 Attract Attention," 10.

26 Les Francis, conversation with author, July 8, 2020; Graham, quoted in John Zeh, "Youth Groups Begin Active Quest to Lower the Voting age," *Rice Thresher* (February 6, 1969), 7.

27 MacGowan, quoted in Carol Ann Ross, "Lobby Mounts Drive to Lower Vote Age," *Atlanta Constitution* (May 25, 1969), 5D.

28 Myer July interview.

29 UoP Press Release, December 20, 1968, LUV Collection.

30 Cohen, quoted in Thomas J. Arrandale, "Coalition Calls for 18-Year-Old Vote," *Congressional Quarterly*, reprinted in *Daily Telegram* (June 11, 1969), 13A. For a comprehensive history of efforts to reform the Electoral College, see Alexander Keyssar, *Why Do We Still Have the Electoral College?* (Cambridge, MA: Harvard University Press, 2020).

31 Francis, quoted in Shepard, "Novices Asking Vote at 18 Attract Attention," 10.

32 YFC pamphlet, 1969.

33 MacGowan, quoted in Ross, "Lobby Mounts Drive to Lower Vote Age," 5D.

34 Paul Minarchenko, quoted in King thesis draft.

35 Ian MacGowan, email correspondence with author, March 4, 2021, and quoted in Ross, "Lobby Mounts Drive to Lower Vote Age," 5D.

36 NEA pamphlet, early YFC pamphlet, and Jim Graham to Dear Friend, April 10, 1969, YFC 1969.

37 NEA pamphlet, early YFC pamphlet, and Jim Graham to Dear Friend, April 10, 1969, YFC 1969.

38 Graham, *Lowering the Voting Age*, 25.

39 NEA pamphlet, early YFC pamphlet, and Jim Graham to Dear Friend, April 10, 1969, YFC 1969.

40 Charles Payne, "Men Led, But Women Organized: Movement Participation of Women in the Mississippi Delta," in *Women in the Civil Rights Movement: Trailblazers and Torchbearers, 1941–1965*, ed. Vicki L. Crawford, Jacqueline Anne Rouse, and Barbara Woods (Bloomington: Indiana University Press, 1990), 1–12.

41 Roy Wilkins to All Branches, March 14, 1969, folder Youth Mobilization 1969, box E18, NAACP Records.

42 "James Brown, Jr. to Dear Reverend," folder Youth Mobilization 1969, box E18, NAACP Records.

43 "Spot Announcements," folder Form Letters 1968–1969, box E12, and publicity materials, Youth Mobilization April 21–22, 1969 Samples, box E18, NAACP Records.

44 Wilkins to Congressmen, draft letters, folder Youth Mobilization 1969, box E18, NAACP Records.

45 "Carolyn Quill[oi]n Plans Youth Meet," *Afro-American* (April 19, 1969), 10.

46 Cushing interview.

47 MacGowan, quoted in King thesis draft.

48 Youth Mobilization Conference Program, folder Youth Mobilization April 21–22, 1969 Samples, box E18, NAACP Records; Mitchell, paraphrased in "NAACP Youth Assembly," *The Crisis* (May 1969), 214.

49 Brooke, quoted in "NAACP Supports Lower Voting Age," *Afro-American* (April 5, 1969), 17, and on "Lowering the Voting Age 18," leaflet, Youth Mobilization April 21–22, 1969 Samples, box E18, NAACP Records.

50 James Brown Jr. to Roy Wilkins and John A. Morsell, April 28, 1969, folder NAACP Youth File James Brown Memoranda, 1969, box E11, NAACP Records.

51 King thesis draft.

52 Stokes, quoted in "NAACP Youth Assembly," *The Crisis* (May 1969), 213.

53 Maureen F. Dillon, "To Lower Voting Age," *New York Times* (May 6, 1969), 46.

54 Brown Jr. to Wilkins and Morsell, April 28, 1969.

55 Quilloin, quoted in "NAACP Youth Assembly," *The Crisis* (May 1969), 214.

56 MacGowan, quoted in King thesis draft.

57 Myer July interview.

58 MacGowan, quoted in King thesis draft.

59 "18-Year Vote," *Yale Daily News* (September 27, 1969), 6.

60 Beatty, quoted in "Backlash Hits Move to Cut Voting Age," *Los Angeles Times* (May 6, 1969), B6.

61 Kelly Alexander, quoted in Tom Gooding, "NAACP Leads Local Fight to Lower the Voting Age," *Daily Tar Heel* (April 13, 1969), 1.

62 Paul Minarchenko, quoted in Shepard, "Novices Asking Vote at 18 Attract Attention," 10.

12. WHERE IT'S AT!

1 Larry Conrad, quoted in Howard A. Coffin, "The 18-Year-Old Vote," *Moderator* (April 1969), 9.

2 Ian MacGowan, quoted in Carol Ann Ross, "Lobby Mounts Drive to Lower Vote Age," *Atlanta Constitution* (May 25, 1969), 5D.

3 California Assembly Interim Committee on Elections and Constitutional Amendments, 1969 Interim Report, "Minimum Voting Age/Age of Majority," 9.

4 Hipple, quoted in Lyn Shepard, "Novices Asking Vote at 18 Attract Attention," *Christian Science Monitor* (April 2, 1969), 10; MacGowan, quoted in King thesis draft.

5 "National L.U.V. Campaign Off to a Big Start," *Pacifican* (January 10, 1969), 2.

6 Dennis King, interview with author, July 12, 2020 (hereafter King interview), and quoted in Mark Simon, "Dennis King: No Madison Avenue Glitter," *Spartan Daily* (September 18, 1972), 1.

7 King interview; King, quoted in Simon, "Dennis King," 1.

8 King interview.

9 Vasconcellos, quoted in "Laws Under Fire," *Stanford Daily* (April 2, 1969), 3.

10 Moscone, quoted in "Backlash Hits Move to Cut Voting Age," *Los Angeles Times* (May 6, 1969), B6.

11 "Lower Voting Age Drive," *Sacramento Observer* (April 10, 1969) and "Teen-Age Vote Loses Ground in Legislature," *Sacramento Union* (April 10, 1969), 10, in folder Michael L. Brodie, 1968–1969, box E10, NAACP Records.

12 Sweetland, quoted in William G. Robbins, *A Man for All Seasons: Monroe Sweetland and the Liberal Paradox* (Corvallis: Oregon State University Press, 2015), 210.

13 "Effort to Get 18-Year-Old Vote Issue on Ballot Begins," *Daily Post-News* (February 17, 1970), 3.

14 King interview; "Drive on to Lower Voting Age," *Times-Advocate* (February 24, 1970), B7.

15 Reagan, paraphrased in Maureen Wade, "Irresponsible Voters," *Spartan Daily* (May 7, 1969), 2.

16 Monroe Sweetland, "Lower the Voting Age," *Fresno Bee* (January 7, 1969), 15.

17 "Research Needed: Voting Age Reform," *Stanford Daily* (January 16, 1970), 3.

18 King interview.

19 *Puishes v. Mann* Appeal, included in "Lowering the Voting Age," *Hearings Before the Subcommittee on Constitutional Amendments of the Committee of the Judiciary, United States Senate*, 91st Cong., 2nd sess., February 16, 17, March 9, 10, 1970 (hereafter 1970 Senate Hearings), quoted on pp. 537, 540, and 517.

20 Chiswell and Marsh, quoted in 1970 Senate Hearings, 118–119.

21 Pugash, quoted in "On the Scene: Teens and the Ballot," *Seventeen* (June 1969), 122–123.

22 "Laverne Endorses 'Vote at 18,'" *Democrat and Chronicle* (December 14, 1969), 4B.

23 James F. Clarity, "Rockefeller Urges Voting Age of 18," *New York Times* (February 23, 1969), 41.

24 "Harnessing the Youth Tide," *New York Times* (June 30, 1968), E12.

25 Douglas, quoted in "Old Enough to Vote," *New Yorker* (April 5, 1969), 29, 31.

26 Rockefeller, quoted in "Governor Will Seek To Reduce Voting Age from 21 to 18," *Farmingdale Observer* (December 18, 1969), 3; Brydges, quoted in "Rockefeller Proposes Cutting the Voting Age to 18," *New York Times* (December 14, 1969), 49.

27 Robert D. McFadden, "R. Peter Straus, Radio Pioneer, Dies at 89," *New York Times* (August 9, 2012), B23.

28 *WMCA Vote at 18 Club v. Board of Elections*, Complaint and Memorandum in Support, reprinted in 1970 Senate Hearings, 577, 604.

29 John Zeh, "18-Year-Old Vote Fight Continues," *Michigan Daily* (February 6, 1969), 3.

30 Forand, quoted in Joey Williams, "Looking for a Battle Plan?," *Moderator* (April 1969), 13; John Coots, "Capitol Crowd Airs Voting Age," *Yale Daily News* (February 6, 1969), 1.

31 Forand, quoted in Williams, "Looking for a Battle Plan?," 13; John Coots, "Legislative Hearing Today on Voting Age," *Yale Daily News* (February 5, 1969), 3.

32 Charles F. J. Morse, "Voting at 18 Passes House," *Hartford Courant* (April 30, 1969), 14; Senators, quoted in Jack Zaiman, "Referendum Will Decide Vote for 18-Year-Olds," *Hartford Courant* (May 8, 1969), 46.

33 Forand, quoted in Morse, "Voting at 18 Passes House," 14, and Zaiman, "Referendum Will Decide Vote for 18-Year-Olds," 46.

34 "Coalition Plans Drive for Lower Voting Age," *Hartford Courant* (October 26, 1969), 10A.

35 Forand, quoted in Williams, "Looking for a Battle Plan?," 13.

36 Forand, quoted in Williams, "Looking for a Battle Plan?," 12.

37 Chris Muzikar, quoted in Dave Lichtenstein, "Student Profiles: Chris Muzikar," *The Independent* (May 2, 1969), 3.

38 Les Francis, "Educator Urges Voting Age of 18 as 'Only Logical Turning Point,'" *Los Angeles Times* (March 3, 1969), C8.

39 Les Francis, NEA interview with Rebecca Login, 2011, in author's possession.

40 Keefer interview.

41 Goldstein, quoted in Mark Gola, "Goldstein '72 Reflects on Role in Lower the Voting Age," College of New Jersey, *Alumni News*, April 2009, online edition, www.tcnjmagazine.com; "Victory for the 'System,'" *Trenton Times* (May 17, 1970), in author's possession.

42 Charles Koppelman, NEA interview with Rebecca Login, 2011, in author's possession (hereafter Koppelman interview).

43 Paul Minarchenko to Lane Ayres, YMCA National Student Caucus, October 17, 1969, YFC 1969.

44 Stuart Z. Goldstein, interview with author, October 10, 2020 (hereafter Goldstein interview).

45 "The Voting Project," *Senior Scholastic* (September 27, 1968), 17; "Two States Say No to Lower Voting Ages," *National Observer*, news clipping, Paul J. Myer personal collection, in author's possession.

46 Keefer interview.

47 Claudia Bernard, "Moratorium, Vote 19 Issues Receive Backing from IFG," *The Post* (October 8, 1969), 1.

48 Goldstein interview.

49 Stuart Z. Goldstein, email correspondence with author, March 24, 2021.

50 Bayh, quoted in Richard Cohen, "'Image' Called Key to Voting Age," *Washington Post* (February 6, 1969), A7; Zeh, "18-Year-Old Vote Fight Continues," 3.

51 Les Francis, conversation with author, July 8, 2020.

52 Pamphlets from Ohio Volunteers for Vote 19 and Citizens Committee for Vote 18, in author's possession.

53 Joel R. Jacobsen, quoted in "State to Consider Referendum for Lowering the Voting Age," *The Independent* (April 18, 1969), 14.

54 Susan Burchfield, "The Golden Age," *Ohio State Lantern* (October 10, 1969), 3.

55 Diana Mardis, "Teens Speak Out on Voting," *Cincinnati Enquirer* (October 18, 1969), Teenager special section, 5.

56 Springer, quoted in Kathy Lang, "Arguments are Aired," *Cincinnati Enquirer* (October 18, 1969), Teenager special section, 5.

57 Burchfield, "The Golden Age," *Ohio State Lantern*, 3.

58 Robinson, quoted in "Two States Say No to Lower Voting Ages," news clipping.

59 Lichtenstein and Levi, quoted in "NSC Reacts to Failure of 18 Year Vote," *The Independent* (November 13, 1969), 1.

60 Bill Sievert, "Two States Reject Younger Vote," *Rice Thresher* (November 13, 1969), 2.

61 Ronald Sullivan, "Vote for 18-Year-Olds Is Facing Trouble in Jersey," *New York Times* (October 13, 1969), 59.

62 "Vote Analysis by Wards," *YFC Bulletin* (November 1969), YFC 1969.

63 *Columbus Dispatch* editorial, quoted in Jim Brewer and Shirley Brownell, "Vote-19 Issue Polled," *Ohio State Lantern* (November 3, 1969), 4.

64 Sullivan, "Vote for 18-Year-Olds Is Facing Trouble in Jersey," 59.

65 "Thumbs Down," *The Post* (November 5, 1969), 2.

66 Wideman, quoted in Jay R. Smith, "Fund Lack, Shaky Image May Kill Vote-19 Drive," *Ohio State Lantern* (October 6, 1969), 1; Pat Keefer, email correspondence with author, May 1, 2021.

67 Sam Brown, "The Politics of Peace," *Washington Monthly* (August 1970), 24–46; Sullivan, "Vote for 18-Year-Olds Is Facing Trouble in Jersey," 59.

68 MacGowan, quoted in *YFC Bulletin*, November 1969, YFC 1969.

13. THE HOUR IS STRIKING

1 Ian MacGowan, interview with Charles Koppelman, 2020, in author's possession (hereafter MacGowan interview).

2 Charles Gonzales, "The 18-Year-Old Vote," *Today's Education* (December 1969), 61; Charles Gonzales, NEA interview, 2011, in author's possession (hereafter Gonzales interview).

3 MacGowan, quoted in William Greider, "Image of Youth Blamed as Bar to Voting Right," *Washington Post* (February 17, 1970), A2.

4 "Two States Say No to Lower Voting Ages," *National Observer*, news clipping, Paul J. Myer personal collection, in author's possession.

5 LeVander, quoted in "Backlash Hits Move to Cut Voting Age," *Los Angeles Times* (May 6, 1969), B6.

6 Myers and Reber, quoted in "Backlash Hits Move to Cut Voting Age," B6.

7 P. W., "Editorial Commentary," *Branding Iron* (February 14, 1969), 4.

8 McGee, quoted in John Zeh, "Youth Groups Begin Active Quest to Lower the Voting Age," *Rice Thresher* (February 6, 1969), 1.

9   Randolph to Ohio Volunteers for Vote Nineteen, telegram, November 3, 1969, YFC 1969.

10 *To Establish Justice, to Insure Domestic Tranquility*, Report of the National Commission on the Causes and Prevention of Violence (Washington, DC: Government Printing Office, 1969), 224.

11 "Report of the Brock Campus Tour," *Congressional Record—Extension of Remarks* (June 25, 1969), E5241.

12 "College Poll: Lack of Direct Participation Frustrates Politically Aware Youth, Students Claim," *Hartford Courant* (November 15, 1969), 17.

13 MacGowan and Mansfield, quoted in *YFC Bulletin* (December 1969), YFC 1969.

14 MacGowan, quoted in *YFC Bulletin* (December 1969), YFC 1969.

15 William F. Buckley, "Questions about Nixon Hope to Lower Vote Age," *Bismarck Tribune* (March 14, 1969), 4.

16 John Zeh, "Nixon's First 100 Days Evaluated," *UCLA Daily Bruin* (May 6, 1969), 1–2.

17 For an excellent explanation of Cox's arguments and the legal and historical significance, see Eric S. Fish's "The Twenty-Sixth Amendment Enforcement Power," *Yale Law Journal* 121, no. 5 (2012), 1168–1235.

18 For a full discussion of this profound constitutional direction, see Alexander Keyssar, *The Right to Vote: The Contested History of Democracy in the United States* (New York: Basic Books, 2000), 216–218.

19 Archibald Cox, "The Supreme Court, 1965 Term—Foreword: Constitutional Adjudication and the Promotion of Human Rights," *Harvard Law Review* 80 (November 1966), 99, 107.

20 Myer July interview.

21 Myer July interview; MacGowan interview; Gonzales interview.

22 Myer July interview.

23 Francis interview; Francis, quoted in Geoff Eastman "Adviser Seeks Assembly Seat," *Spartan Daily* (March 17, 1970), 1.

24 Hester Baker interview.

25 Sandy McConnell, National Hi-Y Council chaplain, to Lane Ayres, YMCA-National Student Caucus, April 9, 1969, YFC 1969.

26 Sheet of messages from Bennett High School students in Marion, Indiana, box CA-38, and LC to Birch Bayh, folder Mail, Jan 1970, box CA-5, Bayh Papers; Jay Berman, interview with author, April 18, 2021.

27 Ian R. MacGowan to YFC Member Organizations, February 2, 1970, folder Student Work—Youth Franchise Coalition, 1969–1970, box 217, Kautz Family YMCA Archives, University of Minnesota Libraries (hereafter YFC 1969–1970).

28 Bruce K. Chapman, "The Right to Vote at 18," *Trial Magazine* (February/March 1970), reprinted in "Lowering the Voting Age," *Hearings Before the Subcommittee on Constitutional Amendments of the Committee of the Judiciary, United States Senate*, 91st Cong., 2nd sess., February 16 and 17, March 9 and 10, 1970 (hereafter 1970 Senate Hearings), 427.

29 Bayh, quoted in 1970 Senate Hearings, 3.

30 Cook, quoted in 1970 Senate Hearings, 71.

31 Cook and Bayh, quoted in 1970 Senate Hearings, 62.

32 Queen, quoted in 1970 Senate Hearings, 152.

33 Randolph, quoted in 1970 Senate Hearings, 14.

34 Kleindienst, quoted in 1970 Senate Hearings, 78.

35 Kennedy, quoted in 1970 Senate Hearings, 157.

36 Sorensen and Gonzales, quoted in 1970 Senate Hearings, 15 and 95.

37 John Lumley, Ramsey Clark, Carl J. Megel, and Jerry Springer, quoted in 1970 Senate Hearings, 93, 103, 126, 112.

38 Bayh and Mead, quoted in 1970 Senate Hearings, 1 and 223; "Age at Which Minors Are to Be Considered Adults for Purposes of Prosecution under Criminal Law," 1970 Senate Hearings, 6–8.

39 Mead, Kleindienst, Randolph, and Lowenstein, quoted in 1970 Senate Hearings, 225, 78, 9, and 115.

40 Queen, quoted in 1970 Senate Hearings, 152–153; Jon Nordheiivier, "15 Are Arrested in Attack on Buses with Negro Children in South Carolina," *New York Times* (March 5, 1970), 19.

41 Lowenstein, MacGowan, and Randolph, quoted in 1970 Senate Hearings, 114, 45, 10–11.

42 Margaret Mead, *Culture and Commitment: A Study of the Communication* (repr., London: Panther Books, 1972), 116.

43 Menninger, quoted in 1970 Senate Hearings, 26.

44 Menninger, Gonzales, and Hayakawa, quoted in 1970 Senate Hearings, 24, 96, and 37–38.

45 Brown, quoted in 1970 Senate Hearings, 151.

46 Rehnquist and Pollack, quoted in 1970 Senate Hearings, 233 and 252.

47 Kennedy, prepared statement and quoted in 1970 Senate Hearings, 163, 158.

48 Goldwater, quoted in 1970 Senate Hearings, 134, 143.

49 Speiser, quoted in 1970 Senate Hearings, 275, 279.

50 "Votes for Blacks and Youths," *Los Angeles Times* (March 17, 1970), A6; John W. Finney, "Kennedy Mapping Vote-at-18 Move," *New York Times* (February 23, 1970), 8.

51 Conyers, Clarence Mitchell, John Mitchell, and Emanuel Celler, quoted in "Congress Delays Extension of Voting Rights Act," *Congressional Quarterly Almanac, 91st Congress, 1st Session* (Washington, DC: Congressional Quarterly, 1969), 422, 425, and 424.

52 Remarks of Senator Edward M. Kennedy 100th Birthday Tribute to Mike Mansfield Washington, D.C. April 2, 2003, 3, JFK Library; Mansfield, quoted in "Extending the Franchise," *Time* (March 23, 1970), 16.

53 Mansfield, "Voting Rights Act Amendments of 1969—Submission of Amendment No. 545," *Congressional Record—Senate* (March 4, 1970), S2938-2929; Mansfield, quoted in "Age of Aquarius," *Newsweek* (March 23, 1970), 24.

54 Ervin, "Voting Rights Act Amendments of 1969," *Congressional Record* 116 (March 4, 1970), 6013.

55 Celler, quoted in "Age of Aquarius," *Newsweek* (March 23, 1970), 25.

14. ENFRANCHISED?

1 Celler, quoted in Floyd Norris, "18-Yr. Old Vote Won't Pass This Year," *The Independent* (March 25, 1970), 5.

2 Cook, quoted in 1970 Senate Hearings, 117; Norris, "18-Yr. Old Vote Won't Pass This Year," 5.

3 John Zeh, "Youth Groups Begin Active Quest to Lower the Voting age," *Rice Thresher* (February 6, 1969), 7.

4 "Enfranchised?," *Wellesley News* (March 19, 1970), 2.

5 Celler, quoted in Richard L. Lyons, "Hill Expected to Approve Vote at 18: Protecting Voting Rights," *Washington Post* (March 17, 1970), A2, and in Marjorie Hunter, "Vote at 18 Nears Full House Test," *New York Times* (March 17, 1970), 18.

6 "Enfranchised?," *Wellesley News* (March 19, 1970), 2.

7 Fred P. Graham, "Lowering Voting Age Is an Idea Whose Time Has Come," *New York Times* (March 29, 1970), 154.

8 John McCormack, quoted in "Congress: Young at Heart," *Newsweek* (June 29, 1970), 22.

9 Alexander M. Bickel, Charles L. Black Jr, Robert H. Bork, John Hart Ely, Louis H. Pollack, and Eugene V. Rostow, "Amendment Favored for Lowering the Voting Age," *New York Times* (April 5, 1970), 171; Pollack, quoted in 1970 Senate Hearings, 255.

10 Edward M. Kennedy, "Kennedy Backs Statute for Lowering the Voting Age," *New York Times* (April 7, 1970), 44.

11 Paul A. Freund and Archibald Cox, "Power of Congress to Lower Voting Age Upheld," *New York Times* (April 12, 1970), E13.

12 Richard Nixon to Speaker McCormack, Majority Leader Albert, and Minority Leader Ford, April 27, 1970, reprinted in 1970 Senate Hearings, 386–389.

13 "Nixon Sees Peril in Voting Age Bill," *New York Times* (April 28, 1970), 22.

14 George Gallup, "Majority of Voters Favor Voting Age Cut," *Hartford Courant* (April 2, 1970), 50; Hazel Erskine, "The Polls: The Politics of Age," *Public Opinion Quarterly* 35 (Autumn 1971), 487, 482.

15 Blumenauer, quoted in 1970 Senate Hearings, 57–58.

16 Malcolm Bauer, "Vote-Age Cut Faces Hurdle in Oregon: Impressive Support," *Christian Science Monitor* (May 19, 1970), 6.

17 William J. Moshofsky, quoted in Paul W. Harvey Jr., "Little Organized Opposition to Vote at 19," *Corvallis Gazette-Times* (May 8, 1970), 14.

18 Blumenauer, quoted in "Commission May Back 19-Year-Old Vote," *Capital Journal* (October 15, 1969), 11.

19 McCall, paraphrased in "Plan to Lower Voting Age Loses in Oregon," *Chicago Tribune* (May 27, 1970), A4.

20 "Backlash Blamed," *Capital Journal* (May 27, 1970), 13.

21 "McCall, Straub Win Handily; Constitution, 19-Vote Go Down," *Lebanon Express* (May 17, 1970), 1.

22 Blumenauer, quoted in "Backlash Blamed," 13.

23 Norman C. Miller, "Bill to Give Vote to 18-Year-Olds May Pass House Test, Go to White House This Week," *Wall Street Journal* (June 15, 1970), 3; Marjorie Hunter, "Democrats Press 18-Year-Old Vote," *New York Times* (April 29, 1970), 17.

24 Celler, quoted in Hunter, "Democrats Press 18-Year-Old Vote," 17.

25 McCulloch, quoted in "18 Year Old Vote Provision Added to Renewed Voting Rights Act of 1965," *Time* (June 29, 1970), 13–14.

26 "Seek to Save Voting Rights Act," *Jet* (July 2, 1970), 6–9; Adams, quoted on 8.

27 Rosalyn Hester, quoted in William Greider, "Non-Rebels with a Cause: 'Kids' Lobby for Vote at 18," *Washington Post* (June 17, 1970), A1.

28 Keefer interview; Hester Baker interview.

29 Hester Baker interview.

30 Hester, quoted in "Youth Organizations Push for 18-Year-old Vote," *NEA News* (March 26, 1970), YFC 1969–1970.

31 George E. Gullen, National Council of the YMCA, to YMCA Board Presidents and Executive Directors, April 23, 1970, and sample letter, YFC 1969–1970.

32 Keefer, quoted in Kathy Lang, "Here's the Latest on Vote 18," *Cincinnati Enquirer* (April 11, 1970), 51.

33 Keefer and MacGowan interviews; Keefer, quoted in Robert Webb, "Local Girl Pushes Voting Issue," *Cincinnati Enquirer* (April 12, 1970), 5.

34 Mitchell, quoted in Greider, "Non-Rebels with a Cause," A1.

35 Myer August interview; MacGowan, quoted in "Youth Organizations Push for 18-Year-old Vote," *NEA News* (March 26, 1970), YFC 1969–1970, and in 1970 Senate Hearings, 47.

36 Senator Warren G. Magnuson, press release, April 28, 1970, folder Student Work—Youth Franchise Coalition, 1970, box 217, Kautz Family YMCA Archives, University of Minnesota Libraries (hereafter YFC 1970).

37 Senator Edward M. Kennedy Replies to President Nixon's Letter on 18-Year-Old Voting, reprinted in 1970 Senate Hearings, 390–391.

38 Chapman, "The Right to Vote at 18," reprinted in 1970 Senate Hearings, 425.

39 Ford, quoted in "Extending the Voting Rights Act of 1965," *Congressional Record* 116 (June 17, 1970), 20196.

40 Colmer, quoted in "Extending the Voting Rights Act of 1965," 20197.

41 Rarick, quoted in "Extending the Voting Rights Act of 1965," 20190.

42 Andrews, quoted in "Extending the Voting Rights Act of 1965," 20164.

43 Celler, quoted in "Extending the Voting Rights Act of 1965," 20160.

44 Mikva, quoted in "Extending the Voting Rights Act of 1965," 20164.

45 Railsback, quoted in "Extending the Voting Rights Act of 1965," 20166.

46 McCormack, quoted in "Extending the Voting Rights Act of 1965," 20196; Greider, "Non-Rebels with a Cause," A1.

47 MacGowan interview.
48 Richard Nixon, Statement on Signing the Voting Rights Act Amendments of 1970, Presidency Project, www.presidency.ucsb.edu.
49 James J. Kilpatrick, "Congress, Nix on Sacrificed Constitution for Vote at 18," *Los Angeles Times* (June 29, 1970), A7.
50 "Veto of Key Bills Mars 91st Congress," *AFL-CIO News* (January 16, 1971), 7; "Votes for Blacks and Youths," *Los Angeles Times* (March 17, 1970), A6; "18 Year Old Vote Provision," 13–14.
51 Christopher Lydon, "Mitchell Gives States to Aug. 3 to Act on Vote at 18," *New York Times* (July 15, 1970), 16.
52 Keefer, quoted in Robert Webb, "'Vote 18' Battle Has Just Begun," *Cincinnati Enquirer* (June 18, 1970), 41.

15. A STEP FORWARD
 1 John Mack Carter, "Editor's Diary: Youth and the Vote," *Ladies' Home Journal* (August 1970), 8.
 2 Quotes from Lynn Lilliston, "Teen-Adult Views of Lower Vote Age: New Voting Age," *Los Angeles Times* (June 29, 1970), E1, E8.
 3 "Real Vote Danger," *Honolulu Advertiser* (June 27, 1970), 18.
 4 Max Johnson, "Lowered Voting Age Brings Opportunities," *Afro-American* (July 11, 1970), 5.
 5 John Lewis, paraphrased in Philip Gailey, "Under 21 Electors Show Little Influence in Two States: Georgia," *Boston Globe* (July 5, 1970), A1.
 6 John S. Saloma, "18-Year-Old Voters," *Boston Globe* (July 5, 1970), A1.
 7 "Some States Tell U.S. They Can't Register 18-Year-Olds," *Chicago Tribune* (July 26, 1970), 20.
 8 Robert Robson, quoted in Mark Brown, "Court Ruling Sought on 18-Year-Old Vote," *Daily Sitka Sentinel* (August 18, 1970), 2.
 9 "Some States Tell U.S. They Can't Register 18-Year-Olds," 20.
10 Fred P. Graham, "U.S. Sues to Uphold 18-Year-Old Vote," *New York Times* (August 18, 1970), 25.
11 "Some States Tell U.S. They Can't Register 18-Year-Olds," 20.
12 "Ruling Sought on Youth Voting," *Hartford Courant* (July 21, 1970), 7; Mark Perkins, quoted in Jackie Ross, "Youths Applaud House Passage of Bill to Lower Voting Age," *Hartford Courant* (June 21, 1970), 44A.
13 Forand, quoted in "Drive Starts to Obtain Vote for 18-Year-Olds," *Naugatuck Daily News* (July 23, 1970), 10; Elaine Orfanos, "Vote 18 Office Opens," *Yale Daily News* (September 29, 1970), 1.
14 Boucher, quoted in Extending the Voting Rights Act of 1965, 20189.
15 LeVander, quoted in "Younger State Voting Age Well Supported," *Daily Journal* (March 3, 1970), 4.
16 "Vote Nov. 3 on Amendment No. 2," *Minneapolis Star* (November 2, 1970), 12A.
17 "Voters' Reactions Varied," *Lincoln Star* (November 7, 1970), 4.

18   "Project 19 Promotes Responsible Youth," *Branding Iron* (October 2, 1970), 20.

19   "Hathaway Comments on 19-Vote Difficulty," *Casper Star-Tribune* (December 19, 1970), 3.

20   Forand, quoted in "Drive Starts to Obtain Vote for 18 Year Olds," 10; Elaine Orfanos, "Vote 18," *Yale Daily News* (April 16, 1970), 2.

21   Rick Hill, quoted in "Group Urges Support for Lower Voting Age," *Hartford Courant* (August 11, 1970), 16.

22   Forand, quoted in "Coalition Plans Drive for Lower Voting Age," *Hartford Courant* (October 26, 1969), 10A and in Joey Williams, "Looking for a Battle Plan?," *Moderator* (April 1969), 13.

23   "Analyzing the Amendments," *Hartford Courant* (November 7, 1970), 18; Forand, quoted and paraphrased in "Leader of Drive for Vote at 18 Discusses Loss," *Bridgeport Telegram* (November 5, 1970), 76.

24   Brown, quoted in "126,000 'Voters' Await Election," *Seattle Spectator* (October 22, 1970), 6.

25   Kramer, quoted in Dale Nelson, "Vote 19 Campaign Hurt by Congressional Action," *Longview Daily News* (July 3, 1970), 2.

26   "126,000 'Voters' Await Election," *Seattle Spectator* (October 22, 1970), 6.

27   Evans, quoted in "Evans Predicts Antiwar Demonstration Oct. 31 May Hurt Chances of Vote 19," *Longview Daily News* (October 7, 1970), 12.

28   Brown, quoted in "126,000 'Voters' Await Election," *Seattle Spectator* (October 22, 1970), 6.

29   "A Problem with the New Left," *The Hilltop* (May 9, 1970), 4.

30   Sam Dixon, quoted in Gailey, "Under 21 Electors Show Little Influence," A1.

31   Mark O. Brown, interview with author, July 9, 2020 (hereafter Brown interview).

32   Rosalyn Hester and Ian MacGowan to YFC Board and Member Organizations, December 1970, YFC 1970.

33   "Bids to Lower Voting Age Lose in 10 of 15 States," *Chicago Tribune* (November 5, 1970), 19; Alan M. Goldberg to James Brown, February 12, 1970, folder Form Letters 1968–1969, box E12, NAACP Records.

34   William O. Billiter Jr., "Under 21 Electors Show Little Influence in Two States: Kentucky," *Boston Globe* (July 5, 1970), A1.

35   "Today's a Big One for Young Washington," *Washington Post* (October 17, 1970), A10.

36   John P. MacKenzie, "Court Urged to Hear Freund on Vote at 18," *Washington Post* (September 26, 1970), A4; King interview.

37   Hester, quoted in "Congress Lowers Voting Age," *Senior Scholastic* (September 14, 1970), 3.

38   Poff, quoted in Warren Weaver, "Measure Lowering Voting Age Presents Political and Constitutional Issues," *New York Times* (June 19, 1970), 17.

39   Hugo L. Black, *Oregon v. Mitchell* (1970), Legal Information Institute, Cornell Law School, www.law.cornell.edu.

40   Ervin, quoted in Ronald J. Ostrow, "Supreme Court OKs Vote at 18 but Only in Federal Elections," *Los Angeles Times* (December 22, 1970), A1; Merlo J.

Pusey, "Court's Clouding of the 18-Year Vote," *Washington Post* (December 30, 1970), A14.

41 *Evening Tribune* (December 23, 1970), B2, *Richmond News Leader* (December 22, 1970), 14, James J. Kilpatrick news clippings, and letters, in folder Oregon v. Mitchell, Case File, 1937–1971, box 434, Series 5: Supreme Court File, 1937–1972, Hugo LaFayette Black Papers, 1883–1976, Library of Congress (hereafter Black Papers).

42 Myer July interview; "Splitting the Difference," *Newsweek* (January 4, 1971), 20–21.

43 "Gift Wrapped," *Christian Science Monitor* (December 24, 1970), news clipping, Black Papers.

44 "Complete Voting Rights Backed for 18-Year-Olds," *UCLA Daily Bruin* (January 12, 1971), 4.

45 "18-Year Voting Approved," *Cornell Daily Sun* (December 22, 1970), 1.

46 "Uniform Registration Urged," *AFL-CIO News* (March 6, 1971), 2.

47 Pusey, "Court's Clouding of the 18-Year Vote," A14.

48 Rosalyn Hester to YFC Board, December 23, 1970, YFC 1970.

16. ON ACCOUNT OF AGE

1 Rosalyn Hester and Ian MacGowan to YFC Board and Member Organizations, December 1970, YFC 1970.

2 "Drive to Register 18-Yr.-Olds Set," *Afro-American* (January 16, 1971), 12; "Youth Vote Drive Begun by South Carolina NAACP," *Afro-American* (February 27, 1971), 6.

3 "High Court Rehearing Urged on Vote at 18," *Washington Post* (January 6, 1971), A13; "NAACP in Plea on Vote for Teens," *Chicago Defender* (January 23, 1971), 14; "Plea Rejected on Vote at 18," *Washington Post* (January 12, 1971), A3.

4 "NAACP Youths In Vote Drive for 18-Year Olds," *Jet* (January 21, 1971), 9.

5 "The Minnesota Youth Franchise Coalition: A Proposal," 1971, Minnesota Historical Society, 3, 23.

6 "Sargent Seeks Lower Voting Age," *Hartford Courant* (January 12, 1971), 30.

7 Rosalyn Hester and Ian MacGowan to YFC Interested Parties, February 4, 1971, YFC 1970.

8 "The Minnesota Youth Franchise Coalition: A Proposal," 1971, Minnesota Historical Society, 24.

9 Mary Ann Madej, "The Great Compromise," *Chicago Tribune* (March 21, 1971), SCL6.

10 Nixon, quoted in "Excerpts from Transcript of Nixon Talk on Youth," *New York Times* (January 15, 1971), 12.

11 Rosalyn Hester to YFC Interested Parties, January 25, 1971, YFC 1970.

12 Ian MacGowan and Rosalyn Hester to YFC Board of Directors, January 22, 1971, YFC 1970.

13 Gardner, quoted in David S. Broder, "Crossing Fingers For Common Cause," *Washington Post* (August 20, 1970), A18.

14 Ian MacGowan and Rosalyn Hester to YFC Board of Directors, January 22, 1971, YFC 1970.

15 Alan Horton, "Pat Leads Vote-18 Fight," news clipping in author's possession.

16 YFC Update (March 30, 1971), YFC 1970.

17 Randolph, "Senate Joint Resolution 7," *Congressional Record—Senate* (January 25, 1971), S140-S141.

18 "Lowering the Voting Age to 18," 92nd Cong., 1st sess., March 9, 1971, *House Report 92-37*, 5.

19 "Lowering the Voting Age to 18: A Fifty-State Survey of the Costs and Other Problems of Dual-Age Voting," 92nd Cong., 1st sess., February, 1971, *Report of the Constitutional Amendments Subcommittee*, US Senate, iii, 20, 22.

20 Mayne, quoted in "Lowering the Voting Age to 18," *Congressional Record—House* (March 23, 1971), H1830; Wiggins, quoted in "Lowering the Voting Age to 18," H1828.

21 Green, quoted in "Lowering the Voting Age to 18," H1834; Ford, quoted in "Lowering the Voting Age to 18," H1833.

22 Allen, "Extension of the Right to Vote," *Congressional Record—Senate* (March 10, 1971), S2883-S2884; Poff, quoted in "Lowering the Voting Age to 18," H1821.

23 Celler, quoted in "Lowering the Voting Age to 18," H1819–H1820.

24 Randolph, quoted in "Extension of the Right to Vote," S2883.

25 Railsback, quoted in "Lowering the Voting Age to 18," H1824; Mikva, quoted in "Lowering the Voting Age to 18," H1832.

26 Howard, quoted in "Lowering the Voting Age to 18," H1824; Grasso, quoted in "Lowering the Voting Age to 18," H1838.

27 "A Modern Father of Our Constitution: An Interview with Former Senator Birch Bayh," *Fordham Law Review* 79 (December 2010), 781–821.

28 YFC Update, March 30, 1971.

29 Paul J. Myer, email correspondence with author, August 20, 2020; King interview.

30 YFC Update, March 30, 1971.

31 Gloster B. Current, quoted in "NAACP Pushes for Youth Vote," *Afro-American* (April 17, 1971), 17.

32 "60% in Poll Favor Local Voting at 18," *New York Times* (April 25, 1971), 4.

33 Celler, quoted in Marjorie Hunter, "House Approves 18-Year Vote," *Duke Chronicle* (March 24, 1971), 3.

34 Delaware House of Representatives, March 23, 1971, recording, Eric S. Fish personal collection, in author's possession.

35 "State Cries 'Foul' in Ratifying Race," *Evening Journal* (March 24, 1971), 1.

36 Legislators, quoted in Connecticut House of Representatives and Senate, March 23, 1971, proceedings, Eric S. Fish personal collection, in author's possession.

37 "Legislators Bicker, but Ratify Vote at 18," *Seattle Post-Intelligencer* (March 24, 1971), 6.

38 Judy Hamilton, "Battles Expected over 18-Year Vote," *Tampa Times* (April 19, 1971), 10A.

39 Tom Goff, "Reagan Sees States' Rights Violation in U.S. Teen Vote Act," *Los Angeles Times* (March 24, 1971), 3.

40 Kate Harris and Ralph Holmes, "18-Year-Old Vote OK Also Has Honor Debate," *Birmingham News* (July 1, 1971), 1.

41 "Jersey Is 27th State to Approve Lowering Age for Voting to 18," *New York Times* (May 4, 1971), 38.

42 Shue, quoted in Public Hearing before the Senate Judiciary Committee, State of New Jersey, April 7, 1971, Eric S. Fish personal collection, in author's possession.

43 Blumenauer, quoted in "Burns' Action Said 'Indefensible,'" *The World* (May 3, 1971), 1.

44 R. W. Apple, "The States Ratify Full Vote at 18," *New York Times* (July 1, 1971), 1.

45 Warren D. Wheat, "Ohio Solons Not Likely to Ratify 'Vote 18,'" *Cincinnati Enquirer* (May 13, 1971), 14.

46 Robert E. Leavitt, quoted in Apple, "States Ratify Full Vote at 18," 43; "26th Amendment: Voting at 18," *Los Angeles Times* (July 4, 1971), B5.

47 Richard Nixon, Statement about Ratification of the 26th Amendment, Presidency Project,www.presidency.ucsb.edu.

48 *New York Times* and *Michigan Daily* (July 1, 1971), 1.

49 Keefer interview.

50 Bond, quoted in John Lewis and Archie E. Allen, "Black Voter Registration Efforts in the South," *Notre Dame Lawyer* 48 (October 1972), 120.

51 Fred Schneider, "First 18-Year-Old Voter Enrolled by Mayor Lindsay," *Columbia Spectator* (January 5, 1971), 3.

52 Bill Kovachs, "Amherst City Fears Youth Vote," *New York Times* (August 2, 1971), 13.

53 "Eighteen Year Old Vote," NAACP 62nd Annual Convention Resolution, July 1971, reprinted in *The Crisis* (March 1972), 7.

54 Goldstein interview.

55 Alex Poinsett, "Debut of the 18-Year-Old Voter," *Ebony* (June 1972), 120–128.

56 *Black Panther* (May 13, 1972) and (June 3, 1972).

57 Gonzales interview.

58 Notice, *Seventeen* (August 1972), 300.

59 Charlie's Girls notice, *Seventeen* (April 1972) 74; Jeans West advertisement, *UCLA Daily Bruin* (October 29, 1971), 8.

60 "Youth Must Be Heard," *Billboard* (March 4, 1972), 3; Special Supplement, *Billboard* (March 11, 1972), 30–33.

61 Nat Freedland, "Industry Unifying to Help Youth Vote," *Billboard* (February 26, 1972), 58.

62 "Youth Must Be Heard," 3; Special Supplement, 30–33.

63 Bobby Hart with Glenn Ballantyne, *Psychedelic Bubble Gum: Boyce & Hart, The Monkees, and Turning Mayhem into Miracles* (New York: SelectBooks, 2015), 189.

CONCLUSION

1   "Analyst's Survey Finds Nixon Hurt by Young Voters," *Hartford Courant* (July 1, 1971), 4; Philip Wagner, "18-Year-Old Vote: Ado about Nothing?," *Hartford Courant* (March 25, 1970), 26.

2   Parsons, quoted in "Youth Group Seeks Antiwar Vote Pledges," *Hartford Courant* (May 16, 1971), 16.

3   "Kennedy Warns of Split in New Youth Vote," *Hartford Courant* (July 30, 1970), 30.

4   "No Exit," *Wellesley News* (May 6, 1971), 2.

5   "Analyst's Survey Finds Nixon Hurt By Young Voters," 4.

6   Seth E. Blumenthal, "Children of the 'Silent Majority': Richard Nixon's Young Voters for the President, 1972," *Journal of Policy History* 27, 2 (2015), 338.

7   Thomas H. Neale, "The Eighteen Year Old Vote: The Twenty-Sixth Amendment and Subsequent Voting Rates of Newly Franchised Voting Groups," Congressional Research Service Report No. 83–103, 1983, Library of Congress, CRS-17.

8   Catherine Kieffer Gervase, quoted in "What Was the First Presidential Election You Voted In?," *At Buffalo* (2021), www.buffalo.edu.

9   Cushing interview.

10 Fred Hechinger, "Students of the Sixties: Salvaging the Youth Movement," *Change* 5 (June 1973), 32.

11 "Youth Turnout Rate Rises to at Least 52%" (Center for Information & Research on Civic Learning and Engagement, Tufts University, November 7, 2008), https://archive.civicyouth.org.

12 Daniel M. Shea and Rebecca Harris, "Why Bother? Because Peer-to-Peer Programs Can Mobilise Young Voters," *PS: Political Science and Politics* 39 (April 2006), 341–345; Dana R. Fisher, "Youth Political Participation: Bridging Activism and Electoral Politics," *Annual Review of Sociology* 38 (2012), 119–137.

13 Myer July interview.

14 Peter F. Nardulli, Jon K. Dalager, and Donald E. Greco, "Voter Turnout in U.S. Presidential Elections: An Historical View and Speculation," *Political Science and Politics* 29 (September 1996), 488.

15 Patricia Keefer, interview with Charles Koppelman, 2020, in author's possession.

16 National Archives and Records Administration, "Amending America: Proposed Amendments to the United States Constitution, 1787 to 2014" (November 12, 2020), https://catalog.data.gov.

17 Dennis King, email correspondence with author, May 2, 2021.

18 Eric S. Fish, "The Twenty-Sixth Amendment Enforcement Power," *Yale Law Journal* 121, no. 5 (2012), 1168–1235; Yael Bromberg, "Youth Voting Rights and the Unfulfilled Promise of the Twenty-Sixth Amendment," *Journal of Constitutional Law* 21, no. 5 (2019), 1105–1166.

19 Jennifer Frost and Eric S. Fish, "The Youth Vote Is Being Suppressed: The 26th Amendment Is the Solution," *Washington Post* (August 14, 2020), www.washingtonpost.com.

20 David A. Strauss, "The Irrelevance of Constitutional Amendments," *Harvard Law Review* 114 (March 2001), 1459.

21 Strauss, "Irrelevance of Constitutional Amendments," 1489; Peter M. Shane, "Voting Rights and the 'Statutory Constitution,'" *Law and Contemporary Problems* 56 (Autumn 1993), 262; Bruce Ackerman, *We the People I: Foundations* (Cambridge, MA: Harvard University Press, 1990), 91.

22 Randolph, quoted in 1970 Senate Hearings, 4.

23 MacGowan, NEA interview with Rebecca Login, 2011, in author's possession; Dennis M. Warren, Class of '70, UoP video interview, 2020.

24 Devin Fergus, *Liberalism, Black Power, and the Making of American Politics, 1965–1980* (Athens: University of Georgia Press, 2009), 10 and passim.

25 David A. Strauss, "The Irrelevance of Constitutional Amendments," *Harvard Law Review* 114 (March 2001), 1489.

26 Jane Eisner, *Taking Back the Vote: Getting American Youth Involved in Our Democracy* (Boston: Beacon, 2004), 10.

27 Rosalyn H. Baker, NEA interview with Rebecca Login, 2011, in author's possession; Myer July interview; Brown interview.

28 Cushing interview; Keefer interview; Greenspun Gale interview.

29 Mae C. Quinn, "Black Women and Girls and the Twenty-Sixth Amendment: Constitutional Connections, Activist Intersections, and the First Wave Youth Suffrage Movement," *Seattle University Law Review* (forthcoming).

30 Blumenauer, quoted in Sarah Zimmerman, "We Are Tired of Waiting for the Adults," *Mail Tribune* (March 28, 2019), https://mailtribune.com.

31 Goldstein interview.

32 Koppelman interview.

33 Cushing interview; Les Francis, personal communication, July 8, 2020.

34 President Barack Obama, "Proclamation 8691—40th Anniversary of the 26th Amendment" (July 1, 2011), https://obamawhitehouse.archives.gov.

INDEX

Abernathy, Ralph, 154

Adams, Farries, 251–252. *See also* Mississippi

AFL-CIO (American Federation of Labor-Congress of Industrial Organizations), 64–65, 163, 257–258, 278; Minnesota campaign, 267; Ohio campaign, 217; YFC and, 186–188, 193, 252

Age, as a social construction, 18, 123, 173, 196, 215, 237, 317–318

Alabama, 71, 105; 26th Amendment ratification, 292; civil and voting rights campaigns, 48, 72, 90, 106–108, 134; *Dixon v. Alabama State Board of Education* (1961), 90; students, 90; white violence, 72, 98, 106–107

Alaska, 53, 74; 19-year-old vote, 53, 74, 83, 158, 171, 212; 18-year-old vote referendum, 203, 226, 258, 266

Alexander, Kelly, 203. *See also* North Carolina

Allen, James, 286

American Civil Liberties Union, 29, 240–241

American Federation of Teachers, 165, 236, 279

Americans for Democratic Action, 188–189, 191, 193; student affiliate, 57

American Samoa, 53, 273; 18-year-old vote, 111; 20-year-old vote, 67, 83

American Youth for Democracy (AYD), 27, 31, 82

Anderson, Terry H., 9

antiwar movement, 121, 126, 137–138, 149, 151, 156, 230, 250, 271; at 1968 Democratic National Convention, 167–170; Moratorium to End the War in Vietnam, 222; Vietnam Veterans Against the War, 291

Arizona, 105, 264, 273, 275

Arnall, Ellis G., 24–26, 29–31, 127; 1943 House hearing testimony, 31–34, 39, 73. *See also* Georgia

Bailey, Beth, 7

Bailey, John M., 75, 82–83

Bayh, Birch, 50, 76, 105, 193; 26th Amendment passage, 288, 306; support for youth voting rights, 50, 128, 131, 157–158, 236; as chair of Senate Judiciary Committee Subcommittee on Constitutional Amendments, 131, 156, 233–235, 242, 246, 285; constituents, 160–161; criticism of, 174–175; Let Us Vote and, 179–180; *Oregon v. Mitchell* and, 274; Voting Rights Act of 1970, 231, 253, 274; YFC and, 186–187, 200, 218, 231, 253, 280

Beatty, Jim, 143, 203. *See also* North Carolina

Berman, Jay, 234

Berman, John A., 83–84

Bickford, Marcus, 17–18, 236

Bishop, Joey, 181–182

Black, Hugo, 29, 102; *Oregon v. Mitchell* decision, 275–277

Blackwell, James E., 93

Congress of Racial Equality (CORE), 72, 92, 95, 106

Congressional hearings, 40, 52, 241–242, 244–245, 285–286; 1943 House hearing, 16, 21, 24, 31–34; 1952 Senate hearing, 39; 1961 Senate hearings, 72–75, 82–83, 163–164; 1968 Senate hearings, 156–160, 174–175; 1970 Senate hearings, 233–241, 246, 249, 254. *See also* Bayh, Birch; Celler, Emanuel

Connecticut, 82–83, 111, 203, 212–214, 265, 282; 18-year-old vote referendum/campaign, 213–214, 226, 269–270; 26th Amendment ratification, 290–291; Connecticut Citizen Coalition Let's Vote 18, 214, 265; Let's Vote—the Connecticut Committee for the 18-Year-Old Vote, 146, 203, 212–214, 269–270; servicemen, 145–146; students, 28, 77, 265; Vindication of Twenty-Eighteen Suffrage (VOTES), 81–85, 111, 146

Conroy, John Patrick, 139. *See also* New York

conservatives/conservatism, 8, 105, 112, 220, 275; political backlash and, 37, 126–127, 132–133, 135, 143, 208, 237, 242; political polarization and, 190–191, 308; youth voting rights and, 126, 141, 176, 211, 220, 240, 249–250, 255, 257, 271–272, 277, 292. *See also* Republican Party; states' rights v. federal power

Conyers, John, 110, 192, 242, 288

Cook, Marlow, 234–235, 243–244, 288

Coriell, Rita, 217. *See also* Ohio

Corneliussen, Steve T., 142; Voting Age Council of North Carolina leadership, 142–143. *See also* North Carolina

Cosgrove, John, 209, 273–274. *See also* California

counterculture/"hippies," 138, 145

Cox, Archibald, 230, 247; federal legislative statute strategy/Morgan approach, 231, 234, 240–241, 245. *See also Katzenbach v. Morgan*

Cushing, Robert (Renny), 301–302, 307–308; McCarthy campaign, 151–152, 167–168; youth franchise movement and, 177, 184–185, 198. *See also* New Hampshire

CUE. *See* New Jersey

Davis, Ken, 136

Delaware, 225; 26th Amendment ratification, 290–291

D'Emilio, John, 7

Democratic Party, 8, 31–32, 37–38, 62, 64–71, 92, 105, 112, 126–127, 150–151, 153, 156, 175, 212, 299, 301, 302; 1964 National Convention and MFDP, 103–105; 1968 National Convention, 167–170, 175; all-white primary, 29–30; "Dixiecrats," 38, 43–44, 292; Young Democrats affiliate, 28, 57, 74, 123, 136, 139, 158–160, 169–170, 177, 186, 190, 205, 267, 270, 305; youth voting rights and, 36, 75, 141, 145, 163–164, 249, 257

Denton, Ralph, 171, 173

Diggs, Charles C., Jr., 45–49, 51–53, 67, 94, 104, 110, 162, 193, 246; Civil Rights Act of 1964 and, 99–102; Kennedy administration and, 68–70; support for youth voting rights, 45–46, 49, 53, 122, 192, 288

Dirksen, Everett, 100, 109, 131

DiScuillo, Alan, 234. *See also* Youth Franchise Coalition

District of Columbia, 21–22, 73, 273, 287–288; 23rd Amendment, 70–71

Dolan, Joseph S., 77, 81–85, 125. *See also* Connecticut

Douglas, Larry, 211. *See also* New York

DuPell, David, 216, 220. *See also* New Jersey

ABOUT THE AUTHOR

Jennifer Frost is a historian of twentieth-century US society, politics, and culture at the University of Auckland in New Zealand. She is the author of *"An Interracial Movement of the Poor": Community Organizing and the New Left in the 1960s* (2001), *Hedda Hopper's Hollywood: Celebrity Gossip and American Conservatism* (2011), and *Producer of Controversy: Stanley Kramer, Hollywood Liberalism, and the Cold War* (2017).